TEILHARD,
SCRIPTURE, AND REVELATION

TEILHARD, SCRIPTURE, AND REVELATION

A Study of Teilhard de Chardin's Reinterpretation of Pauline Themes

Richard W. Kropf

Rutherford • Madison • Teaneck
Fairleigh Dickinson University Press
London Associated University Presses

Associated University Presses, Inc.
Cranbury, New Jersey 08512

Associated University Presses
Magdalen House
136-148 Tooley Street
London SE1 2TT, England

Library of Congress Cataloging in Publication Data

Kropf, Richard W   1932-
Teilhard, Scripture, and revelation.

Bibliography: p.
Includes index.
1. Bible—Criticism, interpretation, etc.—History—
20th century. 2. Jesus Christ—History of doctrines—
20th century. 3. Teilhard de Chardin, Pierre.
I. Title.
BS500.K76 1975   232'.092'4   73-20907
ISBN 0-8386-1481-7

PRINTED IN THE UNITED STATES OF AMERICA

Excerpts from Pierre Teilhard de Chardin's *Human Energy, Activation of Energy*, and *Christianity and Evolution* are reprinted by permission of Harcourt Brace Jovanovich, Inc.; © 1962, 1963, 1969 by Editions du Seuil; © 1971 by William Collins Sons & Co. Ltd. and Harcourt Brace Jovanovich, Inc. Acknowledgment is made to Harper & Row, Publishers, Inc., for the following excerpts:

From THE PHENOMENON OF MAN by Pierre Teilhard de Chardin, translated by Bernard Wall. Copyright 1955 by Editions du Seuil. Copyright © 1959 in the English translation by Wm. Collins Sons & Co. Ltd., London, and Harper & Row, Publishers, New York.
From THE VISION OF THE PAST by Pierre Teilhard de Chardin, translated by J. M. Cohen (Harper & Row, 1966).
From THE DIVINE MILIEU by Pierre Teilhard de Chardin, translated by Bernard Wall. Originally published in French as LE MILIEU DIVIN. Copyright 1957 by Editions du Seuil, Paris. English translation copyright © 1960 by Wm. Collins Sons & Co., London and Harper & Row, Publishers, Inc., New York.
From THE FUTURE OF MAN by Pierre Teilhard de Chardin, translated by Norman Denny. Copyright 1959 by Editions du Seuil. Copyright © 1964 in the English translation by William Collins Sons & Co., Ltd., London and Harper & Row, Publishers, Inc., New York.

To my parents, to my friends both in the United States and in Canada, and to all who seek the "new heavens and a new earth."

Contents

PART III   *The Teilhardian Hermeneutic*

Avant-propos

Parmi les thèses dignes de figurer au "tableau d'honneur" de la Fondation Teilhard de Chardin, je n'hésite pas à compter celle du Révérend Richard W. Kropf. Tout le monde sait que saint Paul (et saint Jean) brillent dans le ciel mental de Teilhard comme des astres de première grandeur, et Kropf, obéissant à un lointain atavisme, a creusé ce thème central avec toute la Gründlichkeit germanique et un admirable déploiement d'érudition exégétique, herméneutique et théologique. Enfin un exposé critique, non pas au sens péjoratif mais universitaire du mot, tel une troupe obligée de se déplacer dans un terrain mouvant et ne suivant que des itinéraires soigneusement balisés!

Nous ne pouvons pas prédire ce qui restera de l'exégèse teilhardienne. Mais on ne peut pas ne pas être frappé, mutatis mutandis, de l'analogie entre saint Paul et Teilhard. Tous deux se sont trouvés en face d'une gnose, assortie de spéculations cosmologiques. Tous deux ont voulu retrouver un Christ plus grand, dont les rayons vaporisent cette rosée pernicieuse. Tous deux ont senti que l'on ne pouvait dévier de l'orthodoxie quand le Christ sortait agrandi de la méditation exégétique ou du théologique. La seule différence est que saint Paul ne pouvait pressentir l'evolutionnisme, alors que celui-ci compte parmi l'une des catégories majeures du penseur du XXe siècle.

Encore une fois, nou ne pouvons pas prophétiser. Mais quelles que soient les spéculations futures des exégètes qui savent couper les cheveux au microtome et se contredire ingénûment ou aggressivement, il semble bien que, d'ores et déjà, Teilhard ait modifié notre sensibilité de croyants: nous ne *pouvons* plus lire saint Paul de la même façon et, tel un flash, ses textes cosmologiques nous éblouissent. C'est l'essentiel.

La contribution du Révérend Kropf doit figurer dans la bibliothèque de tout teilhardien conscient et organisé. C'est, dans la forêt, un rond-point d'où fuient maintes trouées, d'où s'organise et se structure le paysage.

C. Cuénot
Dock. Lit.

Foreword

Among the studies deserving to appear on the honor roll of the *Fondation Teilhard de Chardin*, I do not hesitate to include that of Richard W. Kropf. It is well known that St. Paul and St. John were brilliant stars in the mental universe of Teilhard, and Kropf, following an ancestral urge, has examined this central theme with a profound germanic *Gründlichkeit* and an admirable deployment of exegetical, hermeneutic, and theological erudition. Here at last is a critical statement, not in the pejorative but academic sense of the work, like that of someone obliged to travel across an uncertain terrain, yet following a carefully chosen road.

We cannot predict how much of the Teilhardian exegesis will survive. But no one should be surprised, *mutatis mutandis*, at the analogy between St. Paul and Teilhard. Both were confronted with a gnosis filled with cosmological speculations. Both wished to discover a greater Christ, whose rays would disperse this pernicious dew. Both felt that one would not deviate from orthodoxy if this greater Christ emerged from exegetical or theological meditation. The only difference is that St. Paul did not have to cope with evolutionism, whereas it is one of the major categories of twentieth-century thought.

Again, we cannot prophesy. But whatever the future speculations of exegetes, who know how to split hairs with their microtomes and to argue ingeniously and aggressively, it appears here and now that Teilhard has modified our sensibility as believers: we can no longer read St. Paul in the same fashion and his cosmological texts bedazzle us like lightning. That is the main point.

Father Kropf's contribution should form part of any conscientious and organized Teilhardian library. It is like a crossroads in a forest, leading in many directions, yet organizing and structuring the whole landscape.

C. Cuénot
D. Litt.

Acknowledgments

This study was prepared under the supervision of Roger Lapointe, D.E.S., of the Faculty of Theology of St. Paul University, Ottawa.

The writer is indebted to the Reverend Marcel Patry, O.M.I., Ph.D., Rector of St. Paul University, for the original idea and guidance behind this project, to the Reverends Martin Roberge, O.M.I., L.E.S., D.Th., Vice Rector, Henri Goudreault, O.M.I., S.S.L., D.Th., Léo Laberge, O.M.I., D.E.S., and Pierre Hurtubise, O.M.E., D.Hist, all of the Faculty of Theology of St. Paul University, for their advice and encouragement, and to Sr. Catherine Weibel, I.H.M., M.A., and Sr. Dorothy Smith, S.S.J., Ph.D., whose reading of the manuscript and advice contributed to its final preparation.

Additional thanks are extended to the Fondation Teilhard de Chardin, Paris, for access to much of the unpublished material contained in this study, to the Paris Province of the Society of Jesus for permission to utilize portions of the later Teilhard "Journals," and especially to Père Christian d'Armagnac, S.J., for his assistance in deciphering the same.

Thanks are also due to Robert T. Francoeur, Ph.D., of Fairleigh Dickinson University and Mathilde E. Finch, Editor in Chief of Associated University Presses, Inc., for their help and encouragement in seeing to the publication of this study, and to Dagmar Miller for the typographic work, and to Paul Rentz for additional help in the preparation of the final version of the manuscript.

I also wish to thank the following publishers for permission to quote from copyrighted material:

Curtis Brown, Ltd. for permission to quote from Christopher Mooney, *Teilhard de Chardin and the Mystery of Christ*, published in the United States by Harper & Row, 1966.

quote from Gabriel Moran, *The Theology of Revelation* (copyright Herder & Herder, 1966). Also for permission to quote from Karl Lehman's article "Hermeneutics" and Karl Rahner's article "Revelation" in *Sacramentum Mundi*, vols. 3 and 5 (copyrights, Herder & Herder, 1968, 1969); *Encyclopedia of Theology*, ed. Karl Rahner, 1975.

Palm Publishers Limited for permission to quote from Lucien Cerfaux, *Christ in the Theology of St. Paul* (1959) and *The Church in the Theology of St. Paul* (1959).

Paulist/Newman Press, for permission to quote from Ferdinand Prat, *The Theology of St. Paul* (copyright Newman Press, 1959). Also for permission to quote from Karl Rahner's "On the Theology of the Incarnation," in *Word and Mystery*, edited by Leo O'Donovan, S.J., 1968.

Prentice Hall International, Inc., for permission to quote from Raymond E. Brown, S.S., "Hermeneutics" in *The Jerome Biblical Commentary*, edited by Raymond E. Brown, S.S., Joseph A. Fitzmyer, S.J., and Roland E. Murphy, O. Carm., © 1968, Prentice-Hall, Inc.

Theologische Quartalschrift, for permission to quote Leo Scheffczyk, "Die 'Christogenesis' Teilhard de Chardins und der Kosmische Christus bei Paulus," 1963.

List of Abbreviations

WTW Writings in Time of War:
Ecrits, Ecrits du temps de la guerre 1916-1919

PM The Phenomenon of Man:
Oeuvres, vol. 1 *(Le Phénomène humain)*

AM The Appearance of Man:
Oeuvres, vol. 2 *(L'Apparition de l'homme)*

VP The Vision of the Past:
Oeuvres, vol. 3 *(La Vision du Passe)*

DM The Divine Milieu:
Oeuvres, vol. 4 *(Le Milieu divin)*

FM The Future of Man:
Oeuvres, vol. 5 *(L'Avenir de l'homme)*

HE Human Energy:
Oeuvres, vol. 6 *(L'Energie humaine)*

AE Activation of Energy:
Oeuvres, vol. 7 *(L'Activation de l'Energie)*

MPN Man's Place in Nature:
Oeuvres, vol. 8 *(La Place de l'homme dans la Nature)*

S&C Science and Christ:
Oeuvres, vol. 9 *(Science et Christ)*

C&E Christianity and Evolution:
Oeuvres, vol. 10 *(Comment je crois)*

TF Toward the Future:
Oeuvres, vol. 11 *(Les Directions de l'Avenir)*

Oeuvres, vol. 13 *(Le Coeur de la Matière)*

HU Hymn of the Universe: (Hymne de l'Univers)

T.A. (material from the archives of the Foundation Teilhard de Chardin)

CBQ The Catholic Biblical Quarterly

JBC The Jerome Biblical Commentary

TDNT Theological Dictionary of the New Testament

SM Sacramentum Mundi

ET Encyclopedia of Theology

Introduction

With the abundance of books and articles that have appeared in the last fifteen years dealing extensively with the life and thought of Pierre Teilhard de Chardin (1887-1955), the obvious question is: why yet another study? There are many answers. First is the persisting controversy surrounding this seminal thinker of modern times, whose thought, for better or worse, some have associated with "what promises to become the turning point in the history of theology," to quote the highly qualified estimation of John A. Hardon, S.J.[1] Certainly, anyone whose thought can be construed as causing a "reversal of the Christian perspective," as was Jacques Maritain's opinion,[2] deserves the most extensive examination, even if to categorically reject the premises of this reversal of traditional Christianity.

The second reason, should one be favorably inclined toward the Teilhardian synthesis, would be to uncover more explicitly the premises of such a revolution in Christian thought, in order to extend as much as possible the implications of Teilhard's approach in the direction of further developments—an eventuality that Teilhard himself deemed to be the test of the ultimate value of his work. Judging from the huge number of works along this line in the fields of theology, philosophy, ethics, and spirituality, as well as in the more mundane fields of biology, eugenics, sociology, and even ecology, Teilhard's challenge has been an unqualified success, even if one cannot agree wholeheartedly with the directions toward which some of this development has led. It is impossible to list here the works and articles

1. Cf. John A. Hardon, *Christianity in the Twentieth Century* (Garden City, N.Y.: Doubleday, 1971), pp. 66, 374. Hardon gives the latter opinion as that of Harvey Cox.
2. Cf. Jacques Maritain, *The Peasant of the Garonne* (New York: Holt, Rinehart, Winston, 1968), pp. 116f.

that have appeared in addition to the basic studies. One rather complete bibliography lists some 2,223 items![3]

The third reason is more pressing: even given the exhaustive nature of the types of studies mentioned above, there has been, up to now, a lack of thorough investigation of the specifically scriptural premises on which Teilhard claimed to base his thought, at least from the viewpoint of a study of the exact manner in which Teilhard derived his conclusions. True, there have been, as will be seen, abundant references made to Teilhard's use of Scripture, and even a few beginnings made in the field of exegesis toward a fresh examination of those biblical themes on which Teilhard placed such great emphasis,[4] but with one comparatively short exception,[5] there has not been anything like an exclusive and analytical study of Teilhard's own method of employing Scripture, except a few chapters here and there in general treatments of Teilhard's thought.[6]

This is surprising. Whether Teilhard is considered a theologian or not, as a Christian thinker, he claimed to be influenced by his Christian belief and specifically in his overall synthesis, by revelation in its biblical form.

Should such a study be attempted, however, several possible approaches suggest themselves. The first would be, of course, the route of biblical exegesis itself. But, as witnessed by André Feuillet's excellent book, this would necessarily lead not so much to a study of Teilhard's scriptural methodology as such, but to further consideration of the biblical texts themselves. Another route would be that of positive or historical theology. This, again, has been tried, with excellent results, by George Maloney in his *The Cosmic Christ: From Paul to Teilhard*,[7] a work that admirably situates the thought of Teilhard in the context of a "cosmic theology" that has its roots in Paul and can be traced (as Maloney does trace it) through the patristic writers and some

3. Joan E. Jarque, *Bibliographie Générale des Oeuvres et Articles sur Pierre Teilhard de Chardin* (parus jusqu'à fin Dec. 1969) (Fribourg: Editions Universitaires Fribourg, 1970).
4. André Feuillet, *Le Christ Sagesse de Dieu* (Paris: Gabalda, 1966).
5. Cf. Leo Scheffczyk, "Die 'Christogenesis' Teilhard de Chardins und der Kosmische Christus bei Paulus" in *Theologische Quartalschrift* 143 (1963): 137-74.
6. Cf. particularly Christopher Mooney, *Teilhard de Chardin and the Mystery of Christ* (New York: Harper & Row, 1964), chap. 3, part 3, pp. 87-103; Georges Crespy, *La Pensée theologique de Teilhard de Chardin*, (Paris: Editions Universitaires, 1961); Henri deLubac, *La prière de Teilhard de Chardin* (Paris: Fayard, 1961), chap. 14, 18; *La Pensée religieuse du Père Teilhard de Chardin* (New York: Aubier, 1962), chaps. 5, 7, 8; *Teilhard Explained* (New York: Paulist, 1966), part 1, pp. 7-37; Bruno Solages, *Teilhard de Chardin: Témoinage et étude sur le développement de sa pensée* (Paris: Privat, 1967), p. 355-56. Philippe de la Trinité, *Teilhard de Chardin: foi au Christ universel* (Paris, La Table Ronde, 1968), pp. 214-20; *Teilhard de Chardin: Vision cosmique et Christique* (Paris: La Table Ronde, 1968), pp. 285, 304.
7. (New York: Sheed & Ward, 1968).

medieval theologians up to our present day. But that study, eminently valuable as it is, does not systematically attempt to expound the methodology and stages involved in Teilhard's own process of interpreting Sacred Scripture.

Consequently, a third approach must be taken, that of an analytical examination of Teilhard's own stages of thought in relation to the scriptural passages that he so often quoted. Such a study would retain the primarily generic quality of most studies of Teilhard's thought, differing only in concentrating exclusively on the systematic development of his conclusions as based on the scriptural passages. He claimed that these inspired his synthesis from the very beginning, and confirmed in his own mind its compatibility with the Christian faith. Christopher Mooney faults Teilhard for not having himself given such a systematic exposition. As Mooney puts it, Teilhard neglected "to state explicitly the steps in his reasoning process . . . making simultaneous use of two sources of knowledge, one from phenomena and the other from revelation, without bothering to distinguish between them."[8]

Be this as it may, Mooney, who is quick to point out the biblical sources of Teilhard's synthesis, admits, regarding his own treatment of the subject, that "the purpose of our brief study of St. Paul [or what the critics say about St. Paul] has *not* been to inquire into the *development* of Teilhard's Christology but into its *starting point*."[9]

This starting point will be employed here, but with the express intention of tracing the development of Teilhard's insights into the biblical texts. Further attempts will be made to uncover the process of Teilhard's thinking in such a way as to retrace the interaction in his mind of the data of revelation with those of natural phenomena, thus to remedy the confusion between the two that Mooney believes mars Teilhard's work. This analytical project will occupy Part II below, which follows the introductory section in which the general use of Scripture in Teilhard's writings is surveyed and outlined. Part I also attempts to present a comprehensive picture of the overall theological content of Teilhard's synthesis.

In Part II the analytical study centers on three major Pauline themes that recur in Teilhard's thought; the "Omnis Creatura," derived from the Epistle to the Romans; the "Corpus Christi"; and the "pleroma," as these are derived by Teilhard from the major epistles and, more particularly, as they are related in the captivity epistles. Finally, as something of a corollary, the relationship of these to certain Johannine themes found in Teilhard will be discussed.

Each of these themes, or "theme-clusters," as they appear in Part II,

8. P. 88.
9. *Ibid.*, p. 99. Emphasis mine.

will be treated briefly in the light of biblical exegesis, in that of both Teilhard's day and, to some extent, our own. The reason for this is not only to trace those influences which may have guided his original insights or caused them to be modified as time went on, or simply to contrast these interpretations of Teilhard with those of modern thought, as Scheffczyk has done, but also to uncover the inmost guiding principles that give an overall consistency to Teilhard's approach as distinct from the strict textual analysis of the exegetes.

The real reason for the exegetical review worked into Part II alongside the analysis of Teilhard's incorporation of these biblical themes becomes fully apparent in Part III. While we shall have studied the nuances of Teilhard's interpretations of those scriptural themes exhaustively, it cannot be stressed too much that Teilhard never thought of himself as exegete, certainly not in the usual, more restrictive sense of the word. Instead, he saw himself primarily as a "phenomenological" thinker who attempted to synthesize what he saw. Rather than being concerned with the basic interpretation of texts in their original meaning—generally the primary concern of exegesis—Teilhard was almost exclusively concerned with the *re*interpretation of the texts in terms that "actualize" their meaning in completely contemporary—and for that reason, evolutionary—concepts. Because of this complete reconceptualization on Teilhard's part, and because of its all-pervading influence on his approach to Scripture, I have been tempted to name this whole study, instead of merely the third part, *The Teilhardian Hermeneutic*. Still, broad as the term is, and despite its widespread use today in biblical studies, it would not do justice to the unifying concept of Teilhard's whole synthesis. For it is not Teilhard's subjective approach that is, in the end, my major object, but the objective content of his thought, which is centered in the "ever-growing Christ." Reinterpretation, as it employs hermeneutics, is but the means to this end, which is a fuller understanding of "Christogenesis," the center-pin of all Teilhardian thought. Thus, while this study remains an attempt to expound, in the greatest possible detail, the genesis and development of Teilhard's insights into Scripture and to analyze and criticize this development in terms of its hermeneutical and theological methodology, it even more is an attempt to explore the relationship between this methodology and the process of "Christogenesis" that forms its ontological core.

In reference to sources, while I have made extensive use of almost all of Teilhard's finished manuscripts and some that were not completely finished, I have in addition drawn widely on his correspondence—at least all that is available to the average researcher—and even more on his private notes or "Journals," particularly those of his later years, which up to recently have not been accessible. Unfortunately, due to copyright difficulties, the text of the "Journal" notes cannot yet be quoted to any extent; however, references have been given to these sources in hopes that they will be available for the reader's perusal sometime in the future.[10]

10. The "Journal" notes cited in this study nevertheless do appear (subject to future correction for accuracy) in the earlier version of this study contained in the Canadian National Archives and in the libraries of The University of Ottawa and St. Paul University, Ottawa, Canada. (Cf. Richard W. Kropf, *Christogenesis: A Study of Teilhard de Chardin's Reinterpretation of Pauline Themes*, 1972.)

PART I

A Textual Study of Pauline and Other Related Biblical Citations in the Works of Teilhard de Chardin

1

General Characteristics of Teilhard's Use of Sacred Scripture

In any thorough study of the relationship of the theological aspects of the Teilhardian synthesis to the writings attributed to St. Paul, one cannot help becoming acutely conscious of the great variation in, and wide range of appeals Teilhard has made to recorded revelation in general. Despite his repeated insistence on Pauline and Johannine inspiration as the guiding influence in his theological explorations,[1] Teilhard nevertheless quoted from an astonishingly wide range of biblical sources in a great variety of ways. In order to put his use of Pauline and Johannine material in proper perspective, and to clarify certain preoccupations in his choice of material, it is necessary that first a general survey be made of all the biblical sources in Teilhard's work.[2] This is done here in hopes of approaching the more strictly Pauline and to some extent, Johannine, material (in Part II) without having prejudiced my interpretation by a too selectively Pauline-Johannine concentration before trying to appreciate the full range of Teilhard's appeal to written revelation.

A. THE EXTENT OF TEILHARD'S QUOTATIONS

Let us begin with a combing of Teilhard's works—those presently published and those which will eventually see publication, but not in-

1. There are about seventy-five invocations of St. Paul's name scattered throughout his works, and about a third of these include St. John's name as well. Cf. Appendix C below.
2. See Appendix A for list of biblical citations.

29

cluding his correspondence (even that which is published) or his personal notes.[3] Although the notes and correspondence will play an important part in the later evaluation of his thought and will be occasionally utilized in this preliminary investigation, they cannot be used for statistical purposes because they are only partially available, even to scholars and some are irretrievably lost.[4] To make any judgments based on the proportion of scriptural quotations from any given source, one must then draw only on the works that constitute his more finished thought, those intended for publication or circulation among his friends. The more personal (occasionally tentative in character) correspondence and notes will be more fully utilized later in the analytical stage of the investigation.

Statistically speaking, a search of Teilhard's books and essays reveals some two-hundred and sixty-three biblical quotations (201 explicit and at least 62 implicit) from one-hundred and fifty-four different biblical passages (99 explicitly quoted; 56 or so in more or less implicit quotations). At least twenty-five passages are the subject of reference or "allusion."[5] Direct chapter and verse references are very few and even then, as in the case of one passage, not always accurate.[6] Comparison of a quotation and its reference in a 1921 essay, "Science and Christ," reveals Teilhard's tendency to construct something that he meant to be taken as an explicit quotation. But it was not; he would paraphrase the central passage and incorporate into it verses taken from the immediate vicinity—a characteristic that has, as we shall see, interesting theological implications.[7]

To return to statistics, the Old Testament plays a relatively minor role in Teilhard's work with only fifteen (12 explicit, 3 implicit) texts used, while there are fifty (some 43 of them explicit) quotations from the synoptic Gospels, thirty-six either taken from St. Matthew or betraying a wording that would favor Matthew where synoptic parallels

3. "Journal" entry of Apr. 7, 1955, published in *The Future of Man* (New York: Harper & Row, 1964), p. 305; *L'Avenir de l'Homme*, Oeuvres de Teilhard de Chardin (Paris: Editions de Seuil, 1956): 5:404. Abbreviated hereafter as *FM* and *Oeuvres*, 5 respectively.

4. Cf. Bibliography, n.3.

5. Cf. Appendixes A and B, especially the definitions. An excellent example of the difficulty of determining exactly what constitutes the difference between an "allusion" and a quotation, either direct or indirect (at least for statistical purposes), exists in Teilhard's *The Divine Milieu* in the passage entitled "The Final Solution: All Endeavour Cooperates to Complete the World 'In Christo Jesu.'" The Latin phrase, which appears 164 times in the Vulgate within the Pauline writings, runs as a constant *leitmotiv* through Teilhard's works, but since it lacks any specific reference in terms of chapter and verse in the Epistles, it is not counted statistically in my tables (Appendix A), although in the same passage there occurs an indirect quotation of 1 Cor. 3:22-23, which forms the central thesis of *The Divine Milieu*. Cf. (New York: Harper & Row, 1960), p. 25; *Le Milieu Divin*, Oeuvres de Teilhard de Chardin, 4 (Paris: Editions du Seuil, 1956): 41-42. References to the English language edition, hereafter designated *DM*, will follow the pagination of this first edition.

6. Cf. *Science and Christ* (New York: Harper & Row, 1968), pp. 54, 64 (designated as *S&C* hereafter): *Science et Christ* (*Oeuvres*, 9) (Paris: Editions du Seuil, 1965), pp. 82, 92. The same verse, Eph. 4:10, is first designated as Eph. 4:9.

7. Cf. *S&C*, p. 36; *Oeuvres*, 9:62.

exist.[8] Even if the material found exclusively in St. Luke is subsumed under Pauline themes, which is not entirely the case, this leaves a considerable body of biblical material that is extra-Pauline and extra-Johannine. This would seem to indicate, if nothing else, that Teilhard cannot be accused of narrowly picking and choosing only those parts of Sacred Scripture which suited his claims of Pauline-Johannine inspiration.

The problem of what constitutes a quotation, implicit or explicit, is not always easy to settle. A number of what have been termed quotations consist of but one or two words, which may or may not be set off in quotation marks. The French editions of Teilhard's now published works make extensive use of italics, which, upon comparison with the original manuscripts, generally coincide with Teilhard's extensive use of underlining in his handwritten or typewritten papers. On the basis of typography, one is often reduced to deciding on rather tenuous grounds (for statistical purposes, anyway) what constitutes a quotation. But, as a general rule of thumb, quotations are here considered to be whatever can be traced to a particular biblical passage. In terms of the language employed, although Teilhard generally used Latin in his explicit quotations, this is not universally the case. Thus, 156 out of 201 explicit quotations are in Latin, and five more are in Greek, which is generally accompanied by the Latin or French equivalent. Implicit quotations are usually in French.

The above figures do not include a number of extremely important words or phrases which, although they often appear in quotation marks or italics, do not refer to any one text in particular—or if they do, have acquired a distinct Teilhardian meaning of their own. In ninety-eight instances of such words or phrases, there are eighteen references to the "Omega-Christ" as distinct from the explicit quotation of the phrase "Alpha and Omega" (Apoc. 1:8), thirty-three mentions of the "plérôme," and similarly, some eleven references to the "Parousie."

B. LITERARY CHARACTERISTICS OF TEILHARD'S USE OF SACRED SCRIPTURE

In addition to mere statistical counts, there are a number of literary peculiarities that constitute a major key to understanding Teilhard. Be-

8. Teilhard's frequent use of "Hoc est Corpus Meum" (13 times) is here counted as an implicit quotation of St. Paul inasmuch as it is apparently first of all a quotation from the Roman Canon, as the single parallel quotation "hic est calix sanguinis mei," as well as the liturgical context, would indicate. Cf. "The Priest" in *Writings in Time of War* (London: William Collins Sons &. Co. Ltd., 1968); (New York: Harper & Row, 1968), pp. 207, 208, 210; *Ecrits du temps de la guerre* (Paris: Grasset, 1965), pp. 287, 289 (abbreviated hereafter as *WTW* and *Ecrits* respectively). As shall be seen, the direct extension of the meaning to include the "mystical body" favors this as an implicitly Pauline quotation. (*Ecrits* has been republished as vol. 12 of *Oeuvres de Teilhard de Chardin* by Editions du Seuil, Paris. Page numbers in this study refer to the Grasset edition.)

sides his predeliction for St. Matthew when it comes to a choice between synoptic parallels, there is the matter of variant readings and
transpositions of word order.

The transpositions mean very little as far as the sense of the passages
is concerned; in many cases they may only reflect Teilhard's attempts
to fit phrases, even when in Latin, more consistently into the syntax of
his French sentences. However, along with these transpositions, there
are often variations in wording. Again, this may be of very little consequence to the meaning, as when the phrase from Luke *neque tinea
corrumpit* is rendered *Tinea non corrumpit*, as in the essay "The Heart
of the Matter."[9] But in a number of cases it would appear that Teilhard
was simply quoting from memory, and that his memory did not always
serve him with complete accuracy. Hence it is found that one of his
most frequent quotations, which appears in the Vulgate as "Necesse est
enim ut veniant scandala" (Matt. 18:7) is accurately quoted only once
during the seventeen years in which he cites this passage seven times.
This one time is in *The Divine Milieu*, which went through several re-
dactions that were corrected and criticized by friends before it ever
reached its present form. Teilhard's most common variations of this
text are the substitution of *necessarium* for *necesse* and *eveniant* or
adveniant for *veniant*. This appears to be insignificant in terms of
meaning, but the trait does not recommend Teilhard as a stickler for
accuracy.

It is this characteristic that allows him rather ingenuously to adapt
Scripture passages to his purpose by a simple change of context. Thus,
again, in *The Divine Milieu*,[10] (Matt. 5:18) "Iota unum aut anus apex
non praeteribit a lege" is quoted without the last two words, making
for an easy accommodation to his own purpose, which is to speak of all
the elements and effort contained in the consummation of the universe.
Obviously Teilhard was aware that he was accommodating Scripture at
this point. But was the accommodation facilitated by a lapse of memory
or was the omission deliberate?

Some variations are so obvious as to be undoubtedly intentional, and
in themselves form a fascinating study of the development of Teilhard's
thought. One classic case is another of his favorite passages, Romans
8:28. In his 1916 essay "La Vie cosmique,"[11] a portion of this verse is
quoted correctly: "Omnia cooperantur in bonum." But in his 1917
"L'union créatrice,"[12] it had already become "*Credenti*, omnia
convertuntur in bonum." (Emphasis added; compare VG: "Diligentibus, omnia cooperantur in bonum.") These changes, particularly of
the verb, are decisive, for intentional or not, they pave the way for an

9. "Le Coeur de la Matière" (1950), in *Oeuvres de Teilhard de Chardin* (Paris: Editions du Seuil, 1975), 13:27.
10. Cf. *DM*, p. 117; *Oeuvres*, 4:170.
11. Cf. *WTW*, p. 69; *Ecrits*, p. 57.
12. *WTW*, p. 170; *Ecrits*, p. 191.

accommodation that obviously is intentional, for in 1918, this same reading, repeated in "La foi qui opère"[13] became in "Forma Christi"[14]: "Credenti, omnia convertuntur 'in Christum.'" This same play on words was repeated in *The Divine Milieu*[15] with the sequence "in bonum"–"in Deum"–"in Christum" but with the "Credenti" corrected to "Diligentibus." After this 1927 appearance, Romans 8:28 was not again used in any form. Interestingly, *The Divine Milieu* appears to mark the end of an era in Teilhard's use of Sacred Scripture.

It would appear from these instances—not entirely isolated but characteristic of much of his use of Sacred Scripture—that Teilhard was a writer who felt at home in a very subjective approach to the meanings of biblical words. While he felt justified in his appeal to the written word, the question of complete accuracy was treated with some nonchalance, apparently in the interest of exploiting the fullest potentiality of the passage, even should it require a change or a gloss, much in the time-honored tradition of some of the earliest Church Fathers.[16]

C. THE "SENSES" OF SCRIPTURE IN TEILHARD

The problem arises of whether the word *sense* refers to the words in themselves, to their author (human as well as divine), or to the reader. Thus, in the case of the "literal sense," medieval commentators judged it to be simply the "real" sense (derived from *res*—the "thing" itself) or even the "carnal" sense of the words themselves, without much regard for the intention of the author. What remained was generally lumped together as being the "spiritual" and, by implication, the "true" sense.[17] Modern commentators, on the other hand, generally understand the literal sense as that directly intended by the author, a concept that, although logical enough, immediately presents us with the problem of second-guessing what the author's intention actually was.

13. "Operative Faith," *WTW*, p. 238 (*Ecrits*, p. 320).
14. *WTW*, p. 258 (*Ecrits*, p. 343).
15. *DM*, p. 101 (*Oeuvres*, 4:150).
16. It should be noted that Teilhard's approach to Rom. 8:28 is not without precedent. Two old Jesuit commentaries, with which Teilhard was undoubtedly familiar, quote these words from the Church Fathers:

> *Omnia* porro dicens procul dubio ". . . etiam quae videntur adversa comprehendit; sive enim tribulatio sive paupertas. . . . Deus ea omnia in contrarium vertere potest; ea quippe est ejus potestas, ut onerosa nobis reddat levia et in subsidia (salutis) convertat." (Chrys). Cf. Rudolpho Cornely, S.J., *Commentarius in S. Pauli Ap. Epistolas* (*Cursus Scripturae Sacrae* [Paris: Lethielleux, 1927]), 7:445.

> Cornelius à Lapide, in his *Divi Pauli Epistolarum* (*Commentarius in Scripturas Sacras* [Paris: Vives, 1868], 18:144) adds this sentence from St. Gregory: "Electi . . . in tentatione proficiunt, et quod eis diabolus praeparat ad ruinam, hoc Deus *convertit in gloriam*" (Emphasis added.)

17. In this discussion of the senses of Scripture in Teilhard's works, the divisions of scriptural senses reviewed by Raymond E. Brown in his article "Hermeneutics," in the *Jerome Biblical Commentary* (Englewood Cliffs, N.J., Prentice-Hall, 1968, pp. 605-23), are followed.

This involves one in evaluating the modern commentator's own pre-suppositions. For example, Teilhard will be seen struggling with the weighty problem of what is to be considered the *obvious* meaning of the Pauline phrase "The Body of Christ." Are these words to be taken "literally" at their face value? Or is their literal meaning to be automatically assumed to be in the realm of metaphor, as the adjective *mystical*, appended to the phrase since medieval times, indicates?

1. The "Literal Sense" of Scripture in Teilhard

For the purposes of this discussion, the definition of the literal sense as understood by Brown and that seems to be that implied by the Encyclical "Divino afflantu spiritu" will be adopted: "the sense which the human author directly intended and which his words convey."[18]

The reason for beginning with this rather restricted definition is to place in as great a relief as possible all the "more-than-literal" senses (Brown's terminology) that abound in Teilhard's understanding of Scripture, and in this way to deal first with an objection that is often raised to Teilhard's approach to Christology in general, namely, that he had little or no regard for the historical Christ and hence for the synoptic tradition. Here then another look at the statistics, particularly those involving quotations from the Synoptic Gospels, should be taken.[19] Of some seventy explicit quotations from the Gospels, forty-three are from the synoptics. Thus Teilhard can hardly be charged with ignoring the historical Christ. But he himself answered this charge in a number of places, most notably in his "Introduction to the Christian Life" in 1944:

> As a concrete historical fact, it is indisputable that the living and dominating idea of the universal-Christ first appeared and developed in the consciousness of Christianity from a starting-point in the Man-Jesus recognized and worshipped as God. Even today abandonment of the historical character of Christ (that is, the divinity of the historic Christ) would mean the instant dismissal into the unreal of all the mystical energy accumulated in the Christian phylum during the last two thousand years. Christ born of the Virgin, and Christ risen from the dead: the two are one inseparable whole.[20]

Thus, it is not a question of fact, but of emphasis:

> Confronted with this *factual* situation, a legitimate and "comforting" attitude for the modern believer would appear to be to say to

18. *JBC*, p. 607.
19. Cf. Appendix C.
20. In *Christianity and Evolution* (London: Collins, 1971; New York: Harcourt Brace Jovanovich, 1971), pp. 158-59: *Comment je crois*, (*Oeuvres* [Paris, Editions du Seuil, 1969]), 10:186-87. Note that the 10th volume of the series in English bears a different title from the French edition. The English edition will be henceforth designated *C&E*. This particular essay bears two alternate titles, "Introduction à la Vie chrétienne" and "Introduction au christianisme" respectively.

himself: "Subject to every reservation about the often uncritical way in which pious writers have tried to describe the psychology of the God-man, I believe in the divinity of the Child of Bethlehem *because, in so far as*, and *in the form in which* that divinity is historically and biologically included in the reality of the universal-Christ to whom my faith and my worship are more directly attached."[21]

Accordingly, it should not surprise one when Teilhard chooses not to linger on the historical or the literal accounts, but to seek continually for their fullest meaning.

Consider "Verbum caro factum est." Can there be a single passage in the New Testament, which, if taken literally, has broader implications than this? And so, Teilhard, never content with the status quo, must move on to its extension:

> *Et Verbum caro factum est*. This was the Incarnation. From this first and fundamental contact between God and the human race—which means in virtue of the penetration of the Divine into our nature—a new life was born: an unlooked for magnification and "obediential" extension of our natural capabilities—grace.[22]

For Teilhard there can be no stopping at outward appearances. Every word or phrase of Scripture must be understood in the fullest literal sense it can bear:

> In the first place, he is physically and literally, *He who fills all things. . . .*
> Again physically and literally, he is he who *consummates. . . .*
> Finally, and once more physically and literally . . . it is he who *gives its consistence* to the entire edifice of matter and Spirit. In him too, *"the head of Creation,"* it follows, the fundamental cosmic process of cephalisation culminates and is completed.[23]

It would seem from the above that Teilhard's understanding of the literal sense was something that goes beyond the more restricted meaning that many moderns, such as Brown, have given it. In some ways, Teilhard's understanding of *literal* as being more or less synonymous with *physical* would seem to hark back to the medieval understanding of this sense as *carnal*, but without the apparent depreciation that the medieval adjective implied. Teilhard's stress, on the contrary, seems to contain more than a hint of strong criticism of the very pedestrian and unimaginative understanding that the medieval commentators were also criticizing, but where their appeal was to a more fully "spiritual" understanding, Teilhard's was, on the contrary, to a more daring and realistic application than the medieval theologians and their modern

21. *Ibid.*, p. 159; (French ed., p. 187).
22. "Cosmic Life" (1916) in *WTW*, p. 50; "La Vie cosmique" in *Ecrits*, p. 40.
23. "Super-Humanity, Super-Christ, Super-Charity" (1943) in *S&C*, pp. 166-67; *Oeuvres*, 9:211.

followers have been able to achieve. Whether such an understanding of Scripture is in fact to be considered as truly literal or, lacking any assurance of the original author's real intention, must be considered as "more-than-literal" (to use Raymond Brown's phrase again) must remain problematic, and for the purposes of this study perhaps ultimately irrelevant. Instead, as will be seen in the following glimpse of more-than-literal senses of Scripture in Teilhard, it is not the problem of categorization that should detain one, but of the legitimacy of his understanding of the revealed word of God concerning His Christ.

2. Accommodation and "More-than-Literal" Senses

For determining the legitimacy of Teilhard's interpretations as well as tracing the development of the reasoning that underlies them, it will be necessary to look into other types of understandings and usages of Scripture by Teilhard, considering his use of accommodation and other more-than-literal applications of Scripture—even those he obviously intended to be taken metaphorically. The similarities within his underlying approach to all passages of Scripture and the differences in intent in their application will become clarified. For only by a comprehensive view of all of his scriptural applications—the fanciful as well as the serious—can one begin to appreciate the fullness of his intent.

Mere "accommodation," of course, is not, properly speaking, a "sense" of Sacred Scripture, but merely the utilization of scriptural words and phraseology to convey meanings not intended by either the human author or the Spirit who inspired him. About one-tenth of Teilhard's scriptural "quotations" are clearly by way of accommodation, yet even in these there seems to be a peculiar appropriateness. Who can say that his treatment of Matthew 5:18 ("Iota unum . . .") is completely in disregard of the implications of the original meaning? Or to take an even more startling example, there is his use of "Qui potest capere, capiat" (Matt. 19:12). One would expect this to appear in his much-discussed but little-seen "L'Evolution de la chasteté," but instead it is found in two earlier works in a much different context. In his "Cosmic Life" of 1916 the following passage is found:

> Christ has a *cosmic Body* that extends throughout the whole universe: such is the final proposition to be borne in mind. "*Qui potest capere, capiat.*"[24]

It was in the same spirit of accommodated emphasis that Teilhard closed "The Mystical Milieu" a year later, having first spoken of those granted mystical vision with words borrowed in a similar way:

24. WTW, p. 58; *Ecrits*, p. 47.

In particular, they will recognize the roll of the created thing in the sharpening of sensibility, which gives the warmth that Charity calls for, and the vast cosmic realities that give God his tangible and palpable being here below. *Amictus (mundo) sicut vestimento*—clothed (in the world) as in a garment.

And again, by way of a postscript, he added:

Qui potest capere, capiat.[25]

An ironic accommodation? Perhaps. Yet an arresting one, equally "offensive to pious ears" and to sensibilities as was the original occasion, and concerning the same subject—the role of the flesh.

A rather fascinating bit of accommodation presents itself in the use of the words *Amictus mundo*, a startling phrase that Teilhard used several times in his earlier works and is apparently from Psalm 104 (103): 2. As it first appears in "The Mystical Milieu," the word *mundo*, being a "gloss," is set off in parentheses, but in *The Divine Milieu* (1926) and in "Some Reflections on the Conversion of the World" (1936) the phrase expanded into "Christus *'amictus Mundo'* " and "*Christus amictus mundo*" respectively.[26] But more fascinating yet, in an undated essay believed by Cuénot to date from 1918 or 1919, entitled "En quoi consiste le corps humain?"[27] the same idea was conveyed in a Greek equivalent, *egkekosmismenē*, which is not found in Scripture, but appears to be compounded from *en* (over) and *kosmeō* (to adorn) on the model of *kekosmēmenos* in 3 Maccabees 6:1 or *kekosmētai* as in 2 Maccabees 9:16 and Luke 21:5, but not without a slight root change to bring it in line with the related concept of *kosmos*, hence *egkekosmismemē*.[28] Thus, there seems to be here not only an example of scriptural accommodation, but also of Teilhard's predilection for Greek in his formulation of neologisms.

Whatever one may think of the validity of the practice of "accommodation" in the use of Sacred Scripture, it must be admitted, in the fact of Teilhard's ingenuity, that often his accommodations bordered closely on what Brown terms the "more-than-literal" sense of Scripture, that is, a sense which, although it may not have been intended by the author, has nevertheless had a long history of being accepted as a valid sense of Scripture, often on the basis of parallels drawn by the New Testament itself (e.g., the Passover imagery of John, Paul's interpreta-

25. *WTW*, pp. 148-49; "Le Milieu mystique" in *Ecrits*, p. 167.
26. Cf. *DM*, p. 30; *Oeuvres*, 4:49: S&C, p. 125; "Quelques réflexions sur la conversion du Monde" in *Oeuvres*, 9:164. Finally, in *Oeuvres* 11:105 we have "Deus amictus mundi."
27. S&C, p. 12; *Oeuvres*, 9:34. See note on the date of this essay in Claude Cuénot's *Teilhard de Chardin: A Biographical Study* (Baltimore:Helicon, 1958), p. 451.
28. Cf. G. Kittle, *Theological Dictionary of the New Testament* (Grand Rapids, Mich.: W. B. Eerdmans, 1965), 3:867.

tion of Exodus, etc.) or by the Fathers of the Church, liturgical usage, or even modern appeals to the "decoding rather than the elimination of myth."[29]

Again, apart from the question of the validity of such interpretations, Teilhard's appeals to these "more-than-literal," or what has often been called "spiritual" or sometimes "typical" senses of Scripture are numerous, particularly in his earlier writings. For example, the whole episode concerning Peter's walking on the water to meet Christ (Matt. 14:28-31) was used to introduce the 1918 essay "La foi qui opère,"[30] and was used again in conjunction with Mark 9:25 ("Domine, adjuva incredulitatem meum") in The Divine Milieu,[31] which also uses Luke 18:41 ("Domine, fac ut videam"[32]), all in regard to the gift of discernment of the divine presence in the world. But again, as late as 1947, he used Matthew 8:10 ("What do you fear, O men of little faith?") in his "Faith in Peace," an essay written in an otherwise untheological context.[33]

There is also some use of allegorical interpretation, as in the relating of the stories of Jacob and the Angel at the beginning of "Cosmic Life" in 1916[34] and "The Ascension of Elijah" in much the same manner in "The Spiritual Power of Matter" of 1919,[35] both of which are used to depict mankind's struggle with and victory over the material world, a world that is at the same time an agent and revelation of divine power. At first appearance this allegorical use of Scripture seems to have been strictly for its evocative force of imagery, but as late as 1947, in his essay "Faith in Man"[36] he associated Jacob, along with the stories of Babel, the Titans, Prometheus, and Faust, and, rather surprisingly, even that of the temptation of Christ on the mountain, as all being illustrative of the awakening of life to its powers and the subsequent challenge to submit to a power greater than oneself, for good or for ill. Here there was an appeal to a probative force, not in the teachings of the Church, but to the common experience of mankind. So here again, as in his use of accommodation, this use of a more-than-literal sense seemed prompted by more than just a fortuitous wording or a moralistic penchant. It was certainly more than simply a rifling of the Bible for picturesque imagery. Rather, these more-than-literal applications of

29. Brown, JBC, p. 614, No. 49.
30. WTW, p. 226; Ecrits, p. 307.
31. DM, p. 117; Oeuvres, 4:171.
32. DM, p. 111; Oeuvres, 4:164.
33. The Future of Man (New York: Harper & Row, 1964), p. 149 (designated as FM hereafter); "La foi en la Paix" in L'Avenir de l'Homme (Oeuvres, 5) (Paris: Editions du Seuil, 1959), p. 191.
34. See WTW, p. 14; Ecrits, p. 5.
35. "La Puissance spirituelle de la Matière" in Ecrits, p. 437 (this essay is not published in WTW): also Hymn of the Universe (New York: Harper & Row, 1965), p. 59; Hymne de l'Univers (Paris, Editions du Seuil, 1961), p. 61 (designated HU hereafter).
36. "La Foi en l'Homme," FM, p. 187; Oeuvres, 5:238.

Scripture were employed by Teilhard to reinforce what he insisted was the meaning of Scripture "physiquement et littéralement."

What exactly was Teilhard's understanding of the true sense of Sacred Scripture and the process by which it can be determined? He seems to have entertained no theory of a "sensus plenior" in any explicit way.[37] On the contrary, when he spoke as he did ". . . au sens complet et physique de saint Paul . . . celui in quo omnia constant,"[38] Teilhard seems to be affirming again only what he understood to be the fullest literal sense that the words can bear. But on the other hand, he appears to have admitted that it is only in light of what is now known of the universe that the ancient words of St. Paul and others can begin to be fully understood. Hence, Teilhard's view of this matter might be tentatively described as one of a bi-polar tension between the literal meaning of the words (taken in the medieval or more purely literary sense of the word) and the possible meaning of these words when understood in the light of a modern world view. Yet, for all that, it cannot be said that Teilhard was not concerned with the literal sense in the modern meaning of that word; in fact, the appeal to what he obviously believed was the overall intent of the author is precisely what Teilhard would feel vindicated his interpretation.

How he did this, and the extent to which he did it, is the subject of this book.

D. TEILHARD'S DEPLOYMENT OF SACRED SCRIPTURE IN RESPECT TO THE DEVELOPMENT OF HIS THOUGHT

Now that I have opened this Pandora's box of unsolved problems, it might be well to pause a bit, sitting on the lid, as it were, and calculating the next move, taking into account in greater detail the actual range and variety of the scriptural citations that will be confronted, and organizing them into manageable groups. But before this, let us survey the terrain, the *Sitz-in-Leben* as it might be called, of these citations in the general pattern of Teilhard's works.

I have mentioned earlier that *The Divine Milieu* (1927) marked something of the end of an era in Teilhard's approach to Scripture. This little book represents Teilhard's greatest summary of scriptural appeals, with fifty-four explicit quotations. They range over the whole gamut of possible senses besides being a fair sampling of all the types of peculiarities that characterize his work. This is understandable, for

---

37. Brown defines the *sensus plenior* as "the deeper meaning, intended by God but not clearly intended by the human author, that is seen to exist in the words of Scripture when they are studied in the light of further revelation or of development in the understanding of revelation." *JBC*, p. 616, No. 57.
38. "Réflexions sur le Péché originel" (1947); *C&E*, pp. 190-91; *Oeuvres*, 10:223.

The Divine Milieu was the culmination of Teilhard's efforts, begun early in World War I, to sum up his approach to Christian ascetics and mysticism. Thus, despite its dating from the middle years of his life and thought (those spent in China: 1922-44), *The Divine Milieu* reflects something of the nature of his early writings, particularly those of the World War I period, which tend to be of a highly composite nature, synthetically combining elements of philosophy, theology, history, and, above all, mysticism.

These early writings, and to some extent, *The Divine Milieu*, utilized a wide range of scriptural quotations in a variety of ways, but most noticeably they invoked scriptural passages as "leading" inspirations. It has been seen that the stories of Jacob and Elijah were so utilized, but not these alone.[39] More striking, however, are the introductory verses to "The Struggle Against the Multitude,"[40] a philosophical essay of rather mystical style written in March 1917, shortly antedating a more successful metaphysical effort in "Creative Union" of November 1917.[41] The former essay begins with "Ut unum sint, sicut unum sumus" (John 17:22) and "Si quis vult animam suam salvam facere, perdet eam" (Matt. 10:39), both unusual introductions to a venture into a metaphysics of union. But after "Forma Christi" in 1918,[42] which employs a scriptural verse at the beginning of each major section, Teilhard no longer used this device until the appearance of *The Divine Milieu*, which is dedicated thus:

"SIC DEUS DILEXIT MUNDUM"
For those who love the world[43]

Beginning with the year 1921, a much lower percentage of Teilhard's writings, as listed by Cuénot,[44] is on theological and philosophical subjects. Twenty-five out of twenty-nine titles are on such subjects during the years 1916-20, while in the years 1921-26 only fifteen theological or philosophical essays are listed out of forty-eight titles. None of these 1921-26 essays begins with a scriptural quotation, nor do any others during the rest of his life with the sole exception of *The Divine Milieu* in 1927. The cause of this change can only be speculated upon, but it seems to mirror a number of other changes as well, among them a much stricter division between theological and philosophical speculation on the one hand, and his technical geological and paleontological

39. Cf. "La Maîtrise du monde et le règne de Dieu" (1916) in *Ecrits*, p. 67; *WTW*, p. 74 (Matt. 4:4), also Acts 17:28 in "Le Milieu Mystique" (1917) in *Ecrits*, p. 137; *WTW*, p. 167, and Matt. 14:28, 31 and Heb. 11:1 in "La foi qui opère" (1919) in *Ecrits*, p. 309; *WTW*, p. 226.
40. "La Lutte contre la multitude"; *Ecrits*, p. 113; *WTW*, p. 94.
41. "L'Union créatrice"; *Ecrits*, p. 151; *WTW*, p. 169.
42. *WTW*, p. 248; *Ecrits*, p. 331.
43. *DM*, p. 5; *Oeuvres*, 4:11 (John 3:16).
44. Cuénot, pp. 414-24.

work on the other. No doubt the resumption of his professional scientific training was a major factor in this, but there may have been other factors as well.

Among the changes noticeable after this early period is an increasing tendency to postpone citing Scripture in his theological speculations until well within the text or even at the end, along with markedly reducing the frequency of scriptural quotations.[45] These tendencies are accompanied by a lessening of mere scriptural accommodation and a more sober use of the "more-than-literal" sense, particularly in its allegorical forms. Had he been criticized by one or more of his friends? It may have been so. But that Teilhard differed from some of his friends, particularly in his early period, is evident from a letter to his lifelong friend and advisor, Père Auguste Valensin, S.J. The letter was written on December 17, 1922, in friendly criticism of an article on pantheism that Valensin had written for the *Dictionnaire apologétique de la foi catholique*. It reads in part:

> Note that I understand perfectly the restrictions that the dictionary was imposing upon you.—But all the same you have the right to speak as St. Paul!—This may be said, I repeat, without prejudice of the deep interest your article has afforded me. But, I beg of you, do not just refute! Assimilate! Construct![46]

Thus, despite a modification of his tactics, Teilhard's basic attitude was to change very little.

45. About fifty quotations occur following the 1927 *The Divine Milieu* as against my total of 263 explicit and implicit quotes throughout his writings.
46. Correspondance au P. Valensin, No. 17, Teilhard Archives, Paris. (My translation. See Appendix D, §2, d, ii, for French original.)

2

A General Survey of Biblical Citations in Teilhard's Works

Now that we have examined the general characteristics of Teilhard's use of Sacred Scripture, let us take a closer look at the actual deployment of these texts in relation to the broad thematic areas of his thought. An attempt will be made to adhere to a chronological order within each thematic division, for, as has been seen in the preceding examples, certain texts come into use only during specific periods of Teilhard's writings, others remain perennial, and still others, used in one way earlier in his works, sometimes surface later with a quite different connotation. More often, a slow development takes place, sometimes by stages that are almost imperceptible except through close comparison.

Included in this survey are not only the more important quotations (both explicit and implicit), but also some of the many mentions of or references to certain texts and themes. In opening up this survey to the less explicit type of scriptural mention or allusion, it is necessary to try to determine the extent to which a certain cross-fertilization has taken place in Teilhard's scriptural understanding. It is evident that Teilhard claimed an extensive Johannine as well as Pauline inspiration, yet Pauline outnumber Johannine quotations about five to one (153 vs. 31, to be exact, counting both explicit and implicit quotations, providing that most of the allusions to the "Omega-Christ" are put in a separate category). The many quotations from the synoptic Gospels should also be assimilated into the picture (or set in contrast if and where assimilation is impossible). Again, it is only in relation to the complete picture that Teilhard's understanding of his ostensibly "Pauline" Christ can be fully evaluated.

As for thematic divisions, the sequence suggested by more traditional theology will be followed, modified through the occurrence or
absence of scriptural references in Teilhard's works.[1]

A. FAITH AND REVELATION

Teilhard's meditative use of Matthew 14:28-31 (Peter's walking on
the water to meet Christ) to illustrate man's need for faith as contrasted
to the paralysis induced by doubt has already been observed. This first
occurred in his 1918 "Operative Faith"[2] but here it is not precisely a
theological faith that is being referred to—rather a faith in the future.
Even his use of Hebrews 11:1 on the same page has this same connotation, or more exactly, Christian faith is seen in the end to be the
guarantee of a faith that is viable for the future. More directly theological applications of this same biblical theme in a "spiritual sense" are
found in *The Divine Milieu* along with several other texts to which
Teilhard related it. The phrase "Ego sum . . . nolite timere" from the
preceding verse, Matthew 14:27 (or John 6:20), appears twice in this
work.[3] The second time it has direct application to Christ's Eucharistic
presence in the world, a difficult concept that will be examined later.
The Divine Milieu also uses Mark 9:25 (the sole unmistakable quotation
from Mark in Teilhard: "Domine, adjuva incredulitatem meum") as
well as of Luke 18:41 ("Domine, fac ut videam") and Luke 1:45 ("Beata
quae credidisti").[4] But it is his use of Hebrews 11:1 that should most
attract attention here, because it appears in the form "Fides, *substantia
rerum*" (emphasis mine) without the "sperandarum."[5] Was this a slip or
an intentional omission? Either way, it is interesting in light of a passage in "Le Christianisme dans le monde" written in 1933, where an
editor's footnote focuses attention on a similar transformation of the
meaning of "faith" in these words of Teilhard found under the heading
"La Religion de demain":

> *This endless capacity of harmonising with the whole physical and
> psychological order of our universe* can have but one explanation:
> the Christ who gradually reveals himself to Christian thought is not

---

1. It is advisable to examine the scheme of the 1924 "Mon univers" (*Oeuvres*,
   9:63-114; *S&C*, pp. 37-85) with its broad divisions of "Philosophy," "Religion"
   (speculative theology), and "History." This essay, along with the unpublished
   "Comment je vois" (1946) and "Le Christique" (1955), constitutes Teilhard's most
   important theological summaries. However, both "La Vie cosmique" of 1916 and
   "Le coeur de la Matière" of 1950 (unpublished) remain crucial as semi-
   autobiographical studies of the genesis of his thought.
2. Cf. *WTW*, p. 226; *Ecrits*, p. 307.
3. Cf. *DM*, pp. 50, 117; *Oeuvres*, 4:77, 172.
4. *DM*, pp. 111, 114; *Oeuvres* 4:164, 168 "Lord, help my unbelief" (Mark 9:25);
   "Lord, that I may see" (Luke 18:41); "Blessed are those who have believed" (Luke
   1:45).
5. *DM*, p. 118; *Oeuvres*, 4:173: "Faith, the *substance* of things . . . (hoped for)" (Heb.
   11:1).

a phantasy nor a symbol (*if that were so he would be found in some way wanting or would cease to satisfy us*); he is, or at least he introduces, the reality of what, through the whole structure of human activity, we are awaiting.[6]

This progression of thought is but one reflection of a Teilhardian insight that will have immense implication for his ideas on both Revelation and the Christ "in quo omnia constant." "Fides" is not merely an intellectual attitude, nor a mere projection of wishes into the future; it is ultimately inherence in the person of Christ. It is this "substantialized" faith that corrects the illusion of blind chance in the believer's comprehension of the world. Hence Teilhard could also use 1 John 5:4 ("Haec est quae vincit mundum, fides nostra") in a sense in which faith becomes substantialized in Christ.[7]

It would be a premature undertaking at this point to attempt to assess more closely Teilhard's ideas on the process and nature of Revelation. However, early in his writings, two very important remarks appear with attendant footnotes on this subject in his 1918 "Forma Christi." The first concerns the act of revelation on the part of God, and is in a section that begins with the inscription "Omnia traham ad meipsum" (John 12:32):[8]

> Until God speaks, however much the soul may reflect upon its appetites and desires, it can never discover the nature of the beatifying complement it seeks, *but has not yet risen high enough* to grasp.

It has this footnote (by Teilhard):

> It would appear, nevertheless, that before God's word has been spoken by an inspired Prophet, there already exists in men's minds a pre-formation, or partial divination, of the truths that are to be revealed. Otherwise, it would be difficult to explain the frequent appearance in ancient cosmogonies of the ideas of a divine Triad, a Virgin Mother, or of a just victim. Moreover, if dogmas were not "in the air" at the time the Prophet is speaking, he would not be believed nor understood.[9]

Shortly after, following the quoting of Romans 10:17 ("Fides ex auditu"), come this passage and footnote:

> At that moment, if the soul holds to its faith, its hitherto vague desires *embody themselves* around the new truth. Accompanying faith in the revealed dogma, it feels coming down into it a clearly defined, conscious need for that dogma. All revealed truth, accordingly, including even the distant Trinity, is seen by the soul henceforth to be indispensable to its beatification.

6. *S&C*, p. 110; *Oeuvres*, 9:143.
7. "This is that which conquers the world, our faith"; cf. *DM*, p. 121; *Oeuvres*, 4:177.
8. "I will draw all things to myself": *WTW*, pp. 254-56; *Ecrits*, pp. 339-42.
9. *WTW*, p. 255; *Ecrits*, p. 341.

Without this appeal, belief in this supreme dogma would never go beyond the stage of being strictly an epiphenomenon in our interior life.[10]

In the light of this *preformation*, Teilhard quoted Acts 17:27 three times between the years 1923 and 1927. In *The Divine Milieu* we find the following:

> God tends, by the logic of His creative effort, to make Himself sought and perceived by us: *Posuit homines . . . si forte attrectent eum*.[11]

For Teilhard it is altogether logical that until Christ was revealed, God remained more or less the "Deo ignoto" (Acts 17:23). In using this phrase at the conclusion of his 1920 "Note on Progress,"[12] he seemed to be implying that St. Paul himself was appealing to something resembling a "preformation" of human consciousness.

In much the same spirit, much later in life, Teilhard touched on the problem of the existence of an "ongoing" revelation in a highly speculative essay, "The God of Evolution." Borrowing from the account of Peter's profession of faith in Matthew 16:15-16, he added:

> The gospel tells us that Christ once asked his disciples: "*Quem dicunt esse Filium hominis?*" To which Peter impetuously answered: "*Tu es Christus, Filius Dei vivi*"—which was both an answer and no answer, since it still left the question of knowing what exactly is "the true living God."[13]

There are no scriptural citations directly connected by Teilhard with revelation, but let us look at the "circularity" of faith in Teilhard's synthesis. Faith, as has been seen, guarantees the future. Thus, divine faith gives certainty to human faith. But paradoxically, divine faith is in some way or another dependent on our ability to make sense of the universe in which we find ourselves. Hence, the famous quotation which, taken out of context, proved so scandalous to the Roman authorities:

> If, as the result of some interior revolution, I were to lose in succession my faith in Christ, my faith in a personal God, and my faith in spirit, I feel that I should continue *to believe* invincibly in the world.[14]

10. *WTW*, p. 256; *Ecrits*, p. 341.
11. ". . . So that all nations might seek the deity and, by feeling their way towards him, succeed in finding Him." (Acts 17:27 as translated in *The Jerusalem Bible* (Garden City, N.Y.: Doubleday & Co., 1966). Cf. *DM*, p. 111; *Oeuvres* 4:167.
12. "Note sur le Progrès," *Oeuvres*, 5:37; *FM*, p. 24.
13. "Le Dieu de l'Evolution," *Oeuvres*, 10:289; *C&E*, p. 241. The essay is dated Oct. 25, 1953. The final phrase above appears to be from 1 Thess. 1:9.
14. "How I Believe" in *C&E*, p. 99; "Comment je crois" in *Oeuvres*, 10:120. This passage was singled out in a letter from the Congregation of the Seminaries warning seminary officials to place Teilhard's books on restricted reading. Cf. *The London Tablet* (July 14, 1962), p. 676; also *Acta Apostolicae Sedis* 54 (1962): 526.

No allusion is made here to Romans 1:20 or to Wisdom 13:1-9, but while manner of expression is entirely different, the logic is the same. "Demonstrations" of God's existence (and attributes), if approached by way of rational arguments, depend on the intelligibility of the universe, but for Teilhard this intelligibility is not a question of the past. Ultimately it remains suspended in the outcome of the future. Hence, faith in the divine and faith in the future must meet each other, and together they form what he later terms an "existential exigency."[15] In the end, the two faiths are inseparable. Once, when challenged in a debate by Père D. Dubarle, O.P., on the possibility of a sudden and catastrophic end coming to the humanity that Teilhard envisioned as progressively moving toward maturation (Dubarle suggested that a stray comet might end it all), Teilhard responded: "That will never happen." Dubarle then objected: "That is the answer of a theologian, not of a philosopher." Teilhard's response was: "Our life should be only a life of believing."[16]

B. CREATION AND FALL

For Teilhard, the scriptural quotation par excellence on the subject of creation (and suffering) was Romans 8:22: "Omnia creatura ingemiscit et parturit." This quotation first appeared in his "Cosmic Life" in 1916[17] and after that five more times by explicit quotation and at least six times through indirect quotation or allusion up through the year 1937. This is hardly surprising, considering that at least as early as 1916, in the same essay, he accommodated John 8:32 to proclaim:

> Christ is the term *of even the natural* evolution of living beings; evolution is holy. There we have *the truth that makes free*, the divinely prepared cure for faithful but ardently moved minds that suffer because they cannot reconcile in themselves two almost equally imperative and vital impulses, faith in the world and faith in God.[18]

But it is not the evolution of the world alone that is at stake, for alluding to Colossians 2:19 (cf. Eph. 4:16) he wrote:

> And since Christ was born, and ceased to grow, and died, *everything has continued in motion because he has not yet attained the fullness of his form. The mystical Christ has not reached the peak of his growth—nor, therefore, has the cosmic Christ.*[19]

15. "Journal" 20 (8), p. 59 (July 15, 1954). See note 37 below for more on this notation.
16. "Notre vie ne saurait être qu'une vie de croyant," "Cosmologie et Théologie" (débat Teilhard–Dubarle) Jan. 19, 1947. Cf. *Teilhard Archives*, Paris, and Cuénot, p. 258 (English ed.).
17. *WTW*, p. 66; *Ecrits*, p. 54. Cf. also Appendix A.
18. *WTW*, p. 59; *Ecrits*, p. 47.
19. *WTW*, p. 59; *Ecrits*, p. 48.

Again, in beginning the next section, he affirmed:

"The world is still being created, and it is Christ who is reaching his fulfilment in it."[20]

With this approach, it is not surprising that the creation story of Genesis is hardly quoted at all in Teilhard's works. To be sure, there are allusions to the problems posed by the concept of creation "ex nihilo" and man's formation "ex limo," as well as the problem of polygenism, such as appear in the essay "The Struggle Against the Multitude"[21] and in his major work, *The Phenomenon of Man*.[22] But only one passage (quoted twice) from the book of Genesis other than his allegorical use of the story of Jacob and the Angel is to be found, and that is simply three words from Genesis 1:28:

"Increase and multiply": that, we have hitherto recognized, was the hallowed slogan of organic being. Is it possible that beyond a certain limit the two terms of the formula begin to be mutually contradictory? If multiplication is pushed further, is it not going to extinguish in us, by mechanization, the spark of spontaneity and consciousness that it has taken evolution three hundred million years of life and twenty thousand years of civilization to kindle in each one of us?[23]

Teilhard seems to have been trying, with great circumspection, to avoid any use of the creation story that could give occasion to the charge of an uncritical concordism in his synthesis. But this does not mean that Teilhard avoided biblical thought entirely in its anthropological expressions. Twice in 1917 he rather imaginatively employed the "Legion" of Luke's story of the possessed man at Gerasa (Luke 8:30) to express his philosophical notion of the potential infinitude of the number of created intelligent beings.[24] In the same year, in his "Mystical Milieu" (as the editors of *Writings in Time of War* have pointed out), Teilhard adopted the tripartite division that characterizes St. Paul's anthropology in 1 Thessalonians 5:23: "spiritus, anima, . . . et corpore."[25]

20. *WTW*, p. 60; *Ecrits*, p. 49.
21. See *WTW*, pp. 93-114; *Ecrits*, pp. 108-32.
22. Hereafter designated *PM* (New York: Harper & Row, 1959, 1965); pp. 122, 186, 188; *Le Phénomène humain* (*Oeuvres*, 1, Paris: Editions du Seuil, 1955), pp. 130, 206, 208.
23. "The Rise of the Other" in *Activation of Energy* (hereafter designated *AE*) (London: Collins, 1970; New York: Harcourt Brace Jovanovich, 1970), p. 66; "La Montée de l'Autre" in *L'Activation de l'Energie* (*Oeuvres*, 7) (Paris: Editions du Seuil, 1963), p. 72. The other use of this same phrase from Genesis is to be found in the essay "Comment je vois" (1948) recently published in *Les Directions de l'Avenir* (*Oeuvres*, 11) (Paris: Editions du Seuil, 1973), p. 193; "My Fundamental Vision," in *Toward the Future* (London, Collins; New York, Harcourt Brace Jovanovich, 1975 [hereafter referred to as *TF*]), p. 177.
24. See "The Struggle Against the Multitude" in *WTW*, p. 97; *Ecrits*, p. 116; cf. also "The Soul of the World," *WTW*, p. 181; *Ecrits*, p. 223.
25. See *WTW*, p. 118 n.2; *Ecrits*, p. 138 n.2.

But, because of its Christological overtones, in the matter of the "Fall" and its concomitant suffering Teilhard was unable to avoid the biblical genre; here his Pauline appeals met their greatest difficulties. Nevertheless, he seems to have managed to avoid confronting this problem in any detailed sense until the 1920s. In "Fall, Redemption, and Geocentrism," the quotation "Per peccatum mors" (Rom. 5:12) appears for the first time, with the problem posed in these terms:

> Now, St. Paul is categorical: *"Per peccatum mors."* Sin (original sin) does not explain the suffering and the mortality only of man: for St. Paul it explains all suffering. *It is the general solution of the problem of evil.*[26]

Thus presented, the problem cannot be avoided or judged irrelevant on "existential" grounds, and Teilhard was forced to reject the solution preferred by the more conservative theologians, who would restrict the cause of man's mortality to man's sin alone:

> This first way of solving the problem of its being impossible to pin down original sin is both precarious and humiliating. It avoids criticism by simply giving up; and, what is more serious, it compromises the very content of the dogma.[27]

Although linking death to sin may not be the most important element in St. Paul's doctrine of original sin, for Teilhard it was critical. In another essay, he returned to Romans 5:12:

> "Through sin comes death." In order to get away from evidence that is only too clear, an attempt is now being made to weaken this illuminating phrase. "Death, it is agreed, most certainly existed for animals before man's transgression; and, had man been faithful, even in his case it could not have been averted except by a sort of permanent miracle." However, not only do these distinctions still leave the problem of evil intact, they contradict the obvious meaning of the biblical text. For St Paul, we must remember, the world was only a week old when Adam sinned. Nothing in paradise, accordingly, had yet had time to perish. In the mind of the apostle, it was that transgression which ruined everything for the whole of creation.[28]

26. *C&E*, pp. 39-40; *Oeuvres*, 10:52-53. The following footnote of Teilhard's indicates the situation as he saw it:

> "To admit that there is, anywhere at all, suffering without sin, is to run counter to the thought of St Paul. For St Paul, original sin is so full an explanation of death that the existence of death is in itself sufficient to justify the deduction that there has been sin. I realize that Thomist theologians do not accept this, even though they claim the support of St Paul for their view."

27. "Note on Some Possible Historical Representations of Original Sin" in *C&E*, p. 48; *Oeuvres*, 10:64.
28. "Christology and Evolution" in *C&E*, p. 81; *Oeuvres*, 10:100. This essay dates from the end of 1933.

The problem posed by the biblical (and Pauline) doctrine of original sin always remained one of the major unsolved problems for Teilhard, and much has been written by others on this subject.[29] It is beyond the scope of this study to attempt to solve it; here it will merely be placed in the context of the biblical sources that Teilhard utilized in grappling with the question. In another essay, "Reflections on Original Sin," written in 1947, but only published in 1969,[30] Teilhard attempted to shift the emphasis from the apparent conflict of evolutionary theory and the account of the first sin to a more soteriological concentration on the relationship between the first Adam (Rom. 9:5) and the second Adam "in quo omnia constant" (Col. 1:17). But again the problem devolves on the critical relationship with evil in general, evil that seems to be inevitable within the whole process of evolution, even antecedent to man's appearance. Again Teilhard stressed the "statistical necessity" of evil in an evolutionary universe in his use of the "Necessarium est ut adveniant scandala" from Matthew 18:7.[31]

The existence of evil was no real problem for Teilhard, but there was a major problem in St. Paul's reliance on the account of Genesis and the subsequent implications for his Christology. Sin was, for Teilhard, simply the inevitable (but still freely chosen) complement of failure, which is the unavoidable by-product of evolution.[32] While moral and physical evil are distinct, they are inseparable within the evolutionary process. Thus is found again, in his 1948 Appendix to *The Phenomenon of Man* the text "necessarium est ut scandala eveniant," but this time it is associated with what appears to be an allusion to Romans 8:22:

> Lastly, the least tragic perhaps, because it exalts us, though none the less real: *the evil of growth*, by which is expressed in us, in the pangs of childbirth, the mysterious law which, from the humblest chemism to the highest syntheses of the spirit, makes all progress in the direction of increased unity express itself in terms of work and effort.[33]

This "travail" or "enfantement" is characterized in *The Divine Milieu* thus:

29. Cf. esp. Piet Smulders, *The Design of Teilhard de Chardin* (Westminster, Md.: Newman Press, 1967). Unfortunately, Smulder's excellent book, which was first published in Dutch in 1963 (Bruges: Desclée de Brouwer), was not able to actually cite from Teilhard's three essays that were most concerned with original sin and that were not published until 1969 (*Oeuvres*, 10). Cf. also Robert North's remarks in his *Teilhard and the Creation of the Soul* (Milwaukee, Wis.: Bruce, 1967), esp. p. 60, n.70.
30. "Réflexions sur le Péché originel" in *Oeuvres*, 10:217-30; *C&E*, pp. 187-98.
31. *C&E*, p. 195; *Oeuvres*, 10:227. "It is necessary that scandals will occur." Another citation of this verse from Matthew occurs in "Comment je vois" (1948); *Oeuvres*, 11:213; *TF*, p. 198.
32. Cf. the general discussion of this subject in *The Divine Milieu* (*Oeuvres*, 4), Part II, Section 3.
33. *PM*, p. 312; *Oeuvres*, 1:347.

It is through the collaboration which He stimulates in us that Christ, starting from *all* created things, is consummated and attains His plenitude.[34]

Because of this Christic consummation Teilhard was sure that, despite all appearances to the contrary,

Quite specifically it is *Christ whom we make or whom we undergo in all things.* Not only *diligentibus omnia convertuntur in bonum* but, more clearly still, *convertuntur in Deum* and, quite explicitly, *convertuntur in Christum.*[35]

C. THE "OMEGA-GOD"

Strictly speaking, there is no real attempt at a theology "de Deo Uno et Trino" in the writings of Teilhard, at least in terms of revelation. Although there are a number of rather late references to the concept of *Trinitization* in the course of his final venture into the field of explicit metaphysics,[36] the main thrust of his doctrine of God remains primarily in the field of "theodicy" on the one hand, and "Christology" on the other.

As remarked above, there is a "natural theology" or apologetic concerning the existence of God in terms of what Teilhard called an "existential exigency," which is conceived in terms of projection of evolution toward a supremely personal "Omega-point."[37] This "Omega-point" was so termed after the "Alpha et Omega" of the Apocalypse 1:8, 21:1, and 22:13, and first appeared in Teilhard's writings in his 1917 "The Struggle Against the Multitude":

Thus mankind, in its teeming mass of souls, each one of which concentrates a world, is the starting point of a higher Spirit: the Spirit that will shine forth at the point on which purified souls will concentrate, the Spirit that will represent, in its supreme simplicity, the Multitude of multitudes that have been tamed and unified. It will be the most simple because the most comprehensive, the needle-sharp peak on which the whole Multitude will have con-

34. *DM*, pp. 30-31; *Oeuvres*, 4:50.
35. *DM*, p. 101; *Oeuvres*, 4:150.
36. "Mais, afin que ce Centre initial et final (i.e., Point Oméga) subsiste sur lui-même en son splendide isolement, force est de nous le représenter (conformément au donné "révélé"—*deuxième temps*) comme s'opposant trinitairement à lui-même." "Comment je vois," *Oeuvres*, 11:208-9. Again, Teilhard speaks of Pleromization as "la réalisation de l'être participé par arrangement et totalisation—apparaît comme une sorte de réplique ou de symétrique à la Trinitisation." *Ibid.*, p. 210. (*TF*, pp. 193-94, 195.)
37. The conjoining of the phrase "existential exigency" with the concept of "Omega" can be traced to a Journal note of June 23, 1954 ("Journal" 20 [8]: 59), where God is characterized as being "indemonstrable" in an evolutionary universe except as the agent of "irreversible totalization," something that itself is indemonstrable, strictly speaking, but that derives from the exigency or existential demand for the survival of the "All" (a totalization of union) "Forever" (irreversibility).

verged, there to remain suspended. It will be Unity triumphing over Non-being: it will be α and ω.[38]

Thus, what began as a quotation of Apocalypse 1:8(b) ("Celui qui est" . . . "Celui qui devient") in "Cosmic Life" in 1917[39] was reduced shortly after to "Alpha et Omega," or even simply "Omega." But there are exceptions. In his 1921 "Science and Christ" is found:

He is the alpha and the omega, the principle and the end, the foundation stone and the keystone, the Plenitude and the Plenifier. He is the one who consummates all things and gives them their consistence.[40]

And in his 1936 "Some Reflections on the Conversion of the World," the whole phrase is repeated:

In fact, the more one thinks about it, the clearer it becomes that to "universalise" Christ is the only way we have of retaining in him his essential attributes (alpha and omega) in a fantastically enlarged Creation.[41]

All this gives witness to something of a progression, but it is a progression whose term is already fixed in advance. In Teilhard's thought there were three meanings for the term *Omega*:

1. The "Omega-point": the hypothetical term toward which all evolution advances.

2. The "Omega-God": the personal center of the universe that already preexists, or from which all creation is "suspended."

3. The "Christ-Omega": the hypostasis of the Divine Omega with his "personalistic universe," a union that is consummated in the God-man, Christ.[42]

In addition to the terms *Alpha*[43] and *Omega*, there is one other very

38. *WTW*, p. 98; *Ecrits*, p. 116.
39. *Ecrits*, p. 42; *WTW*, p. 52.
40. *S&C*, p. 34; *Oeuvres*, 9:60.
41. *S&C*, p. 124; *Oeuvres*, 9:163.
42. Teilhard generally speaks of two "Omegas" or two focal points of the universe, which ultimately coincide. (Cf. *S&C*, p. 164; *Oeuvres*, 9:209.) However, in *Le Phénomène humain* (*PM*, p. 270; *Oeuvres*, 1:301.) it is clear that first "Omega" can be viewed as both immanent in as well as transcendent of creation, *before* any identification with Christ. In his 1918 "Mon Univers" (*Ecrits*, p. 274) he designated the natural term of the universe as "o" (omicron), while the supernatural term, which he already identified with Christ, as "ω" (omega).

The existence of a fourth "Church-Omega" is postulated by Donald P. Gray (*The One & The Many: Teilhard de Chardin's Vision of Unity* (New York: Herder, 1969), pp. 100-102) as a logical extension of Teilhard's meaning. Thus, the Body of Christ ("Church-Omega") is to its divine head ("Christ-Omega") as the evolutionary goal ("Omega-point") is to its transcendent support (the "Omega-God").
43. In keeping with Teilhard's general "Phenomenological" approach, the term *Alpha* is never used alone, for it is in a sense both an "Unknown God" (unknown except through the Incarnation) and an "unknown point" in relation to the appearance of the universe, which no matter how far back science takes us, finds us with something already given; i.e., this evolutionary phase of the Universe, "the only known

important biblical phrase that Teilhard utilized extensively in his concept of God—the God "in quo vivimus et movemur et sumus" (Acts 17:28). This verse occurs some ten times in Teilhard's works, always by way of explicit quotation and always in Latin. It first appears in 1916 in "Cosmic Life," where evolution is seen heading toward a final consummation, but the final product depends on something outside the evolutionary series itself:

> If we look at this world, we see that the fundamental substance within which souls are formed, the higher environment in which they evolve—what one might call their own particular Ether—is the Godhead, at once transcendent and immanent, *in qua vivimus et movemur et sumus*—in whom we live and move and have our being.[44]

His devotion to and exposition of this God of Acts 17:28 can be traced and receives a Christological and even Eucharistic manifestation in the following texts:

> "In eo vivimus, movemur, et sumus." Christ operates, he exerts his living pressure, on the believer who can act and believe rightly, through all the surface and depth of the world.[45]

> In a secondary and generalised sense, but in a true sense, the sacramental Species are formed by the totality of the world, and the duration of the creation is the time needed for its consecration. *In Christo vivimus, movemur et sumus.*[46]

D. TEILHARD'S CHRISTOLOGY

The emphasis has now shifted to the central subject of this study, that of Teilhard's Christology. Here this term is to be understood in a very broad and nontechnical sense, not as opposed to, or even parallel to "soteriology," but as an attempt to find a more traditional, yet sufficiently comprehensive term to cover Teilhard's concept of Christogenesis. However, since the major portion of Part II will be devoted to a more critical study of this Christogenesis in its biblical foundations and its Teilhardian development, an attempt will be made here only to enumerate those texts which, taken together, will form the basis of deeper investigation. Before this can be done, however, these texts must be properly catalogued and located within the development of his thought.

to us." (Cf. the 1924 "My Universe", *S&C*, p. 45; *Oeuvres*, 9:73-74.) In contrast, the term *Omega-Christ* is used over a score of times apart from the quotation from the Apocalypse itself, not counting all the other times the term *Omega* is used in a not strictly theological context.
44. *WTW*, p. 47; *Ecrits*, p. 37.
45. Cf. *S&C*, p. 71; "Mon Univers" (1924) in *Oeuvres*, 9:100.
46. *DM*, p. 104; *Oeuvres*, 4:154. See Appendix A for other listings of this text.

1. The Divine Word

Teilhard had little to say about the preexistent Word of God: from the outset his emphasis was eminently incarnational. Looking a second time at the sole citation of John 1:14 in his works, one discovers that it is more concerned with theological anthropology than the Incarnation as such.

> Et Verbum caro factum est. This was the Incarnation. From this first and fundamental contact between God and the human race—which means in virtue of the penetration of the Divine into our nature—a new life was born: an unlooked for magnification and "obediential" extension of our natural capabilities—grace.[47]

The terms word or The Incarnate Word were used infrequently by Teilhard beyond this, and were almost entirely confined to his early writings.[48] In one of these, entitled "L'Ame du monde," written in 1918, the Word was both given the attributes listed in "The Litany of the Sacred Heart" and identified as being "The Soul of the World":

> Through the soul of the world, and through that soul alone the Word, becoming incarnate in the universe, has been able to establish a vital, immediate, relationship with each one of the animate elements that make up the cosmos.[49]

In the same year of 1918, Teilhard spoke of the task of the priest as being "to offer to the incarnate Word an increase of reality and consistence. . ."[50] and, again, in "Forma Christi," he alludes to that action as ". . . the encompassing and unifying activity of the incarnate Word."[51] After this, explicit use of the Johannine word became increasingly rare, and in one of his last uses of it, Teilhard made no real distinction between "le Verbe Incarné" and the "Centre universel christique." Significantly, both terms occur beneath the heading: "LE CHRIST-OMEGA."[52]

In inverse proportion to this trend away from Johannine terminology, his 1917 "Creative Union" gives indication of the slow reconceptualization of the Word in terms of the Christ of the Pauline Epistles, especially that of Colossians. Yet the Johannine implications are very evident. In this essay is found the statement: "In him, 'the plenitude of the universe,' omnia creantur because omnia uniuntur—all things are

---

47. WTW, p. 50; Ecrits, p. 40.
48. Out of twelve such allusions to "the Word," ten are before 1928. Cf. Appendix A, n.3.
49. WTW, pp. 186-87; Ecrits, p. 228.
50. WTW, p. 217; Ecrits, pp. 296-97.
51. WTW, p. 253; Ecrits, p. 338.
52. "Super-Humanité, Super-Christ, Super-Charité" (1943) in Oeuvres, 9:210; S&C, p. 165.

created because all things are made one. . . ."[53] The italicized words
tie together this allusion to Colossians 1:16 ("Plénitude") to an extremely important philosophical insight of Teilhard, one summed up in
his footnote in the same essay:

> there would somehow be two divine creative acts: the first, *quasi-organic*, conclud-
> ing in the appearance of pure Multiple (= the effect in conflict with the divine one-
> ness); the second, *quasi-efficient*, unifying the Multiple (= creation properly so
> called).[54]

Also, in his "Mon univers" of 1918 (not to be confused with the 1924
essay of the same title) is found a similar appeal to Colossians 1:16, this
time under the heading: "La philosophie de l'Union":

> Should it be admitted that Christ coincides with the Universe, hav-
> ing the quality of a *universal Center* for both cosmic progress and
> gratuitous sanctification, still it remains to be seen if one can go
> much further in the explanation of his divine coextension with the
> world, that is to say an application of the law of transformation of all
> things *in Ipso* and *per Ipsum*—in Him and through Him.[55]

Thus, it can be seen that from the outset the Divine Word was identified with the Universal Christ, not because He did not preexist the
Incarnation (or creation, for that matter) but because in a theology that
took both the phenomena of creation and the phenomenon of revelation as its starting points, this creation, which is *a continuing process of
unification*, cannot be separated from the Incarnation of the Divine
Word who appears as the principal agent of this unification.

2. The Incarnation

What then of the Incarnation as a historical event? Of this Teilhard
did not speak extensively, but when he did, he preferred to employ
Pauline language. The following text is decisive. In section "C" entitled
"L'animation du monde par le Christ universel" in "Mon univers" of
1924, which speaks of the Incarnation as a historical event in relation to
the preexistence of Christ (i.e., the Word), are found these statements:

> The first act of the Incarnation, the first appearance of the Cross,
> is marked by the plunging of the divine Unity into the ultimate
> depths of the Multiple. . . . It is because Christ was "inoculated" in
> matter that he can no longer be dissociated from the growth of
> Spirit: that he is so engrained in the visible world that he could
> henceforth be torn away from it only by rocking the foundations of

53. *WTW*, p. 174; *Ecrits*, p. 196. In his earlier essay "La Lutte contre la multitude"
speaks of "la fonction rédemptrice du Verbe, que celle d'unification de toute chair
en un même Esprit." An editor's footnote calls attention to this idea and its parallel
in John 11:51-52. (Cf. *WTW*, p. 106; *Ecrits*, p. 124.)
54. *WTW*, p. 164, n.10; *Ecrits*, p. 186, n.10.
55. Cf. *Ecrits*, p. 276. Not published in *WTW*. (My translation)

the universe. . . . Not only "in ordine intentionis" but "in ordine naturae," "omnia in eo condita sunt"—"all things are contained in him," not only "in the order of intention" but also "in the order of nature."[56]

But this reference to Colossians 1:16 is followed by another Pauline allusion, that of the "Kenosis" (i.e., "emptying-out") of Philippians 2:7:

> Then there began for him a second phase of effort and suffering on the Cross: the only phase we can in some degree understand, because it is the only one which corresponds to what we are now conscious of ourselves: the phase, after that of 'Kenosis' in matter, of human "co-feeling."[57]

It would appear from this text, when read in its entirety, that this "kenosis" is primarily the Incarnation itself, understood as the first phase of Christ's redemptive suffering, while the second phase, the death and resurrection of Christ, generally remains in Teilhard's writings subsumed under the first. Thus, Teilhard's emphasis always appears to have been "Christological" in the incarnational sense of the word, rather than "soteriological" in its narrower sense.

In the same sense of the historical Incarnation of the Word, Teilhard twice utilized in his early works the formula of Ephesians 4:9-10 in slightly modified forms. This is seen particularly in his "Pantheism and Christianity," where in 1923 he again cited "in Eo omnia constant" (Col. 1:17), but added:

> The Incarnate Word could not be the supernatural (hyperphysical) centre of the universe if he did not function *first* as its physical, natural, centre. Christ cannot sublimate creation in God without progressively raising it up by his influence through the successive circles of matter and spirit. That is why, in order to bring all things back to his Father, he had to make himself one with all—he had to enter into contact with every one of the zones of the created, from the lowest and most earthly to the zone that is closest to heaven. *"Quid est quod ascendit in coelum, nisi prius quod descendit in ima terrae ut repleret omnia."*[58]

Curiously, but logically enough, Teilhard seemed to be thinking of this same text when he quoted the "descendit ad inferos" of the Creed, but he applied it to the Eucharistic presence in the world[59] and later on to the baptismal rite as a symbol of the Incarnation.[60] Thus there should be no surprise at Teilhard's readiness to employ the consecratory formula of the Eucharistic liturgy in most of his early writings concerning the "Body of Christ."

56. *S&C*, pp. 60-61; *Oeuvres*, 9:88-89.
57. *S&C*, pp. 61-62; *Oeuvres*, 9:90.
58. *C&E*, p. 71; *Oeuvres*, 10:88.
59. Cf. *DM*, p. 103; *Oeuvres*, 4:153.
60. Cf. "L'Evolution de la chasteté," *Oeuvres*, 11:79; *TF* p. 73.

3. *The Body of Christ*

Probably the most single important document in contributing to a fuller understanding of Teilhard's concept of the Body of Christ is an undated and apparently unfinished essay entitled "Note on the Physical Union Between the Humanity of Christ and the Faithful in the Course of Their Sanctification,"[61] believed to have been written late in 1919 or 1920. While that essay did not employ the "Hoc est corpus meum" formula, direct reference was made to the Eucharist in terms of its physical instrumentality.

This little essay is noteworthy for a number of points, but its grouping of the Johannine theme of the Vine with the "Mystical Body" (and the pleroma, as will be seen), the Eucharist, and the historical Christ, first captures interest here. Teilhard's interpretation of John 14:9 at the end most illuminates Teilhard's concept of the historical Christ, and, for that matter, the Divine Person of the Word.

> In the first place, when we extend all around us the domain of Christ's humanity we have no reason to fear that we are veiling from ourselves the face of the Godhead. Since we adhere to Christ *"in ordine vitali"*—in the order of life—he is *not an intermediary* separating us from God, but a *medium* uniting us to God. *"Philippe, qui videt me, videt Patrem"*—"He who has seen me, Philip, has seen the Father."[62]

A *milieu* rather than an *intermediary*: this is a concept to be stressed and remembered, for it corresponds closely to Teilhard's views of matter and spirit as not two kinds of "things" but two aspects of one and the same "Weltstoff." This is not to imply that the Godhead is itself such in nature, but it does more than imply that for an Incarnate God, physical matter is more than a mere means to an end; it is a vital component of that union which is the end.

In this same context, "Materia matrix," one of Teilhard's most frequent nonbiblical phrases, is crucial, and his incarnational "Amictus mundo" should be understood in conjunction with it. If after 1927 he no longer employed "Hoc est corpus meum," it is not because it had ceased to be the "single word" and the "single act . . . filling the universality of things,"[63] but probably because, as with the term *mystical Body*, he found this language too charged with restrictive overtones. While he continued to use the latter as late as 1933, it was usually with quotation marks and often without the adjective *mystical*. But long before this he had begun utilizing the language of Paul without modifica-

---

61. "Note sur l'Union physique entre l'Humanité du Christ et les Fidèles au cours de la sanctification," *Oeuvres*, 10:19-26; cf. *C&E*, pp. 15-20.
62. *S&C*, pp. 19-20; *Oeuvres*, 9:26.
63. "My Universe" in *S&C*, p. 66; *Oeuvres*, 9:94.

tion. In the "Mon Univers" of 1924, the appeal of literal boldness is again found:

> At that moment, St Paul tells us (I Cor. 15. 23 ff.), when Christ has emptied all created forces (rejecting in them everything that is a factor of dissociation and superanimating all that is a force of unity), he will consummate universal unification by giving himself, in his complete and adult Body, with a finally satisfied capacity for union, to the embrace of the Godhead.[64]

The process by which this is accomplished by us was expressed by Teilhard in terms strongly modeled on the language of the Apostle. In *The Divine Milieu* he underscored these Pauline verbs: *"Collaborare," "compati," "commori," "con-ressucitare."*[65]—the language of one who took the Incarnation extensively as well as literally. When Teilhard quoted Colossians 3:17 " 'Whatever you do,' says St. Paul, 'do it in the name of Our Lord Jesus Christ' "[66] this "in the name of" is to be taken in its full biblical and incarnational sense, that is, in the same sense that Teilhard used, times beyond counting, the Pauline phrase "in Christo Jesu," and which phrase he interpreted in his "Forma Christi" (1918) in a distinctively nonjuridical sense:

> If things are to find their coherence *in Christo*, we must ultimately admit that there is *in natura Christi*, besides the specifically individual elements of Man—and in virtue of God's choice—some *universal physical reality*, a certain cosmic extension of his Body and Soul.[67]

In this same consciousness of our incorporation in Christ, Teilhard quoted Galatians 2:20: "Vivo ego—jam non ego: vivit in me Christus,"[68] but again, not content with verbatim quoting, Teilhard constantly elaborated this theme in various combinations:

> *Quidquid patimur, Christus agit* et *Quidquid agimus, Christus agitur*[69]
> Quidquid patimur, Christum patimur.
> Quidquid agimus, Christus agitur.[70]
> Whatever we do, it is to Christ we do it. Whatever is done to us, it is Christ who does it.[71]

---

64. *S&C*, p. 85; *Oeuvres*, 9:113-14.
65. *DM*, p. 18; *Oeuvres*, 4:32. ("To work, to suffer, to die and rise together with.")
66. *Ibid.*
67. *WTW*, p. 252; *Ecrits*, p. 338. Cf. chap. 1, n.5 above.
68. *WTW*, p. 259; *Ecrits*, p. 344. "I live now not with my own life but with the life of Christ who lives in me" (*Jerusalem Bible* translation).
69. "Whatever we suffer, (it is) Christ (who) acts, and whatever we do, it is done to Christ." Cf. "Mon Univers" (1918), *Ecrits*, p. 275. (My translation)
70. "Whatever is done to us, it is Christ who does it; whatever we do, it is to Christ we do it." "Forma Christi," *WTW*, p. 259; *Ecrits*, p. 344.
71. "My Universe" (1924), *S&C*, p. 74; *Oeuvres*, 9:102.

And modeled on Romans 14:7-8 is found:

> No man lives or dies to himself. But whether through our life or through our death we belong to Christ.[72]

Further, if another step in Teilhard's reasoning may be anticipated:

> Whether he lives or dies, *by* his life and *by* his death, he in some sense completes his God.[73]

4. The Pleroma and the Universal Christ

With Teilhard, as with so many others who have pondered the meaning of certain Pauline texts, there was a certain difficulty that had to be overcome—namely the relationship between Christ as the head of his body, the Church, and his primacy over the whole of creation. Teilhard's inclination was to absorb the one function into the other, as witnessed in his phrase describing Christ as "Caput creationis et Ecclesiae," a statement apparently modeled on Colossians 1:18 and found in this precise form only in the crucial "Note on the Physical Union between the Humanity of Christ and the Faithful in the Course of Their Sanctification."[74]

That this identification between Christ's ecclesiastical "headship" and his cosmic attributes may be criticized as oversimplified and hasty Teilhard seemed well aware, for his 1924 "Mon Univers" he confronts such objection in the section entitled "Christ is Identical with Omega," where he cites four texts that to his mind illustrate two great truths about the Pauline Christ and that together lead to a conclusion, also illustrated by a Pauline text, something in the manner of a syllogism:

> In order to demonstrate the truth of this fundamental proposition, I need only refer to the long series of Johannine—and still more Pauline—texts in which the physical supremacy of Christ over the universe is so magnificently expressed. I cannot quote them all here, but they come down to these two essential affirmations: "In eo omnia constant" (Col. 1. 17), and "Ipse est qui replet omnia" (Col. 2. 10, cf. Eph. 4.9), from which it follows that "Omnia in omnibus Christus" (Col. 3. 11)—the very definition of omega.[75]

The major premise is his most frequently used text from the Pauline corpus. To judge from the next section of this same essay, that entitled

---

72. *"The Divine Milieu"* (1927), *DM*, p. 89; *Oeuvres*, 4:133.
73. "Human Energy" in *Human Energy*, London: Collins; New York: Harcourt Brace Jovanovich, 1969, p. 155; *L'Energie humain (Oeuvres*, 6) (Paris: Editions du Seuil, 1962), p. 192. (Designated *HE* or *Oeuvres* 6 hereafter.)
74. Cf. *C&E*, p. 15; *Oeuvres*, 10:21.
75. *S&C*, p. 54; *Oeuvres*, 9:82.

"The Influence of Christ-Omega. The Universal Element,"[76] where Teilhard also quoted the "qua sibi omnia possit subjicere" of Philippians 3:21, he seems to have been already resisting, in the major of this syllogism, a "juridicist" interpretation of Christ's dominance of the universe that is commonly understood in conjunction with a stress on the "mystical" nature of his headship over the Church, robbing the "in eo constant" of Colossians 1:17 of any true organic meaning. Such an interpretation would either restrict this universality of Christ to the divine nature of the "Logos" while ignoring the "Theandric Christ" (which Teilhard saw to be the whole context of Colossians 1:15f.) or would reduce Christ's incarnate "Lordship" to a strictly legal interpretation of Philippians 3:21 (probably the reason he did not cite this text along with Colossians 1:17).

The second premise of his argument, which serves as something of a "minor," is the "Ipse est qui replet omnia" of Colossians 2:10, accompanied by a reference to Ephesians 4:9. Here the emphasis would seem to be on the "replet" rather than the "omnia," thus reinforcing the nonjuridical character of the "in eo . . . constant" of the major premise by introducing the "pleromic" element and thus enabling Teilhard to move to his conclusion, which is a fully organic interpretation of Colossians 3:11. In this way he would subsume any ecclesially understood "headship" of Christ under the Christic fulfillment of the universe in Ephesians 4:10. Possibly the source of this confusion is due to the French *remplir*, which is used to translate both the active and the passive forms of the Latin and Greek. But the slip is curious nevertheless, and, if nothing else, serves as an instructive introduction to Teilhard's concept of the *pleroma*.

The use of this word appears first in Teilhard's writings in "The Priest" of July 1918:

> Life and death, unity and plurality, element and totality, possession and quest, being and becoming . . . such is the *Pleroma* of the world and of Christ.[77]

It is this double "plénitude" (the word he more generally used in these early writings) that must be reconciled.

> You who are yourself the *plenitudo Entis creati*, the fulness of created being, you, Jesus, are also the *plenitudo entis mei*, the fulness of my own personal being, and of all living creatures who accept your dominion.[78]

76. *S&C*, pp. 56-57; *Oeuvres*, 9:85: ". . . by which He is able to subject all things to himself" (Phil. 3:21).
77. *WTW*, p. 214; *Ecrits*, p. 293. (Emphasis added)
78. *WTW*, p. 211; *Ecrits*, p. 291.

Again, and this time with a Johannine twist, the same word is found in "Forma Christi" (Dec. 1918):

> Jesus Christ *never establishes himself in a void*—at *Cana* did he not tell them first to fill the jars with water?—It is *by substituting his plenitude for another* that he wins us—that is, by taking *within us* the place of our own self, and substituting his own embrace for the universal embrace of created being that encloses us.[79]

It is primarily in terms of a dialectic that this early *pleroma* is first conceived, as again is seen in "Le Prêtre":

> If men could only see that in each one of them there is an element of the *Pleroma*, would not that, Lord, effect the reconciliation between God and our age? If only they could understand that, with all its natural richness and its massive reality, the universe can find fulfilment only in Christ; and that Christ, in turn, can be attained only through a universe that has been carried to the very limit of its capabilities.[80]

But the distinctively Pauline vision of this reconciliation was not long in coming. Turning again to his "Note on the Physical Union . . . ," we find this explanation:

> A solid basis for the demonstration, or rather the suggestions, we have in mind may profitably be sought in a consideration of the consummated mystical body (that is, the *Pauline pleroma*). . . . since the pleroma is the kingdom of God in its completed form, the properties attributed to it by Scripture must be regarded as specially characteristic of the entire supernatural organism, even if they are to be found only in an ill-defined form in any particular preparatory phase of beatification.[81]

In this extraordinary passage Teilhard's insistence on the physical reality of Christ's presence in humanity can again be seen, not just as a means to an end, but as an end as such. If there is any doubt about this, the following passage corroborates it:

> In the first place, it is quite certain that the eucharist, of which many of the elect will have been unable to partake during their life on earth, is not the only means by which the faithful can achieve contact—contact which is necessary as a "necessary" means—with Christ's humanity: the contact which is to ensure their integration in the *pleroma*. We become members of Christ before any external contact with his sacramental body.[82]

79. *WTW*, p. 264; *Ecrits*, p. 349.
80. *WTW*, p. 220; *Ecrits*, p. 299. (Emphasis added)
81. *C&E*, p. 16; *Oeuvres*, 10:22. (Emphasis added)
82. *C&E*, p. 17; *Oeuvres*, 10:23-24. (Emphasis added)

As has been noted in the first quotation from this crucial essay, Teilhard's concept of "Matter-Spirit" is of critical importance, but the obvious connection in its Eucharistic aspects between this passage and the sixth chapter of St. John's Gospel, on the one hand, and I Corinthians 10:17, on the other, should not be overlooked. From this point on there seems to have been little hesitation in Teilhard's elaboration of his vision of the pleroma. On the more strictly Christological side, the pleroma is but an extension of Christ, who is both the "Plénitude et Plénifiant."[83] At the same time it involves Christ in a union in which "les liaisons du Corps mystique" are conceived "en termes physiques," which at the same time involves

> conceiving a "graduated" type of union for the pleroma (modified by the very excess of its physical perfection), such that, without losing anything of their subsistence or personality, the elect would be *physically* incorporated in the organic and "natural" whole of the consummated Christ.[84]

Concerning its created aspects, the following statements are found: ". . . the development of the Pleroma (that is, the bringing of the universe to maturity),[85] or ". . . the consummation of the world (the Pleroma, as St. Paul says),[86] or "the *evolutionary structure* of the universal unity (of the 'Pleroma,' as St. Paul has said),"[87] or in terms of the evolutive end of the process, ". . . the constitution of the pleroma . . . must necessarily make itself apparent to our minds by a progressive advance of spirit."[88]

Thus, the pleroma, like the Omega, has its double aspect—the created and the uncreated, the fullness of evolving nature and the divine consummation. Just as the Omega point is ultimately one, so too there is ultimately "a 'monocephalous' Pleroma in Christ."[89] The Universal Christ is nothing other than "a synthesis of Christ and the universe."[90] In reality or in retrospect, the two terms *Omega* and *pleroma* represent the same reality approached from different starting points. *Omega*, the consummation toward which the universe strives, is simply the phenomenological counterpart of the revealed *pleroma*, and Christ is the Divine and human embodiment of each. If from the evolutive aspect Teilhard can speak of ". . . the mystery of the creative

---

83. "Science and Christ" (1921), S&C, p. 34; Oeuvres, 9:60.
84. "Pantheism and Christianity" (1923), C&E, p. 70; Oeuvres, 10:85-86.
85. "My Universe" (1924), S&C, p. 59; Oeuvres, 9:88.
86. The Divine Milieu (1927) p. 25. The French reads "Univers" in place of "world," cf. Oeuvres, 4:43.
87. ". . . cette notion de la *structure évolutive* de l'unité universelle (du 'plérôme' dirait saint Paul) . . ." in "La Route de l'Ouest: Vers une mystique nouvelle" (1932); Oeuvres, 11:62; TF, p. 57.
88. "Christology and Evolution" (1933); cf. C&E, p. 83; Oeuvres, 10:102.
89. Cf. "Note sur la notion de perfection chrétienne" (1942), Oeuvres, 11:116. ("Un Plérôme 'monocéphale' in Christo.") cf. TF, p. 104.
90. Cf. "Comment je crois" (1934), C&E, p. 126; Oeuvres, 10:149.

union of the world in God or Pleromization,"[91] he can at the same time speak in the same terms of salvation history: ". . . it is not precisely either Creation, or Incarnation, or Redemption, . . . but Pleromization."[92] Or operationally speaking, he can say in 1948 that the Parousia (the return of Christ), when seen as the reunion of the phenomenal and celestial worlds, involving the unification of humanity with itself (in Christ), is nothing but the pleroma described by St. Paul.[93]

5. Pantheism, Pan-Christism, and the "Third Nature" of Christ

How do the meanings assigned by Teilhard to the Pauline pleroma relate to his more explicit appeals to Holy Scripture? While his citations of the revealed Word are insistent and repetitious enough, for all that, they serve only as so many springboards to deductive leaps of frightening depth and dizzying complexity. Nevertheless, there actually is a point, even scripturally speaking, where everything aims at one final target, one final frame of reference, or one final quotation, although even that, as is usually the case in Teilhard, is not without its correlative appeals.

The quotation in question is that of 1 Corinthians 15:28 (or variations of the same), and its conceptual framework is that of pantheism: "d'un 'Panthéisme' chrétien, ἔσται ὁ Θεὸς πάντα ἐν πᾶσιν.' "[94] As early as 1916, in his "Cosmic Life" Teilhard spoke of his own attraction to "the pantheist aspiration for fusion of all in all."[95] He was convinced, despite all advice to the contrary, that he was not "off base" in describing mankind's whole religious drive, and its fulfillment in Christianity as pantheism of one form or another. Hence, even in *The Divine Milieu*, which he prepared with utmost caution to pass the Roman censors unscathed, he did not hesitate to quote this one verse boldly—and, lest there be any doubt, in two languages—at the same time sharply distinguishing between this and any "false" or "monistic" pantheism:

> Christianity alone therefore saves, with the rights of thought, the essential aspiration of all mysticism: *to be united* (that is, to become

91. Cf. "Christianisme et Evolution" (1945), *C&E*, p. 213; *Oeuvres*, 10:183.
92. Cf. "Réflexions sur le péché originel" (1947), *C&E*, p. 230; *Oeuvres*, 10:198.
93. Parousie = apparition—retour du Christ attente d'un événement humain = monde phénoménal doit rejoindre monde céleste
    +
    opérer unification de l'humanité sur elle-même = plérôme de St. Paul. "Foi humaine—Foi spirituelle": Notes taken by Solange Lemaitre. *TA*, #117.
94. Cf. "Panthéisme et Christianisme" (1923), *Oeuvres*, 10:91; *C&E*, p. 75.
95. *WTW*, p. 15; *Ecrits*, p. 6. P. Henri deLubac makes note of Teilhard's propensity to translate the "en pasin" of 1 Cor. 15:28 in terms of a personalistic "en tous" ("in all") rather than as "en tout" ("in all things") as did F. Prat. However, as will be seen, Teilhard did not always do so. Cf. H. deLubac, *Teilhard de Chardin: The Man and His Meaning* (New York: Hawthorne, 1965), p. 34, n.17.

the other) *while remaining oneself.* More attractive than any world-Gods, whose eternal seduction it embraces, transcends, and purifies—*in omnibus omnia Deus (En pasi panta Theos)*—our divine milieu is at the antipodes of false pantheism. The Christian can plunge himself into it whole-heartedly without the risk of finding himself one day a monist.[96]

Why then, if he was already so aware of the possible misunderstanding that his use of the word *pantheism* was apt to cause, did he resume using the word in subsequent works? The only answer to this seems to be in the particular Christological interpretation that he insisted belongs to 1 Corinthians 15:28. Thus, in 1930 he reiterated in terms more closely resembling Colossians 3:11: "Le Christ est celui en qui tout devient tout."

> Let us return to St. Paul; let us recall that the supernatural nourishes itself from all, and let us accept to their conclusion these magnificent perspectives according to which the Christ of St. Paul appeared to us as the One *in whom everything is created* and the One in whom the entire world, with all its *depth*, its *width*, its grandeur, its *length*, its physical being, its spirituality, attains and holds its consistence.
>
> We foresee that in this Christianity, thanks to the power of Christ, we have the two elements required by human consciousness; first of all, a total and deep unity, an organic unity which nevertheless conserves individual relationships, that is to say, which manifests in itself those perfections in that unity which is deformed by pantheism: *"The Christ is the one in whom all becomes all"* (St. Paul). Likewise, in this more complete understanding of Christ, we are able to satisfy our optimistic desires concerning all of creation. We have everything that we need in our Christian traditions and Scripture in order to have the right, as Christians, to believe that the world, whatever be its need for atonement, is above all a work of creation continued in Christ. But why has there not been a return to these great and deep sources according to the needs of the present; the "nova et vetera"—both new and old—as the Gospel says?[97]

Two years later, in his "La Route de l'Ouest: Vers une Mystique nouvelle," Teilhard added, à propos the fear of a certain "monism":

> There is no longer a danger of monism in a Christianity that has been openly westernized. But is there not, without doubt, a similar idea which, in us and around us, gradually drawing a cosmic unity

96. Cf. *DM*, pp. 93-94; *Oeuvres*, 4:139-40. This particular variation "En pasi panta Theos," while retaining the general "flavor" of 1 Cor. 15:28 appears to reflect somewhat the word order of Col. 3:11 ("ta panta kai en pasin Christos"). The omission of the final *n* on "pasi" follows the plural dative ending of the masculine and neuter forms in classical "Attic" Greek, indicating Teilhard's tendency to construct his own paraphrases rather than to quote verbatim.

97. "Essai d'intégration de l'homme dans l'Univers," Dec. 10, 1930—The fourth of four conferences given at Chadefaud to the "Groupe Marcel Legaut." Unpublished, *TA*, #92, p. 10. (My translation, emphasis added. Cf. Appendix D §1, 6, for French original.)

towards a universal convergence, resounds in the depths of the
modern soul—the eternal and profound tune which lulled all pantheisms? But has there ever been, even by definition, a true mysticism without something of a pantheism? "And then" says St. Paul in
speaking of the consummated Incarnation, "God will be all in all: *en
pasi panta Theos.*"[98]

Nevertheless, undaunted by this spectre of a monistic misunderstanding of his type of "Panthéisme chrétien," he insisted a few months later
that:

> the strength of pantheism is realized, God is all in all things, and it
> is even more so as they are unified in their purest essence. For St.
> Paul, for example, the representation of the world is nothing but a
> creation which gravitates around Christ who has descended upon the
> world as if in a great baptism: he takes hold of the essence of the
> world, its purest things, concentrating them in himself and thus re-
> turning them to his Father.[99]

Despite the obvious problems and discomfort that this position
would continue to raise for Teilhard, he never seems to have backed
down from this position linking the Pauline Pleroma and his allusions
to 1 Corinthians 15:28. In his 1944 "Introduction to the Christian Life"
he stated:

> Ultimately, God is not alone in the totalized Christian universe (in
> the pleroma, to use St Paul's word); but he is all in all of us ("*en
> pasi panta theos*"): unity in plurality.[100]

This same text of St. Paul forms the basis for the distinction he utilized
to defend this "pantheism" that was essential to his vision of God and
the universe, a pantheism that was not

> pantheism of identification, at the opposite pole from love: "God is
> all,"

but rather:

> pantheism of unification, beyond love: "God all in all."[101]

Thus, rather than having toned down his language, Teilhard seems
to have sharpened the sense of shock this terminology would produce.

---

98. Sept. 8, 1932. *Oeuvres,* 11:59. (My translation.) cf. *TF,* pp. 53-54.
99. From "Orient et Occident: la Mystique de la Personalité" (1933), unpublished, *TA*
    #118, p. 2. (My translation; cf. Appendix D §1, c, for French original.)
100. *C&E,* p. 171; *Oeuvres,* 10:200.
101. Cf. "A Clarification: Reflections on Two Converse Forms of the Spirit" (1950), *AE*,
    p. 223; "Pour y voi clair: Réflexions sur deux formes inverses d'Esprit," *Oeuvres,*
    7:231-32.

But he seems to have wished to make this same point even more expressively Christological when he admitted to a kind of "Panchristisme" in the 1924 "My Universe"[102] and again in his 1934 "How I Believe":

> For, unlike the false monisms which urge one through passivity into unconsciousness, the "pan-Christism" which I am discovering places union at the term of an arduous process of differentiation. I shall become the Other only by being utterly myself. I shall attain spirit only by bringing out the complete range of the forces of matter. The total Christ is consummated and may be attained, only at the term of universal evolution.[103]

Tying this notion in with several biblical themes at once, Teilhard wrote in 1936:

> If Christianity is to keep its place at the head of mankind, it make itself explicitly recognisable as a sort of "pan-Christism"—which, in fact, is simply the notion of the mystical Body, taken in its fullest and most profound sense, and the extension to the universe of the attributes already accorded (particularly with reference to human society) to Christ the King.[104]

Let us now turn to the problem posed by Teilhard's supposed "Third Nature" of Christ. The Christologically speaking heterodox suggestion is, taken in its context, more properly a soteriological preoccupation of Teilhard, which appears in his essays only in conjunction with his speculation over the problem presented by Romans 6:9 ("Christus jam non moritur . . ."). He first referred to this verse in his "Chute, Rédemption, et Géocentrie" of 1920. The problem was this:

> In all probability mankind is neither "unica" [unique] nor "singularis" [singular] but is "one among a thousand." How, then, is it that, against all probability, this particular mankind was chosen as the centre of the Redemption? And how, from that starting-point, can Redemption be extended from star to star?
> All that I can entertain is the possibility of a multi-aspect Redemption which would be realized, as one and the same Redemption, on all the stars—rather as the sacrifice of the mass is multiplied, still the same sacrifice, at all times and in all places. Yet all the worlds do not coincide in time! There were worlds before our own, and there will be other worlds after it. . . . Unless we introduced a relativity into time we should have to admit, surely, that Christ has still to be incarnate in some as yet unformed star? . . . And what, then, becomes of "Christus iam non moritur" [Christ dies no more]?[105]

102. Cf. S&C, p. 59; Oeuvres, 9:87.
103. C&E, p. 129; Oeuvres, 10:149.
104. "Some Reflections on the Conversion of the World" in S&C, p. 124; Oeuvres, 9:163.
105. C&E, p. 44; Oeuvres, 10:57.

His only answer at that time was:

> . . . yet one thing in the Catholic creed is more certain than any-
> thing: that there is a Christ *"in quo omnia constant."* All secondary
> beliefs will have to give way, if necessary, to this fundamental arti-
> cle. Christ is all or nothing.[106]

The problem then is hardly minor, and by 1953 in Teilhard's "A Sequel to the Problem of Human Origins: The Plurality of Inhabited
Worlds"[107] the probability of our having to face the soteriological question posed by the existence of other intelligently inhabited planets had
become a virtual certitude in Teilhard's mind.

He discarded three suggested solutions as unacceptable, namely:

1) That death, as the "Index" of the presence of Original Sin, does not exist in other
inhabited worlds—the absurdity of the nonuniversality of the Fall in this sense.
2) That these worlds, despite their enormous apartness, are somehow miraculously
"informed"—the actual sinfulness or culpability of one race automatically affecting the intelligent races of other worlds.
3) That we accept the "humiliation" of retreat from such a difficult problem.

Instead, he struck out boldly in another direction on the basis of two
suppositions:

1) That in virtue of their convergent nature (the law of complexity-consciousness), all intelligent beings be considered ultimately "centered," that is, destined for an "Omega-
point."
2) That Christ is "universalized" by his Resurrection:

> No doubt (as happened earlier at the end of geocentrism) it is in-
> evitable that the end of "monogeism" (or perhaps one should say
> "geo-monism"?) may well oblige us to revise a good many of our
> theological "representations" and make them more flexible; but
> these adjustments matter little provided that, ever more structurally
> and dynamically coherent with all we are now discovering in connex-
> ion with cosmogenesis, one thing remains solidly established: the
> dogma which sums up all dogmas:
> *"In Eo Omnia constant."*[108]

As will be seen in chapter 5, the solution to this problem had for
some time been taking shape in Teilhard's mind, and it was to be the
tentative postulation of a "third Nature" of Christ, a cosmic nature that
would serve as the focal point of a pleroma that extends to all possible
worlds.[109]

106. *Ibid.*
107. *C&E*, p. 229f.; *Oeuvres*, 10:273f.
108. *C&E*, pp. 234-35; *Oeuvres*, 10:280.
109. Cf. the comment of N. M. Wilders (editor of *Oeuvres*), *ibid.*, p. 282, n.12 (p. 236).

E. IRREVERSIBILITY AND THE PAROUSIA

Leaving behind the strictly Christological aspects of Teilhard's synthesis, we now turn to one of the most pervasive of his concerns, the search for the "irreversibility" of things. According to his autobiographical essay, "Le Coeur de la Matière,"[110] in 1950, this quest for the imperishable—that which "tinea non corrumpit" ("no moth devours," Luke 12:33)—dominated his thought from his childhood and was probably responsible for his great interest in rocks, which was later to bloom into his career as a geologist and paleontologist. According to this essay, this quest for the lasting, the imperishable "heart of matter" led him to look beyond these most concretized of the natural and biological sciences, with their petrified and fossilized relics of the past, and drove him toward an overriding concern for the future—for the preservation of all that is worthy and of lasting value in the evolution of the universe and of man. It is a search for what he terms *ktēma eis aei,* a phrase that appeared first in "Cosmic Life"[111] in 1916 and again, a year later, in "The Mystical Milieu"[112]—which in 1945, in "Action and Activation," he identified as coming from Thucydides:

> In a more literal sense than the worthy Thucydides could have hoped for his history, man, in his internal mechanism, is so constructed that he cannot be set in motion except under the magnetic attraction of a *ktēma eis aei,* of a treasure that will never perish.[113]

It is curious but not strange that Teilhard appears to have shied away from using the *"thēsaurous en ouravōi"*[114] of Matthew 6:20, which would appear most apt, employing instead this classical Greek phrase. In a 1950 letter to a friend he stated:

> I had also noticed, last Sunday, the lesson: "Do not worry about material things . . . God will provide." I generally do not like especially this part of the Gospel, because too many people interpret it as a warning that the further development of Earth and Man is not in the genuine line of Christianity.[115]

In light of this uneasiness with the Gospel formulation, it was natural for him to turn at an early date to the more "materialistic" symbolism of the Book of Revelation. As in his 1923 "Pantheism and

110. *Oeuvres,* 13:19-91.
111. Cf. *WTW,* p. 58; *Ecrits,* p. 44.
112. *WTW,* p. 140; *Ecrits,* p. 159.
113. *S&C,* p. 177; *Oeuvres,* 9:224.
114. "Treasure in heaven."
115. *Letters to Two Friends* (New York: New American Library, 1968), p. 218. This letter was written in English to Rhoda De Terra on Sept. 8, 1950. However, the "tinea non corrumpit" of Luke 12:33 does appear in the 1950 essay "La Coeur de la Matière," *Oeuvres,* 13:27.

Christianity,"[116] he had used a portion of Apocalypse 21:23, so, accompanied by a footnote quotation of the same in his 1924 "My Universe," the following question is found:

> Is it not in the heavenly Jerusalem that the elements of the new earth will be so transparent, reflecting so brilliantly, that nothing, seemingly, will subsist but the rays, materialised in us, of God's glory?[117]

What was this "heavenly Jerusalem" for Teilhard? In *The Divine Milieu* (1927) man's quest for permanence, the concern that "opera sequuntur illos" (Apoc. 14:13), is found as the first element of its composition. Second, there is the element of completion, as phrased in the following words borrowed from 2 Corinthians 5:4: "Non volumus expoliari, sed supervestiri."[118] Likewise, as has been noted, he was not above borrowing and using even more freely the "iota unum aut unus apex non praeteribit" from Matthew 5:18 to illustrate this point![119]

But what of the catastrophic end pictured in the apocalyptic verses of the synoptics, particularly that of Matthew? Teilhard had taken notice of these in *The Divine Milieu*, but they were transformed from words of destruction to a prophecy of consummation,[120] of "aggregation," and of "segregation."

> And, under the finally liberated action of the true affinities of being, the spiritual atoms of the world will be borne along by a force generated by the powers of cohesion proper to the universe itself and will occupy, whether within Christ or without Christ (but always under the influence of Christ), the place of happiness or pain designated for them by the living structure of the Pleroma. *Sicut fulgur exit ab Oriente et paret usque ad Occidentem. . . . Sicut venit diluvium et tulit omnes. . . . Ita erit adventus Filii hominis.* Like lightning, like a conflagration, like a flood, the attraction exerted by the Son of Man will lay hold of all the whirling elements in the universe so as to reunite them or subject them to His body. *Ubicumque fuerit corpus congregabuntur et aquilae.*[121]

It is doubtful if the italicized words have ever been interpreted more literally in the history of biblical exegesis! When Teilhard quoted Psalm 104 (103):30 in this same work and capitalized "RENOVABIS FACIEM

116. *C&E*, p. 56; *Oeuvres*, 10:84.
117. *S&C*, p. 75; *Oeuvres*, 9:103.
118. *DM*, pp. 24, 82; *Oeuvres*, 4:41, 122: "[Their] work follows them. . . We do not wish to be unclothed, but rather clothed over."
119. *DM*, p. 116; *Oeuvres*, 4:170: "One jot or tittle shall not pass."
120. Teilhard expressed his interpretation of the Parousia much later as being "more akin to a maturing than to a destruction." Cf. "The Stuff of the Universe" (1953), *AE*, p. 382; *Oeuvres*, 7:405.
121. *DM*, p. 134; *Oeuvres*, 4:196. The Latin verses are from Matthew 24:27f.: "Just as the lightning comes out of the east and appears even in the west . . . just as the flood comes and sweeps away all . . . so shall be the coming of the Son of Man. . . . Wherever the body shall be, there shall the eagles be gathered."

TERRAE,"[122] he meant to be taken seriously. With regard to another apocalyptic phrase (the wording is that found in 2 Peter 3:13) we find the following statement in "The Salvation of Mankind: Reflections on the Present Crisis," written in the prelude of World War II:

Not only do "the new heaven and the new earth" anticipated by the gospel, open up (if we are prepared to "homogenise" them with our modern representations of the world), unexpected horizons to the physics of matter—but they provide the only space in which one of the most essential qualities of our psychological being can be deployed—irreversibility in progress and ambitions.[123]

Not only does the interpretation that Teilhard advanced guarantee in classic Christian terms a final triumph of good over evil; it is also the very condition of all human progress here and now.

But alongside this optimistic guarantee of "irreversibility" must be raised the question of the conditions that will actually bring about the advent of the Parousia. It has been seen how Teilhard was convinced that the end of man's present world will not be the result of a chance accident or catastrophe from outside. On the other hand, what part will man's own actions play in this final chapter of the world's evolution?

As early as 1916 Teilhard called attention to the traditional idea of a judgmental Second Coming in his "Mastery of the World and the Kingdom of God":

The Parousia, we know, is promised as a dawn that will rise over a supreme onslaught of error. . . . Life, at any rate, will neither openly approve nor find excuses for the lack of faith that will mark those last days.[124]

Even as late as 1942 this less-than-optimistic warning appears when in his "Christ the Evolver" he parallels the "frigescit caritas multorum" of Matthew 24:12 with the warning (which he saw underlined by the then-current Papal Encyclicals) that we were now living in "these last centuries 'in which faith has been growing cold.' "[125] Still, at an early date Teilhard saw this negative element as only an aspect of something more general—the maturity of the universe and its resultant capacity for the ultimate growth of both good and evil.

When the end of time is at hand, a terrifying spiritual pressure will be exerted on the confines of the real, built up by the desperate efforts of souls tense with longing to escape from the earth. This pressure will be unanimous. Scripture, however, tells us that at the same time the world will be infected by a profound schism—some

122. *DM*, p. 112; *Oeuvres*, 4:164: "You shall renew the face of the earth."
123. "Sauvons l'Humanité: Réflexions sur la crise présenté" (1936) in *Oeuvres*, 9:189; *S&C*, p. 148.
124. *WTW*, p. 91; *Ecrits*, pp. 83-84.
125. *C&E*, p. 147; *Oeuvres*, 10:172.

trying to emerge from themselves in order to dominate the world even more completely—others, relying on the words of Christ, waiting passionately for the world to die, so that they may be absorbed with it in God.

It is then, we may be sure, that the Parousia will be realised in a creation that has been taken to the climax of its capacity for union.[126]

The result of this schism was already alluded to in a reference to Romans 8:22 in Teilhard's 1922 "Note on Some Possible Historical Representations of Original Sin" in which he kept in mind the great apostasy predicted by St. Paul in 2 Thessalonians 2:3-11. In contrast to an Original Sin in the remote past, Teilhard was compelled to assert:

The supreme transgression, committed by an as yet inarticulate mankind, is not to be found behind us: would it not be better to look for it ahead, when mankind has at last become fully conscious of its powers and will split into two camps, for God or against him?[127]

However, a return to Teilhard's *The Divine Milieu* of 1927 must be made to grasp the full implications of this divine-human causality of the Parousia. Here this process is termed a "metamorphosis," which at the individual level is at once both a divine and human operation: "I work . . . the Father works always" (John 5:17). [128]

But the same reciprocity holds true at the collective level:

There are as many sur-animations by God of secondary causes as there are forms of human trust and human fidelity. Although essentially single in its influx, Providence is pluralised when in contact with us—just as a ray of sunlight takes on colour or loses itself in the depths of the body which it strikes. The universe has many different storeys and many different compartments: *in eadem domo, multae mansiones*.[129]

This surprising use of John 14:2 is consistent, if unusual, but Teilhard had already stated that within this process

the heart of God is boundless, *multae mansiones*. And yet in all that immensity there is only one possible place for each one of us at any given moment, the one we are led to by unflagging fidelity to the natural and supernatural duties of life.[130]

Why this insistence, even to the point of taking liberties with this verse, generally understood to refer to heavenly rewards? Teilhard was

126. "My Universe" (1924), *S&C*, p. 84; *Oeuvres*, 9:113.
127. *C&E*, p. 53; *Oeuvres*, 10:69.
128. Cf. *DM*, p. 112; *Oeuvres*, 4:164.
129. *DM*, p. 123; *Oeuvres*, 4:180: "In the same house . . . many mansions;" a paraphrase of "in domo Patris mei mansiones multae sunt." (John 14:2).
130. *DM*, p. 96; *Oeuvres*, 4:142.

apparently concerned with a "false mysticism"; that is "to *confuse* the different *planes* of the World, and consequently to mix up their activities."[131] For Teilhard this was to some extent the error of the first Christians, as evidenced in St. Paul's letters to the Colossians and Thessalonians. But out of this, according to Teilhard, came an opposite and equally unfortunate reaction:

> A rather childish haste, combined with the error in perspective which led the first generation of Christians to believe in the immediate return of Christ, has unfortunately left us disillusioned and suspicious. Our faith in the Kingdom of God has been disconcerted by the resistance of the world to good. A certain pessimism, perhaps, encouraged by an exaggerated conception of the original fall, has led us to regard the world as decidedly and incorrigibly wicked. And so we have allowed the flame to die down in our sleeping hearts.[132]

What is this "fire" that has been lost? Nothing other than the "Expectation of the Parousia."[133] For Teilhard this is the scandal of Christianity today, because without this expectation Christianity has become a religion turned toward the past rather than the future—a loss of perspective that falsifies its very nature, which in another place he has defined as:

> the *definitive religion* of a world which has suddenly become conscious of its dimensions and its course, both in space and in time.[134]

Having seen Christianity preeminently in this light, he appropriately closed *The Divine Milieu* on a positive and insistent note, which recalls the "Maranatha" of early Christians and is the closing prayer and affirmation of the Apocalypse. For Teilhard this prayer and affirmation were more than that; they represent a primary condition for the fulfillment of the universe.

> He came. Yet now we must expect Him—no longer a small chosen group among us, but all men—once again and more than ever. The Lord Jesus will only come soon if we ardently expect Him. It is an accumulation of desires that should cause the Pleroma to burst upon us.[135]

F. THE CHURCH: THE "PHYLUM" OF LOVE AND UNITY

Teilhard's approach to the Church was highly Incarnational and Eucharistic. Consequently, there was little or no mention of the "con-

131. *DM*, p. 95; *Oeuvres*, 4:141.
132. *DM*, p. 135; *Oeuvres*, 4:197-98.
133. "L'Attente de la Parousie," the title of the epilogue of *Le Milieu divin*.
134. "The Christian Phenomenon" (1950): cf. *C&E*, p. 208; *Oeuvres*, 10:242.
135. *DM*, pp. 134-35; *Oeuvres*, 4:197.

stitutional" texts of Scripture (i.e., those dealing with the place of Peter or the Apostles, etc.). Instead, his doctrine of the Church was more or less implicit in his doctrine of the Body of Christ and was definitely subservient to his tendency, already seen, to extend the concept of the Body of Christ to the whole of creation. This does not mean that in Teilhard's mind the Church became unidentifiable within the mass of humanity. Although his intention was to describe a more final and apocalyptic judgment, the words that he borrowed from Matthew 22:14 ("pauci electi") in "Forma Christi"[136] and the allusion to John 15:2 ("He is the sword that mercilessly cuts away such of the body's members as are unworthy or decayed") in "The Priest"[137] indicate that the Parousial processes of "aggregation" and "segregation" begin here in this life. And the focal point of this process is the Body of Christ, in both its initiation and consummation. In his "Note on the Physical Union between the Humanity of Christ and the Faithful . . ." are found these seminal passages:

> Briefly, the state of beatitude must be understood as a state of *permanent eucharistic union* in which we will be raised up and maintained *as a body* (that is to say *"per modum unius"*—as one single being) and *"in corpore Christi"* (in the body of Christ).[138]

And again, these words that have already been seen: "We become members of Christ before any external contact with his sacramental body."[139] Further, in relation to the "state of grace" (which is also a union with the Body of Christ),

> long before any communion, a first and *permanent* connexion through the operation of baptism is formed between the Christian and the body of Christ. And after each communion, in spite of the disappearance of the sacred species which had, for a time, raised it to a special degree of intimacy and importance, this connexion persists—more strongly established, even though in a less concentrated form.[140]
> The more familiar we become with this idea of a physical influx continually emanating (with an admixture of grace) for souls from the humanity of Christ, the more we realize how closely it harmonizes with the very numerous scriptural passages in which our possession of the Father is strictly subordinated to our *permanent* union with the incarnate Word; the more wonderful, too, become the depth and clarity of the evangelical precepts, in particular those which insist on communion and charity.[141]

In his 1924 "My Universe," the corporate aspect as well as the corporeal nature of the Eucharistic communion was again stressed, but

136. 1918; see *WTW*, p. 265; *Ecrits*, p. 349.
137. 1918; *WTW*, 209; *Ecrits*, p. 289.
138. *C&E*, pp. 16-17; *Oeuvres*, 10:23.
139. *C&E*, p. 17; *Oeuvres*, 10:23.
140. *Ibid*.
141. *C&E*, p. 18; *Oeuvres*, 10:25.

with an even greater emphasis on the assimilative properties of the Eucharist. After quoting St. Gregory of Nyssa on this point, he went further to say:

> The Flesh of Christ is fed by the whole universe. The mystical Milieu gathers up everything that is made up of energy. Nothing in the world is completely lacking in power, and nothing is rejected, except that which turns its back on the unification of spirit.[142]

To this a footnote was added:

> One cannot over-emphasise the fact that the sanctification of souls, however personal it may be, is still essentially collective. We are spiritualised by being carried along by the spiritualisation of all things. We are united to Christ by entering into communion with all men. We shall be saved by an option that has chosen the whole. And the beatific vision will be not so much an individual vision as a specific act of the Mystical Body, the Divine revealing itself to each one of us through the eyes of Christ.[143]

There is affirmed here a Body of Christ that transforms the elements of this world and is itself increased through this transformation—an idea that most literally translates what Teilhard believed to be the meaning of the eucharistic "Hoc est corpus meum" and that also explains the liberty he took with 1 Corinthians 13:12 in *The Divine Milieu* when he paraphrased the latter as "Quomodo comprehendam ut comprehensus sum?"[144] in a context that is definitely eucharistic. For as he had already said:

> When the priest says the words *Hoc est Corpus meum*, his words fall directly on to the bread and directly transform it into the individual reality of Christ. But the great sacramental operation does not cease at that local and momentary event. . . . In fact, from the beginning of the Messianic preparation, up till the Parousia, passing through the historic manifestation of Jesus and the phases of growth of His Church, a single event has been developing in the world: the Incarnation, realised, in each individual, through the Eucharist.
> All the communions of a life-time are one communion.
> All the communions of all men now living are one communion.
> All the communions of all men, present, past and future, are one communion.[145]

Seen in this manner, the "Communion of Saints" becomes but an aspect of the incarnate and universalized Christ. Indeed, in his 1936 "Sketch of a Personalistic Universe," Teilhard went on to extend this relationship even further:

> The essence of Christianity is neither more nor less than a belief in the *unification of the world in God by the Incarnation*.

142. *S&C*, p. 77; *Oeuvres*, 9:105.
143. *S&C*, p. 77, n.11; *Oeuvres*, 9:105-6.
144. *DM*, p. 105; *Oeuvres*, 4:155: "How shall I comprehend as I am comprehended?"
145. *DM*, p. 103; *Oeuvres*, 4:150-51.

To be the alpha and omega, Christ must, without losing his precise humanity, become *co-extensive with the physical expanse of time and space*. In order to reign on earth, He must "superanimate" the world.[146]

Exactly where does the Church as an organization fit into this cosmic movement toward unity? In his Epilogue to *The Phenomenon of Man*, Teilhard described Christianity, in terms analogous to that of the evolution of species, as a "Phylum," or again, as a "Spearhead" (in the French, "la *flèche* de la Biogénèse).[147] In his "Introduction to the Christian Life," written in 1944, this concept is more explicitly developed in a section entitled bilingually in the French original "L'essence du Christianisme: A 'Personalistic Universe' ":

From the realistic and biological point of view which is eminently that of Catholic dogma, the universe represents: (1) The arduous, personalizing unification in God of a tenuous mass of souls, distinct from God, but in subordinate dependence on him, (2) by incorporation in Christ (incarnate God), (3) through the building up of collective humano-Christian unity (Church).

"When all things are subjected to him, then the Son himself will also be subjected to him who put all things under him, that God may be everything to every one" (1 Cor. 15:28).

From this it follows that a threefold faith is necessary, and sufficient, as a foundation for the Christian position:

1. Faith in the (personalizing) personality of God, the focus of the world.

2. Faith in the divinity of the historic Christ (not only prophet and perfect man, but also object of love and worship).

3. Faith in the reality of the Church *phylum*, in which and around which Christ continues to develop, in the world, his total personality.[148]

And as for his "phylum Eglise," it must be seen as a phylum of love, for ". . . the dominating and ultimate energy of the whole system can only be a person-to-person attraction: in other words, a love attraction."[149] Thus, in Teilhard's writings, the subject of love, in one form or another, gradually began to dominate his thought. As far back as 1917, when he described the "ut unum sint, sicut unum sumus" of John 17:22 as the ". . . the definitive formula which gives us the key to the Gospel and to the world,"[150] the problem has to be confronted as to how complete unity can be achieved without the annihilation of personality, or as he later formulated it, in terms of "union" as distinct from "fusion," or—to put it even more strongly—between a "Panthe-

146. "Esquisse d'un Univers Personnel" in *Oeuvres*, 6:113; cf. *HE*, p. 91. (Emphasis added)
147. Cf. *Oeuvres*, 1:332; *PM*, p. 298.
148. *C&E*, pp. 151-52; *Oeuvres*, 10:179-80.
149. *C&E*, p. 152; *Oeuvres*, 10:180.
150. "The Struggle Against the Multitude" in *WTW*, p. 113; *Ecrits*, p. 131.

ism of Identification" and a "Pantheism of Unification."[151] The only answer, of course, is love, which he understood as the basic unitive energy of the universe. True union, unlike mere amalgamation, differentiates.[152] This was one of Teilhard's basic phenomenological laws. "Convergence" with organic "complexity" is correlative to greater "consciousness" because this true unity is "center to center," or, on the human level, "person to person." It would require a chapter or two simply to summarize the reasoning and observations that Teilhard had put into these formulations; indeed, they form the whole underlying theme of books like *The Phenomenon of Man* and major essays such as "Centrology" (1944) or "Outline of a Dialectic of the Spirit" (1946).[153] Yet it was because of insights like this, of universal application, that he could speak with such assurance when he quoted John 13:34 in "The Atomism of the Spirit" (1941):

> "Love one another": it seemed as though all that was finest in morality must have reached its peak and be summed up in that precept once and for all. . . . The "Lord's precept" does not disappear under the harsh light of modern criticism: rather does it leave the domain of sentiment, to become the leading instrument of evolution. "It leaves the world of dreams, to enter into the system of universal energies and essential laws."[154]

But in addition to being the moving force of evolutionary progress, this same precept is also a challenge to the moral energies of the Church. The "Manete in dilectione mea" (John 15:10), the "one thing necessary" (Luke 11:42) of *The Divine Milieu*[155] cannot be taken passively. As he was to write in "The New Spirit" (1942):

> "Love one another . . ." Hitherto the evangelical precept has seemed simply to mean, "Do not harm one another," or, "Seek with all possible care and devotion to diminish injustice, heal wounds and soften enmities in the world around you." In such an order of things no man can love his neighbour without drawing nearer to God— and, of course, reciprocally (but this we knew already). But it is also impossible (this is newer to us) to love either God or our neighbour without assisting the progress, in its physical entirety, of the terrestrial synthesis of the spirit: since it is precisely the progress of this synthesis which enables us to draw closer together among ourselves, while at the same time it raises us towards God.[156]

In 1945 Teilhard turned his attention to the text of Luke 10:27 (cf. Deut. 6:5) in "Christianity and Evolution." In this text he proclaimed

151. Cf. "Pour y voir clair" (1950), *Oeuvres*, 7:231-32; *AE*, p. 223.
152. "La véritable union ne fond pas: elle différencie et personnalise. *Oeuvres*, 7:230; *AE*, p. 222.
153. Both essays appear in *Oeuvres*, 7 (*AE*).
154. *AE*, pp. 51-52; *Oeuvres*, 7:58-59.
155. *DM*, p. 99; *Oeuvres*, 4:147.
156. *FM*, p. 95; *Oeuvres*, 5:124-25.

the key to a reconciliation of love of God and a love for the evolving universe:

> love of evolution is not a mere extension of love of God to one further object. It corresponds to a radical reinterpretation (one might almost say it emerges from a recasting) of the notion of charity. "Thou shalt love God." "Thou shalt love thy neighbour for the love of God." In its new form, "Thou shalt love God in and through the genesis of the universe and of mankind," this twofold gospel commandment is synthesized into a single meaningful act, with an as yet unparalleled field of application and power to make new.[157]

Or again, in the final essay of his life, "Le Christique," he spoke of the three major "evidences" of the truth of Christianity: "coherence," "contagious power," and "superiority." Note the second of these:

> —Next the evidence of the *contageous power* of a form of Charity in which it becomes possible to love God "not only with all his body and all his soul," but with the whole Universe in evolution.[158]

However, lest it be thought that Christianity for Teilhard was merely a community or "phylum" of love without its own structure or visible boundaries, there exists at least one essay (besides numerous references in his letters and notes) where this subject was broached with clear allusion by way of parallel to Colossians 1:18 and Ephesians 1:10 and also to the theme of John 15:1-6.

> Biologically, it behaves as a "phylum"; and by biological necessity it must, therefore, have the structure of a phylum; in other words, it must form a coherent and progressive system of collectively associated spiritual elements.
>
> That being so, it is evident that *hic et nunc* there is nothing within Christianity except Catholicism which possesses such characteristics.
>
> There are, no doubt, many individuals outside Catholicism who recognize and love Christ, and are therefore united to him, as much as (and even more than) some Catholics. But these individuals are not grouped together in the "cephalized" unity of a *body* which reacts vitally, as an organic whole, to the combined forces of Christ and mankind. They benefit from the sap in the trunk without sharing in its early development and youthful surge at the heart of the tree. . . . Everything goes to show that if Christianity is in truth destined to be, as it professes, and as it is conscious of being, the religion of tomorrow, it is only through the living, organic axis of its Roman Catholicism that it can hope to measure up to the great modern humanist currents and become one with them.

---

157. *C&E*, p. 184; *Oeuvres*, 10:214-15.
158. March 1955. (My translation.) *Oeuvres*, 13:116.

To be Catholic is the only way of being fully and utterly Christian.[159]

Perhaps the above passage may strike post-Vatican II readers as being a little too rigid and unappreciative of other Christian communities, or a little too aggressive concerning what Teilhard had sometimes called "The Roman Axis" of Christianity. Perhaps it was a case of a man who had suffered too much at the restrictions imposed by this authority "protesting too much" in his efforts to remain loyal. Nevertheless, this view, whether given a more rigid or more lenient interpretation, was consistent in its logic.

G. THE CROSS AND HUMAN SUFFERING

As noted before, Teilhard's synthesis, theologically speaking, was primarily "Christological" rather than "Soteriological." This was mainly because of the difficulties represented by the historical doctrine of original sin and the problem of its relationship to the universal evolutionary phenomenon of death. Consequently, Teilhard was constrained to assimilate, as much as he found possible, the redemptive death of the historic Christ to the general effort demanded by the evolutive process, and in turn, to see that historic death and resurrection, by virtue of the universality of the Incarnation, as transforming all death and suffering throughout the evolution of the universe. To recall again the words of "Mon univers" (1924) concerning the "kenosis" of Christ as understood by Teilhard, let it be noted that, while he interpreted Christ's death in the same terms as did St. Paul in 1 Corinthians 15:55, another element takes precedence:

> We had, intellectually and vitally, to overcome the horror with which destruction fills us. By subjecting himself to the trial of individual death, by his blessed acceptance of the death of the world, Christ effected this reversal of our outlook and fears. *He vanquished death.* He gave it, physically, the value of a metamorphosis: through which the world, with him, entered into God.
> And then Christ rose again. We are often too inclined to regard the Resurrection as an isolated event in time, with an apologetical significance, as some small individual triumph over the tomb won in turn by Christ. It is something quite other and much greater than that. It is a tremendous cosmic event. It marks Christ's effective assumption of his function as the universal centre. Until that time, he was present in all things as a soul that is painfully gathering together its embryonic elements. Now he radiates over the whole universe as a consciousness and activity fully in control of themselves. After being baptised into the world, he has risen up from it. After sinking

159. "Introduction to the Christian Life" (June 1944), *C&E*, p. 168; *Oeuvres*, 10:196-97.

down to the depths of the earth, he has reached up to the heavens."
Descendit et ascendit ut impleret omnia" (Eph. 4. 10).[160]

It is primarily in relation to this understanding of the death and resurrection of Christ that Teilhard's view of every human's suffering in
this world and each one's death must be understood. There are frequent references to Gospel texts such as Matthew 10:39 ("Anyone who
finds his life shall lose it") and Matthew 16:24 (cf. Luke 9:23, Mark
8:34): ("If anyone wants to be a follower of mine, let him renounce
himself"). Both of these texts, as well as John 12:24 ("Unless a wheat
grain falls on the ground and dies, it remains only a single grain . . ."),
were quoted in the 1917 "The Struggle Against the Multitude"[161] in
what is a rather metaphysical context, thus at a very early date tying
Teilhard's view of Christian asceticism to his theory of creative union.
This theory he was to describe in his "Creative Union" of November of
that same year as ". . . the philosophy of the universe expressed in
terms of the notion of the mystical body,"[162] and was to formulate
metaphysically as "plus esse = plus, et pluribus, uniri."[163] But in the
earlier essay he had already described this same theory in terms of
ascetical-mystical theology:

> Once a man has resolved to live generously in love with God and
> his fellow-men, he realizes that so far he has achieved nothing by
> the generous renunciation he has made in order to perfect his own
> inner unity. This unity in its turn must, if it is to be born anew in
> Christ, suffer an eclipse which will seem to annihilate it. For in
> truth those will be saved who *dare to set* the centre of their being
> *outside themselves*, who dare to love Another *more than themselves*,
> and in some sense become this Other: which is to say, who dare to
> pass through death to find life. *Si quis vult animam suam salvam fa-
> cere, perdet eam.*[164]

This union, which, as has been seen ". . . gives us the key to the
Gospel and to the world,"[165] is also the key to the mystery of suffering.
While in *The Divine Milieu* the doctrine was expounded in terms of
Christian activity and its complement of the suffering of passivity, the
full reintegration of these themes is found in a much later essay with
the long, long title:

> What the World is Looking for from the Church of God at this
> Moment: A Generalizing and a Deepening of the Meaning of the
> Cross.[166]

160. *S&C*, pp. 63-64; *Oeuvres*, pp. 91-92 (Emphasis added; cf. also 1 Cor. 15:55).
161. Cf. *WTW*, pp. 112-13; *Ecrits*, pp. 130-31. (*Jerusalem Bible* translations).
162. *WTW*, p. 174; *Ecrits*, p. 196.
163. *WTW*, p. 155; *Ecrits*, p. 177: "To be more = more, and by many, united."
164. *WTW*, p. 112; *Ecrits*, p. 130.
165. *WTW*, p. 113; *Ecrits*, p. 130.
166. "Ce que le Monde attend en ce moment de l'Eglise de Dieu: Une généralisation et
un approfondissement de sen de la croix" (Sept. 14, 1952) in *Oeuvres*, 10:251-61;
C&E, pp. 212-20.

In this essay, after summarizing the traditional views of the cross as primarily a symbol of reparation and expiation, which notions are dominated by a "catastrophic" view of the supernatural and of creation, Teilhard counterposed an evolutionary view of the universe and what he saw to be the inescapability of suffering in a universe that by its very structure entails hard work, the statistical inevitability of failures, the biological necessity of death, and the psychological need of an "amorizing" process that demands the price of sacrifice on the "reflective" level of existence. Given these structural necessities of a universe that is in a true state of evolution, it seemed altogether logical for Teilhard to expand the traditional vision of the cross in terms that surpass the usual categories of soteriology, and, in so doing, to expand the meaning (and wording) of John the Baptist's acclamation in John 1:29:

> is not the God of evolution—the God for whom our neo-humanism is looking—precisely and simply, taken in the fullest sense of the words and in a generalized form, the very God of expiation?
> And this because, if we consider the matter carefully, "to bear the sins of the guilty world" means precisely, *translated and transposed into terms of cosmogenesis*, "to bear the weight of a world in a state of evolution."[167]

H. CONCLUSION

Should a count be made, some one-hundred and twenty instances of Teilhard's employment of quotations, both explicit and implicit, as well as direct references and various allusions drawn from Sacred Scripture, have been utilized in this general survey. Less than half of the occasions in which this wealth of material occurs has been illustrated. A great deal of additional material that belongs to the more strictly ascetical and mystical aspects of his work has been bypassed as well, not because it is not noteworthy, but because it does not so directly relate to the Christological development of his thought as do the examples cited. However, much of this latter class of material is not without its Christological overtones.

In an era of growing concern for literal exegesis, Teilhard is seen to have been a surprisingly free and unrestricted user of Sacred Scripture, and this at times in a manner that could only cause the professional biblical scholar to shudder. This could be said about his apparent ignorance—particularly during his long exile in China—of much of the work that was being done in the field.[168]

---

167. *C&E*, pp. 218-19; *Oeuvres*, 10:259-60.
168. A story was once related by a fellow Jesuit, here unnamed, that Teilhard, on a visit to England during a rare journey back home, criticized a biblical scholar for the lack of serious studies on the Pauline texts that so interested Teilhard. He was supposedly shown, to his embarrassment, a whole list of such material, of most of which he had been unaware. His 1944-55 "Journals" and the accompanying bibliographical notations show little evidence of further reading in this direction.

But the boldness and logic of his insights are striking. The principal problem is the process by which such insights, amounting at times to a virtual reinterpretation of Scripture, could occur. Not that reinterpretation in itself is any great phenomenon! The hetereodox have never suffered any lack of inspiration in their reading of Sacred Writ. The warning of 2 Peter concerning the difficulty and opportunities for misinterpretation in the writings of St. Paul should be recalled, and as for the Book of Revelation, little need be said. But in the case of Teilhard there seems to be an insight that is strikingly consistent with a whole tradition of biblical theology, for the most part long forgotten in the West, but one that, as George Maloney, S.J.,[169] has so amply shown, is still alive and well in the Christian East. And yet, as any analysis of a positive-historical nature will show, this Eastern theology is equally, if not more so, as Johannine as Pauline, and is certainly a product, intellectually and psychologically, of a vastly different milieu from that of a twentieth-century man of the world of empirical science.

Further, whatever the happy coincidence between the insights of Teilhard and those of a number of the Greek Fathers and even of a handful in the West—such as Irenaeus (who of course was by birth and education an Oriental and reputedly a disciple, once removed, of St. John), or later figures such as the Christian pantheist Erigena or the famous scholastic protagonist John Duns Scotus—the fact that Teilhard has had such illustrious theological predecessors does not in itself establish the validity of his project. On the contrary, there are those who see in the whole drift of Incarnational Christology a radical break with the Christ of the synoptics, and it is worth noting that among the earliest of the Eastern theologians to extol the cosmic Christ was Origen, who was both judged as being heterodox and who had his theological roots, at least, in the Alexandrine school of scriptural interpretation, hardly noted for its adherence to the literal sense of Scripture.

The three major Pauline themes previewed above will now be traced in detail. Each of these the "Omnis Creatura" (Rom. 8:22f.), the "Corpus Christi" (particularly in 1 Cor. and Eph.), and the "pleroma" (manifested in Ephesians and Colossians, and as Teilhard saw it reflected in 1 Cor. 15:28), is eminently Christological and, as Teilhard interpreted them, bound inextricably with his understanding of evolution as ultimately one vast "Christogenesis." Within the context of these themes (and their relationship to his selection of Johannine material), the very heart of Teilhard's call for a reinterpretation of the Scriptures and, indeed, for the reorientation of the whole Christian vision, can most directly be discovered.

---

169. *The Cosmic Christ: From Paul to Teilhard* (New York: Harper & Row, 1968).

PART II

Teilhardian Reinterpretation and the Verdict of Modern Exegesis

3

Omnis Creatura

Of the three major Pauline themes that formed the core of Teilhard's Christology, the one that at first was most closely bound up with his dynamic approach (hence with Christology understood in terms of "Christogenesis") had its origin in the moving image given by St. Paul in Romans 8:19-25. In it, the "expectatio creaturae" (Rom. 8:20) was delineated in terms of hope contrasted to "vanity" or purposelessness; and Teilhard saw the destiny of all creation to be bound up in the redemptive promise of Christ.

Typically, Teilhard tended to quote only the simple phrase taken from verse 22: "Omnis creatura ingemiscit et parturit."[1] While the latter part of the phrase seems first to have captured his attention, still, never neglecting this latter part, his emphasis seems gradually to have shifted to the first part—namely, that nothing in creation, no matter how material and thereby seemingly insignificant, will be without its place in the great redemptive design of God. A certain evolution was to take place in Teilhard's mind concerning this verse as well as the section of Romans in which it is situated (including the enigmatic Rom. 5:12: "In quo omnes peccaverunt"). This evolution was to affect all his subsequent elaboration of "Christogenesis" and will be crucial to all further evaluation of his synthesis. Apart from this matter, and apart from the hermeneutical judgment that Teilhard was to bring to bear upon it, his whole "Christogenic" vision of the cosmos becomes shipwrecked on the rock of "concordism," leaving nothing but a scattering of theological flotsam hardly worthy of salvage.

Indeed, while the problem of evil in general and sin would continue

1. "The entire creation . . . has been groaning in one great act of giving birth. . . ." (*Jerusalem Bible* translation).

83

to plague Teilhard's speculations for the rest of his life, it was here, in the relationship of physical in respect to moral evil, that his earliest inspirations from Scripture were to receive their severest test, and, consequent upon this test, to be freed to open the way toward their fullest integration in the revelation of a "pleromic" universe.

A. THE USE OF ROMANS 8:22
IN THE WRITINGS OF TEILHARD

Attention has earlier been called to the fact that Teilhard explicitly quotes Romans 8:22 at least eight times in his writings between the years 1916 and 1936. Added to this are one clearly implicit quotation and at least five equally clear allusions to this Pauline theme.[2]

The first occasion in which this text appears is in "Cosmic Life" in 1916. In chapter 4 of this essay, "Communion with God through Earth," the quotation appears in part B, entitled "The Holiness of Evolution," section 3, "The Meaning of the Cross."

> A price has to be paid for the struggle. The earth groans in travail with Christ. *Omnis creatura ingemiscit et parturit*—like a wagon that creaks and grinds, progress advances painfully, bruised and tearful.[3]

In the rest of this section, Teilhard goes on to elaborate the implications of this view:

> If he is to act in conformity with his new ideal, the man who has determined to admit love of the world and its cares into his interior life finds that he has to accept *a supreme renunciation*.
> He must agree to be, some day, the fragment of steel on the surface of the blade that flies off as soon as a blow is struck, the soldier in the first wave of the attack, *the outer surface, made use of and sacrificed, of the cosmos in activity*.[4]

It can be seen that Teilhard was here primarily using Romans 8:22 to expound an ascetical principle, but a principle not in any way that of suffering for suffering's sake, that is, a kind of negative purification from the world. Instead:

> Eagerly and wholeheartedly, the soul has offered and surrendered itself to all the great currents of nature. When it reaches the term of all that it has gone through and when at long last it can see things with a mature eye, it realizes that no work is more effective or brings greater peace than to gather together, in order to soothe it and offer it to God, the suffering of the world; no attitude allows the

2. Cf. Appendix A, Rom. 8:22.
3. *WTW*, pp. 65-66; *Ecrits*, p. 54.
4. *WTW*, p. 66; *Ecrits*, p. 55.

soul to expand more freely, than to open itself, generously and tenderly—with and in Christ—*to sympathy with all suffering*, to *"cosmic compassion."*[5]

From this can also be seen that this grand travail of the cosmos was given an explicitly Christological interpretation. It is not simply a moral comparison of evolution with Christ's cross and our own suffering. It is an identification, a *"com*passion." And this connection, this co-suffering of creation, is intrinsic to the nature of the universe, not simply due to the inevitable failures and setbacks of the evolutionary process, but apparently because of an innate gap that separates nature as it is from its "telos" or final perfection. Thus, in "The Priest" (1918) is found this implicit quotation: "Thus the universe groans, caught between its *passionate desire* and its impotence,"[6] and again: "I can feel that all the strain and struggle of the universe reaches down into the most hidden places of my being."[7]

A year later, in "The Names of Matter," a very interesting use of Romans 8:22 appeared in a context both reminiscent of the metaphysics of "Creative Union" (1917) and somewhat predictive of the "Ultraphysics" of *The Phenomenon of Man* (1937). Speaking of the three states of matter, which he termed "Matter A, B, and C," Teilhard stated:

A. *Living Matter.—Matter A (or Living Matter)* involves the still unifiable (spiritualizable) but not yet unified portion of the Universe.

Of this Matter A, the principal part is formed by human souls themselves, taken collectively. Achieved and autonomous so that it may be a spiritual soul, it does not exist as isolated in the world and is not made for separate existence. Our souls represent, in reality, the elements, the atoms, of a further construction, even more elevated in spirituality beyond themselves. But in awaiting this superior unification under a single Spirit, their multiplicity undergoes the inconveniences of all incompletely organized plurality. . . . And we ourselves, plunged into this *spiritual Matter* ["*Matière d'esprit*"], cruelly experience all the painful discordances and invincible mutual exteriority that are involved in this state. . . . Who does not experience the tearing apart of nature wherein contrary tendencies develop simultaneously through a rending of the Spirit in their antagonistic growth?—All this belongs to the fecund pain, a suffering of aggregation, an evil of growth ["un mal de croissance"], involved in being. *Omnis creatura ingemiscit et parturit*.[8]

This passage has been quoted at length because of its great importance concerning what he termed the "materia matrix" in the next

5. *WTW*, p. 57; *Ecrits*, p. 68.
6. *WTW*, p. 206; *Ecrits*, p. 286. (Emphasis added.)
7. *WTW*, p. 215; *Ecrits*, p. 295.
8. "Les noms de la Matière" in *Ecrits*, pp. 424-25 (not published in *WTW*). (My translation.)

paragraph, and then a paragraph later where he added (with a footnote included):

> By its nature, living Matter is destined to be diminished, to lose its Materiality. [Footnote: i.e., by this troublesome *Materiality* is to be understood the shocks, the exteriority of parts, and the determinisms involved.] But, I repeat, in the Spirit the *formal Materiality* (and thus the "Unifiability") would not disappear, but find its consummation. Throughout this whole section, it should not be forgotten, it is a question of Materiality *in relationship* to our soul.[9]

Thus, Matter A (living matter) must pass through the second stage, that of Matter B.

> —Matter B is *Dead Matter* or *Inverted Matter*, which results from the desegregation (whether culpable or not, but always painful) of *Living Matter*.[10]

While this inanimate or dead matter, because of its seeming imperishability, has the appearance of immortality, it is, in terms of Teilhard's theory of creative union, quite the opposite, for tending toward "The Pure Multiple" ("Le Multiple pur," which is also the equivalent of pure nothingness),[11] Teilhard renamed Matter B, "la Matière mauvais":

> In principle ("Ex dogmate"), *Bad Matter*, which is, initially, what is in *some sense* evil (in the sense of disintegration) seems to have *taken concrete form* ["pris corps"] finally in a group of *potentialities* and of fallen monads which constitute, in opposition to God, a *real pole* of attraction as opposed to dissociation.[12]

9. *Ecrits*, p. 425. Note *"in relationship"* above: This whole section 5 of "Les noms de la Matière" deals with "Matière relative," i.e., matter in its relationship to our own personal evolution. The same remark applies to the paragraphs from this essay that follow below.

10. *Ibid*.

11. Cf. "Creative Union" in *WTW*, pp. 162-64; *Ecrits*, pp. 184-86. That "Les noms de la Matière" may have been written partly as a sequel to "L'Union créatrice" as well as something of an introduction to "La Puissance spirituelle de la Matière" (Cf. *Ecrits*, pp. 417, 435-36) seems possibly indicated by a remark in a letter to Teilhard's cousin Marguerite (cf. *The Making of a Mind* [New York: Harper & Row, 1961], p. 245) written Oct. 3, 1918. In any case, it is known that Teilhard was quite unsatisfied with his "metaphysical" speculations as they appeared in "L'Union créatrice." Whether "Les noms de la Matière" actually helps clarify some of these notions is for the reader to judge.

12. *Ecrits*, p. 427. *"Potentialities"*: Teilhard here used the Latin term "habitus" (repeated in the French below as "habitudes"), apparently in something of the same sense in which the scholastic theologians used the term, as denoting a more or less permanent capacity in a being. Teilhard seems to have here been groping toward a formulation of the principle of evil in the universe, however impersonally expressed, as opposed to the more nonsubstantial scholastic conception of evil as "an absence of good."

Thus "Matière B" in this stage of his thinking seems to have been associated with a theory of a "pre-cosmic fall." Later on, as shall be seen, he associated this pure multiplicity with the first stage of creation, in contrast to the organization of the elements, i.e., creation properly speaking. However, at this point, the retrogressive aspects of death (the inversion of matter to multiplicity) appears to have been dominant in his thought.

What then is Matter C? It is

a kind of *secondary or New Matter*, engendered not through a lapse or regression of being, but through a progressive and normal play of spiritual activity.

One primary source of *Matter C* in us is the functioning of our faculties *according to their activities*. . . .

To this primary Materiality, which is "secreted" *in itself* under the form of "Potentialities" through its own proper activity, there should be joined another (exterior to ourselves, but nonetheless unyielding), but this time as a result of our own freedom, *our own choice*.[13]

But thus seen, the outcome is still in doubt:

From the midst of *Matter which is not yet spiritualized* (Matter A), to the foundation of the Spirit *in the process of continual materialization* (Matters B and C), the human aspiration has never varied: "Who shall deliver us from this body of death?"[14]

The above question, an explicit quotation of Romans 7:24, is associated, as it should be, with his equally extraordinary use of Romans 8:22. The answer is also extraordinary, worth quoting in full:

Rightly, this reanimation of the solidified (materialized) Spirit does not seem to be impossible. In fact, for the immense portion of the Cosmos (Matter B) which,—by nature or by fault—, is incapable of ascending to the level of the Spirit, our emancipation from the determinisms of matter would appear to be unrealizable here below. To be liberated Man must die, that is to say, to be finally isolated from all which is not destined to survive with him. To attain the higher circles of existence, the mixed organism (formed from what is both mortal and what is immortal intertwined) from which the terrestrial life is woven must be dissolved.—*Matter C* constitutes essentially the fallen part (the chrysalide) of ourselves, that from which we can rid ourselves only so much as we let it fall aside. But at the same time, strangely enough, it is discovered that we are pushed from such deep roots in our birth in the spirit that it [i.e., matter] cannot be rejected entirely. Even in our "separated" souls, matter exists according to that part of itself which is capable of being *revived*.[15]

For Teilhard, then, even as early as this essay of 1919, evolution reaches its completion in resurrection, or in the consummation of the incarnation, as he put it in his "Note on Some Possible Historical Representations of Original Sin" of 1922:

The incarnation of the Word (which is in process of continual and universal consummation) is simply the final term of a creation which

13. *Ecrits*, pp. 427-28.
14. *Ecrits*, p. 428.
15. *Ecrits*, p. 430.

is still continuing everywhere and does so through our imperfections (*"omnis creatura adhuc ingemiscit et parturit."*)[16]

Again, a year later in "Pantheism and Christianity" (seen in part above in conjunction with Eph. 4:9), the Christological element in his interpretation of Romans 8:22 is just as strong, but the emphasis on the union of all creation with its Creator ("la tendance panthéiste fondamentale") has now taken precedence over the earlier concern for the transformation of the material as such.

> The Incarnate Word could not be the supernatural (hyperphysical) centre of the universe if he did not function *first* as its physical, natural, centre. Christ cannot sublimate creation in God without progressively raising it up by his influence through the successive circles of matter and spirit. That is why, in order to bring all things back to his Father, he had to make himself one with all—he had to enter into contact with every one of the zones of the created, from the lowest and most earthly to the zone that is closest to heaven. *"Quid est quod ascendit in coelum, nisi prius quod descendit in ima terrae ut repleret omnia."* Even therefore, in that aspect of its evolution which is regarded as the most "natural," it is towards Christ that the universe, since all time, has been moving as one integral whole. *"Omnis creatura usque adhuc ingemiscit et parturit."* Has any evolutionist pantheism, in fact, ever spoken more magnificently of the Whole than St Paul did in the words he addressed to the first Christians?[17]

At this point the development of Teilhard's understanding of Romans 8:22 reached its Christological apex; indeed, this is where it merged into his concepts of the Body of Christ and of the pleroma. From this point on, only two more explicit quotations of this text appeared, the first being this summary in *The Divine Milieu* where, again, the term of this development is the pleroma:

> It is through the collaboration which He stimulates in us that Christ, starting from *all* created things, is consummated and attains His plenitude. St. Paul himself tells us so. We may, perhaps, imagine that the Creation was finished long ago. But that would be quite wrong. It continues still more magnificently, and in the highest zones of the world. *Omnis creatura adhuc ingemniscit et parturit.* And we serve to complete it, even by the humblest work of our hands. That is, ultimately, the meaning and value of our acts. Owing to the inter-relation between matter, soul and Christ, we lead part of the being which He desires back to God *in whatever we do*. With each one of our *works*, we labour—atomically, but no less really—to build the Pleroma; that is to say, we bring to Christ a little fulfilment.[18]

16. *C&E*, p. 53; *Oeuvres*, 10:69.
17. *C&E*, pp. 71-72; *Oeuvres*, 10:88.
18. *DM*, pp. 30-31; *Oeuvres*, 4:50.

The final explicit quotation of Romans 8:22 is a very short but telling one. For Teilhard, the need for the world to sense the worth of its endeavor has become essential to its psychic health—and it is at the same time its form of adoration as well. Christianity's possession of this touchstone of faith for modern man is itself a mark of its credibility.

> That such a religion is exactly in line with what the modern world is looking for as its God, and regards as its specific form of worship: a God who justifies, sets the crown upon, and receives as a supreme tribute, the incessant ("adhuc parturit") labour of the consummation, even on earth, of man.[19]

Christologically, as has been said, Teilhard's explicit comments on what has been termed the "Expectatio creaturae" (the topic of the whole section of Rom. 8:18-25) came to an end with the 1936 passage quoted above. However, there were a few further allusions, one of which is of theological importance even though it occurs as a mere footnote at the end of a paleontological essay of January 1925 entitled "The Transformist Paradox" and subtitled "On the Latest Criticism of Transformism by M. Vialleton":

> Is it necessary to recall that far from being incompatible with the existence of a Primal Cause, transformist views, as set out here, present its influx in the noblest and most heartening manner possible? For the Christian transformist, God's creative action is no longer conceived as an intrusive thrusting of His works into the midst of pre-existent beings, but as a *bringing to birth* of the successive stages of His work in the heart of things. It is no less essential, no less universal, no less intimate either on that account.[20]

Without involvement in the intricacies of the problems presented in Teilhard's system by the notion of creation, how account for the decreasing use of Romans 8:22 in his writings, and its complete absence in any explicit way after 1936? Could it be that the terms used by St. Paul no longer suited his purpose or in some way obscured it? Based on the varying uses of the words *creation, birth, genesis,* and *evolution,* the evidence is not clear or is at least ambiguous.[21] While the quotation cited immediately above gives some hint of the problem, a passage in an unpublished address of 1930 affirms his position:

19. "Some Reflections on the Conversion of the World" (1936), *S&C*, p. 123; *Oeuvres*, 9:162.
20. *The Vision of the Past* (London: Collins; New York: Harper & Row, 1966), p. 102; *La Vision du Passé* (*Oeuvres*, 3) (Paris: Editions du Seuil, 1957), p. 142. (English version will be designated *VP*.)
21. In a note entitled "Profession of Faith" written in English to a friend, Lucille Swan, Sept. 28, 1933, Teilhard associated the two terms *evolution* and *birth*:
     "The Evolution or Birth of the Universe is of a '*convergent*' (not of a divergent) nature:—towards a final Unity." (unpublished, *T.A.*, #107)
     But in a remark made in the course of a talk given by Teilhard, "Sur le Règne de Dieu" (1946), he stated that while formerly the idea of "naissance" dominated the concept of the beginnings, it is now the idea of "Genèse," of the world as "materia matrix," that is foremost. (*T.A.*, unnumbered, p. 1, ¶3.) Yet again, in a Journal note of Jan. 6, 1955 ("Journal" 21 [9]: 17), writing in another context, Teilhard wrote that the problem of the evolution of dogma becomes distorted by the classic confusion between the notions of "Evolution" and of "Genesis."

If we should accomplish this transformation of the notion of the Incarnation, of Christ, of Communion, which is at the foundation of the great work of a creation in union with God . . . we foresee that in an Incarnation well understood as creation continued throughout the whole universe there will always be a place for the expiation of failure and also a place for laborious effort and progress. Accordingly the Cross, the expression of redemptive suffering, is, to begin with, the symbol of creative but laborious effort, of a humanity which climbs toward the Christ whom it awaits.[22]

But two years later in "La Route de l'Ouest" he put it this way: "The divine Unity surmounts the plural by sur-creation, not by substitution."[23] And in the same essay he scored what he considers a distortion in Pauline thought, where

exactly as in the case of asceticism and mysticism, a certain contamination still seems to exist in the Christian cosmogonies, involving both Eastern and Western views. In spite of the fact that they are associated in a single perspective by St. Paul, the ideas of an absolutely contingent first creation (and thus hardly explainable), taken along with that of an equally contingent general fall (and thus hardly honorable respecting the Creator), do not accord well with the ideas of an Incarnation leading to a kind of mutual enfolding ["réplétion"] of the One and of the Multiple. One detects, in this ensemble, the mixture of elements borrowed from preoccupations or from the lines of solutions which are quite different or even opposed. A separation and rechoice between these elements, leading finally to a Christian Cosmogony which would be vast in its horizons and pure in its lines,—worthy of Christ in whom is its crown,—this effort represents the necessary task.[24]

What appears here is perhaps one of the earliest recorded reservations in Teilhard's mind about the adequacy of all aspects of Pauline thought for transposition to the situation of an evolutionary universe. While Teilhard was unsparing in his use of the more openly Christological texts of St. Paul's letters, he appears to have been considerably less enthusiastic over what he believed to be the Pauline view of creation and its close connection with the vexing problem of an original Fall.

For this reason, when Teilhard made further allusions to this text from Romans, they seem to fall into two distinct usages that are not closely connected. The first is the repetition of the phrase *mal de croissance* in association with the term *enfantement* as it is found in the 1948 appendix to *The Phenomenon of Man*.[25]

This "Evil of Growth" is distinguished in *The Phenomenon of Man* from three others: "The Evil of Disorder and of Failure" and its par-

22. "Essai d'intégration de l'Homme dans l'Univers," Conférence 4, Dec. 10, 1930, unpublished, *TA* #92, p. 10. (Cf. Appendix D §1, 6, for French text.)
23. "La Route de l'Ouest; Vers une Mystique nouvelle," Sept. 8, 1932, *Oeuvres*, 11:54. (My translation.) Also in *TF*, p. 48f.
24. *Ibid.*, pp. 63-64, *TF*, p. 58-59.
25. *PM*, p. 312; *Oeuvres*, 1:347: quoted in chap. 2, §2 above.

ticular specification in the "Evil of Decomposition," and again, from the particularly human problem of the "Evil of Solitude and Anxiety."[26]

Without forgetting the relationship that Teilhard establishes between Romans 8:22 and Romans 8:28 ("Omnia cooperuntur in bonum") and the particular Christological interpretation that he gave the latter,[27] we should note that it is precisely the evil of growth that is singled out, in terms reminiscent of Romans 8:22, as apart from that of disorder, decomposition, and human anxiety. These latter can coexist with a more or less static or cyclical universe, but it is only from a universe that is in the throes of progress that they take on a more than passive meaning. Accordingly, Teilhard's early ascetical interpretation of Romans 8:22, is reintegrated with the more evolutionary viewpoint in his 1952 essay "What the World is Looking for from the Church of God: A Generalization and a Deepening of the Meaning of the Cross":

> If the Cross is to reign over an earth that has suddenly awoken to consciousness of a biological movement drawing it ahead, then at all costs and as soon as possible it must (if it is to be able to co-exist with human nature which it claims to save) present itself to us as a sign, not merely of "escape," but of progress.[28]

Thus, while there was no renewed appeal to Romans 8:22 in this later essay, Teilhard's concern lest the mystery of suffering be construed in the sense of an "escape"[29] harks back directly to his earliest claim that Romans be understood in terms of a cosmic "passion" that sees all creation in expectation of redemption in Christ.

On the other hand, the final allusion (if it is such) appears in quite a disparate sense and context. It is in the 1951 essay "Reflections on the Scientific Probability and the Religious Consequences of an Ultra-Human" and deals with the concept of evolution as being more universal than mere Darwinian transformism:

> In the new and magnificent sense of the word, let us insist once more, evolution has become for science something very different— something much bigger and much more certain than that. It is an expression of the structural law (both of "being" and of knowledge) by virtue of which *nothing, absolutely nothing*, we now realize, can enter our lives or our field of vision except by *way of birth*—which means, in other words, the pan-harmony in space-time of the phenomenon.

---

26. *PM*, pp. 311-12; *Oeuvres*, 1:346.
27. "Credenti, omnia convertuntur 'in Christum' " as in "Forma Christi" (*WTW*, p. 258; *Ecrits*, p. 343; cf. also *DM*, p. 101; *Oeuvres*, 4:150).
28. *C&E*, p. 217; *Oeuvres*, 10:258.
29. Teilhard himself added the English word *escape* in parentheses after the French *évasion* (see *Oeuvres*, 10:258).

The attached footnote concerns the phrase *by way of birth* (par voie de naissance):

> That is, as a function of antecedents which are themselves linked with the totality of earlier states of the universe.[30]

Here is the nub of the conflict that underlay, at least in part, Teilhard's increased restraint in employing Romans 8:22 in any explicit way, for, as he said in the preceding paragraph of this same essay:

> it has become impossible to present the world to us in the form of an established harmony: we now see unmistakably that it is a system in movement. It is no longer an *order* but a *process*. No longer a cosmos but a cosmogenesis.[31]

True, St. Paul's cosmos is one that is in the process of being redeemed, of being born to a new life. But as early as 1920, in "Fall, Redemption, and Geocentrism," Teilhard had already sensed that he would not be able to accept all the facets of St. Paul's overall treatment of the problem of sin and death in the universe.

> Let me say frankly what I think: it is impossible to universalize the first Adam without destroying his individuality. Even if we conceive mankind as *"singularis"* or *"unica"* (a point we shall be discussing later), we can no longer derive the whole of evil from one single hominian. I must emphasize again that long before man death existed on earth. And in the depths of the heavens, far from any moral influence of the earth, death also exists. Now, St Paul is categorical: *"Per peccatum mors."* Sin (original sin) does not explain the suffering and the mortality only of man: for St Paul it explains all suffering. *It is the general solution of the problem of evil.*[32]

30. "Réflexions sur la probabilité scientifique et les Consequences religieuses d'un Ultra-Humain," *Oeuvres*, 7:282; *AE*, p. 272.
31. *Ibid.*
32. *C&E*, pp. 39-40; *Oeuvres*, 10:52-53. That Teilhard was to remain convinced that St. Paul's position was altogether so uncompromising seems indicated by the Journal note of April 29, 1949 ("Journal" 16 [4]: 51), which queried another but closely related concept taken from the same verse (Rom. 5:12) as the "Per peccatum mors" cited above. The note questions the true meaning of the "en ōi pantes hēmarton"—"in quo omnes peccaverunt" in a sense to be understood differently from that understood by St. Augustine. Teilhard's apparently inadvertent substitution of *en* in place of *eph* did not help reduce his puzzlement. Prat, however (*Théologie de St. Paul* [Paris: Beauchesne, 1912], 1:256-57; *idem*. pp. 296-97, in the 1909 edition) clearly states that even the "in quo" of the VG can be, and in this case must be, translated as meaning "because," and this would be equally true even if the Greek reading were *en hōi*. (Cf. Kittle, *TDNT*, 2:538, and Moulton & Milligan's *The Vocabulary of the Greek New Testament* [Grand Rapids, Mich.: Eerdmans, 1963]), pp. 234, 210, regarding the similar use of *en* and *epi* in the causative or explanatory sense.) The whole cause of the confusion probably goes back to St. Augustine (as Teilhard seems to have suspected himself) in that Augustine's understanding of "in quo omnis precaverunt" (Rom. 5:12) seems not to be based on the passage that he quoted, but rather more on 1 Cor. 15:22 ("Et sicut in Adam omnes moriuntur . . ."). Cf. Prat, *ibid.*; cf. English ed., *The Theology of St. Paul* trans. from the 10th French ed. by John L. Stoddard (Westminster, Md.: Newman Press, 1952) 1:215-16, esp. n. 1.

Whatever Teilhard's later speculations were to be concerning the Pauline account of the appearance of death and physical evil, it is clear that, in the light of what evolution had to say about the origin of the cosmos, he would be forced to abandon any claim that Romans 8:22 in any literal way described a situation that could be equated with the concept of a *cosmogénèse* in the way in which he understood it. Thus, while Teilhard's use of this text had begun with an ascetical interpretation of the evolutive process and quickly moved toward a directly Christological emphasis, all his efforts to interpret this text in a cosmological sense (no matter how hypothetical in form, as in his "Les noms de la Matière") were to run into headlong conflict with the Pauline adoption of the Genesis account of the original sin, within the context of which Romans 8:22 is inextricably situated. Thus, in the end, Teilhard seems to have been resigned to associating this text, in a more or less general way as he did at first, with the struggle against evil, but not without wresting from his effort one concession or step toward coherence: if the universe is in labor, its pains are the pains of progress and not of futility. Of this he was convinced, for ultimately the product of that labor would be the Cosmic Christ. If Romans 8:22 could not give expression to this fact all by itself, it might mean more caution in his interpretation, but it could hardly result in the loss of his vision. If part of the problem lay in the milieu in which St. Paul wrote, that could be understood. But the real problem lay in the philosophical presuppositions of those who would claim to theologize on the basis of what they thought St. Paul meant—and for this Teilhard had little patience; to the frank statement given above from "Fall, Redemption, and Geocentrism," Teilhard was to feel obliged to add this critical footnote:

> To admit that there is, anywhere at all, suffering without sin, is to run counter to the thought of St. Paul. For St Paul, original sin is so full an explanation of death that the existence of death is in itself sufficient to justify the deduction that there has been sin. I realize that Thomist theologians do not accept this, even though they claim the support of St Paul for their view.[33]

Not that Teilhard was without his own presuppositions, but he seems to have been slowly learning not to assume that St. Paul shared them. Now, striking out boldly by means of a startlingly (for his time) untraditional hypothesis—but quite in line with his earlier essays, particularly "The Struggle Against the Multitude" and "Creative Union"—he wrote (again in "Fall, Redemption, and Geocentrism"):

> Original sin is the essential reaction of the finite to the creative act. Inevitably it insinuates itself into existence through the medium of all creation. It is the *reverse side* of all creation. By the very fact that he creates, God commits himself to a fight against evil and in conse-

33. *C&E*, p. 40; *Oeuvres*, 10:53, n.2.

quence to, in one way or another, effecting a redemption. The specifically human Fall is no more than the (broadly speaking, collective and eternal) actualizing of this *"fomes peccati"* which was infused, long before us, into the whole of the universe, from the lowest zones of matter to the angelic spheres. Strictly speaking, there is no first Adam. The name disguises a universal and unbreakable law of reversion or perversion—the price that has to be paid for progress.[34]

B. TEILHARD'S UNDERSTANDING OF ROMANS 8:22 IN THE LIGHT OF EXEGESIS

In the preceding study of Romans 8:22 as it occurs in the writings of Teilhard we saw that two major problems arose, either of which may have caused him to change his mind concerning the suitability of using this text in a cosmological mode of understanding. The first was the connection in St. Paul's mind between man's original Fall and the presence of death (and all other physical evil) in the universe. Consequent upon this discovery, which throws in doubt the possibility of any adaptation of Pauline "cosmology" to a contemporary understanding of the universe, is a closely related exegetical question concerning whether St. Paul in any way intended to convey an eschatological vision of a final restoration of the physical universe.

Since Teilhard took a physical restoration of the universe for granted from the very beginning, it would seem advisable to examine this exegetical presupposition first in the light of those commentators who may have most influenced Teilhard in the course of his education, and thence to proceed to the question of the tie between original sin and physical evil in the universe, first from the commentaries of these earlier authors, and then in the light of more recent exegetes, beginning about the time of Teilhard's death.

As for what educational influence may have shaped Teilhard's own approach to these exegetical questions, we are forced merely to speculate. There is little or no reference to his studies in the collections of letters addressed to his parents during the years of his philosophical and theological training; the few allusions to his intellectual activities that do exist are mainly concerned with his budding interest in paleontology, and to some extent, to the influence that Henri Bergson's *Creative Evolution* was beginning to exercise on his thought.[35] There is

34. *Ibid.*, pp. 40-41 (pp. 53-54). To this same passage is attached this footnote of Teilhard's:
   According to this hypothesis, moral evil is indeed (as St Paul holds) bound up with physical evil, but in virtue of an immanent sanction, the latter being a necessary accompaniment of the former. Progress-creation, transgression-fall, suffering-redemption, are three physically inseparable terms, which mutually counterbalance and vindicate one another—and the *three must be taken together as one* if we are fully to understand *the meaning of the Cross*.
35. Regarding Bergson, cf. especially Madeleine Barthélemy-Madaule, *Bergson et Teilhard de Chardin* (Paris: Éditions du Seuil, 1963).

no reference whatsoever to his scriptural courses, despite the relative prominence of two of his professors in this field.[36] It must be remembered that Teilhard's theological training took place during the height of the modernist crisis, and that the full liberation of Catholic biblical studies took place during the latter years of his life. But during those critical years when Catholic scholarship began to take its first steps toward closing the gap between itself and the advanced state of Protestant exegesis, Teilhard was nearly totally engaged in the more scientific aspects of his paleontological studies, as well as being, for the most part, in more or less total exile from the locus of these pioneering attempts.

In the light of what evidence is available, a guess must be made as to what biblical exegesis Teilhard was exposed during his studies by which he may have been influenced either positively or negatively. The standard exegetical work of the more formative years would have been, it may be presumed, the two great Jesuit standbys, the great summa of scriptural scholarship of Cornelius a Lapide and the more contemporary *Cursus Scripturae Sacrae*, first published just before the turn of the century. In addition, notice should be taken of the writings of F. Prat (his *Théologie de St Paul* was first published in 1909) and perhaps that of M.-J. Lagrange, whose *Epître aux Romains* received its "imprimatur" in 1915. Teilhard's friend and fellow Jesuit Joseph Huby may have also supported him. Beyond these, and with the single exception of a late reference to the work of Lucien Cerfaux, Teilhard's probable sources can only be conjectured from the opinions that he himself expressed without reference to authorship. Unsatisfactory as this may be, it is the best that can be done at present.[37]

1. Commentators of Teilhard's Formative Period

Inasmuch as Teilhard often claimed that what he was doing was to return to the understanding of the early Church Fathers in the matter of the transformation of the universe in Christ,[38] it would seem likely

36. Teilhard's theological studies took place in the Lyon Provinces' temporary house of studies "in exile" located at Ore Place, Hastings, Sussex (England). Here his professors in Scripture were the Old Testament scholar Fr. Albert Condamin, and also Fr. Alfred Durand, whose studies on the Gospels, particularly St. John, were to receive some notoriety.

37. Teilhard made no reference to either of his Scripture professors (Frs. Condamin and Durand), nor to any of the texts he may have used during the duration of his theological studies, in the collection of letters published under the title *Lettres d'Hastings* (Paris: Aubier, 1967; Eng. trans. *Letters from Hastings* [New York: Herder, 1967]). Except for two rather brief journeys to Europe and America in the years 1934 and 1937, Teilhard was continually in China and Southeast Asia from 1926 to 1946. With the exception of the "Journal" begun in July 1944, all his notes that would normally contain a record of his reading material during these years have been lost.

38. Cf. "Some Reflections on the Conversion of the World" (1936), *S&C*, p. 122; *Oeuvres*, 9:161. "Super-Humanity, Super-Christ, Super-Charity" (1943), *S&C*, p. 166; *Oeuvres*, 9:210; "Catholicism and Science" (1946), *S&C*, p. 189; *Oeuvres*, 9:189.

that it was the opinions of Cornelius a Lapide that most influenced his thinking in this direction. If his treatment of this whole section of Romans (i.e., Rom. 8:19-25) is examined, copious references to the opinions of patristic writers, of both the East and the West, will be found. Commenting on the words *expectatio creaturae*, Lapide made a decisive point, which he backed by references to Chrysostom and Augustine:

> Note the emphasis: It does not say: "The creature expects," but, "The expectation of the creature expects"; which is to say that the creatures so avidly expect this glory that they may be seen to be this very expectation.[39]

Finally, in commenting on verse 21, Lapide cited Chrysostom again to stress the glorification of all nature subsequent to man's glorification:

> It is because of or in commendation of the liberty and glory of the sons of God . . . that the other creatures which serve man will participate in the glory given to man, as Chrysostom has said.[40]

Thus, while it would appear that the Church Fathers genuinely taught a future glorification of the whole universe, it is a glorification that is subsequent to and dependent upon the glorification of man. Note should also be taken at this point of the opinions of M.-J. Scheeben, the dogmatic theologian whose ideas were gaining ground even before Teilhard's birth. In his *Dogmatik*, which was translated into French as far back as 1877, there is growing evidence of his espousal of this early patristic interpretation. In section 996, paragraph 3, Scheeben stated:

> In the natural order, the creature only has its happiness and peace in coordination with God. . . . In the supernatural order, God so attracts creatures to himself, that he himself, as the supreme good, is the object of their possession and of their joy.[41]

39. "Nota emphasim: Non dicit: Creatura expectat, sed, Expectatio creaturae expectat; q.d. Creaturae ita avide hanc gloriam expectant, ut videantur esse ipsa expectatio." Tom 18, *Divi Pauli Epistolarum* (Vivès: Paris, 1868), p. 138. True, the author does cite Chrysostom and Theophylactus as to the essentially "personified" nature of verse 22, but still, in his analysis of verse 19, he even cites Western authorities like Augustine, Gregory the Great, and Cajetan:
    omnis creatura, inquiunt, id est omnis homo, qui est nodus et vinculum omnis creaturae, et microcosmus, et mundi miraculum, ut aiebat Trismegistus: quia nimirum homo ab omnibus creaturis aliquid participat.
    Furthermore (citing Augustine again):
    > Verum apostolus loquitur hic de liberatione a corruptione, non peccati in hac vita, sed mortalitatis in futura. (*Ibid.*, p. 139.)
40. ". . . Id est *propter*, vel in commendatione libertatis et gloriae filiorum Dei . . . cum homo gloria donabitur, hanc ejus gloriam caeterae creaturae, quae homini servierunt, participabunt, inquit Chrysostomos." (*Ibid.*).
41. M.-J. Scheeben, *La Dogmatique*, trans. L'abbé P. Bélet (Paris: V. Palmé, 1881), p. 473. (My translation.) That Scheeben intended to include all of material creation becomes clear in his *Die Mysterien des Christentums*, ed. Josef Höfer (Freiburg: Herder, 1865), but it did not see translation into French until much later, well after

Teilhard would also have been able to point to the opinions of Cornely as equally indicative of an exegesis that admits of a transformation of material creation, but even more than Cornelius a Lapide, Cornely stressed that this change is brought about not by a glorification of creatures in their own right, but by reason of their share "in the liberty of the glory of the sons of God."[42] Nevertheless, Cornely clearly affirmed that for Paul as much as for Peter there would be a "positive perfecting" of the creaturely world to the extent that there could truly be said to be "new heavens and a new earth" awaiting us.[43]

In his treatment of verse 22, Cornely further strengthened the case for this perfecting of the world of creatures in his agreement with St. Ambrose that at least two of the words in the verse have been poorly translated, *sustenazei* being better translated by "congemiscit" than "ingemiscit" and *sunōdinei* as "comparturit" rather than simply "parturit," both of which improved translations tend to bring out more clearly the collective nature of salvation for the whole universe.[44]

On the other hand, Ferdinand Prat, S.J., during this same era espoused an opinion that appears to be diametrically opposed to Cornely's regarding the matter of the future of the material universe, at least in the context of Romans 8:19-22. While Prat seemed to be willing to admit that the *su* prefixes of the two verbs in verse 22 express "a *collective* sentiment rather than a sentiment *shared* with us," this opinion is nevertheless safely hedged by the reminder that the whole text is a personification.[45]

But perhaps more encouraging for Teilhard, if he had seen it, would

Teilhard's theological training. It is noteworthy that Rom. 8:16-30 is explicitly mentioned in Section 96 "Die Verklärung der materiellen Kreatur." But that this glory is achieved precisely through the glorification of man, in virtue of his supernatural end, was made most explicit. Also noteworthy is his statement, that this glorification is analogous to that of the transfiguration of the human body:

> Pursuing the analogy of the transfiguration of the human body, we must stop at saying that it consists, on the one hand, of a suppression and repression of materiality, particularly of the corruptibility, inconstancy, and perishableness resulting therefrom, and on the other hand, of a communication of supernatural beauty and energy.

The Mysteries of Christianity (London, St. Louis: B. Herder Book Co., 1946), p. 683.

42. quod creatura non in gloriam, sed *in liberatatem gloriae filiorum Dei* translatum iri dicatur, i.e. illam in libertatem, quam gloria filiorum Dei secum creaturae afferet . . . In hanc autem libertatem gloriam filiorum Dei homo ipse quoque transferatur oportet.
Cornely, *Ad Romanos* (*Cursus Scripturae Sacrae*, 8) (Paris: Lethielleux, 1927), p. 432.

43. Quae autem futura sit positiva perfectio creaturae aeque parum Paulus docet ac S. Petrus, qui nos novos coelos et novam terram, in quibus justitia habitet, secundum divina promissa expectare dicit (2 Pet. 3:13). *Ibid*.

44. Cf. *ibid*., p. 433.

45. Cf. Fernand Prat, English ed. 1:238. Additional quotations from Prat's work, in footnotes, will be given in the original French, as below:
"Un mot d'une intraduisible énergie (*apokaradokia*) nous la représente la tête dressée, le front tendu, l'oeil ardemment fixé sur le terme encore lointain de son espérance. Ne cherchons toutefois dans cette hypothèse que ce que l'Apôtre a voulu y mettre. Il ne parle nulle part d'une rénovation physique de la nature.

have been the opinion of M.-J. Lagrange.[46] The *hupetagē* of verse 20 (i.e., "subjection") is apparently an allusion to Genesis 3:17f. The stress is on the "liberation of the Sons of God" in verse 21. Consequent on this is a kind of association of all creation in this liberation, in both a positive and negative sense. In the positive sense, this liberation, according to Lagrange, will extend to material creation, but in a sense that is distinctly dependent upon and subservient to the liberty of the children of God.[47]

On the negative side, this future liberation is presently contradicted by the deliverance of material creation into the power of universal death and corruption in the *physical* sense. This would not be merely a moral corruption, that is, creatures' subjection to misuse by corrupted man, as Lagrange seemed to detect in Cornely, but which predominates even more in Prat's interpretation. It would follow, according to Lagrange's understanding of the text, that the reversal of this corruption is not a matter of a restoration of individual creatures to a prior state of incorruptibility, but simply a cancellation of the *law of death* on a universal scale in such a way that the place of material creation in the service of redeemed man will be in some way assured.[48]

What becomes more and more apparent in St. Paul is that whatever his particular vision might be of the nature and extent of the restoration of the material universe, it remains dependent on the future of man himself; and the mode of this restoration is in some way the corresponding inverse of that curse which God wrought upon material creation in consequence of man's sin.

Although Teilhard never directly quoted Romans 8:20, the interpretations of the exegetes already cited are—with some variations—almost unanimous. There is that of Cornelius a Lapide, for example, who appears to have favored the interpretations endorsed by St. Thomas:

> Les nouveaux cieux et la nouvelle terre, de quelque manière qu'on les entende, sont étrangers à son eschatologie. Il se fait seulement l'interprète des voeux de la création, certain que l'état violent où le péché l'a mise cessera au moment marqué pour notre transformation glorieuse." (1:286; cf. also 1909 ed., p. 330.)

French quotations from Prat's *Théologie de St Paul* will generally be taken from the revised and expanded edition of 1912, although occasionally differences as well as similarities in this edition and that of 1908 (or the single-volume 1909 printing) will be noted.

46. M.-J. Lagrange, *St Paul: Epître aux Romains* (Paris: Gabalda, 1931).
47. Dans le sens positif, Paul ne peut vouloir dire que la créature jouira elle-même de la liberté des enfants de Dieu. Elle ne peut être mise sur le même pied; elle jouira donc de la liberté afférente à l'état de gloire où seront les enfants de Dieu; ils seront dans la gloire; elle recouvre sa liberté avec les privilèges de cet état nouveau. . . . (*Ibid.*, pp. 208-9.)
48. Le côté negatif se comprend plus aisément par opposition. La créature est délivrée de la servitude de la corruption, c'est-à-dire qui appartient à l'état de corruption, qui en est le résultat. *Phthora* ne peut vraiment pas s'entendre d'une corruption morale, comme si la créature était affranchie du service des hommes corrompus (contre Corn.). Car dans Paul il a toujours le sens de corruptibilité ou de corruption au sens naturel: . . . Paul ne se demande pas si c'est, pour chaque créature, un esclavage que d'être destinée au changement, mais parle de l'esclavage envers un pouvoir de mort auquel la créature est soumise en général. (*Ibid.*, p. 209.)

man, who is a microcosm of all creation, has become mortal, being subjected to that same mutability which is characteristic of all creation, and this is directly due to the curse of God, which his sin deserved.[49] Cornely's opinion is that all creation is subjected to "corruption" because of this same divine sentence on man, which is a condition that did not afflict it to begin with: ". . . creatures from the beginning were not involved in the reign of vanity. . . ."[50]

On the other hand, the twentieth-century exegetes Prat and Lagrange saw the "vanity" as more of the moral than of the physical order; yet Prat paradoxically emphasized that "creation" in this verse is explicitly ". . . the material creation, with the exception of rational beings."[51] Lagrange did not exclude man himself as the subject of the sentence, but preferred to speak of "the moral association of nature with the destinies of man . . ." and consequently preferred not to speculate on the condition of physical nature before man's fall.[52] Prat appears to have maintained a similar silence about the physical condition of nature before man's fall and, like Lagrange, to have stressed man's culpability rather than God's curse.[53]

Thus, try as he might, Teilhard was faced with the inescapable fact that any understanding of St. Paul's "cosmology" is ultimately linked to his concept of the Fall. Instead of some quasi-moral servitude to man's misuse of nature, Teilhard saw that St. Paul's understanding of corruption includes physical evil, and most of all, death. This corruption is the consequence of man's original sin; and it is this concept, this ". . . fundamental dogma . . . the *universality* of the corruption let loose by the initial human fault,"[54] that Teilhard found to be incompatible with the known evolutionary history of the world. It was this realization that sparked his first speculations on a revised understanding of the nature of original sin. It led to the censuring reprisals that he suffered at the hands of his superiors in the 1920s. It was this fundamental incompatibility of what he took to be the exegetical understanding of St. Paul in opposition to a scientific understanding of our universe that eventually caused him to forge his way independently of the exegetes and the then-current exegesis, as is evidenced by his remarks

49. Cf. Cornelius a Lapide, 18:138-39.
50. ". . . creaturas ab initio ad regnum vanitatis non pertinuisse. . . ." Cf. Cornely, 8:427; also pp. 426-30.
51. *Theology of St. Paul*, 1:238, n.2: ". . . la création matérielle à l'exclusion des êtres raisonnables." (Cf. French, 1912 ed., 1:285, also 1909 ed., p. 330, esp. n.1.)
52. ". . . association morale de la nature aux destinées de l'homme. . . ." (Lagrange, p. 206.)
53. Prat's stress on material nature as "Maintenant asservie à un maître qui la profane et la prostitue" (1:286) allowed him to maintain that "*la création matérielle*, associée jadis malgré elle à notre déchéance, a le presentiment et la promesse qu'elle sera un jour associée à notre glorification" (*ibid.*, p. 285), and yet at the same time to claim that St. Paul ". . . no parle nulle part d'une rénovation physique de la nature" (*ibid.*, p. 286), as has already been noted (1909 ed., p. 330). Cf. English ed., 1:238.
54. "Fall, Redemption, and Geocentrism" (1920), *C&E*, p. 37; *Oeuvres*, 10:50.

about "a certain contamination . . . in the representations of Christian cosmogonies. . . . associated in a single perspective by St. Paul."[55]

Since this is the case, whatever else may be said about exegetical development from this period on becomes for us something of an exercise in purely retrospective comparison. Exegetical studies had no real effect on what Teilhard subsequently had to say on the linking of physical evil and death to man's sin, and its consequent effect on the understanding of the nature of the future of the cosmos. Nevertheless, for assessing the validity of Teilhard's interpretation, as well as ultimately trying to understand the principle that governed it, such a comparison may prove valuable.

2. More Recent Commentators and Exegetes

Teilhard's rather pessimistic conclusion concerning the effect of St. Paul on Christian "cosmogony" was perhaps somewhat premature. In 1954, the year before his death, appeared a comprehensive article by J.-M. Dubarle entitled "Le gémissement des creatures dans l'ordre divin du cosmos (Rom. 8:19-22),"[56] which reviews the further development in the understanding of this difficult text, and which, had Teilhard chanced to read it, might have confirmed him in what he had deemed to be his more independent approach.

Père Dubarle began his article by noting that it has been the dilemma posed by modern science's discovery of the relatively late appearance of man on the face of the earth that has propelled modern exegetes and theologians to reexamine the meaning of Romans 8:19-22 as a whole. It is in the light of the apparent difficulty posed by what has been generally taken to be the literal sense of Paul's text (the direct causal linking of creation's corruption to man's Fall) that two major groups of interpreters can be distinguished: those who still accept this literal interpretation, and those who seek some other interpretation and attempt to justify it as being equally true to the literal sense.

In the first group are G. Salet and L. Lafont, whose joint work, L'évolution régressive, appeared in 1943.[57] They hold this direct causality to be the sense intended by Paul and apparently themselves believe in this literal interpretation! In this first group also are E. C. Rust and D. Dubarle (J.-M.'s brother), who believe that the literal meaning of Paul should be understood in the sense that man, through his own culpable Fall, somehow added a new dimension—a kind of "ratifica-

---

55. "La Route de l'Ouest: Vers une Mystique nouvelle" (1932), *Oeuvres*, 11:63. (Cf. *TF.*, p. 58.)
56. Cf. *Revue des Sciences Philosophiques et Théologiques*, #38 (1954), pp. 445-65.
57. Cited by Dubarle, *ibid.*, p. 446.

tion" or "confirmation"—to a preexisting disorder (of diabolic origin?) in the universe.[58]

In the second group are those who take a radically different approach, one that makes God the primary cause of physical evil in the universe. Numbered among these is N. P. Williams, whose *The Idea of the Fall and Original Sin*[59] appeared in 1927, and whose concept is (in terms reminiscent of Teilhard's WW I essays) that evil in the physical sense is simply the price paid for the rupture of God's solitary unity through the act of creation. Karl Barth's *Der Römerbrief*[60] (1919) expressed the same idea in more existential terms: that the innate disorder of creatureliness was a tension between its separation from God and its eternal aspirations. Finally, Dubarle mentions C. E. Raven's *Natural Religion and Christian Theology* (1953)[61] which apparently, with no hesitations, ascribes the whole problem directly to the will of God and sees in St. Paul at least a groping attempt to understand the evolutionary process.

Between these two general schools of thought we have Emil Brunner,[62] whose work of 1950 posits the hypothesis of a creation of the universe more closely corresponding to God's prevision of the human Fall.

To all this speculation, J.-M. Dubarle, taking his cue from the more strictly exegetical efforts of A. Viard, H. Lietzmann, H. M. Biedermann, and P. Benoît,[63] suggests that St. Paul's understanding of the fall of creation along with that of man must be understood in the light of several different approaches to an understanding of the world as evidenced within the Old Testament itself and as elaborated by the rabbinical schools. He asserts that, while Paul rejects the idea that the fall of creation is in any way attributable to the fall of the angels (one opinion found in some Patristic authors) Paul nevertheless did understand that in some way all creation had been subjected to a slavery that was similar to, but not commensurate with, man's sin.[64] The main ingredient, however, according to Dubarle, is Paul's conviction of the overall goodness of material creation and its eventual deliverance from the "vanity" described in Qoheleth. He goes on to conclude, in line with what we already know about Hebraic thought patterns concerning causality, coupled with the not-entirely-unanimous attitudes concerning the world evidenced in the Old Testament, that Romans 8:19-22 remains ambiguous. In view of this, Dubarle favors a view that does not tie corruption too closely with man's sin.[65]

58. *Ibid.* E. C. Rust, *Nature and Man in Biblical Thought* (1953) and D. Dubarle, "La théologie du cosmos," vol. 2, chap. 8, in *Initiation Théologique* (1952).
59. Cited by Dubarle, *Revue des Sciences. . . ,* p. 446.
60. Dubarle, *ibid.,* p. 448, cites the 6th ed., pp. 290-95.
61. Cited by Dubarle, *ibid.,* p. 448.
62. *Die christliche Lehre von Schöpfung und Erlösung,* cited by Dubarle, *ibid.,* p. 449.
63. Cf. Dubarle, *ibid.,* p. 450.
64. *Ibid.,* p. 451.
65. *Ibid.,* p. 458. Un fait est affirmé, la sujétion de la création à la vanité et à la corrup-

In terms of what has taken place in the understanding of this text since Teilhard's death, there has been a shift in emphasis from a discussion of the how and why of creation's subjection to "vanity" or futility, to a renewed stress on the future hope of redemption. This, of course, parallels much of what has been the current emphasis on the theological scene, much of it centering on "The Theology of Hope," a development that, although having come about quite independently in the Protestant world on the basis of a somewhat "Marxist" approach to the Scriptures, has not been long in discovering the relevance of Teilhard's thought.

While much of this development belongs to the late 1960s, there were signs even before that of this new emphasis. In an article published in 1960,[66] the eminent Catholic scriptural scholar Stanislaus Lyonnet lists what he considers three essential characteristics of Pauline thought concerning this matter:

1 That the redemption of the Universe is but a *consequence* of the redemption of man.

2 That more precisely, it is one *consequence of the redemption of man's body*.

3 That therefore the Universe cannot be considered simply an instrument of man's redemption, but an *object of redemption* in its own right.

From these Pauline principles, Lyonnet draws these conclusions: first, the Christian conception of salvation is essentially collective; second, it extends to the whole Universe; and third, it is dependent ultimately on the redemption of man.[67]

In Protestant circles, a similar emphasis has initiated a debate centering on the "eschatology" of Paul. R. Bultmann stresses the "apocalyptic" nature of Paul's early letters (vs. the more "realized" eschatology of the remainder); Käsemann prefers to see the foundations of Christian theology firmly embedded in the mature eschatology of St. Paul.[68]

T. W. Manson, in his 1963 work *On Paul and John*, quotes with approval C. H. Dodd's summary of Romans 8:18-25:

This experience of the Spirit (an experience of sonship to God, of life, of freedom, of the Love of God) is a ground of hope for the

tion. Il n'est précisé expressément de quelle cause il dépend: de l'action créatrice de Dieu, ou de la perturbation apportée par le péché, bien que des présomptions générales doivent jouer en faveur de la première hypothèse.

66. "Rédemption de l'Univers" in *Lumière et Vie* #48 (1960) pp. 43-63. See also "The Redemption of the Universe" in *Contemporary New Testament Studies*, ed. Sr. M. Rosalie Ryan, C.S.J. (Collegeville Minn.: Liturgical Press, 1965) pp. 425-28.

67. Cf. *Lumière et Vie*, #48, pp. 50-51ff.

68. See the summary of this debate by John G. Gager Jr. in "Paul's End-Time Language," *Journal of Biblical Literature* 89, no. 3 (Sept. 1970): 325-37. Prof. Gager also calls attention to the article of H. Hommel, "Das Harren der Kreatur" in *Schöpfer und Erhalter* (1956), were Hommel admits the universal meaning of "ktisis" (creation) in its classical context, but sees it used in Paul principally of man. Note, however, that this does not contradict the conclusions of Lyonnet, outlined above.

whole universe, since man cannot be isolated from the rest of Nature. The Universe too is waiting for something. . . . If we are able to state in prosaic terms of metaphysics what Paul thought would happen, we must say that he shared with many of his contemporaries the belief that, in the Good Time Coming, the material universe would be transfigured into a substance consisting of pure light or glory, thus returning to its original perfection as created by God.[69]

This quotation would certainly have been encouraging to Teilhard in his conviction of the universal participation of creation in the final consummation of the Parousia, at least if the above words were not understood in a dualistic sense. Still, if Paul's vision was one of a universal "restoration" to a primeval perfection that existed before man's Fall, then Teilhard must be understood as differing radically from the Apostle on this point. As he made clear in his 1922 "Note on Some Possible Historical Representations of Original Sin," if there is *"no acceptable place for Adam"* in any literal sense, due to what we know about the origins of the human race, then there is *"still less place, in our historical picture, for the earthly paradise."* Following this latter heading (which like the former, begins one of the preliminary statements of "Difficulties in the Traditional Representation"[70]), the following statement makes his position very clear:

> The earthly paradise is intelligible only as a *different way of being* for the universe (which fits in with the traditional meaning of the dogma, which sees in Eden "another world"). Yet, however far back we look into the past we find nothing that resembles this wonderful state. There is not the least trace on the horizon, not the smallest scar, to mark the ruins of a golden age or our cutting off from a better world. As far as the mind can reach, looking backwards, we find the world dominated by physical evil, impregnated with moral evil (sin is manifestly "in potency" close to actuality as soon as the least spontaneity appears)—we find it *in a state of original sin*.[71]

Thus, Teilhard concluded, any serious attempt to read the biblical account on the same level with modern scientific accounts of man's origin and the situation that prevailed before man's appearance will issue only in making us "certainly victims of an error in perspective."[72]

On the positive side, however, the biblical accounts, Paul's in particular, are not to be rejected out of hand as having no real importance for our view of the universe in terms of its incorporation in the

---

69. The *Moffatt New Testament Commentary* (London, 1934), as cited by T. W. Manson, *On Paul and John*, Studies in Biblical Theology, #38 (London: SCM press, 1963), p. 25.
70. Cf. *C&E*, p. 46; *Oeuvres*, 10:62.
71. *C&E*, pp. 46-47; *Oeuvres*, 10:63.
72. *C&E*, p. 47; *Oeuvres*, 10:63.

Parousia. When it comes to speaking of its future in respect to the final glorification of Christ, however, Teilhard remained equally insistent:

> if Christ is (in the words of St Paul) to incorporate all things in himself and then to return to the bosom of the Father "with the world gathered up in himself," it is not enough (as, maybe, we used to think it was) that he supernaturally sanctify a harvest of souls—he must do more, and in that same movement, he must creatively carry the noogenesis of the cosmos to the natural term of its maturity.[73]

3. Conclusion

In the light of the exegesis considered, Teilhard may have been correct in his adherence to conviction of a universal consummation of the material universe in Christ. Likewise, his own particular vision of man as the summit of biological evolution led him to a more theologically sound agreement with the scriptural view that the destiny of the material creation is more or less consequent upon man's fidelity to God's redemptive plan for him. Therefore his understanding of Romans 8:22 remained implicitly what it was from the very beginning—*"The Cosmic compassion"*[74] of the Christ who, "starting from *all* created things, is consummated and attains His plenitude."[75]

On the other hand, concerning the connection of the present state of the universe in regard to physical evil (pain, suffering, and death), Teilhard clearly rejected the Pauline account, which appears to make physical evil consequent upon man's sin; and for this reason he also ultimately had to reject the Pauline eschatological cosmology, inasmuch as it is conceived as a "restoration" of material beings to a primitive state of innocence and incorruption.

Given this partial rejection of the Pauline understanding of the origin of evil in relation to man's Fall, Teilhard was forced to consider two

---

73. Cf. "A Mental Threshold Across Our Path: From Cosmos to Cosmogenesis" (1951), *AE*, p. 264. "Un Seuil mental sous nous pas: du Cosmos à la Cosmogénèse," *Oeuvres*, 7:272. It might be noted here that Teilhard's insistance on the cosmic dimensions of the redemptive plan of God seems to find backing in F. X. Durwell's interpretation of Rom. 8:21-22 in his *The Resurrection: A Biblical Study* (New York: Sheed & Ward, 1960); originally *La Résurrection de Jésus: mystère de salut* (Paris: Editions Xavier Mappus, 1958), p. 292, where Jewish and Christian apocalyptic is seen as incorporated into "the liberty of the glory of the children of God." This wedding of human redemption and cosmic eschatology would seem to be in the line of that interpretation of late Jewish apocalyptic writing which Jürgen Moltmann (*Theology of Hope* [New York: Harper & Row, 1967]; originally *Theologie der Hoffnung* [Munich: Kaiser Verlag, 1965]) sees as neither a reversion from prophetic eschatology into the realm of cosmic myth (G. von Rad) nor as an early attempt to translate this eschatology into a cosmic predetermination of history (K. Koch and W. Pannenberg), but rather as "an eschatological and historical interpretation of the cosmos." Thus read, the prophetic promise, having become truly cosmic in dimension, sees the "eschaton" not as "a repetition of the beginning, nor as a return from the condition of original estrangement and the world of sin to the state of original purity, but as a state that is ultimately wider than the beginning ever was." Pp. 135-36.
74. Cf. *WTW*, p. 68; *Ecrits*, p. 57.
75. Cf. *DM*, p. 31; *Oeuvres*, 4:50.

other possibilities. The first of these was an adaptation of the theory of the "Alexandrine School" as to some sort of "precosmic fall," while the second solution remained not too radically different: it simply saw the act of creation itself as tantamount to a "fall" into pure multiplicity, out of which the struggle toward organized being would inevitably involve pain, conflict, death, and, in the case of man, sin. In any case, the universe of the Parousia could not in any way be thought of as a "restoration" except in the sense of a "pleromization," which will in some way complement the primeval unity of God. But this is to anticipate another stage in his thought.

In the face of the difficulties raised by the problem of original sin as he grappled with it in the 1920s, Teilhard turned his attention more emphatically to his concern for the future of the Universe in Christ, believing that St. Paul's vision of the cosmic Christ should not be jeopardized by the limited scope of Paul's cosmology, dependent as it apparently was on Paul's view of the origin of evil in the universe. Thus, while Teilhard's "Journals" contain many references to the problem of original sin during the years just prior to his 1947 essay "Reflections on Original Sin,"[76] the problem is one that far transcends this particular difficulty (at least in the sense of the problem of the historicity of the original sin). What is at stake is the whole Christian *Weltanschauung*, the central dogmatic "axis" of which demands a certain *"homogeneity"* and *"coherence"* that seem to be missing in the traditional (and largely Pauline-influenced) concept of original sin.[77]

Teilhard's attempt at a solution was ingenious. It remained essentially Pauline: it was to interpret the place and the sin of the first Adam in a way that is entirely relative to Christ. It was a matter of divining the principal axis of Christian belief and thus "to maintain Christ *to the measure of and at the head of creation.*"[78] It is in terms of this central concern that Teilhard went on to say:

> Our attempt to do so is all the more warranted, we should note, in that the same obligation to rethink the dogma of original sin is imposed on us from a third quarter of human thought: it comes not from science, nor from theology, but from Scripture. The most recent advances in exegesis insist that what we should look for in the first chapters of Genesis is not "visual" information about man's *history* but teaching about his *nature*.
> So we have a clear road ahead.[79]

There is no need to become further involved in the more intricate aspects of Teilhard's solution to this particular problem. Within this

76. Cf. *C&E*, pp. 187-98; *Oeuvres*, 10, pp. 217-30.
77. Cf. *C&E*, p. 188; *Oeuvres*. *10:219-20*.
78. *C&E*, p. 190; *Oeuvres*, 10:222.
79. *C&E*, p. 191; *Oeuvres*, 10:223.

approach, the problem of original sin and the problems posed by the literal meaning of Romans 8:22 and its immediate context were no longer central to Teilhard's thought, even if they cannot be described as peripheral. Teilhard was no longer concerned with finding evidences of a cosmogenesis in St. Paul; it was more than enough to have discovered a Christogenesis.

4

The Body of Christ

If the text of Romans 8:22 can be said to have provided the key to a dynamic vision of the universe in the process of redemption in Teilhard's synthesis, the central and ever-persisting image of the Body of Christ can be said to have inspired the very core of all of Teilhard's vision of "Christogenesis." Indeed, as many have noted, the whole atmosphere of his earliest "mystical" essays, such as the tripartite "Christ in the World of Matter: Three Stories in the Style of Benson,"[1] as well as his later (1923) "The Mass on the World,"[2] are permeated with the presence of the Eucharistic Body of Christ, which knows no bounds in its ever-growing assimilation of the universe. Even to the end of Teilhard's life, this same dynamic presence of Christ, now described in its pleromic future, remained his dominant inspiration, especially in his final essay, "Le Christique" (March 1955).

The many facets of this complex theme, ranging from Teilhard's metaphysical concept of "creative union," through his "hyperphysical" analysis of the relation of spirit to matter, leading in the end to his integral understanding of the pleroma, must now be explored.

A. THE DEVELOPMENT OF THE CONCEPT OF THE BODY OF CHRIST IN TEILHARD'S THOUGHT

Given these diverse aspects of Teilhard's thought in relation to his understanding of the Body of Christ, we can roughly divide them ac-

1. Cf. "Le Christ dans la Matière: Trois histoires comme Benson," *Hymne de l'Univers (HU)* (Paris: Editions du Seuil, 1961), pp. 39-52; *Hymn of the Univers* (New York: Harper & Row, 1965), pp. 42-50.
2. "La Messe sur le Monde," *HU*, pp. 13-32 (English ed., pp. 11-32).

cording to the periods marking the stages of the development that his writings evidence. Most of his thought concerning this subject occupies the years that center on World War I; however, it is possible even to subdivide these years into more or less distinct periods, ranging from the earliest years in which he expressed his basic insight, through the mid-war period (in which the more metaphysical aspects hold the foreground), to the late period of the war when, as seen above, the problem of spirit-matter occupied his attention. However, two more periods can also be detected: the early postwar period, when he attempted to relate his early insights more explicitly to his ideas on the Eucharist, and later, the 1920s, when his thought on this subject reached its fullest development in the face of his growing consciousness of the difficulties presented by the doctrine of original sin. This development in turn marks the gradual merger of his understanding of the Body of Christ into his growing awareness of the Pauline pleroma.

1. The Early World War I Period (1916): The Initial Insight

Teilhard's first mention of the Body of Christ despite the Pauline nature of the phrase, contains one explicit Johannine quotation, another implicit Johannine quotation, one more Johannine allusion, and finally, a paraphrased quotation from the Apocalypse.[3] This may appear rather strange, until it is realized that his "Cosmic Life" is partly autobiographical in nature, and that in it he attempted to trace the outlines of the dialectical process that had begun to bear fruit in his own mind, a process that revolves around the multifaceted problem of matter vs. spirit, God vs. the world, pantheism vs. personalism. The first of these Johannine citations (John 1:14, "Et Verbum caro, factum est") has been seen twice (see esp. chap. 2, §D, 2, above), but now let it be viewed in the context of the passage that goes before:

> Minds that are afraid of a bold concept or are governed by individualistic prejudices, and always try to interpret the relationships between beings in moral or logical terms, are apt to conceive the Body of Christ by analogy with human associations; it then becomes much more akin to a social aggregation than to a natural organism. Such minds dangerously weaken the thought of Scripture and make it unintelligible or platitudinous to thinking men who are eager to trace out physical connexions and relations that are specifically cosmic. They unjustifiably diminish Christ and the profoundly real mystery of his Flesh. The Body of Christ is not, as some unenterprising thinkers would have us believe, the extrinsic or juridical association of men who are embraced by one and the same benevolence and are destined to the same reward. It must be understood with boldness, as St John and St Paul and the Fathers saw it and loved it. It consti-

3. "La Vie cosmique" (1916); Ecrits, pp. 39-42; WTW, pp. 49-53: see §B of chap. 3.

tutes a world that is natural and new, an organism that is animate and in motion, one in which we are all united, physically and *biologically*.

The exclusive task of the world is the physical incorporation of the faithful in the Christ who is of God.[4]

How is this "physical incorporation" to be carried out? The next paragraph gives the answer.

At the source of its developments an operation was called for, transcendent in order, to graft the Person of a God onto the human cosmos, under conditions that are mysterious but physically governed. This would give immanence to or "immanentize," in our universe the principle around which a predestined body of the chosen is to achieve its segregation. *Et Verbum caro factum est*. This was the Incarnation.[5]

It can be seen that for Teilhard's purpose, which was to stress the *physical reality* of the Body of Christ as the foundation of a *biologically* understood organism, the Johannine emphasis on the physical reality of the Incarnation is useful to root out any legalistic or extrinsic interpretations of the Pauline concept of the Body of Christ. In this way, Grace is conceived as the "magnification and 'obediential' extension of our *natural* capabilities [emphasis added]. . . ," but in terms that mix both Johannine and Pauline themes:

Grace is not simply the analogous form found in a number of different immanencies, the life, uniform and at the same time multiple, shared by living creatures. It is the unique sap that starts from the same trunk and rises up into the branches, it is the blood that courses through the veins under the impulse of one and the same Heart, the nervous current that is transmitted through the limbs at the dictate of one and the same Head: and that radiant Head, that mighty Heart, that fruitful Stock, must inevitably be Christ.[6]

After speaking of Sacramental Communion as that by which Christ "consummates the union of the faithful in Himself through an individual and integral contact of soul with soul, flesh with flesh. . . ,"[7] he returned to the subject of grace and the Body of Christ:

When our activity is animated by grace it is as effective and "creative" as life, the Mother of Organisms, and it builds up a Body in the true sense of the word. This is the Body of Christ, which seeks to be realized in each one of us.

The mystical Body of Christ should, in fact, be conceived as a physical Reality, *in the strongest sense the words can bear*.[8]

4. *WTW*, pp. 49-50; *Ecrits*, p. 39.
5. *WTW*, p. 50; *Ecrits*, p. 40.
6. *Ibid*. Cf. John 15:1f.; Col. 1:18; also Eph. 1:22; 4:15-16; 5:23.
7. *Ibid*.
8. *WTW*, p. 51; *Ecrits*, p. 41. Cf. Col. 2:19; Eph. 4:16.

Given this emphasis on the physical reality of the Body of Christ (already there seems to have been a hint of dissatisfaction with the term *mystical*, although Teilhard would continue to use it for some time), there still remained a certain tension in his thought. Nearer the end of the same section he spoke of (again in Johannine terms)

> the *living Water* of your precious Essence, in which he who loses himself finds his soul and the soul of all other men made one with his own.[9]

But in ending the next paragraph, he again mixed Pauline and Johannine imagery (this time taken from Apoc. 1:8):

> Your Body, Jesus, is not only the Centre of all final repose; it is also the bond that holds together all fruitful effort. In you, side by side with *Him who is*, I can passionately love *Him who is becoming*.[10]

The tension here is not so much between the divine and the human, although it should be noted that the "living water" was here spoken of as being of God's "Essence" while the human contribution to the physical reality of the Body was described as being effected "with the rigour and harmony of a natural evolution."[11] Rather, the subject is basically the unresolved tension between spirit and matter, between the "Communion with Earth" (Part II) and "Communion with God" (Part III). Thus, Section A of Part III sharpens this conflict in terms of the duality expressed in the title "The World of Souls" (Section A) as against "The Body of Christ" (Section B). The resolution of this conflict is offered in Part IV ("Communion with God through Earth") as being precisely "The Cosmic Christ" (Part IV, Section A).

> By grace, Jesus Christ is united to all sanctified souls, and since the bonds that link souls to him in one single hallowed mass end in Him and meet in Him, and hold together by Him, it is He who reigns and He who lives; the whole body is His in its entirety. Souls, however, are not a group of isolated monads. As the "cosmic view" specifically shows us, they make up one single whole with the universe, consolidated by life and matter. Christ, therefore, cannot confine his body to some periphery drawn within things; though he came primarily, and in fact exclusively, for souls, he could bring them together and give them life only by assuming and animating, with them, all the rest of the world; through his Incarnation he entered not only into mankind but also into the universe that bears mankind—and this he did, not simply in the capacity of an element associated with it, but with the dignity and function of directive principle, of centre upon which every form of love and every affinity converge. Mysterious and vast though the mystical Body already be,

9. *WTW*, p. 52; *Ecrits*, p. 41. Cf. John 4:14.
10. *WTW*, p. 52; *Ecrits*, p. 42.
11. *WTW*, p. 50; *Ecrits*, p. 40.

it does not, accordingly, exhaust the immense and bountiful integrity of the Word made Flesh. Christ has a *cosmic Body* that extends
throughout the whole universe: such is the final proposition to be
borne in mind. *"Qui potest capere, capiat."*[12]

The above paragraph should be considered the central theological intuition of all of Teilhard's work, and, as far as he was concerned, the
central truth of Christianity!

But as the key to the understanding of Christianity, the Incarnation
itself remains a mystery, not just in the supernatural sense of the word,
but because it is bound up in the mystery of the meaning of the universe.

> The Incarnation is a making new, a restoration, of *all* the
> universe's forces and powers; Christ is the Instrument, the Centre,
> the End, of the *whole* of animate and material creation; through
> Him, *everything* is created, sanctified, and vivified. This is the con-
> stant and general teaching of St John and St Paul (that most "cos-
> mic" of sacred writers), and it has passed into the most solemn for-
> mulas of the Liturgy: and yet we repeat it, and generations to come
> will go on repeating it, without ever being able to grasp or ap-
> preciate its profound and mysterious significance, bound up as it is
> with understanding of the universe.[13]

Yet at the same time, it is the mystery of the universe itself that is
revealed in the Incarnation. It is the key to the understanding of evolution:

> *everything has continued in motion because he has not yet attained*
> *the fullness of his form.* He has not gathered about Him the last
> folds of the garment of flesh and love woven for him by his faithful.
> *The mystical Christ has not reached the peak of his growth—nor,*
> *therefore, has the cosmic Christ.* Of both we may say that *they are*
> and at the same time *are becoming*: and it is in the continuation of
> this engendering that there lies the ultimate driving force behind all
> created activity. By the Incarnation, which redeemed man, the very
> Becoming of the Universe, too, has been transformed. Christ is the
> term *of even the natural* evolution of living beings; evolution is holy.
> There we have *the truth that makes free*, the divinely prepared cure
> for faithful but ardently moved minds that suffer because they can-
> not reconcile in themselves two almost equally imperative and vital
> impulses, faith in the world and faith in God.[14]

2. *Mid-World War I Period (1917):*
The Metaphysics of Union

Following the initial insight expressed in "Cosmic Life," which was
to remain Teilhard's most extensive manifesto on the Body of Christ,

---

12. WTW, p. 47; *Ecrits*, pp. 57-58. Note the parallel with Col. 1:16-17 at the beginning. Final quotation is from Matt. 19:12.
13. WTW, p. 58; *Ecrits*, p. 48.
14. WTW, p. 59; *Ecrits*, pp. 48-49.

there remained the task of refining this position in terms of the problems that were raised.

The basic metaphysics involved was the first of these to occupy Teilhard's attention. Similarly to "Cosmic Life," "The Struggle Against the Multitude" draws primarily from Johannine themes, where he described John 17:22 ("Ut unum sint, sicut unum sumus") as "the definitive formula which gives us the key to the Gospel and to the World."[15] While there is in this essay no explicit reference to the concept of the Body of Christ (there is an allusion, in ascetical terms, to the vine motif of John 15:1f. on page 130 [p. 112], the connection is nevertheless there:

> Let us read the gospel boldly and we shall see that no idea can better convey to our minds the *redemptive function of the Word* than that of a unification of all flesh in one and the same Spirit.[16]

In the same year, however, the identification of this metaphysics of union with the doctrine of the Body of Christ became more explicit in "The Mystical Milieu," where this milieu was identified with the Body of Christ. He wrote:

> Since first, Lord, you said, *"Hoc est corpus meum,"* not only the bread of the altar but (to some degree) everything in the universe that nourishes the soul for the life of Spirit and Grace, has become *yours* and has become *divine*—it is divinized, divinizing, and divinizable. . . .
>
> In the mystery of your mystical body—your cosmic body—you sought to feel the echo of every joy and every fear that moves each single one of all the countless cells that make up mankind.[17]

Finally, in confirmation of this linkage of the doctrine of the Body of Christ with his theory of "creative union," Teilhard in "L'Union créatrice" explicitly linked his metaphysics with revelation, after having made it clear that it is the function of morality and its moral power of love to bring about more than just an extrinsic relationship between beings. (Teilhard used the word *physique* as opposed to *extrinsèque*, but as the editor notes, he meant this in the original Greek sense of "natural" or "organic" as opposed to "superficial" or "artificial."[18]) Thus he went on to write in the concluding section:

> In him, "the plenitude of the universe," *omnia creantur* because *omnia uniuntur*—all things are created because all things are made

---

15. WTW, p. 113; Ecrits, p. 131. (Cf. also initial invocation, *ibid.*, p. 94 [113].)
16. WTW, p. 124; Ecrits, p. 106. The editor of the volume added a footnote to this passage that curiously misquotes John 11:51-52 in the effort to identify Teilhard's reference to the Gospel, but the inference seems legitimate enough.
17. WTW, p. 146; Ecrits, pp. 164-65. Here also he first employs his gloss on Ps. 103 (104):2 (Amictus mundo sicut vestimento), *ibid.*, p. 148 (p. 167) as well as invoking in his conclusion a paraphrase of John 6:44 ("Personne ne vient a moi si je ne le prends et ne l'attire moi-même . . ."), *ibid.*
18. Cf. WTW, p. 171; Ecrits, p. 193.

one—and there we meet again the precise formula of creative union.[19]

But he further specified (speaking of his "système ontologique"):

Without knowledge of Christ, this exposition would be extremely vulnerable and hypothetical, particularly in the extrapolation that led us to anticipate a spirituality, still to be realized, that is to be born from the sum of our souls. *With* knowledge of Christ, this almost delirious dream becomes to some degree a Reality known by faith. As the reader must have seen for some time, the philosophy of creative union is simply the development—generalization, extension to the universe—of what the Church teaches us about the growth of Christ. *It is the philosophy of the universe expressed in terms of the notion of the mystical body.*

All these reachings-out that draw beings together and unify them constitute the *axis* of all individual and collective life. It is in virtue of that axis that we see that Christ has not only a *mystical*, but a *cosmic body*, the most impressive description of whose chief attributes we owe to St Paul—even if he never uses the actual term. And this Cosmic Body, to be found in all things, and always in process of individualization (spiritualization) is eminently the *mystical Milieu*.[20]

3. *The Late World War I Period (1918)*

Having reached a certain metaphysical understanding of the Body of Christ in terms of his theory of creative union, Teilhard then shifted his perspective to the old problem of spirit-matter dualism, as was evidenced by the essays of 1919 ("L'Elément universel," "Les noms de la Matière," and "La Puissance spirituelle de la Matière," studied in part in the previous chapter[21]). It should be noticed here, however, that his relevant 1919 statements seem to have been influenced by what he had already formulated in more or less Christological terms the year before. This is evidenced in his concern with the manner by which "*a certain coextension* of Christ with the Universe can be admitted. . . ," as is found in his 1918 "Mon univers."[22]

This essay, which, like the 1916 "Cosmic Life" appears to have been written as an attempt to resolve his psychological "preoccupation *to unify my* interior *vision*. . . ,"[23] evidences a new turn toward a more distinctively Pauline mode of expression in its emphasis on a "faith in the Plenitude of Christ" and "the fundamental vision *of Christ in all things.*"[24] These two rather oblique allusions to Ephesians 1:23 are the first appearance of the concept of the pleroma in Teilhard's writings in

19. *WTW*, p. 174; *Ecrits*, p. 196. Compare with Col. 1:16.
20. *WTW*, pp. 174-75; *Ecrits*, pp. 196-97.
21. Chap. 3, §A above.
22. *Ecrits*, p. 272. (Not published in *WTW*; my translation.)
23. *Ecrits*, p. 278.
24. *Ecrits*, p. 273.

a way that distinguishes the Body of Christ in its present state from its final completion. But his concern here was principally Christianity's goal. He went on to say:

> In a general manner, I think that the coextension of Christ and the World ought to be understood throughout as a physical, organic influence exercised by Christ upon the essential movement (or the sum of essential movements) which makes the Universe to grow (—a creative or transforming action).
> This being posed, if we should ask for a simplification: — o = the natural goal (x) of human (and cosmic) progress; — ω = the supernatural goal of the Kingdom of God (the plenitude of Christ).[25]

It would be in virtue of this resolution (of o and ω) that he would be able to say (modeled on Rom. 14:7-8?):

> Really and literally, in the hypothesis of Christ adopting and supernaturalizing the natural evolution of the World, quidquid patimur, Christus agit et quidquid agimus, Christus agitur.[26]

Returning to his idea of creative union, Teilhard said he was seeking "an idea of the law of transformation of all things in Ipso and per Ipsum." If found, this "better philosophy, for me, will always be that which permits me all the more to think [with] Christ, necessarily, and everywhere."[27]

Significantly, this 1918 "Mon Univers" ended in a mood of questioning, with a call to summon all our reserves to overcome that dualism which Teilhard complained of in primarily psychological terms, but which is at the same time metaphysical (ontological) and epistomological, being a conflict between the Universe of experience and the God of revelation.[28]

Having thus posed this project for himself, Teilhard's next few essays began to grapple more intensively with the problem of the "physical" aspects of the concept of the Body of Christ. Whereas his 1917 "The Mystical Milieu" and "Creative Union" may be rather ambiguous in this matter (if indeed the latter does not represent even a slight retreat in the direction of a "spiritualistic" interpretation), his next 1918 essay, "The Priest," returned to the realism of the "Hoc est Corpus meum" formula.[29]

25. Ecrits, p. 274.
26. Ecrits, p. 275. Cf. chap. 2 above, n.69.
27. Ecrits, pp. 276-77. Of the two Pauline phrases above, the first ("in . . . per Ipsum") comes from Col. 1:16 and the second ("sentir . . . Christ") appears to be adopted from Phil. 2:5.
28. Ecrits, p. 278. As noted before, this particular essay was not published in the English translation of Ecrits, although no reason is given. Perhaps it is because there are two Mss. of the original, which, along with the re-use of this same title in 1924, combine, retrospectively, to indicate the essay's provisional character.
29. WTW, p. 208; Ecrits, p. 287. This formula, taken directly from the Liturgy, was first used by Teilhard in "Le Milieu mystique" (WTW, p. 146; cf. Ecrits, p. 164) but

Even though Teilhard had already anticipated his own challenge in the first two highly speculative 1918 essays, in which he attempted to unify his vision of the goal of evolution ("o") with the divine "Omega" ("ω") through a better understanding of the Incarnation and its extension through the "Mystical Body," the matter remained unresolved. Teilhard had already sought to reconcile this apparent duality through his postulation of the existence of a kind of pantheistically conceived "soul" ("L'Ame du Monde"—the title of an earlier 1918 essay[30]), that in some way receives its completed form from Christ:

> it is Christ who has the function of cementing the definitive concentration of the universe. The world, that is to say our substance, is centred on God *in Christo Jesu*.[31]

Just what was Teilhard trying to say? Observe these two paragraphs:

> Through the soul of the world, and through that soul alone the Word, becoming incarnate in the universe, has been able to establish a vital, immediate, relationship with each one of the animate elements that make up the cosmos.
> The soul of the world, whose life is drawn from the Word infused into it, is at the same time the purchase-point required for the Incarnation. It supplies ready to hand the matter destined to form the mystical body—and it is that soul, again, hidden beneath the countless multitudes of created beings, that envelops us in a living network charged with grace and spirituality.[32]

It would seem that the "Soul of the World" (which in some way is the hypothetical summation of all created souls) supplies the "matter" that is to become the Mystical Body. Is the Body then ultimately a "spiritual" organism, that is, physical only in the organic sense, transcending "matter"? At the very end of the same year, in his "Forma Christi," he attempted to clarify the problem further, and in doing so gave what amounted to a preview of his final position on matter and spirit.

As for the term *forma* in this last essay of 1918, nowhere is a specific definition given; instead, at the beginning of Part A is found a quotation with the following reference:

Secundum potentiam (δύναμιν) *qua possit Ipse omnia sibi subjicere.* Phil. 3:21.[33]

here is also coupled with "Hic est calix Sanguinis mei" (*WTW*, p. 210; *Ecrits*, p. 289). But in these cases the application is more ascetical-mystical than in its initial use. "Le Prêtre" also contains the first explicit use of the word *Plérôme* in Teilhard; but again, the highly mystical tone of this essay makes it extremely difficult to determine the exact sense of the term until the resolution of the matter-spirit problem.
30. *WTW*, pp. 177-90; *Ecrits*, pp. 217-32. See esp. the introduction by the editor.
31. *WTW*, p. 186; *Ecrits*, p. 228. The French has "Création" in place of "universe."
32. *WTW*, pp. 186-87; *Ecrits*, p. 228.
33. "According to the power through which He is able to subject all things to himself."

Taking his cue from this verse, he described this concept in functional terms:

> In Scripture Christ is essentially revealed as invested with *the power of giving the world*, in his own person, *its definitive form*. He is consecrated for a cosmic function. And since that function is not only moral but also (in the most real sense of the word) physical, it presupposes *a physical basis* in its humano-divine subject.
>
> If things are to find their coherence *in Christo*, we must ultimately admit that there is *in natura Christi*, besides the specifically individual elements of Man—and in virtue of God's choice—some *universal physical*[34] *reality*, a certain cosmic extension of his Body and Soul.[35]

In this sense, Teilhard viewed the whole history of the world as being that of "the progressive information of the universe by Christ."[36]

The next section of "Forma Christi" begins with another quotation, this time from John 12:32 ("Omnia traham ad meipsum"—"I shall draw all things to myself"), but immediately in the sentence following is found the Pauline term "Caput Creationis," that is, "The Head of Creation," presumably from Colossians 1:18. Teilhard was apparently willing to allow this text to be taken, for the moment, in its dynamic sense (parallel to the Johannine quotation and to his title for this section: "L'Attraction."[37] But significantly, in section 3 ("C" in *WTW*), in which he returned to the term *Mystical Milieu* (i.e., "L'Etablissement du Milieu mystique"), he not only employed his favorite quotation of Acts 17:28 ("*In eo vivimus, et movemur, et sumus*"), but introduced his bold paraphrase of Romans 8:28 ("*Credenti, omnia convertuntur 'in Christum' *").[38] Also in this context of a literal "physicism," Teilhard was evidently paraphrasing Romans 14:7-8 when he repeated the couplet that appeared earlier: "Quidquid patimur, Christum patimur—

WTW, p. 251; *Ecrits*, p. 337. The actual text in Greek has *energeian*, not *dynamin*, and in Latin "operationem" instead of "potentiam." No variants are listed in the Merk, Nestle, or Kurt Aland critical texts. However, the word *dynamin* appears in a similarly constructed phrase in Eph. 3:20.

34. Note that the editor has inserted another footnote (*WTW*, p. 252; *Ecrits*, p. 338, n.3) reminding the reader of Teilhard's "Greek" understanding of the word *physical*. However, it would appear (note the words in the parenthesis in the preceding paragraph) that Teilhard here was stressing the material aspect of the organism.

35. *WTW*, p. 252; *Ecrits*, p. 338. In the introduction to this essay Teilhard went so far as to state that ". . . pour saint Jean et saint Paul notamment, le Christianisme était essentiellement une Cosmogonie. . . ," (*WTW*, p. 250; *Ecrits*, p. 335). An overstatement, to be sure, but understandable enough during this period when he still thought of Romans 8:22 in such terms.

But again, this must be understood in terms of Teilhard's dynamic view of matter and spirit. All energy is ultimately psychic in nature (not "physical" as was the mistranslation in one edition of *The Phenomenon of Man*).

36. *WTW*, p. 254; *Ecrits*, p. 339.

37. Section B, *WTW*, pp. 254-56. In *WTW* this section is retitled "The Magnetism of the Spirit" (*Ecrits*, pp. 339-42).

38. *WTW*, pp. 257-58; *Ecrits*, pp. 342-43.

Quidquid agimus, Christus agitur,"[39] and again in beginning the next section (§4, "La double respiration de l'âme"), when he utilized in the same literal way the text of Galatians 2:20, "Vivo ego—jam non ego: vivit in me Christus."[40]

The whole thrust of these quotations suggests that Teilhard was intending here to replace the rather vague concept of a *soul* of the universe as it appeared in the essay "The Soul of the World" with an analogy based on the scholastic distinction between *matter* and *form*. Following this line of thought, he suggested that

> in truth, Christ acts upon us *as a form*, and the *totality of souls* ready to receive it is the *matter* which interiorly (substantially) takes on form in him. [41]

Yet, much as this analogy appealed to him, he was not entirely satisfied with it, for if this is the case, then what of the doctrine of the Resurrection? Would it not become a superfluous and nonsensical fantasy? The flesh must be seen as something more vital than that. Responding to this difficulty, Teilhard returned to his original insistence on the corporality of redemption, but this time with considerably more precision as well as emphasis:

> "the mystical body of Christ is something more than a totality of souls; because, without there being present in it a specifically material element, souls could not be physically gathered together in Christ."
> Matter, it is true, is not the *formal* instrument of the union and interplay of the monads; but it is matter that gives the things of this world their radical capacity of entering into higher or lower syntheses, under one and the same Spirit. The essence (the formal effect) of materiality would appear to be *to make beings capable of unification*. In this regard, there is no difference between the lower natural world and the new world that is being formed around Christ. [42]

Drawing a parallel between the world of nature below us and the world that is being formed around Christ, Teilhard concluded:

> If that is so, if every collective soul is born in *our* world through the instrumentality of a body, then Christ can consummate our unity in the Centre *that stands firm above us*—the Centre, that is, which is his Spirit—only if he first encloses us in a material network

39. In "Mon univers" of 1918, *Ecrits*, p. 275.
40. *WTW*, § "D: The Phases in the Growth of the Soul" (pp. 259-64; *Ecrits*, pp. 344-49).
41. *WTW*, p. 266; *Ecrits*, p. 351.
42. *WTW*, p. 167; *Ecrits*, p. 352. Both paragraphs end with "Jésus" in the French, which would seem to emphasize the humanity of Christ.

underlying our *"esse corporeum."* If he is to be the soul of our souls, he must begin by being the flesh of our flesh.

Hence the importance of the Eucharist.[43]

In his "Note on the 'Universal Element' of the World," written in part on the day he completed "Forma Christi" and on the day after (Dec. 22 and 23, 1918), Teilhard attempted to reformulate what he had written in "The Soul of the World" in the light of "Forma Christi" and his earlier "Creative Union" (Nov. 1917). Reaffirming the basic legitimacy of the "pantheist" principle in its spiritual manifestations, he nevertheless postulated that in order to achieve their "absolute" character, the "forms" (i.e., souls) must also be conceived as tending to something "transcendent."[44] If for the Christian this transcendent term is not a mere "aggregate" but an organic whole ". . . of a higher entitative order than that of the elements considered in isolation," which is achieved in Christ, then this universal element can be understood as:

> the principle of super-individualization *"quo unumquodque ens perficitur, entitative, sub ratione adoptionis suae in tali universo"*—"by which each and every being is perfected, entitatively, in virtue of its reception into such a universe."[45]

For Teilhard, this "universal element" is ". . . the penetrating influence of Christ - ω, of Christ - 'Forma Mundi.' "[46]

Defending his basic insight against the misunderstanding of his broader use of the word *pantheism* elsewhere, he concluded in part with this clarification and an attached footnote:

> Thus, instead of being, as it is in pantheism, a lower universal basis—the matter of Matters—the universal element is seen to be *the higher Centre common to all developments, the Form of Forms.**
>
> *Is not this precisely the definition of the *Word*?
> —In short, one may say this: instead of looking for the *universal element* in an *informable principle* of the world, we should recognize it in an *informing* supreme *principle*. If that principle is not operative, we immediately have multiplicity.[47]

The editor of *Ecrits* (who remains unnamed) points out that this whole note attached to "Forma Christi" was crossed out in the original manuscript, probably because of its tentative character and also because another essay was to be written two months later having a very similar title.[48] Nevertheless, this "Note" is an important milestone in the journey in which Teilhard attempted to arrive at an understanding of the Body of Christ that would allow him to combine in somewhat

43. *WTW*, p. 268; *Ecrits*, p. 352.
44. *WTW*, p. 273; *Ecrits*, p. 360.
45. *WTW*, p. 274; *Ecrits*, p. 361.
46. *Ibid.*
47. *WTW*, p. 275; *Ecrits*, p. 362.
48. *WTW*, p. 271; *Ecrits*, p. 357.

metaphysical terms the abstract and "spiritual" interpretation of the "Mystical Body" with his recast doctrine of the Body of Christ in terms boldly physical and more universally "pleromic."

These essays of 1918 represent a strengthening of Teilhard's conviction that the old problem of the apparent dualism between spirit and matter could be solved, and this on the basis of the insights provided by the traditional doctrine of the Body of Christ. There remained still one major problem in his mind when it came to setting up a neat progression from the Incarnation through the Eucharistic, Ecclesial, and Cosmic extensions of this same organic understanding of Christ. To put the problem squarely, it centered on the Eucharist and that "body" formed by the Eucharist—the Church.

4. The Early Post-World War I Period (1919 to mid-1920)

Although the first few months of 1919 saw Teilhard's thought progressing in several directions at once,[49] sometime in that year he applied himself directly to deepening his understanding of the relationship between the Eucharistic and Ecclesial manifestations of the Body of Christ. As noted above, Teilhard's use of the "Hoc est corpus meum" formula was patterned after the liturgical concept of consecration, but as extended to the whole universe. Following the Pauline direction of development, which sees the Eucharistic Body as formative of a more extensive body (as in 1 Cor. 10:16-17), Teilhard's treatment of this idea tends to pass directly to all that is "divinisable" in creation. The reason for this was not simply his penchant for a "Universal Christ." At least part of it is rooted in his very concept of the body (or any corporeal entity) in itself. For this reason the essay that deals most directly with the Eucharistic-Ecclesial theme, the unfinished work entitled "Note on the Physical Union between the Humanity of Christ and the Faithful in the Course of Their Sanctification,"[50] should be read in conjunction with another short undated work believed to be of this period: "What Exactly Is the Human Body?"[51] In the latter essay, Teilhard set forth an insight that was unobtrusively present in much of his later thinking: the "coextensivité" of being. As he put it:

the limited, tangible fragments that in common usage we call monads, molecules, bodies, are *not complete* beings. They are only the nucleus of such beings, their organisational centre. In each case,

49. Cf. "Note pour servir à l'Evangélisation des temps nouveaux," Jan 8, 1919 (Ecrits, pp. 355-62): "Terre promise," Feb. 1919 (Ecrits, pp. 383-96; WTW, pp. 271-76): "L'Elément universel," Feb. 21, 1919 (Ecrits, pp. 397-414; WTW, pp. 289-302).
50. C&E, pp. 15-20; Oeuvres, 10:19-26.
51. "En quoi consiste le corps humain?" in Oeuvres, 9:31-35; S&C, pp. 11-15 (probably from Sept. 1919). Cf. also Cuénot, p. 451.

the real extension of these bodies coincides with the full dimensions of the universe.[52]

Lest the implications of this view escape notice, let the question he asked to begin with be pondered: "What, in Christ, is the matter which undergoes the hypostatic union, what is the *matter which claims our worship*?"[53]

Teilhard seemed actually to be incapable of giving an answer to this question at the moment; among the suggestions he made appears that curious word translated as *rooted in the cosmos* ("enracinée dans le cosmos"—Editor's translation):

> In (the) future, we shall say that the Body is the very Universality of things, in as much as they are centred on an animating Spirit, in as much as they influence that Spirit—and are themselves influenced and sustained by it. For a soul, to have a body is to be ἐγκεκοσμισμένη.[54]

The second essay, which the editors of his works believe may have been written about January 1920, shows a definite concern to correlate the above insight (which is not mentioned explicitly) into a more explicit delineation of the relationship between the life of grace and the relationship to the Eucharistic and Ecclesial bodies of Christ. Indeed, the very first sentence of the essay begins with a combined quotation from John 15:1 and 14:6 ("Vitis et Vita vera") balanced with a single adaptation of Colossians 1:18, which is rendered as "Caput creationis et Ecclesiae" (cf. Vulgate: "caput corporis ecclesiae . . . ut sit in omnibus ipse primatum tenens"). Obviously, Teilhard's understanding of the latter half of Paul's sentence was here (as elsewhere) taking literal precedence over the title of "caput ecclesiae." The reason for this apparent discrepancy is not hard to see, for Teilhard rejected the "extrinsicist" or "nominalist" interpretations of Christ's headship over creation and

---

52. (Paragraph H), S&C, p. 13; Oeuvres, 9:35. Cf. also "Forma Christi," WTW, p. 253; Ecrits, p. 339. This "coextensivity," mentioned many times in his "Journals" in various ways (as the "Principe de Coexistence" in Journal 14 [2]: 75; "coextent" in Journal 15 [3]: 39; "processes coextensif" in Journal 15 [3]: 81; "coextensivité" in Journal 17 [5]: 97), apparently entered into Teilhard's conceptual framework via Bergson's Evolution créatrice, which Teilhard read while he was a student at Hastings. (Cf. Henri Bergson, Creative Evolution (New York: Modern Library, Random House, 1944), p. 222.) The concept itself is derived from Descartes, Spinoza, and Leibnitz, and was also shared by the physicist Faraday (cf. Bergson, ibid.) Curiously enough, another scientist-philosopher, A. N. Whitehead, adopted the same view, which he termed his principle of "universal relativity." Contradicting Aristotle on this point, Whitehead held that "an actual entity is present in other actual entities. In fact, if we allow for degrees of relevance, and for negligible relevance, we must say that every actual entity is present in every other actual entity." Process and Reality (New York: Harper Torchbooks, 1960), p. 79.
53. S&C, p. 11; Oeuvres, 9:33. N. B. again the French original (stressing the humanity involved in the incarnation) has "Jésus" rather than "Christ."
54. S&C, p. 12; Oeuvres, 9:34. See discussion of egkekosmismenē" in chap. 1, §C, 2, above.

church. But the "intrinsic" or "natural" (i.e., "organic") approach can be divided—some see this organism as an animation (or superanimation) of souls in virtue of their relationship with the Word (i.e., "qua divinitate Christi"); others see it as a "physical" relationship dependent on the humanity of Christ. Teilhard obviously chose the second interpretation.[55]

Even with this choice, Teilhard sought further preciseness. Viewed retrospectively from the end-point of the pleroma, which Teilhard here defined as the "Corps Mystique consommé,"[56] the Body of Christ, he noted, is described by Scripture principally in organic terms, but almost exclusively in relation to the supernatural end of man. Revelation tells us little about this organic relationship in terms of "l'action physique et personnelle du Christ théandrique" outside of any other reality than the Church triumphant. This he saw as being indicative of the "collective" nature of salvation as opposed to an "individually" understood Divine contact with man. In effect:

> the state of beatitude must be understood as a state of *permanent eucharistic union* in which we will be raised up and maintained *as a body* (that is to say *"per modum unius"*—as one single being) and *"in corpore Christi"* (in the body of Christ).[57]

Arguing that the process of salvation must be accomplished in a manner commensurate with its exalted goal, Teilhard concluded:

> Since beatification coincides with a certain degree of physical incorporation in the created being of our Lord, we must inevitably admit that in the course of his meritorious life the believer is introduced into, and progresses further in, a certain state of physical connexion with the humanity of Christ the Saviour. If we are not to establish an unwarranted disparity between the state of grace and the state of glory, we must say that grace does more than attach us by its spiritual instillation to the divinity of the Word: it brings with it a certain progressive inclusion in a created organism, physically centred on the humanity of Christ.[58]

What Teilhard meant by *physical* here is definitely something more concrete, namely, organic in the biological sense of the word. Still, lest some recoil from a wrongly construed interpretation (like the crowd

---

55. See *C&E*, pp. 15-16; *Oeuvres*, 10:21-22.
56. Cf. *C&E*, p. 16; *Oeuvres*, 10:22. Although Teilhard continued to use, because of this retrospective approach, the term *plérôme* interchangeably with both "le Royaume de Dieu" and "Corps Mystique," the word as it appears in this essay will not be considered in terms of the concept of the Pleroma (the subject of chap. 5 below), but simply as the eschatological extension of the Body of Christ, inasmuch as it is the relationship between the Eucharist and the Ecclesial Body of Christ that is the object of this essay.
57. *C&E*, pp. 16-17; *Oeuvres*, 10:23. "Per modum unius" here is opposed to "per modum unius potentiae" on the preceding page: i.e., one single being or organism as opposed to a collection of individuals united under a single power.
58. *C&E*, p. 17; *Oeuvres*, 10:23.

described in John 6:53f.), he hastened to point out that the physical contact between the communicant and the Eucharistic Body is something more than a mere consumption of the species; it "is effected *on a physical plane that is very different* from that on which the evident quantitative contact between our body and the Host takes place."[59]

Understood in this manner, the physical reality of the contact in Holy Communion is not the initiation of a physical incorporation into Christ, but a continuation and intensification of that union:

> In that case, how should we approximately represent eucharistic (sacramental) union?—simply as the tightening, specially chosen and favoured, and wonderfully active, of a looser (but real) link established and maintained *"perenniter"* (constantly) by the state of grace. Long before any communion, a first and *permanent* connexion through the operation of baptism is formed between the Christian and the body of Christ.[60]

Even though the Church is not mentioned explicitly in this latter part of the essay (which ends with an unfinished sentence), the general implication is clear. For if by virtue of the Incarnation Christ's presence is physically extended through all of creation, the object of this Incarnation is the formation of a single organism whose "form" or "head" is the Christ, precisely in respect to his human nature. But because this organism is "centered" on the physical humanity of Christ, contact with His humanity becomes the only means ("nécessaire de 'nécessité' de moyen") of insuring one's incorporation into the pleroma, so much so that "we become members of Christ before any external contact with his sacramental body."[61] Is not this statement too strong, particularly if one understands "members of Christ" here in the ecclesial sense? But Teilhard understood it as a relationship or law of "annexion progressive"[62] or intensification. It is not a case of the rest of humanity, or even of the cosmos being out of contact with this coextensive Incarnation; rather

> the immediate practical corollary of this law is that, *for the just man*, God's general presence is constantly backed by a particular presence of Christ *"secundum suam naturam humanam"* (according to his human nature)—a presence which is prior (*in ordine naturae*, in the order of nature) to the indwelling of the divine persons in the sanctified soul.[63]

59. *C&E*, p. 18; *Oeuvres*, 10:24.
60. *Ibid.*
61. *C&E*, p. 17; *Oeuvres*, 10:24.
62. *C&E*, p. 17; *Oeuvres*, 10:23.
63. *C&E*, p. 25; *Oeuvres*, 10:18-19. A Journal entry of July 30, 1948 ("Journal" 15 [3]: 139) which, although it does not appear to be directly intended in terms of the Body of Christ, nevertheless speaks of "the two bodies": first, that which is "cosmic," coextensive with Time-Space, and second, that which is "organic," i.e., to be measured in terms of its centric complexity. The text is not entirely legible, despite its brevity.

It might be rightly asked if there was not a contradiction here between the "coextension" of the essay "What Exactly Is the Human Body?" and the progressive view of the Incarnation in the "Note on the Physical Union. . . ," rather than a true correlation. In one sense, yes, but only if the coextension is taken in a temporally static and spacially homogenous sense, a sense that Teilhard's evolutionary framework precludes. In terms of his law of complexity-consciousness, the physical coextension of Christ's humanity is relative, because its influence is to be conceived in terms of a radiating point. To repeat a phrase from the first of these two essays, the body (in this case the Body of Christ)

> is the very Universality of things, in as much as they are centred on an animating Spirit, in as much as they influence that Spirit—and are themselves influenced and sustained by it.[64]

Thus, in speaking of our own corporality he went on to say:

> My own body is not these cells or those cells that *belong exclusively* to me: it is *what*, in these cells *and* in the rest of the world feels my influence and reacts against me. *My* matter is not a *part* of the universe that I possess *totaliter*: it is the *totality* of the Universe possessed by me *partialiter*.[65]

From this it can be inferred that Christ's corporeal presence is not given in a static state through the Incarnation; rather, this presence increases in intensity in proportion to His effective "information" of the universe. This point is confirmed in the second of these essays when Teilhard applied the same insight to the Eucharistic relationship between the Christian and Christ:

> In short, the Christian's whole life, on earth as in heaven, can be seen as a sort of perpetual eucharistic union. The Divine comes to us only as "informed" by Christ Jesus: that is the fundamental law of our supernatural life.[66]

By way of a corollary, he went on to add, speaking of a Christian's activities in the world:

> But this is not all: since this presence grows in proportion with the state of grace in us, it is capable not only of enduring but also of being *intensified* by the whole miscellaneous body of what we do and what we suffer. It is literally true that "*quidquid agit Christianus, Christus agitur*"—whatever the Christian does, it is to Christ it is done.[67]

64. *S&C*, p. 12; *Oeuvres*, 9:34 (Paragraph E).
65. *S&C*, p. 13; *Oeuvres*, 9:34 (Paragraph G).
66. *C&E*, p. 18; *Oeuvres*, 10:25.
67. *C&E*, p. 19; *Oeuvres*, 10:25.

Teilhard confined this latter essay to the discussion of the physical relationship of the Christian to Christ, but the fact that "Grace" remains a principal activator of this union, or as he put in one phrase "this idea of a physical influx continually emanating (with an admixture of grace) for souls from the humanity of Christ"[68] allowed him to speak of the Christian as not only the object of this union but also *"the just man."*[69] Through the vagueness of his use of the words *influx* and *grace*, Teilhard left the way open for reintroducing in later essays an understanding of the Incarnation that went beyond the confines of the Christian soul or even all humanity, at least potentially. This is intimated by the closing remarks:

> Nor need we fear, again, that we are putting too great a strain on the limits that define the lower nature in which the Word is incarnate. However boundless the power we must attribute to this nature if its influence is to radiate continually over each one of us, such magnitude should not alarm us. By the horizons it opens up for us on to the power hidden within created being, and more particularly on to the heart of Jesus Christ, this overplus is seen to be, on the contrary, one of the most magnetic aspects of . . .[70]

From the foregoing, it may be inferred that Teilhard understood the Incarnation as that act by which the Word not only united itself hypostatically with a human nature in the historical person of Christ, but also united itself with the whole cosmos in such a way that through His body Christ possesses the *whole universe partially*, which union must be intensified through the *informative function of grace* until the *whole universe is possessed* by Christ *totally*. It is within this framework that all Teilhard's subsequent references to the Eucharist (which remains the means "par excellence" of building up this Cosmic Body of Christ) must be located, and also his references to the Church. This Church, which in his later writings was to be characterized as the "Phylum of Love," represents that "informed" portion of humanity which is fully conscious of its participation in the Incarnation and whose vocation is to engage itself fully in the progressive "humanization" of mankind "in Christo Jesu."[71] While strong intimations of this view of the Church are already present in his January 1919 "Note pour servir à l'évangélisation des temps nouveaux,"[72] the real key to the comprehensive view of Christianity would seem to lie in a passage which paves the way for an ever-extending view of the Body of Christ. This view

68. *Ibid.*
69. *Ibid.*
70. *C&E*, p. 20; *Oeuvres*, 10:26. The final word in this unfinished manuscript appears to be "Christianisme," according to the editor of *Oeuvres*.
71. Cf. esp. "Introduction to the Christian Life," *C&E*, pp. 151-72; *Oeuvres*, 10:177-200.
72. *Ecrits*, pp. 363-81; cf. esp. p. 374.

serves not to mark off the Church as a special preserve of God's activity with its own exclusive mediator to the Father, but as a special manifestation of that Incarnational activity uniting the whole universe in a relationship to God that is successively eucharistic, ecclesial, and cosmic.

> In the first place, when we extend all around us the domain of Christ's humanity we have no reason to fear that we are veiling from ourselves the face of the Godhead. Since we adhere to Christ "*in ordine vitali*"—in the order of life—he is *not an intermediary* separating us from God, but a *medium* uniting us to God. "*Philippe, qui videt me, videt Patrem*"—"He who has seen me, Philip, has seen the Father."[73]

As much as these two essays ("What Exactly Is the Human Body?" and "Note on the Physical Union . . .") enabled Teilhard to progress in working out his more fully organic understanding of the Body of Christ, they were of a highly provisional nature. There still remained the task of more systematically explicating his theory of matter and spirit, which still suffered from the classical overdose of dualism and still tended to affect his manner of expression. His more developed "hyperphysics," which would lead to his formulation of one single "Weltstoff" displaying the two faces of matter and spirit in a dynamic relationship, was yet a long way off, as is evidenced by his gropings in this direction in "Les noms de la Matière"[74] and "La Puissance spirituelle de la Matière,"[75] both written in mid-1919.

It seems likely that this correlative view of the Incarnation and the Body of Christ as both "coextensive" and "progressive," forged out in the year or so between early 1919 and mid-1920, had a major influence on the "hyperphysics" that would be formulated in his *Phenomenon of Man* years later in the 1930s. This doctrine of the Body of Christ, particularly in its Eucharistic aspects, may have been as much of a challenge to his future "hyperphysics" as it was an inspiration to his metaphysics of creative union. Yet much work remained to be done.

5. The Early 1920s

The bulk of Teilhard's speculations on the Body of Christ took shape during the years of World War I and immediately after, but as for the scriptural texts used to support his position, there appears to have been little exegetical argument. The texts themselves are more explicitly Johannine than Pauline, and are employed primarily as leading inspirations and quotational highlights of what is mostly metaphysical and even "hyperphysical" exploration in a theological context.

73. *C&E*, pp. 19-20; *Oeuvres*, 10:26. (The quotation is from John 14:9.)
74. *Ecrits*, pp. 415-32. Cf. chap. 3, §A, above.
75. *Ecrits*, pp. 433-46; for Eng. trans., *HU*, pp. 57-71.

Yet during that earlier period taken as a whole (§§ 1-4 above), a more Pauline mode of expression did begin to emerge. For example, the rather fleeting citation of Colossians 1:16 in the 1918 "Mon univers" (cf. chap. 2, §D, 1, above) seems to be almost something of an afterthought, while in the January 1920 "Note on the Universal Christ," the same quotation emerges as a principal point of argument:

> We have (since the earliest times, and fortunately) lavishly accorded to Christ the attributes of universal mediation: *"Omnia in ipso, per ipsum. . . ."* Has it been noted that, as the universe is seen to be more immense in its determinisms, its past, and its extension, so those attributes become an uncommonly heavy burden for our classical philosophy and theology?[76]

The question posed in this essay is a reformulation, in Pauline terms, of that same challenge expressed a year earlier in 1919 in his "Note pour servir à l'évangélisation des temps nouveaux," when he wrote:

> We often had the example of men who vowed themselves to study *in* Religion, *in order to* honor or defend Religion. But when will the priests and religious be seen who, overcoming this extrinsicism, will search and study *through* religion, *religiously*; that is to say, with the distinct and professed consciousness that the least of their natural achievements, because through them souls are nourished, serves definitively to make the Body of Christ grow?[77]

As he was to put it a few pages later:

> The Christian option, then, ought to be presented as a choice, not precisely between Heaven and Earth, but between two efforts to complete the Universe, either *within* or *outside of Christ*.[78]

Teilhard's answer to this dilemma facing Christianity in his 1920 "Note on the Universal Christ" was, of course, to call for an understanding of Christ that is truly universal "(. . . in other words, he is gradually consummated from all created being)."[79] This rather surprising sentence indicates a more-than-passing relationship of the world in relation to the pleroma, which he had already defined during this earlier period as the "Corps mystique consommé."[80]

76. "Note sur le Christ universel" in *Oeuvres*, 9;40; *S&C*, p. 15.
77. *Ecrits*, pp. 375-76 (My translation). Note the mention of "extrinsécisme," a target of Bondel's writings about that time. The reader is recommended to consult the enlightening exchange of views between Teilhard and Blondel through their mutual friendship with P. Auguste Valensin, S.J. as published in *Blondel et Teilhard de Chardin*, ed. Henri de Lubac (Paris: Beauchesne, 1965) (English: *Pierre Teilhard de Chardin—Maurice Blondel: Correspondence* [New York: Herder & Herder, 1967]). Robert Hale, O.S.B. Cam., in his excellent little book *Christ and the Universe: Teilhard de Chardin and the Cosmos* (Chicago: Franciscan Herald Press, 1973), believes that Blondel's influence over Teilhard may have been even more considerable still, extending to Teilhard's whole "pan-christic" outlook (Cf. pp. 51-56).
78. *Ecrits*, p. 379.
79. *S&C*, p. 16; *Oeuvres*, 9;41.
80. *C&E*, p. 16; *Oeuvres*, 10:22. Cf. chap. 2, §D.4 above.

However, during this new period, which began in mid-1920, most notably with his "Fall, Redemption, and Geocentrism" of July of that same year, Teilhard switched his emphasis from the mediating Christ to the Christ of Colossians 1:15-19, whose humanity is *"prima super omnes,"* "the head of humankind," *"in quo omnia constant."*[81] In citing these passages, as well as the "ut repleret omnia" of Ephesians 4:10,[82] Teilhard was now endeavoring to launch the new approach he had been advocating for some time but had held back until he was convinced that the Incarnation does not represent a means of liberation from matter but rather a transformation of it.

But such a new approach, as he then realised, was more easily advanced than proven. The real obstacle was to be not so much that ancient dualism separating spirit from matter, but the old problem of evil. Within the Pauline mode of understanding evil is not only bound up with the occurrence of sin, but is also woven through the concept of the Redemption and the preeminence of Christ as Lord of Creation and Head of His Body. In "Fall, Redemption, and Geocentrism," Teilhard had to face this problem squarely:

> The *spirit* of the Bible and the Church is perfectly clear: the *whole* world has been corrupted by the Fall and the *whole* of everything has been redeemed. Christ's glory, beauty, and irresistible attraction radiate, in short, from his *universal* kingship. If his dominance is restricted to the sublunary regions, then he is eclipsed, he is abjectly extinguished by the universe. *"Qui descendit, nisi qui ascendit, ut repleret omnia?"* [Eph. 4:10: "He who descended is he not who also ascended . . . that he might fill all things?"].
> *The Church cannot measure up to the truth except by universalizing the first and the second Adam.*[83]

What had taken Teilhard back to the problem of sin and redemption was not simply the problem of how Christ can be considered the "second Adam" in relationship to the human race, but how the second Adam can be related in any meaningful way to a universal primacy over all creation, more specifically over a world and a humanity which *"in all probability* is neither 'unica" [unique], nor 'singularis' [one], but is 'one among a thousand.' " In such an overwhelming expansion of our horizon, he asked, what becomes of St. Paul's "Christ who dies no longer?"[84]

Teilhard's first attempt at a solution to this problem is rather startling. It has already been seen how he rejected the Pauline cosmology, inextricably bound up, as Teilhard thought, with the attribution of all physical evil to the Fall of man.[85] But how preserve the significance of

81. *C&E*, pp. 41, 42, 44; *Oeuvres*, 10:54, 55, 57.
82. Cf. *C&E*, p. 39, 43; *Oeuvres*, 10:52, 56.
83. *C&E*, p. 39; *Oeuvres*, 10:52.
84. *C&E*, pp. 43-44; *Oeuvres*, 10:57. Cf. Rom. 6:9.
85. Cf. chap. 3, §A (latter part), above.

the "second Adam," or even that of the "first Adam"? In his "Note on Some Possible Historical Representations of Original Sin," written before Easter of 1922, Teilhard first mentioned his interest in an "Alexandrian" theory of original sin, that of a "precosmic" fall.[86] While this hint remained buried in the subsequent discussion of the "historical representations" and their difficulties, it would nevertheless continue to exercise a certain fascination for Teilhard's mind.

But what would happen to the concept of the "first Adam" within the Alexandrine system? As he later explained in his 1947 "Reflections on Original Sin,"[87] Adam would have to be conceived as some sort of perfect prototype, whose existence predates history (i.e., is "transhistorique") and in whose image, once fallen, the rest of creation comes to be! Obviously, this can be no solution for an evolutionary paleontologist. But then what was its attraction for Teilhard? The answer may lie in the similarity of the concept of a precosmic fall to Teilhard's earlier and rather tentative formulation of the existence (real or merely conceptual?) of a certain "pure multiple" or multiplicity, which he held to be the product of God's *first* act of creation in contradistinction to a *second* act of creation ("creation" properly speaking), which is by its very nature a unifying movement.[88]

In the 1947 "Reflections on Original Sin," Teilhard went on positively to identify the Fall in Genesis with the dissociated state of pure multiplicity, and thus to identify evil and original sin as merely that force or tendency in nature, once it has achieved some unity within its complexity, to drift back into the state of disunity.[89] But obviously there are major difficulties in such a solution and in the 1922 "Note on Some Possible Historical Representations of Original Sin" Teilhard underscored them as being:

> a. that we have to abandon an individual Adam and an initial fall, unless we regard as "principal transgression" the moral crisis which apparently accompanied the first appearance of intelligence in man;
> b. that, in consequence, it confuses in duration the two phases of fall and recovery; these are no longer two distinct periods, but two components which are constantly united in each man and in mankind.[90]

86. Cf. *C&E*, p. 45; *Oeuvres*, 10:61.
87. Cf. *C&E*, pp. 191-93; *Oeuvres*, 10:223-26.
88. In this matter Teilhard seemed unable to make himself clear. In "L'Union créatrice" he spoke of a sort of "Néant positif," which exists as a "multiple pur" at the antipode of God's existence—a concept that he admitted "redolet manichaeismum." (Cf. *Ecrits*, pp. 184-85; *WTW*, pp. 162-63.) However, his discussion of this difficult idea has a footnote attached, which appears to modify his position:
> Il y aurait ainsi, en quelque façon, deux actions, créatrice divines: la première, *quasi-organique*, aboutissant à l'apparition du Multiple pur (= *effet antagoniste de l'Unicité* divine); la deuxième, *quasi efficiente*, unifiant le Multiple (= création la deuxième, *quasi efficiente*, unifiant le Multiple (= création proprement dite). (*WTW*, p. 164, n.10; *Ecrits*, p. 186, n.10.)
89. Cf. *C&E*, pp. 193-98; *Oeuvres*, 10:226-30.
90. *C&E*, pp. 52-53; *Oeuvres*, 10:68.

Having thus stated them negatively (he had first put them more gently in a positive manner), he hastened to point out:

> Creation, Fall, Incarnation, Redemption, those vast universal events no longer appear as fleeting accidents occurring sporadically in time—a grossly immature view which is a perpetual offence to our reason and a contradiction of our experience. All four of those events become co-extensive with the duration and totality of the world; they are, in some way, aspects (distinct in reality but physically linked) of one and the same divine operation. The incarnation of the Word (which is in process of continual and universal consummation) is simply the final term of a creation which is still continuing everywhere and does so through our imperfections ("*omnis creatura adhuc ingemiscit et parturit*"). The supreme transgression, committed by an as yet inarticulate mankind, is not to be found behind us: would it not be better to look for it ahead, when mankind has at last become fully conscious of its powers and will split into two camps, for God or against him?[91]

Does this view make the moment of the Incarnation unlocatable in the course of history? Not so, in Teilhard's mind, at least according to his later protestation against the misinterpretation of his views. But what he wrote in this essay of 1922 was enough to suggest his being reassigned to do paleontological work in China. Significantly, the same view is still favored in his 1947 essay on the same subject, except that the threefold operations of Creation, Incarnation, and Redemption are summed up as but phases of one movement, that of "pleromization."[92] Thus, while Christ remains the "second Adam," this is clearly in a sense not foreseen by Paul.

6. The Later Years (The China Period)

Teilhard embarked for China on April 6, 1923. Although he was to return to Paris for a relatively short period (Oct. 1924 to May 1925) he may have had a foreboding that his views were soon to cause consternation, if they had not already. In any case, the change in his life circumstances was significant enough for him to write, in the spring of 1924, what stands as one of his most significant essays of a theologically global nature, the larger of the two essays entitled "Mon Univers." In terms of his understanding of the Body of Christ, he admits that he

---

91. *C&E*, p. 53; *Oeuvres*, 10:69.
92. *C&E*, p. 198; *Oeuvres*, 10:230. Rather significant of the daring of this essay, and its instrumentality in Teilhard's "exile" to China, is the fact that in Cuénot's biography this "Note sur quelques Représentations historiques possibles du Péché originel" was assigned the bibliographical reference number 452 (the preceding and succeeding numbers are 47 and 49 respectively), which would seem to indicate that the editors of his works deemed it prudent to keep this manuscript under "wraps" for some time. It was finally published in 1969. "Réflexions sur le Péché originel" was assigned a number (477) that is likewise chronologically out of order. Cf. Cuénot, pp. 419, 441.

held a view at the opposite pole from what most theologians had to say about the "Mystical Body" and most exegetes had to say about Colossians 1:15f.:

> As regards the weakened interpretation of the Apostle's words, I dismiss it simply because it is less in conformity with the spirit of St Paul as it animates the body of his Epistles, and less, too, in conformity with my general view of the world. However, I have given up hope of converting those who reject my version. I have, in fact, become convinced that men include two irreconcilable types of minds: the physicalists (who are "mystics") and the juridicists. For the former, the whole beauty of life consists in being organically structured; and in consequence Christ, being pre-eminently attractive, must radiate physically. For the latter, being is embarrassing as soon as it disguises something vaster and less patient of definition than our human social relationships (considered from the point of view of their artificial content). Christ, accordingly, is no more than a king or a great landowner. These (the juridicists), logically inconsistent with their theology of grace, will always understand "mystical" (in "mystical body") by analogy with a somewhat stronger family association or association of friends. The physicalists, however, will see in the word mystical the expression of a hyper-physical (supersubstantial) relationship—stronger, and in consequence more respectful of embodied individualities, than that which operates between the cells of one and the same animate organism. The two types of mind will never understand one another, and the choice between the two attitudes must be made not by reasoning but by insight. For my own part, it has been made, irrevocably and as long as I can remember. I am a physicalist by instinct: and that is why it is impossible for me to read St Paul without seeing the universal and cosmic domination of the Incarnate Word emerging from his words with dazzling clarity.[93]

This lengthy passage stands as perhaps Teilhard's single most important statement on this whole question, and marks the beginning of a search for a whole new mode of expression within which the Pauline term *pleroma* increasingly comes to the fore.

But Teilhard was not about to abandon the term *Body of Christ* entirely to the "juridicists"; however, during the following years, with very few exceptions, he avoided using the adjective *mystical*. Accordingly, in *The Divine Milieu* of 1926, although he took a less aggressive tone than in the 1924 "Mon Univers," he made his position clear:

> We should not be content to give this destination of our being in Christ a meaning too slavishly imitative of the legal relationship which in our world links an object to its owner. Its nature is altogether more physical and deeper. Because the consummation of the world (the Pleroma, as St. Paul says) is a communion of persons (the Communion of Saints), our minds no doubt require that we

93. *S&C*, pp. 55-56; *Oeuvres*, 9:83-84.

should express the relationship with the help of analogies drawn from society. Moreover, in order to avoid the perverse pantheism and materialism which lie in wait for our thought whenever it applies to its mystical concepts the powerful but dangerous resources of analogies drawn from organic life, the majority of theologians (more cautious on this point than St. Paul) do not favour too literal an interpretation of the links which bind the limbs to the Head in the Mystical Body. But there is no reason why caution should become timidity.[94]

In this same spirit of cautious compromise (Teilhard was steadfastly determined to try to have *The Divine Milieu* published), he spoke again of "The mystical Christ, the universal Christ of St. Paul."[95] A few pages later, though, his continuing use of the term gave evidence of his persisting discomfort with the usual formulation.

In spite of the strength of St. Paul's expressions (formulated, it should be remembered, for the *ordinary run* of the first Christians) some readers may feel that we have been led to strain, in too realist a direction, the meaning of "Mystical Body"—or at least that we have allowed ourselves to seek esoteric perspectives in it.[96]

The next appearance of the traditional phrase in Teilhard's writings was not until 1933, in a short essay entitled "The Significance and Positive Value of Suffering." Here quotation marks were employed, but the passage itself indicates that Teilhard had not set aside interest in the possibilities of a meaningful utilization of the concept, particularly when applied specifically to man's spiritual life within the Church.

In the collective man formed by all men together and subordinated to Christ within the "mystical body," there are, as St. Paul has told us, different organs and functions. What part can we imagine to be more specially entrusted with the task of sublimating and spiritualizing the general work of progress and conquest? The contemplatives and prayerful no doubt. But also, most certainly, the sick and suffering.[97]

The two remaining major exceptions to Teilhard's discontinuance of the term *Mystical Body* occurred in the years 1936 and 1940. They fully indicate that, despite the disclaimer in the 1924 "Mon Univers," Teilhard had not given up the struggle to try to convince others that the Body of Christ should be understood in a fully organic sense in re-

94. *DM*, pp. 25-26; *Oeuvres*, 4:42-43.
95. *DM*, p. 95; *Oeuvres*, 4:141.
96. *DM*, pp. 101-2; *Oeuvres*, 4:150.
97. "La Signification et la Valour constructrice de la Souffrance," *HE*, p. 50; *Oeuvres*, 6:64. It should also be noted that this essay appears to have been written specifically for the publication *Trait d'Union*, the magazine of L'Union catholique des Malades, an organization founded and directed by Teilhard's invalid sister, Marguerite-Marie.

spect to the whole universe. The first exception occurs in a paper written in answer to a request that specified that it be sent on to a member of the hierarchy in Rome. Accordingly, the paper, entitled "Some Reflections on the Conversion of the World," calls for an expansion of our theological categories in consonance with the exigencies of modern thought concerning the universe. *Mystical Body* is linked to those concepts which boldly proclaim his cosmic view of the Incarnation—but not until after Teilhard had used the occasion to stress the orthodoxy (as well as the necessity) of his views:

> In taking on universality, Christ is not lost in the heart of the universe (as he was in those forms of modernism that were condemned): he dominates and assimilates the universe by imposing upon it the three essential characteristics of his traditional truth —the *personal* nature of the Divine; the manifestation of this supreme Personality in the *historical Christ*; the *super-terrestrial* nature of the world consummated in God. The "universalised" Christ takes over, correcting and completing them, the energies that undoubtedly lie hidden in modern forms of pantheism. He grows greater by remaining what he was—or, to put it more exactly, *in order to* remain what he was.
>
> In fact, the more one thinks about it, the clearer it becomes that to "universalise" Christ is the only way we have of retaining in him his essential attributes (alpha and omega) in a fantastically enlarged Creation. If Christianity is to keep its place at the head of mankind, it must make itself explicitly recognisable as a sort of "pan-Christism"—which, in fact, is simply the notion of the mystical Body, taken in its fullest and most profound sense, and the extension to the universe of the attributes already accorded (particularly with reference to human society) to Christ the King.[98]

Feeling that he had little to lose once he had spoken out so boldly to the highest authorities in the Church, Teilhard continued on his own way, but not without one last appeal in which he attempted again to link his concepts with the more traditional formulation of the "Mystical Body" of Christ. This last appeal occurs in "La Parole attendue" ("The Expected Word"), an essay that attempts to analyze the major crisis facing humanity at the beginning of World War II in terms of the "crisis of growth" in human development and the present failure of mankind to integrate the goals of its own development with those traditionally advanced by Christianity. But as section IV of the essay indicates ("The Great Remedy: The Manifestation of the 'Universal Christ'"), the real answer (and by implication the real failure of the Church in avoiding its responsibility in this matter) lies in the welding of the "nova et vetera" in new elaboration of the doctrine of a truly

---

98. "Quelques Réflexions sur la Conversion du Monde," *S&C*, pp. 123-24; *Oeuvres*, 9:163.

universal Christ in the dimensions of the Pauline pleroma.[99] Indeed, he notes, the Church has already made a start in this direction:

In fact, it appears that, directed by a divine instinct and similar to the mounting of modern humanitarian aspirations, the Christian sap may be already rising, leading toward a blossoming of the bud which has been dormant for so long. Beginning just two centuries ago, surrounding the cult of The Heart of Jesus, there has taken shape a movement that in its depths gives evidence in the Church of an adoration of Christ considered in his influences upon the Mystical Body, and likewise upon the whole human social organism. The love of Christ: it is the energy wherein is gathered, without confusion, all the chosen elements of Creation. Finally, through a deed that characterizes a decisive stage in the elaboration of a dogma, Rome has interpreted and consecrated, in the form of Christ the King, this irresistible advance of the Christian consciousness toward a more universal and realistic appreciation of the Incarnation.[100]

But much remained to be done, and Teilhard was still determined to make his contribution.

In the years to follow, the concept of the Body of Christ no longer explicitly appeared in Teilhard's writings. But there can be no doubt that his early enthusiasm for this concept continued to inspire much of his thought, especially that concerning the pleroma.

Negatively, it is possible to see why the continued restriction by theologians of the Body of Christ to its Eucharistic and Ecclesial manifestations would force Teilhard to adopt the more comprehensive idea provided by the more abstract word, even though he was to take great pains to see that his own expression of the pleroma would retain the organic and physical connotation derived from his understanding of the Body of Christ.

Positively, the transition was facilitated, at least theologically, through Teilhard's perception of Christ's position as "Head," or as he had put it in his "Note on the Physical Union Between the Humanity of Christ and the Faithful . . . ," paraphrasing Colossians 1:18: "Caput creationis et Ecclesiae."[101] Now older and wiser, he steered away from such easy and uncritical accommodations of Scripture, but at the same time he was totally convinced that no other conclusion was possible unless he was to sacrifice his lifelong struggle to insist that the universe is truly "monocephalous"—that in order to make any sense at all, the goal of evolution and the goal of salvation had to be one and the same. Thus, in his 1951 "A Mental Threshold Across Our Path: From Cosmos to Cosmogenesis," Teilhard reaffirmed this conviction:

however ultra-gratuitous be the depth to which the heart of God opens up for us at this time, that God must . . . satisfy the condition

---

99. *Oeuvres*, 11:106; also in *Cahiers de Teilhard de Chardin*, 4 (Paris: Editions du Seuil, 1963): 26, and *TF*, p. 97.
100. *Ibid.*, pp. 106-7 (*Cahiers*, 4:27). (My translation.) Cf. also *TF*, pp. 97-98.
101. *C&E*, p. 15; *Oeuvres*, 10:21.

of being *the one* peak of a universe which is henceforth recognized by us as structurally monocephalic and evolutively incomplete.[102]

Less than two years before his death, an apparent allusion in "The God of Evolution" is found to Ephesians 1:10 with Teilhard's ever-present complaint that our theology (like the "mystical"-"social" narrowing of the Body of Christ concept) has been outstripped by the exigencies of man's vision:

> In the eyes of everyone who is alive to the reality of the cosmic movement of complexity-consciousness which produces us, Christ, as still presented to the world by classical theology, is both too confined (localized) astronomically, and evolutively too extrinsic, to be able to "cephalize" the universe as we now see it.
> And further, there is undoubtedly a most revealing correspondence between the shapes (the pattern) of the two confronting Omegas: that postulated by modern science, and that experienced by Christian mysticism. A correspondence—and one might even say a parity! For Christ would not still be the Consummator so passionately described by St Paul if he did not take on precisely the attributes of the astonishing cosmic pole already potentially (if not as yet explicitly) demanded by our new knowledge of the world: the pole at whose peak the progress of evolution must finally converge.[103]

Passages like the last two, which are among the more striking of many that abound in his later writings, make it clear that Teilhard was convinced that what he himself was advocating was consonant with the thought of St. Paul, whatever the verdicts of biblical exegetes or the restricted interpretations of theologians. Such a position involves some real difficulties, among which come to mind such problems as: What was Paul's real meaning in speaking of the Church as Christ's Body? In what sense did Paul intend Christ to be understood as "Lord" of all creation? In what sense does Christ complete this Body of his, or can this be understood in the reverse sense of the Body completing Christ? These and related questions will be examined—some in the second part of this chapter, others, like the last, waiting for a more complete evaluation in chapter 5.

B. TEILHARD'S CONCEPT OF *THE BODY OF CHRIST* IN THE LIGHT OF PROFESSIONAL EXEGESIS

To state more precisely the three major problems bearing on an evaluation of Teilhard's interpretation of the Pauline "Body of Christ," it will be necessary to make finer distinctions, some of which may

102. *AE*, p. 264; *Oeuvres*, 7:272.
103. *C&E*, p. 242; *Oeuvres*, 10:290.

never have occurred to Teilhard in his enthusiasm to see this concept understood globally in terms of a *Cosmic Body of Christ*.

The first, the question of a mystical versus a physical interpretation of the Pauline image, may be stated thus: Is there a "Mystical Body" expounded in the writings of St. Paul apart from the historical and resurrected body of Christ?

The second, St. Paul's meaning in his description of Christ as "Lord" of Creation, involves a distinction, of which Teilhard was aware, between Christ's position as "Head" of His Body and "Lord" of the Universe. This distinction requires a better grasp of what is meant by Christ's position as "firstborn" of all the dead.

The third major problem, which must be understood in the light of the previous ones, is how Christ completes, or is completed by, his Body. This question will receive fuller discussion in pleromic terms in the next chapter.

While these three problems are likewise not always clearly distinguished or given equal emphasis by the exegetical commentaries that we examined in the previous chapter, we will nevertheless find that they emerge with increasing clarity, particularly in the treatment of F. Prat, whose work was highly influential with S. Tromp, the principal theological contributor to the 1943 encyclical "Mystici Corporis." Although note will be made of the pioneering efforts of M.-J. Scheeben, the work of Emile Mersch[104] remains an unknown factor with regard to Teilhard, as well as the opinions of such Protestant interpreters as Barth and Robinson. Most important in terms of a retrospective judgment on Teilhard's thought is the work of such contemporaries as L. Cerfaux and P. Benoît.

1. Early Formative Influences

There is little or no mention of the sources of Teilhard's views in his writings, but Cornelius a Lapide, as the most venerable of Jesuit authors, takes precedence because of his heavy reliance on patristic tradition, along with J. Knabenbauer, and his contributions to the turn-of-the-century *Cursus Scripturae Sacrae*.[105] Since the Pauline text to which Teilhard most often alluded in his early writings is Colossians 1:15-19, it will be well to examine the opinions of these two authors regarding the meaning of these verses as bearing on the doctrine of the Body of Christ.

First, Teilhard quoted the "omnia creata per ipsum" once and

104. Robert Hale (pp. 41-42) believes that the line of thinking developed in Mersch's 1933 work *Le Corps mystique du Christ* and his later *La Théologie du Corps Mystique* must have been known to Teilhard by means of his two close friends P. Charles, S.J., and J. Maréchal, S.J., both of whom were Mersch's teachers at Louvain. In any case, it was through friends such as these that Teilhard was aware of the patristic tradition that favored his own line of thought.
105. Vols. 7, 8, and 9 (Paris: Lethielleux, 1911-12).

quoted (directly or indirectly) the "Per ipsum . . . in ipso" of this same verse several times in his essays collected in *Writings in Time of War*[106] and in his "Note on the Universal Christ."[107] According to Cornelius a Lapide (following the opinion of Anselm), this text indicates the "immensity of the Son, inasmuch as the Son is everywhere through (his) essence, presence, and power . . . he occupies and fills everything. . . ."[108] Certainly the similarity between this interpretation and the attributes that Teilhard assigned to Christ in his "Forma Christi" is striking.

Likewise, Knabenbauer stated that this passage describes Christ as the "efficient cause and the final cause, the beginning and the end of everything," and in the same passage he went on to link this verse, even more explicitly than did Teilhard, with the "alpha and omega" of Apocalypse 22:13.[109] Even more remarkable, Knabenbauer drew a parallel between the "omnia in ipso constant" of Colossians 1:17 (which Teilhard often paraphrased as "in quo omnia constant") and Teilhard's other often-quoted Pauline phrase: "in ipso vivimus, movemur et sumus" (Acts 17:28).[110]

However, there is one significant difference in Teilhard's use of Colossians 1:16, 17, and it becomes most apparent in Cornelius a Lapide's comment on verse 18, where he made a sharp distinction between the divinity of Christ treated in the preceding verses and the humanity in the verses that follow.[111] While Teilhard did not deny this attribution of verses 16 and 17 to be in virtue of Christ's divinity, his emphasis was quite otherwise. In fact, where Cornelius a Lapide[112] saw verses 16 and 17 to be determined by the meaning of verse 15 "primus super omnes" (equating the "et ipse est ante omnes" of verse 17 in the same way with the preexistent Word), Teilhard was adamant in stressing the humanity of Christ. According to his 1920 essay "Chute, Rédemption et Géocentrie":

> The case of the second Adam is completely different. There is, it is clear, no lower centre of divergence in the universe at which we could place the first Adam. On the contrary—the universe can and must be conceived as converging towards a point of supreme confluence. In virtue, moreover, of its universal and increasing unification, it possesses this property, that each of its elements is organically connected with all the others. In these circumstances, there is no-

106. See pp. 57, 174; *Ecrits*, pp. 47, 196, 276.
107. Cf. *S&C*, p. 15; *Oeuvres*, 9:40.
108. C. a Lapide, 19:76: "immensitatem Filii, scilicet Filium esse ubique per essentiam, praesentiam et potentiam . . . omnia occupat et replet. . . ."
109. Knabenbauer, *Cursus Scripturae Sacrae*, 9:289: "causa efficiens et causa finalis, principium et finis omnium."
110. *Ibid*.
111. "18. ET IPSE EST CAPUT CORPORIS ECCLESIAE.—Hactenus egit de Christo ut Deo, ejusque divinitatem ostendit, jam agit de Christo ut homo est, et Christi hominis dignitatem ostendit. Christus enim qua homo est, non qua Deus, est proprie caput Ecclesiae." (19:77.)
112. Cf. *ibid.*, pp. 76-77.

thing to prevent a human individual nature from having been so chosen, and its omni-influence having been so elevated, that from being *"una inter pares"* it has become *"prima super omnes."* Just as in living bodies a cell, at first similar to the other cells, can gradually come to be preponderant in the organism, so the particular human-ity of Christ was able (at least at the Resurrection) to take on, to acquire, a universal morphological function.[113]

This perspective, caused Teilhard to insist in his 1924 "Mon univers" that he was

> very well aware that there are two loopholes by which timid minds hope to escape the awesome realism of these repeated statements. They may maintain that the cosmic attributes of the Pauline Christ belong to the Godhead alone; or they may try to weaken the force of the texts by supposing that the ties of dependence that make the world subject to Christ are juridical and moral, the rights exercised by a landowner, a father or the head of an association. As regards the first subterfuge, all I need to do is to refer to the context, which is categorical: even in Col. 1. 15 ff, St Paul quite obviously has in mind the theandric Christ; it was in the Incarnate Christ that the universe was pre-formed.[114]

In contrast to Lapide's restricting the headship of Christ to his Church in his remarks on Colossians 1:18, Teilhard deliberately para-phrased this verse in his "Note on the Physical Union . . ." to read "caput creationis et ecclesiae"—Head of *Creation* and of the Church.[115] How is such a change to be justified?

In answering this question, it is worthwhile to note that Knaben-bauer, in his treatment of the latter part of Colossians 1:18 (". . . qui est principium, primogenitus ex mortuis, ut sit in omnibus ipse primatum tenens") appears to agree with Durand (Alfred Durand, 1858-1928?) that in a real sense, but one presently limited to the spiritual order, all the faithful are already risen in Christ. In this sense, many see the term *firstborn of the dead* as little different from *head of the Body of the Church.* But then the question arises concerning Co-lossians 1:17 as to why the *prōtotokos* (firstborn) of this verse should be understood only in a temporal sense if indeed Christ truly possesses a dignity and preeminence that must be understood also in terms of the "omnia in ipso condita sunt . . . et omnia per ipsum et in ipsum creata sunt" (verses 16, 17).[116] However, Knabenbauer himself understood the latter part of verse 18 as not applying to all of creation (in response to the question noted by Durand) but only to saved humanity, an in-

113. *C&E*, p. 41; *Oeuvres*, 10:54-55.
114. *S&C*, pp. 54-55; *Oeuvres*, 9:82-83.
115. Cf. *C&E*, p. 15; *Oeuvres*, 10:21.
116. Cf. Knabenbauer, *Cursus Scripturae Sacrae*, 9:300.

terpretation that would make verse 18 analogous, but not equivalent to verse 15.[117]

Although Teilhard never directly quoted the word *prōtotokos* or *primogenitus*, it may still be assumed that he would have seen the relationship between the "primogenitus omnis creaturae" of verse 15 and the "primogenitus ex mortuis" of verse 18 neither as equivalent nor as a mere literary parallelism born of an analogy between the preexistent word and the risen human nature of Christ. On the contrary, rather than quoting Colossians 1:15-19 on this point, he made a distinctic n between two phases of the same function, using Ephesians 4:10 to drive home his point:

> And then Christ rose again. We are often too inclined to regard the Resurrection as an isolated event in time, with an apologetical significance, as some small individual triumph over the tomb won in turn by Christ. It is something quite other and much greater than that. It is a tremendous cosmic event. It marks Christ's effective assumption of his function as the universal centre. Until that time, he was present in all things as a soul that is painfully gathering together its embryonic elements. Now he radiates over the whole universe as a consciousness and activity fully in control of themselves. After being baptised into the world, he has risen up from it. After sinking down to the depths of the earth, he has reached up to the heavens. "descendit et ascendit ut impleret omnia" (Eph. 4. 10).[118]

As to the meaning of the word *head* as it appears in Colossians 1:18, which Teilhard insisted on understanding as applying to creation as well as the Church, Knabenbauer, as might be expected, is much more cautious. But he was not merely "juridical" in his interpretation. He appears to have been convinced that St. Paul was speaking of a truly organic relationship of some sort between Christ and His Church, which Church is not merely the sum of its individual members, as might be possibly construed from the reading of verse 18 (*sōmatos, tēs ekklēsias*, "[the] body, the Church") but which in verse 24 of the same chapter is rendered more concretely (*sōmatos autou, ho estin he ekklēsia*, "his body, which is the Church.") Knabenbauer remained convinced that Christ's relationship was more than a simple domination or superiority over the Church. Instead, it should be understood in terms that represent a new level of that same activity described by ver-

---

117. Christus igitur est principium et fons vitae gratiae et vitae gloriae, idque similiter exprimitur: *primogenitus ex mortuis*, designatur iterum in primogenito praeter rationem temporis prioris dignitas et eminentia et dominium idque ratione mortuorum, id est totius generis humani, mortui per peccatum et debitum mortis corporalis solventis. Ut vocatur v.15 primogenitus ratione habita creaturae in universum, ita nunc ratione creaturae novae novique ordinis. (*Ibid.*)
118. "My Universe" (1924), in *S&C*, pp. 63-64; *Oeuvres*, 9:92.

ses 16 and 17, verses that contain those words which Teilhard so often quoted: "in quo omnia constant."[119]

Regarding verse 19 of this same passage of Colossians 1, as has been already seen, Teilhard began to make a few references to the "plénitude" and even to the "plérôme" as far back as 1920, but in a way definitely subsidiary to the concept of the Body of Christ, at least until 1924. But his characterization of the pleroma as "the consummated Mystical Body"[120] already showed a departure from the interpretation of Lapide or Knabenbauer. For the former this "plenitude" is simply "all perfection" or, as in Ephesians 1:23 "(the) complement, i.e., The Church, as the body, is the complement of Christ as head. . . ."[121] Knabenbauer was even more restrictive, refusing to see the ecclesial meaning in Colossians 1:19. However, in the context of Ephesians 1:23, Knabenbauer, after repeating his words about the nature of this ecclesial body stressed that this pleroma can be understood both actively as well as passively, as the phrase *tou panta en pasin plēroumenou* "fills all in all" indicates. Hence, it is more than just a case of the Church completing Christ; it is also of Christ completing his Church.[122]

Let us look at two other verses from Ephesians that Teilhard has cited. The first is Ephesians 1:10, which is rarely quoted in any direct form by Teilhard but from which his expression "celui qui consomme"[123] is taken, and which in another place is rendered by the word *céphaliser*.[124] According to Knabenbauer, the *anakephalaiōsasthai* of Ephesians 1:10 has been rendered variously as "ab initio (a capite) renoventur," (or thus in its Syriac equivalent); "instaurare" (Vulgate); "restaurare" (Vict. Ambr. variant); "ad initium revocare" (in Tertullian), and "recapitulare" (Irenaeus). Knabenbauer called attention to the fact that its immediate derivation is from *kephalaion*, not *kephalē*, thus indicating a sort of "summing up" rather than any direct translation as "cephalization" in Teilhard or the idea of "bringing to a head" as in Chrysostom.[125] Still, Knabenbauer did call special attention to the

119. Cf. Knabenbauer, 9:299. Caput autem non dicitur significatione praefecti aut domini aut solum superioris, sed ad naturalis capitis similitudinem Christus est caput mysticum ecclesiae, quia erga eam simili ratione se habet atque caput naturale ad corpus suum; quippe in cuius membra singuli ex capite, quod quasi sedes et centrum est omnium virium vitalium, virtus omnis diffundatur, ita ut ex capite membra habeant non tantum quo nutriantur, conserventur, crescant, agant, et etiam quo inter se ad unum corpus constituendum compingantur et uniantur (cf. Eph. 4, 15.16; 5, 23.29). Uti in antecedentibus designatus tamquam creator et conservator omnium (v. 16.17), ita nunc *ipse* (et non alius) declaratur esse etiam novae creaturae creator, seu auctor et effector reparationis et redemptionis omnium. (*Ibid.*)
120. See *C&E*, p. 16; *Oeuvres*, 10:22.
121. C. a Lapide, 18:78, 589.
122. Unde quemadmodum ecclesia Christum complet, ei tamquam capiti praebens membra, ita Christus sua ex parte ecclesiam complet omnibus membris illa subministrans quibus agere possint. (Knabenbauer, 9:65.)
123. "He who consummates"; cf. "Super-Humanity, Super-Christ, Super-charity" in *S&C*, p. 166; *Oeuvres*, 9:211.
124. "Cephalize"; cf. "The God of Evolution" in *C&E*, p. 242; Oeuvres, 10:290.
125. See Knabenbauer, 9:47.

prefix *ana* and its implication of the recall of the scattered elements of creation into their pristine order, much as is described in Colossians 1:20.[126] In this regard, Lapide gave special attention to the "recapitulation" theory of Irenaeus, who saw Christ as taking upon himself all nature through the "microcosmos" that is man.[127]

In the other verse from Ephesians (or verses, but usually in a shortened and combined form, the passage from 4:9-10: "Quid autem ascendit nisi quia et descendit . . . ut omnia impleret"), the "in inferiores partes terrae," which Teilhard generally left out, is according to Knabenbauer usually understood as referring to the same concept as the "descendit ad inferos" of the creed. But, according to many moderns, it may just as well refer to the descent to the earthbound condition involved in the Incarnation. Knabenbauer liked this interpretation, which is obviously jn the direction of Teilhard's use of the text.[128] But in Teilhard, even when the latter part of this combined verse is unstated, the emphasis remains on the "impleret," something that ties it closely with Ephesians 1:23, and, for that matter, with Ephesians 3:18, both of which are attestations of the "pleroma" in its active (i.e., transitive) sense.

Further, there is Teilhard's appeal to Philippians 3:21, which began the essay "Forma Christi" in 1918 and is repeated at least four more times in the course of his works.[129] Again the stress is on the energy or power (note again that Teilhard substituted the *dynamin* of Ephesians 3:20 for the *energeia* of Philippians 3:21) by which Christ draws all things to himself as to a pole. Elaborating this idea in his predictably literal way, Teilhard wrote of this power in the 1924 "My Universe" as being that with which ". . . the universe is physically impregnated"[130] and in *The Divine Milieu* of ". . . the physical and overmastering contact of Him whose appanage [i.e., lot] is to be able *omnia sibi subjicere*."[131] But what is even more surprising is Knabenbauer's linkage of this same text with the "omnia subjecta sunt ei" of 1 Corinthians 15:27 (by way of 1 Cor. 15:44, 53),[132] for it comes close to linking this text also with what for Teilhard was the ultimate of pleromic texts: "Ut Deus sit omnia in omnibus" ("That God might become all in all": 1 Cor. 15:28).

2. The Exegetical Positions of Prat

Of all the exegetes contemporary with Teilhard, Ferdinand Prat, S.J. (1857-1938), whose influence can be seen in the Encyclical of Pius XII,

126. See *ibid.*, p. 48.
127. Cf. Lapide, 19:592.
128. Cf. Knabenbauer, 9:116. For the relationship of this text to "kenosis" in Teilhard, see chap. 2 §D, 2, above.
129. Cf. *WTW*, p. 251; *Ecrits*, p. 337. Cf. also Appendix A.
130. *S&C*, p. 57; *Oeuvres*, 9:85-86.
131. *DM*, p. 103; *Oeuvres*, 4:152.
132. Cf. Knabenbauer, 9:259.

"Mystici Corporis,"[133] is probably the most important. Because Prat's opinions were known to Teilhard,[134] they will be considered in some detail.

Of particular interest is Prat's treatment of Colossians 1:15-19. In it he made a strict division between the "preexistent Christ" of verses 15-17 and the "incarnate Christ" of verses 18-20.[135] In a footnote, Prat had already admitted, consistent with his later statement, that verses 18-23 refer to Christ's human life, "or rather to his theandric life, as head of the Church and firstborn among the dead."[136] In the 1912 edition (however, not in the 1908 edition) Prat categorically states that " 'first-born of every creature' has nothing in common with 'first-born among the dead.' "[137] Yet he admitted the temptation to understand "all things have been created by him" (v. 15) and "all things have been created in him" (v. 16) as applying to the Word made man, a tendency warranted by Origen and Hippolytus in line with the prologue of St. John's Gospel. It is the same temptation to which Teilhard succumbed, but Prat felt constrained to resist it.[138]

In the chapter that follows his discussion of the Christology of the Epistle to the Colossians, Prat outlined his principal opinions concerning the theology of the "Mystical Body" in the writings of St. Paul. His first point was that this body is *distinct* from the natural body of Christ (although the natural body is part of the mystical body).[139]

In discussing the development of the concept in the course of Paul's writings, Prat concluded that the "head" or headship described in Colossians 1:18 is probably a simple "preeminence," because the same title in Colossians 2:10 is manifestly used without any relationship with "the allegory of the human body."[140] Prat believed that it is only in Ephesians that this headship is described in relationship to the body of

---

133. This encyclical, issued on June 29, 1943, was principally the work of S. Tromp, S.J., whose own book (the first of three) *Corpus Christi quod est Ecclesia* holds much the same exegetical interpretations as Prat.

134. The noted geologist George B. Barbour has recollected that in the autumn of 1949 Teilhard spoke of Prat's *Theology of St. Paul*. Cf. George B. Barbour, *In the Field with Teilhard de Chardin* (New York: Herder & Herder, 1965), p. 129.

135. This division appears most clearly in a footnote on p. 401 of the 1908 ed. and reappears on p. 347 of vol. 1 of the 1912 ed. (Cf. 1:291 of the English translation.)

136. *Ibid.* (1908 ed.), p. 398; (1912 ed.) 1:343; cf. Eng. ed., 1:287.

137. *Ibid.*, 1:347 (Eng., 1:290).

138. *Ibid.* (1908), p. 403; (1912), 1:349. "On serait donc tenté de rapporter ce titre au Verbe fait homme auquel tout l'univers est subordonné comme à l'envoyé et au mandataire de Dieu; mais, dans la phrase de saint Paul, le passage de la nature divine à la nature humaine ne s'étant pas produit encore, mieux vaut s'en tenir au sens le plus simple." (Eng., 1:292).

139. "Le Christ naturel, le Verbe incarné, le prêtre-victime du Calvaire, est une partie et la principale du Christ mystique; ce n'est pas le Christ mystique tout entier." *Ibid.* (1908), p. 419; (1912) 1:359 (Eng., 1:300).

140. *Ibid.* (1908), p. 421; (1912) 1:362; Eng., 1:302. Note that Prat generally used the term *allégorie* although the term *théorie* appeared in the 1908 edition (p. 425) to describe a "métaphore" in which the "analogie" of the human body is employed. Cf. *ibid.* (1908), p. 417; (1912) 1:360 (Eng., 1:302-3).

the Church, which Church is the "pleroma" in which Christ "se complète en tous."[141]

Finally, basing his argument on Ephesians 4:12-16, Prat in 1912 characterized the whole nature of the Mystical Body as being "d'une personnalité collective" (a phrase not used in the 1908 edition),[142] the growth of which must be understood primarily not in extensive but rather *intensive* terms.[143] As can readily be seen, the adjective *mystical*, so regularly used by Prat, refers primarily and almost exclusively to the realm of grace and special "charismae."

It is noteworthy that there is little or no discussion of the relationship of the texts of Romans and 1 Corinthians in Prat's treatment of the Mystical Body, except in the 1912 chapter on the Sacraments where he clearly began his discussion of the eucharist in St. Paul with the statement: "If baptism gives birth to the mystical body, the Eucharist feeds it and makes it grow."[144] But that such a strong statement is not made in the chapter on the Mystical Body as such would seem entirely consistent with his denial of any doctrine, at least on a Pauline basis, that would hold to a physical restoration of the universe. Thus, it would seem in Prat's interpretation of Paul that the sacramental Body of Christ has no real physical relationship to the Mystical Body except perhaps as a means to an end, but the end is of another order altogether.[145]

In Teilhard's favor it should be noted that Prat gave special attention to the Pauline phrases *in Christo* and *in Christo Jesu*. These words, so

141. Note that this last phrase is translated as "completes himself" in the English edition of Prat's work. (Cf. 1:303.) While the 1912 French ed. employs the above-quoted phrase, the 1908 ed. has "se complète entièrement en tous" (cf. p. 422). In an appendix giving alternate translations from the French, the English ed. suggests "fulfills himself" (cf. 2:480).

142. Cf. *ibid.* (1912), 1:368 (Eng., 1:306). In the 1908 ed. in which the latter part of this chapter is quite different, Prat was taken up more with the idea that: "Il nous apprend que toute l'humanité est destinée désormais à former une même famille dans la maison d'un commun Père, une même théocratie sous le sceptre d'un même roi." (cf. p. 427). However, this rather juridical point of departure into "Le Grand Mystère" was also balanced in the same chapter of the 1908 edition by a strong linkage of the "Mystical Body" with "la vigne allégorique de saint Jean," a more organic note that parallels Teilhard's early Johannine approach to the subject. (Cf. *ibid.*, pp. 424-25.)

143. Cf. *ibid.* (1912), 1:368 (Eng., 1:306).

144. *Ibid.* (1912), 2:317 (Eng. 2:263).

145. In his explanation of the term *mystical*, Prat makes it clear why he preferred to speak of the whole Pauline image as a "metaphor" that employs an "analogy": "C'est une réalité de l'ordre moral, mais une réalité véritable, puisqu'elle est le sujet d'attributions, de propriétés et de droits. Mystique n'est pas l'opposé de réel et il y a des réalités en dehors de ce qu'on palpe et de ce qu'on pèse. Il faut remarquer toutefois que cette réalité s'exprime par une métaphore, comme tous les objets immatériels et suprasensibles. . . ." *Ibid.* (1908), p. 417; (1912) 1:360; (Eng. 1:300-1).

Again, in 1912, Prat further elaborated this view: "Si on l'appelle *mystique* ce n'est pas pour dénier les propriétés réelles, c'est pour le distinguer du corps *physique* pris par le Verbe au sein de Marie, pour marquer son rapport avec ce que Paul nomme le *Mystère*, et surtout pour exprimer certaines propriétés *mystérieuses* de l'ordre surnaturel qui, parce qu'elles échappent à la vérification de l'expérience sensible, n'en sont pas moins des réalités." *Ibid.* (1912), 2:344 (Eng., 2:285).

often repeated by Teilhard, Prat deemed to be definitely connected with the Pauline doctrine of the Body of Christ, so much so that these phrases were for Paul, according to Prat, the means of constantly referring to that great mystery of Christ: "The Mystery *par excellence*" in which Christ is considered "as an element in which the life and activity of the Christian are exercized."[146]

Whether Prat's exegetical positions had any effect on Teilhard—positive or, as is much more likely, negative—must remain a matter of conjecture. But it would seem that, despite Prat's understanding of the Mystical Body as altogether based on the Pauline doctrine of the Redemption and the "second Adam," there is within his general understanding at least an orientation with which Teilhard could heartily agree: the idea of the up-to-now incompleteness of Christ:

> The head is helpless without the body; the organism can function normally only if it possesses every one of its organs. So Christ without the Church would be an incomplete being; incomplete as a Redeemer, since the grace which he possesses for the purpose of bestowing it would remain inactive; incomplete also as second Adam, because he is so only by his representative character; incomplete even as Christ, for Christ is also, in St Paul, a collective personality. Thus Christ "is completed in all in every way": in the members of the sacred hierarchy as Head of the Church, and in the humble faithful as Saviour and Sanctifier.[147]

But this understanding of the Redemption, as is clearly seen in Prat's estimation, remains confined to the supernatural order and has no direct connection with the consummation of the material universe as Teilhard understood it. Consequently, there seems to have been little incentive for Teilhard to attempt to grapple any further with an exegetical approach to the Pauline theory (or theories) of Redemption, which appears to hinge on a literal understanding of the Genesis account. However, Prat himself appears to have taken a slightly stand-offish attitude when he discussed Paul's literal adaptation of the Genesis account, inasmuch as it is not clear how Paul arrived at his own understanding concerning an "original sin," something that does not seem altogether clear in Genesis to begin with. Nevertheless, according to Prat, it is clear that the Epistle to the Romans is very definite in its

---

146. *Ibid.* (1912), 1:370 (Eng., 1:308-9). Prat also devotes a special note to this subject: Note T in the 1908 ed., pp. 434-36; Note M in the 1912 ed., 2:476-80; Eng., 2:391-95. Cf. also Oepke's remarks on *"en Christōi Iēsou, en Kyriōi* and Related Formulae" in Kittle's *Theological Dictionary of the N.T.* Among the meanings assigned to the formula Oepke states: "Comprehensively it denotes the *gathering of the many into one, Hen sōma esmen,* R. 12:5; *heis este,* Gl. 3:28; Eph. 3:21f.; *ekklesia(i),* Gl. 1:22; 1 Th. 1:1; 2; 14; *of creation,* Col. 1:16f.; *of the summing up of the whole cosmos,* Eph. 1:10. . . ." (Grand Rapids: Erdmans, 1964), 2:54. (Emphasis added.)

147. *Ibid* (Eng.), 2:283-84; Fr. (1912), 2:342.

presentation of original sin and "real justice."[148] His opinions open the
way to less literal understandings of the problem of original sin in that
he concludes that St. Paul was not attempting to prove the existence of
original sin, but was merely making use of the universality of the Fall
(as commonly understood and accepted on the testimony of the Scriptures) to stress the universality of the Redemption.[149] But on the other
hand, in his analysis of the theme of the two Adams, Prat (drawing on
1 Cor. 15:44-49) stated that for St. Paul

> Adam and Christ summarize the two periods of humanity; they do
> not merely symbolize them, they realize them in their person by a
> mysterious identification.[150]

While this "summing up" of humanity may be quite in line with
what Teilhard envisioned regarding Christ in virtue of the Redemption,
in Teilhard's opinion to equate this too closely with the idea of a first
Adam who mysteriously summarizes unredeemed humanity would be
to jeopardize the truly fundamental doctrine of the Christian faith:

> There are times when one almost despairs of being able to disen-
> tangle Catholic dogmas from the geocentrism in the framework of
> which they were born. And yet one thing in the Catholic creed is
> more certain than anything: that there is a Christ "*in quo omnia
> constant.*" All secondary beliefs will have to give way, if necessary,
> to this fundamental article. Christ is all or nothing.[151]

For that matter, Teilhard would also appear to be calling not only for
the rejection of the "traditional" conceptualization of the doctrine of
original sin, but also for serious reconsideration of the almost exclusive
emphasis of past theology on the redemptive mission of Christ and to
some extent even suggesting that St. Paul's own preoccupation with
man's Fall and this restoration might be deemphasized as well. Yet, at
no point does Teilhard attempt to suggest that God might have become
man irrespective of man's need for redemption.[152] On the contrary,
Christ's function in the universe is, according to Teilhard, precisely to

148. "Justice réelle"; cf. *ibid.* (1912), 1:260 (Eng., 1:218); also *ibid.* (1908) n. M, pp.
303-7; (1912), Appendix G, 1:514-18 (Eng., 1:438-42). The 1908 note and 1912 appendix are not identical.
149. Cf. *ibid.* (1912), 1:255 (Eng., 1:214).
150. *Ibid.* (1912), 2:203 (Eng., 2:171).
151. "Fall, Redemption, and Geocentrism" (1920) in *C&E*, p. 44; *Oeuvres*, 10:57.
152. Cf. Prat (1912) 2:212, n.1 (Eng., 2:177). Prat denied that there is anything in Paul
that would indicate any other motive for the Incarnation other than the redemption.
Somewhat less credibly, Prat claimed that none of the Church Fathers assign any
other motive for the Incarnation, and claims that St. Thomas held the same (S.T.
IIIa, qu. I, art 3). However, he [Prat] neglects to cite St. Thomas's admission of the
Incarnation as a kind of completion to God's creative act. Cf. St. Thomas's *Compendium Theologiae*, Part II, chap. 201. Likewise, that Scotus's speculations in this direction represent a Western revival of a long-neglected Eastern tradition is neglected by Prat. Cf. Gabriel M. Allegra, *My Conversations with Teilhard de Chardin
on the Primacy of Christ* (Chicago: Franciscan Herald Press), 1970.

bring about unity in the face of that disunity of which man's sin is the most culpable element. But Teilhard saw this primarily as an evolutive function of Christ, of which human redemption is only a part (albeit the most important part).

Speaking of God's desire to share his being, being that outside of God is essentially *multitude*, Teilhard wrote in his 1920 "Note on the Modes of Divine Action in the Universe":

> 1. First of all, it appears contradictory (to the nature of partici-pated being) to imagine God creating an *isolated* thing. Only one being can exist in isolation: *Ens a se* (Being which exists only in it-self). Everything which is not God is essentially multitude—multitude organized in itself, and multitude organizing around it-self. If God, then, is to *make a soul*, there is only one way open to his power: *to create a world*. . . . For now at last we can see that if God wished to have Christ, to launch a complete universe and scat-ter life with a lavish hand was no more than he was obliged to do.[153]

What Teilhard was saying in such passages did not come into full light until three years later, in his "Pantheism and Christianity," but it is in the light of this "fundamental religious tendency" (i.e., pantheism) that the Redemption must be understood. Hence, in 1933, in his "Christology and Evolution," he proclaimed:

> My profound conviction, born of the experience of a life spent simultaneously in the heart of the Gentile world and in that of the Church, is that at this very moment we have reached a delicate point of balance at which a readjustment is essential. It could not, in fact, be otherwise: our Christology is still expressed in exactly the same terms as those which, three centuries ago, could satisfy men whose outlook on the cosmos it is now physically impossible for us to accept.[154]

The principal obstacle to this overdue renewal of Christology is, with-out a doubt as far as Teilhard was concerned, the doctrine of original sin, and the problem with this doctrine is not so much the question of the historicity of Adam and Eve and such related issues, but something much more basic in our thinking:

> To my mind, the answer is that if the dogma of original sin is con-stricting and debilitating it is simply because, as now expressed, it represents a survival of obsolete static views into our now evolution-ary way of thinking. Fundamentally, in fact, the idea of Fall is no more than an attempt to explain evil in a fixed universe.[155]

153. *C&E*, p. 32; *Oeuvres*, 10:42-43.
154. *C&E*, p. 77; *Oeuvres*, 10:96.
155. *C&E*, p. 80; *Oeuvres*, 10:99.

In spite of the subtle distinctions of the theologians, it is a matter *of fact* that Christianity has developed under the overriding impression that all the evil around us was *born from an initial transgression*. So far as dogma is concerned, we are still living in the atmosphere of a universe in which what matters most is reparation and expiation.[156]

To recast the doctrine of the Redemption, not to eliminate it, is what Teilhard had in mind. But it must first be understood that the meaning of evil, and the idea of an original Fall, as "a *secondary* distortion of the world . . . in a universe which is presumed to have issued *fully formed* from the hand of God,"[157] simply no longer fits:

> In these circumstances, evil is not an unforeseen accident in the universe. It is an enemy, a shadow which God inevitably produces simply by the fact that he decides on creation. New being, launched into existence and not yet completely assimilated into unity, is a dangerous thing, bringing with it pain and oddity.[158]

> Christ, it is true, is still he who bears the sins of the world; moral evil is in some mysterious way paid for by suffering. But, even more essentially, Christ is he who structurally in himself, and for all of us, overcomes the resistance to unification offered by the multiple, resistance to the rise of spirit inherent in matter. Christ is he who bears the burden, constructionally inevitable, of every sort of creation. He is the symbol and the sign-in-action of progress. The complete and definitive meaning of redemption is *no longer only* to expiate: it is to surmount and conquer.[159]

The need for a total reevaluation of the problem of evil and its supposed origin in the Genesis-Pauline conception of original sin may have caused Teilhard, in despairing of an answer that could be provided by biblical exegetes, to despair of converting theologians to a more "physical" understanding of the Body of Christ. The connection between this double rejection of the then long-standing tradition was certainly more than a case of a psychologically compounded defiance. May not the definitive rejection of all "juridical" interpretations of the "Mystical" Body of Christ and the renunciation of further efforts to convert the

---

156. *C&E*, p. 81; *Oeuvres*, 10:100.
157. *C&E*, 80; *Oeuvres*, 10:99.
158. *C&E*, p. 84; *Oeuvres*, 10:103. To the above Teilhard added this footnote by way of argument:

> Is not this precisely the truth adumbrated in all the myths in which the ideas of birth and evil are associated? We may say that all that would be needed to modernize Christology would be to clarify the notion of *sin*, as used in theological and liturgical formulas, by that of *progress*: in short, to explain smoke by fire. That is not asking much, surely? (*Ibid*.)

159. *C&E*, p. 85; *Oeuvres*, 10:104.

theologians that figures in his 1924 "My Universe" have been logically connected with his 1922 rejection of the common understanding of the doctrine of original sin? Would not such an "extrinsicist" explanation of the problem of evil (i.e., evil, death, and suffering as imposed on an otherwise finished and perfect universe through the "accident" of mankind's Fall) also lead to an extrinsic notion of grace, which in turn would logically lead to an equally extrinsic (in this case "juridical") understanding of the relationship of Christ as Head in respect to his Body, thus restricting the potential extension of his Body to redeemed "souls" rather than to fully cosmic dimensions?[160]

Although such a direct connection between the Pauline mode of understanding evil and sin and the scholastic concept of grace and the subsequent common interpretation of the "Mystical Body" seems never to have been traced in such negative terms by Teilhard, the sequence seems logical enough even though he may have confronted it in reverse order. While none of his fulminations against "Aristotelianism" or scholastic theology blame this extrinsicism directly on the influence of the Bible as such, neither did he believe that modern biblical exegesis would ever be capable of correcting, at least by itself, this unfortunate situation in theology, in Christology in particular. For underneath the metaphysical position of the scholastics lie cosmological presuppositions that are out of touch with reality;[161] and likewise, despite its eschatological dynamism, there were in the Redemption theology of St. Paul certain cosmological presuppositions that render a total acceptance by modern man impossible.

3. More Recent Exegesis on "The Body of Christ"

Foremost among recent Catholic exegetes to wrestle with the Pauline concept of the Body of Christ are Lucien Cerfaux and Pierre Benoît. As Joseph T. Culliton[162] pointed out, the positions of theologian E. Mersch and exegete A. B. Allo differed but little from the earlier views of F. Prat. Like Prat, both distinguished clearly between the risen body of Christ and the "Body" of the Church that is formed by way of sacramental participation "in Christo." Likewise, both saw a clear distinction based on the supposed division of Colos-

160. Indeed, it is in §B (Part II) of the 1924 "Mon Univers," where Teilhard treated the subject of "L'Influence du Christ-Oméga: L'Elément universel," that Teilhard criticized the "infra-substantiel" understanding of grace (*Oeuvres*, 9:86; *S&C*, p. 58). It is noteworthy that this section was placed between §A of Part II, where he rejected the "juridical" understanding of the Body of Christ, and §C of Part II, where he took up the matter of Redemption and the problem of evil.
161. Cf. "Pour y voir clair" (1950), where Teilhard repeated his criticism of the scholastic understanding of grace as "un simple 'accident'" and saw this as being consonant with the fact "qu'à l'intérieur d'une conception aristotélicienne de l'Univers il est simplement impossible à aucune véritable vision universaliste de se développer à l'aise. (*Oeuvres*, 7:234-35; *AE*, p. 225.)
162. "Lucien Cerfaux's Contribution Concerning 'The Body of Christ'" in *CBQ* 29 (1967): 41-59.

sians 1:15-17 from 18-20—between Christ as Lord of the Cosmos and
Christ as Head of the Church. Similarly, they would clearly distinguish
the "pleroma" in the sense of the fullness of divinity in Christ (Col.
1:19) from the "pleroma" in the sense of the Church as the "complement" of Christ, filled with his graces (Eph. 1:23). In this they differ
slightly from Prat, who sees Col. 1:19 as a fullness of graces accruing to
the risen Christ.[163] But while Mersch warns against a too-easy identification between the mystical Christ and the Church, Allo tends toward
such an identification, to be understood in the sense of a "collective
Christ."[164]

While Cerfaux, in his later work *Christ in the Theology of St.
Paul*,[165] makes a similar division between the creative activity of Christ
and his salvific activity (Col. 1:15-16 vs. 18b-19, verses 17-18a being
transitional), he rejects the tendency to see in Ephesians 1:10f. and
22f., as some do, any extension of the pleroma to the cosmos and
beyond.[166] This position, however, does not militate against that of his
earlier work, *The Church in the Theology of St. Paul*,[167] the first edition of which was published shortly before the appearance of the Encyclical "Mystici Corporis" and which differs radically in some aspects
from that of the encyclical. The basic conclusion, based on Cerfaux's
painstaking reconstruction of the development of the concept of the
Body of Christ in St. Paul's thought, is that there is no basis for seeing
in Paul's thought the existence of a "Mystical Body" that is distinct
from the real body of Christ or from Christ as a person.[168]

The reason, parodixically enough, is that there are actually two distinct images of the body in the Pauline writings: the earliest is contained in the major epistles, the mortal body of Christ to which Christians are united in the Eucharist; the later is that Body described in the
captivity epistles—the risen body of Christ. True, according to Cer-

163. Regarding the very complex question as to the origin of Col. 1:15-20, which has of
    late generally been considered to have been a preexisting liturgical hymn incorpo-
    rated by Paul into his Epistle, but probably altered by him to suit his purposes, the
    reader is referred to the articles of James M. Robinson, "A Formal Analysis of Col.
    1:15-20" in *The Journal of Biblical Literature* 76 (1957): 270-87, and of Bruce Vaw-
    ter, "The Colossians Hymn" in *CBQ* 33 (1971): 62-81.
164. Cf. Culliton, pp. 42-43.
165. *Le Christ dans la Théologie de S. Paul*, (Paris: Editions du Cerf), 1951, pp. 298-301;
    Christ in the Theology of St. Paul (New York: Herder, 1959), pp. 397-400.
166. *Ibid.*, p. 322 (Eng., p. 428).
167. *La Théologie de l'Eglise suivant Saint Paul* (Paris: Editions du Cerf), 1942: *The
    Church in the Theology of St. Paul* (New York: Herder & Herder, 1959).
168. Thus we cannot say: "In your Christian life you are like a human body," for mysti-
    cism goes beyond the content of this formula. Neither can we say: "You are *the
    body* of Christ" (with the definite article so that we have *to sōma tou Christou*),
    thinking directly and exclusively of the physical body or the body in the Eucharist,
    for this mode of expression breaks the logical connection with the development of
    the comparison. Much less can we say: "You are *the body* of Christ," thinking of a
    mystical Christ as distinct from Christ as a person: here again we should be break-
    ing the connection, and we should be giving to the word *sōma* a meaning which it
    can never admit. And so it remains for us to translate: "You are a body, a body
    which is that of Christ (dependent on him, and in which his life flows)."
    (*Ibid.*, p. 277: 3rd. French ed., p. 233).

faux, the first, the essentially sacramental image, provides the basis for a "simile" (Cerfaux denies that it is an allegory) in which the Church is described in terms of the relationship of one member to another. But on the whole this first body image of the great epistles is to some extent incompatible with that of the epistles of the captivity, in which the Church is identified with the glorious and risen person of Christ.[169]

The basis for this denial of a mystical Christ as apart from Christians sharing a "mystical identity" `with the person of Christ appears to be rooted in exegetical considerations based on the great epistles. Here Cerfaux, agreeing with Huby, denies that the word *Christ* can be understood in any "collective" sense.[170] Thus after reviewing many exegetical opinions, Cerfaux concludes:

> For similar reasons we refuse to see in *sōma* the meaning of "social body." The Church is a body only by way of allusion to the principle of unity which is the body of Christ, and *sōma* without anything to which it is referred, and even more *hen sōma*, means a human body or the body of Christ, but always a physical person.[171]

What then of the "body" described in the epistles of the captivity? Cerfaux appears to understand this body primarily in terms of the "pleroma," which "plenitude" is to be understood in the passive sense, yet dynamically, as being the grace which flows from Christ to his members, just as he himself possesses the fullness of divinity "corporaliter" in his risen body.[172]

Consequently, viewed in terms of the pleroma as thus passively understood in the order of grace, the headship of Christ, as introduced in Ephesians, is seen first (Eph. 1:22f.) as an extension of the simile used in the great epistles and then in a more juridical sense in the husband-wife comparison of Ephesians 5:23f. Cerfaux believes that this same juridical or dominative understanding takes on "cosmic" overtones in Colossians, but somewhat in the "political" sense of the body image as found in Stoic thought.[173] Understood in this manner, Cerfaux rejects the interpretation of P. Allo, whose proposed view of the Church in pleromic terms in his article "L'évolution' de l'évangile de Paul" would have met with Teilhard's enthusiastic approval had he read it:

> the concept of the Church is capable of prodigious enlargement, even to the point of becoming cosmic, embracing spiritual and material creation in its totality.[174]

169. Cf. *ibid.*, pp. 334-35; French ed., pp. 281-82. Cerfaux here uses the phrase "*partiellement inconciliables.*"
170. Cf. *ibid.*, p. 269; French ed., pp. 228-29, n.2.
171. *Ibid.*, p. 274; French ed., p. 232.
172. Cf. *ibid.*, pp. 322-25; French ed., pp. 272-75.
173. Cf. *ibid.*, p. 331; French ed., p. 279.
174. As quoted by Cerfaux (*ibid.*, [Fr.] p. 285) from *Vivre et Penser*, ler série (1941), p. 166. (My translation.)

Instead, citing Huby's opinion concerning Colossians 2:10, Cerfaux chooses to see no connection between this verse and the element of vital influx into the body suggested by Colossians 1:18. Rather, Cerfaux interprets Christ's supereminence over "the principalities and powers" to be something of an entirely different order.[175] Thus, while he judges the connection between the risen body of Christ and the body that is his Church as being of the "mystical" order,[176] no real connection can be construed between Christ as head of the Church and Christ as Lord of creation (much less as "head of creation" as Teilhard would have it).[177]

Nevertheless, Cerfaux's work may be considered favorable to Teilhard's insights in several ways, notably in his overall insistence that there is no such "mystical" Body of Christ apart from the risen body of Christ, and that the foundation of this mystical identification between the Church and Christ's risen body is in the Christian's sacramental sharing in the real body of Christ. Still, the general import of Cerfaux's interpretation would discourage Teilhard's idea of a "Cosmic" Body of Christ in any sense. While Cerfaux believed that the key to our understanding of the Pauline doctrine of the Body of Christ lies in our understanding of the pleroma, this pleroma is understood strictly on the supernatural plane. With Teilhard, on the contrary, it was just the opposite: the pleroma is to be understood as an extension of the Body of Christ, historically incarnate in Jesus Christ, sacramentally shared by the faithful, and becoming progressively coextensive in time and space through the power of the Resurrection.

In the light of this basic difference between the two, Teilhard broke his usual silence about biblical exegetes to complain of Cerfaux by name.[178]

The other principal Catholic exegete whose understanding of the Body of Christ must be given attention is Père Pierre Benoît, O.P. Of all current exegetes, Benoît in the analysis in his long article "Corps, Tête et Plérôme dans les Epîtres de la captivité"[179] comes perhaps closer than anyone else to vindicating Teilhard's views. Rejecting both the theory of a Stoic origin (Wickenhauser and J. Dupont) or that of even a partly Gnostic origin (H. Schlier and E. Käsemann) as untenable, Benoît finds the concept of the Body of Christ in St. Paul growing

175. *Ibid.*, pp. 341-42; French ed., p. 286.
176. Cf. *ibid.*, p. 343; French ed., p. 287.
177. In his earlier *Christ in the Theology of St. Paul*, Cerfaux indicates that the intermediate verses 17-18a of the Colossians hymn only indicate the transition from the order of creation to the order of salvation: "Primacy in creation was a preparation for a primacy in the order of salvation." (P. 400; cf. French ed., pp. 299-300.)
178. Je suis resté stupéfait de la minimisation que Cerfaux (qui est-il?) fait subir à la notion de Plérôme! Très instructif de se rendre compte qu'un certain Christianisme réput´ "avancé" en est encore là!
   Remark from a letter of Teilhard to Jeanne Mortier, March 21, 1951. *TA*, Correspondence Teilhard-Mortier, #58.
179. In *Revue Biblique* #63 (1956) pp. 5-44 and republished in his collection *Exégèse et théologie*, 2 (Paris: Editions du Cerf, 1961), pp. 107-53.

naturally out of a sacramental understanding of the union between Christ and the Christian, thus rejecting the concept of a mystical union apart from the sacramental one.[180] But since this basic position is taken from the first letter to the Corinthians, Benoît believes that there is some development in Paul's thought that must be accounted for as it appears in the captivity epistles.

This development centers on the understanding of "Body" as it appears in the captivity epistles, where, as Benoît carefully draws out, the "grand réalisme" of the concept of the physical union of the Christian with Christ in the great epistles gradually becomes expanded in the captivity epistles to the point where it embraces "ultimately, in an indirect fashion, the whole Cosmos."[181] The source of these ideas is to be found, he says, in two related Old Testament concepts, the first being that of the individual who "represents" (or contains within himself?) the collectivity and is by that fact a sort of "corporate personality"[182] (a concept revived by Paul in the New Testament, particularly under his figure of Christ as the "new Adam"), and, second, the basic Hebrew concept of the person, which idea transcends the body-soul dualism of Greek thought and, particularly in its eschatological dimensions, involves a great deal more than just the individual organism.[183]

But the precise relationship between the risen Christ and his extended body is not one simple identification.[184] Benoît makes this clear in his treatment of the concept of Christ as "Head." There are, according to him, two factors that account for this distinction. The first is the obvious gap that exists between the condition of Christ's members on earth and Christ's own personal glorified state in heaven.[185] Paul's is not a simple, realized eschatology. The second reason has to do with the evolution of Paul's understanding of Christ as head in relation to

180. ". . . Je doute que Paul ait jamais pensé à une "union mystique" du chrétien au Christ autrement que sous la forme d'une union physique (sacramentelle) du corps du chrétien au corps individuel du Christ." *Ibid.*, in *Exégèse et Théologie*, 2:109.
181. *Ibid.*, 2:114-15 (my translation).
182. Benoît (*ibid.*, p. 122) uses the English expression "corporate personality" as taken from T. W. Manson's *The Servant-Messiah* (Cambridge, n.p., 1951). However, the source of much of this line of thinking seems to have been H. Wheeler Robinson's *Corporate Personality in Ancient Israel* (Philadelphia: Fortress Press, 1965). A year after Manson's book, however, J. A. T. Robinson's *The Body* (London: S.C.M., 1952) was published, which, following the line suggested by the earlier Robinson (H. W.) and others, maintains: ". . . that when Paul took the term *sōma* and applied it to the Church, what it must have conveyed to him and his readers was (to employ a distinction which itself would have surprised him) something *not corporate but corporal.* . . . The body that he has in mind is as concrete and as singular as the body of the Incarnation. His underlying conception is not a suprapersonal collective, but of a specific personal organism" (pp. 50-51). Benoît, however, in an article evaluating J. A. T. Robinson's book, does have reservations about the latter's understanding of the "pleroma," among other things, with relationship to this body. (Cf. *Exégèse et Théologie*, 2:169.)
183. Benoît, 2:122-23.
184. Cf. *ibid.*, 2:128.
185. Cf. *ibid.*, 2:129.

the circumstances surrounding the writing of the epistle to the Colossians.[186] Without going into these, let it merely be said that Paul first uses the term *head* to express Christ's domination over the various "demonic" powers of the universe. This is entirely in consonance with the Hebraic metaphoric use of the word *resh* (head) and is already found in 1 Corinthians 11:3f., where the same understanding of headship is applied thus: ". . . Christ is the head of every man, man is the head of woman, and God is the head of Christ" (*Jerusalem Bible* trans.).[187] But this use of *head* in Colossians becomes quite naturally expanded in Ephesians to a more dynamic notion regarding the relationship of Christ as head to his body, the Church. This new development, according to Benoît, is derived from Greek (esp. medical), rather than Hebrew concepts.[188]

The great advantage of his new development in Paul's thought leads, naturally, into his revival of another ancient Hebrew idiom, that of God's people as "bride" or "spouse," for it is here in Ephesians (Eph. 5:22-32) that the two images of Christ as head of his Church and as bridegroom combine in a dynamic way and, rather than being contradictory, become fully complementary in the most advantageous and fully biblical way, affirming both the identity and the distinction between the risen Christ and his Church.[189]

But does not this double meaning of "head," thus unified in Ephesians in Paul's doctrine concerning the Church, naturally raise the question as to whether he is not similarly extending this same double understanding (of domination and of organic relationship) to the cosmos as a whole? According to Benoît, this is not the case. Aside from the necessity of finding Stoic ideas in such a concept (a source that Benoît has already ruled out regarding the Church as a social body), it contradicts what is manifestly the whole basis of the Pauline understanding of the physical extension of Christ in his members, this basis being primarily that of a sacramental union. Far from being extendable directly to the rest of creation, it is, in fact, not extended even to the unsaved portion of humanity, but only to those who are baptized and who partake in the Eucharistic Body of Christ. But this is not to say that Christ's influence is not extended indirectly to all creation, even so far as to include the "cosmic forces." But this extension is not in any sense part of his body; only the "new man" who has "put on Christ"

186. Cf. *ibid.*, 2:132.
187. Cf. Benoît, *ibid.*, 2:131.
188. Cf. *ibid.*, 2:133. According to Benoît, this concept of head as the vital principle, mover, etc. of the body would, in Hebrew terminology, be the properties of the "heart."
189. Cf. *ibid.*, 2:134. Cf. also the excellent article of Paul Andriessen, "La nouvelle Eve, corps du nouvel Adam" in *Recherches Biblique* 7 (Paris, Bruges, 1964): pp. 87-109.
   Andriessen sums up these complementary images in the traditional "two in one flesh" concept of marriage. "Le Christ et l'Eglise sont pour l'Apôtre deux personnes, ou, ce qui pour lui revient au même, deux corps qui sont unis ensemble dans un corps conjugal" (p. 109).

through participation in his death and Resurrection can lay claim to that.[190]

However, further on, in his discussion of the pleroma, Benoît refuses to see a strict division between the two strophes of Colossians 1:15-19 that would in any way assign the first part to the Divine Word and the second part to the human nature of Christ. Rather, somewhat like Cerfaux, the subject of the whole hymn is the "Person of Jesus" in his dual role of "créateur et recréateur."[191] But, as he leads up to this subject, Benoît treats Colossians 2:10 more positively than does Cerfaux, seeing in Christ's role as head of the angelic and cosmic powers something indirectly connected with his redemptive role, at least in the sense that the powers are somehow included in the universal reconciliation, even if by way of subjection.[192]

Accordingly, Benoît sees something of a parallel relationship between Christ as head of the Church and head of creation, a parallel better expressed in the mysterious "recapitulation" of Ephesians 1:10.[193]

Despite this somewhat more positive note, Benoît's exegesis of the concept of the Body of Christ in St. Paul's epistles is, at least in its conclusions, substantially the same as Cerfaux's.[194]

4. Conclusion

Consideration of the opinions of these two contemporary authorities on the thought of St. Paul indicates that, despite their overall insist-

190. "Le 'Corps du Christ' reste toujours pour lui limité au groupe des *hommes* sauvés, qui est l'Eglise; pour évoquer l'extension de l'oeuvre du Christ, il use d'un autre terme, celui de "Plérôme. . . . Il ne doit pas cette expression à la métaphore stoïcienne, qui de soi permettrait un élargissement cosmique; il la doit à sa conception proprement chrétienne de l'union physique des corps des chrétiens au corps mort et ressuscité du Christ par le moyen des sacrements. Dans cet horizon de pensée, il n'y a pas de place dans le Corps du Christ pour d'autre êtres que pour les hommes sauvés. . . ." (Benoît, 2:136.)
191. Cf. *ibid.*, 2:141.
192. "A ce titre, les Puissances cosmiques ou angéliques sont certainement intéressées à la rédemption du Christ. Mais c'est à titre indirect. Elles ne font pas partie du Corps. . . . Elles sont bien comprises dans la "réconciliation" universelle de Col. I.20, mais il est permis de penser que ce terme vise proprement le salut de l'humanité (cf. v.22 et II Cor., V, 18-20; Rom., V, 10s.; XI, 15) et ne s'applique au cadre cosmique que dans un sens large impliquant le retour à l'ordre et n'excluant pas la réduction à l'impuissance des éléments hostiles." (*Ibid.*, 2: 137-38.)
193. "A ce titre, le parallèle Eph., I, 10, avec son *anakephalaiōsasthai* est plus expressif et plus exact: tout doit être ramené sous le Christ comme sous un Chef unique, chef reconnu et même tête nourricière pour les uns, chef imposé de force pour les autres." (*Ibid.*, 2:138.)
194. Benoît (*ibid.*, 2:115, n.2) nevertheless expresses his basic agreement with the propriety of the term *mystical* as used in the 1943 encyclical, as conditioned by the historical development of the term, and the need to express something midway between a gross misinterpretation of the word *physical* (as we usually take it) and a mere "moral" understanding of the Body of Christ. In this sense, Benoît would be apparently asking for an understanding of the word *mystical* that would imply something of the same concept as Teilhard's use of the word *physical* in the wider, classical sense of "organic." However, it would seem that unfortunately the gap cannot quite be closed between the two terms, even when stripped of their popularly misconceived meanings, because there is still quite a difference between a "mystical"

ence that the Body of Christ be understood not so much in terms of a "mystical Body" apart from the real body of Christ, which is sacramentally shared and thus mystically identified with the Church, nevertheless their general import would severely limit Teilhard's claim to see this body understood as somehow "coextensive" with all of creation. Thus, despite Benoît's more positive linking of the pleroma with the *body-Head* themes, the "Body of Christ which is the Church" appears to stand in a completely different order from the "pleroma" in St. Paul's writing, even though it is the same "plenitude of divinity" that overflows in different ways to establish them in a parallel order of relationship.

For Teilhard, even though he had long since given up his attempt to express this relationship in terms of the Body of Christ—which he saw not as a parallel relationship in the orders of nature and grace, but as a continuum of divine influx into all orders of existence—the prevailing views of the pleroma would likewise present similar problems. For what lay at the heart of this division of the Body of Christ (as others saw it) from the pleroma (as he now sought to understand it) was not so much the division of grace from nature, but even more basically, the separation of matter from spirit. It is this dualism in our concept of reality, as well as in the verbal expression of St. Paul, that was at the root of Teilhard's failure to compete successfully with the prevailing view of the mystical Body of Christ. Ultimately it proves to be the principal obstacle, hidden beneath all others, to adequate comprehension of Teilhard's major expression of the unity of the universe in Christ—the pleroma.

organism existing strictly in the order of a spiritually understood "grace" and an organism that finds its root in the sharing of a transformed, but still physically real body.

5

The Pleroma

A. THE DEVELOPMENT OF THE PLEROMIC CONCEPT IN THE WRITINGS OF TEILHARD DE CHARDIN

If "Christogenesis" is the underlying theme of Teilhard's understanding of Scripture (as well as of all reality, theologically speaking), then the concept of the pleroma represents the maturation point not only of his Christology but of all of his grand synthesis. The appearance of this concept in Teilhard's writings is gradual. True, the word appeared in his writings as early as 1919, but the fully developed meaning that was to emerge in his mature thought took at least another five years to reach the point where it began "to stand on its own feet." Indeed, the emergence of this concept was like a birth, with its preliminary stages of conception and gestation; and even after its parturition, a relatively long period remained when its life was dependent on the earlier theological concepts from which it took its origin.

1. *Early Phases (1916-1924)*

Even before the first appearance of the word *pleroma* in Teilhard's writings, there are sure indications of what was to come. Groping as his first expression may have been, Teilhard was manifestly in love with the concept of a universal Christ, even before he could seize upon a single name to express it. In his 1916 "Cosmic Life," the idea quickly rose to the surface, in what amounted to one of his earliest and boldest expressions of his "panchristic" tendencies, phrased in what he would later describe as his "physicist" understanding of the Body of Christ. The passage in question merits a second examination:

Souls, however, are not a group of isolated monads. As the "cosmic view" specifically shows us, they make up one single whole with the universe, consolidated by life and matter. Christ, therefore, cannot confine his body to some periphery drawn within things; though he came primarily, and in fact exclusively, for souls, he could bring them together and give them life only by assuming and animating, with them, all the rest of the world; through his Incarnation he entered not only into mankind but also into the universe that bears mankind—and this he did, not simply in the capacity of an element associated with it, but with the dignity and function of directive principle, of centre upon which every form of love and every affinity converge. Mysterious and vast though the mystical Body already be, it does not, accordingly, exhaust the immense and bountiful integrity of the Word made Flesh. Christ has a *cosmic Body* that extends throughout the whole universe: such is the final proposition to be borne in mind. *"Qui potest capere, capiat."*[1]

And again, in rapid succession on the following pages:

The Incarnation is a making new, a restoration, of *all* the universe's forces and powers; Christ is the Instrument, the Centre, the End, of the *whole* of animate and material creation; through Him, *everything* is created, sanctified, and vivified.[2]

And since Christ was born, and ceased to grow, and died, *everything has continued in motion because he has not yet attained the fullness of his form.*[3]

But not until 1918, in his first "Mon Univers," did the word that in French perhaps best translates *pleroma* appear in such a context; having spoken already of *"a certain* coextension of Christ with the Universe,"* Teilhard asserted his faith "in the 'Plénitude' of Christ"[4] and again, reasserting "The fundamental vision *of Christ in all Things*,"[5] he went on to say in the passage that follows closely:

$- o =$ the natural goal (x) of human (and cosmic) progress; $- \omega =$ the supernatural goal of the Kingdom of God (the *plenitude* of Christ).[6]

While in neither of the above cases was "plénitude" marked off by Teilhard with any particular signs of emphasis, they certainly appear to be the first expression in Teilhard of the Pauline pleroma. But, after speaking once in the 1918 "The Priest" of "the plenitude of your incarnate word"[7] he added with distinct emphasis:

1. *WTW*, pp. 57-58; *Ecrits*, p. 47.
2. *WTW*, p. 58; *Ecrits*, p. 48.
3. *WTW*, p. 59; *Ecrits*, p. 48.
4. *Ecrits*, pp. 272-73, (my translation.)
5. *Ibid.*, p. 273.
6. *Ibid.*, p. 274. (Emphasis added.)
7. *WTW*, p. 206; *Ecrits*, p. 286.

> You who are yourself the *plenitudo Entis creati*, the fulness of created being, you, Jesus, are also the *plenitudo entis mei*, the fulness of my own personal being, and of all living creatures who accept your dominion.[8]

Having distinguished these two plenitudes, he went on to describe a third:

> a third plenitude is added to the other two. In a very real sense, Lord Jesus, you are the *plenitudo entium*, the full assemblage of all beings who shelter, and meet, and are for ever united, within the mystical bonds of your body.[9]

After having so spoken, he then employed the full Pauline terminology:

> Life and death, unity and plurality, element and totality, possession and quest, being and becoming . . . such is the *Pleroma* of the world and of Christ.[10]

And again, in the concluding section of this same essay, which deals with "The Apostolate," he affirmed:

> If men could only see that in each one of them there is an element of the *Pleroma*, would not that, Lord, effect the reconciliation between God and our age? If only they could understand that, with all its natural richness and its massive reality, the universe can find fulfilment only in Christ; and that Christ, in turn, can be attained only through a universe that has been carried to the very limit of its capabilities.[11]

If these first appearances of the themes of plenitude and the *plérôme* in Teilhard's thought heralded the beginning of a promising new idea, still, during the early postwar years, there occurred a slow growth, almost imperceptible at times, and almost always implicit, in which the initial idea began to develop a shape of its own while at the same time remaining entirely dependent upon the concept of the Body of Christ.

In the first of his postwar essays, "Forma Christi," dated December 22, 1918, after asserting that matter is the formal instrument of union and interaction, he made this statement close to the end:

> If that is so, if every collective soul is born in *our* world through the instrumentality of a body, then Christ can consummate our unity in the Centre *that stands firm above us*—the Centre, that is, which

8. *WTW*, 211; *Ecrits*, p. 291.
9. *WTW*, p. 212; *Ecrits*, pp. 291-92.
10. *WTW*, p. 214; *Ecrits*, p. 293. (Emphasis added.)
11. *WTW*, p. 220; *Ecrits*, p. 299. The editor rightly notes that in this last passage Teilhard was defining his own special vocation as he saw it—a prophetic statement, in view of this very early use of this Pauline word in this essay. (Emphasis added.)

is his Spirit—only if he first encloses us in a material network *underlying* our *"esse corporeum."* If he is to be the soul of our souls, he must begin by being the flesh of our flesh.[12]

These words were written concerning the necessity of the Eucharist in the Christian life. Yet, in a new essay, "The Universal Element," written two months later as a replacement for the discarded appendix to "Forma Christi" (which appendix he had entitled "Note sur l'Elément Universel"), Teilhard attempted to pin down more precisely what he was attempting to say in the former essay when he referred to "un réseau matériel." Thus, he began to speak of "a *universal physical element* in the world, which establishes, at all times and in all things, a relationship between themselves and the Absolute—both in them and around them."[13]

What Teilhard appears to have been trying to account for here is the likelihood of an organic substratum of man's cosmic consciousness: "Somewhere there must be *something* that corresponds to cosmic 'abstraction' and consciousness."[14] He envisioned two possible solutions to this psychic phenomenon and its physical counterpart: the first solution was immanentist in nature—to identify the Absolute with the multiple, either in a material sense, that is, a homogeneous pantheism, or by ab-158 'ion of the multiple into a single universal soul, that is, monism; the other solution was basically transcendental, that is, with the Absolute conceived as being distinct from creation. But this latter, or "Christian," position can only explain and satisfy man's cosmic consciousness provided that somehow all creation is, in the end, "aggregated" and "consummated" to this transcendent Absolute. How is this to come about?

> this probability would become a certainty, if we knew that, in virtue of its nature, the universe was moving toward a *total end*. If such an end does in fact exist, then every being (in as much as it is *essentially* an element of such a universe) has its own particular essence crowned by a certain quality, a certain *form* (common to all) which makes it an integral, rightly adapted, part of the single Whole with which it shares a natural harmony, *"qua constituitur elementum talis Universi."*[15]

The concrete answer to this search is, for the Christian, not hard to find:

> In virtue of even the natural properties of the Universal Centre, the mystical Body of Christ is haloed by a *cosmic body*, that is to say

12. *WTW*, p. 268; *Ecrits*, p. 352.
13. *WTW*, p. 290; *Ecrits*, p. 401.
14. *WTW*, pp. 291-92; *Ecrits*, p. 402.
15. "by [or through] which element such a universe is constituted." *WTW*, p. 296; *Ecrits*, p. 407.

by *all things* in as much as they are drawn by Christ to converge upon him and so reach their fulfilment in him, in the *Pleroma*.

In our world, when it is supernaturalized, the Universal Element is ultimately Christ, in as much as everything is integrated to it and consummated in it. It is the living *Form* of the incarnate Word, universally attainable and perfectible.[16]

But why this continued use of the scholastic term *form*? It would appear that Teilhard had in mind much the same idea as that explicated in "Forma Christi" regarding the "matter" that makes up the Body of Christ (cf. chap. 4, §A, 3 above):

On the one hand, *if we have faith*, the irresistible forces of life and matter become *for us*, in very reality, the organizing activity of Christ assimilating us to himself. On the other hand, since all well-ordered activity here below is directed *towards Spirit*, and Spirit *towards Christ*, our *total* human effort (*the more* it is undertaken with *good intention*) collaborates in the plenitude of the Incarnation. All Christian imperturbability in the face of earthly vicissitudes, and all human enthusiasm in the face of a world to be conquered, are reconciled in those who have built their lives in the "mystical milieu" constituted by the Universal Element.[17]

There are two elements here (corresponding to "matter" and "form"): thus the "universal element" is not the "matter," rather, it would appear to be the "form" ("Forma Christi").[18] It is "all . . . activity," "our total human effort," which was here conceived as "matter"; only together with this "form" is the "plenitude of the Incarnation" brought about. Put more precisely:

= The Universal Element makes *the transcendent immediate; it unifies, by differentiating, the Multiple*; it allows us *to complete what already exists and to win full possession of what we already hold; it detaches us from the world by attaching us to it*.[19]

16. *WTW*, pp. 297-98; *Ecrits*, pp. 408-9.
17. *WTW*, p. 300; *Ecrits*, p. 411. Note the similarity of this progression of thought to that contained in *The Divine Milieu* some six years later, including the parallel with the implicit quotation of 1 Cor. 3:21 (cf. *DM*, pp. 25-28; *Oeuvres*, 4:41-48). Note also that it is in the line of the general evolution of Teilhard's thought that this "milieu mystique" later became "le milieu divin."
18. In a footnote in this same essay, Teilhard returns to the "soul" analogy employed in the earlier 1918 essay "L'Ame du Monde" (cf. chap. 4 §A, 3, above) to further elaborate this application of the scholastic notion of "matter" and "form":

It is possible in fact that side by side with our *supernatural unification* in Christ a *natural unification* of Spirit may be taking place in the world (= the work of natural human effort, the natural term of progress), the latter providing the *foundation* for the former. On that hypothesis, Christ would act vitally upon the universe by means of (by taking the place of) what would almost be a "Soul of the World." (*WTW*, p. 298, n.7; *Ecrits*, p. 409, n.7.)

19. *WTW*, p. 301; *Ecrits*, p. 412.

This understanding of the action of God through Christ on this world Teilhard called in this essay a new kind of "intégrisme," not just an "integrism in purity" (i.e., "the authentic Christ"):

> But *integrism*, too, *in universality*—not a single element of created energy, not one iota of the redeemable world, must be lacking to the plenitude of Christ.[20]

And again, with a fully "pleromic" emphasis, he concluded:

> Not only so that no chosen particle may be omitted from the Pleroma (nothing is so small as to be inessential to its totality) but so that the universe *may be given its* true *form under the influence* of Christ, *we must* bring about the reign of Christ even—indeed, above all—*in the continually nascent fringe of the world.*[21]

In this so laboriously worked-out sense must be understood the reasoning contained in the undated and incomplete essay "Note on the Physical Union Between the Humanity of Christ and the Faithful in the Course of Their Sanctification." In the course of this essay, the *plérôme* was mentioned three times, twice in the following paragraph:

> A solid basis for the demonstration, or rather the suggestions, we have in mind may profitably be sought in a consideration of the consummated mystical body (that is, the Pauline *pleroma*). In the first place, since the *pleroma* is the kingdom of God in its completed form, the properties attributed to it by Scripture must be regarded as specially characteristic of the entire supernatural organism, even if they are to be found only in an ill-defined form in any particular preparatory phase of beatification. Secondly, in no other reality is the physical and personal action of the theandric Christ made manifest to us by revelation more than in the Church triumphant.[22]

But, rather than allowing a "spiritualistic" interpretation of Scripture to prevail regarding the Pleroma, Teilhard argued, on the basis of the Eucharist, just the opposite:

> If we are not to establish an unwarranted disparity between the state of grace and the state of glory, we must say that grace does more than attach us by its spiritual instillation to the divinity of the Word: it brings with it a certain progressive inclusion in a created organism, physically centred on the humanity of Christ.[23]

But in terms of the Eucharist, such a position involves an apparent difficulty: to his mind physical contact with the humanity of Christ remains "a 'necessary' means" for incorporation into the pleroma,

20. *Ibid.*
21. *WTW*, p. 302; *Ecrits*, pp. 412-13.
22. *C&E*, p. 16; *Oeuvres*, 10:22. (Emphasis added.)
23. *C&E*, p. 17; *Oeuvres*, 10:23-24.

nevertheless this physical contact is established in the life of the Christian, and for that matter in the life of any of the "just," long before or even without any reception of the Eucharist.[24] But it is apparent from the whole tenor of this essay that the Eucharistic union between Christ and the believer has a central function in the elaboration of the pleroma.[25]

It would seem that this apparent difficulty caused Teilhard to leave the final paragraph of this essay incomplete—if indeed it was to have been the final paragraph. Nevertheless, this paragraph, even as it now stands, gives evidence of his determination not to allow his pleromic vision of the universe, as it was then taking shape, to be deterred by such difficulties.

Further light on Teilhard's determination is evidenced by at least two passages in a letter to Auguste Valensin written on February 2, 1920 (which would be within a week or two of the probable date of the unfinished essay). In this letter Teilhard argued even more strongly than in the above essay for his case concerning the "physicéité" of the Eucharist and his extended understanding of the Body of Christ.

> As you have thought, he (Fr. Léonce) would wish to affirm, more than I have, the essential distinction (*at the same time* as the common *physical nature*) between the contacts through grace and the Eucharist. Now this can only be done by treating the question from a more general point of view, that is to say in distinguishing *a whole series of* successive *zones* in "communion" or real union with Christ, all of these zones being *physical*, but each in a special order,—(the diverse orders not being fortuitous, but *drawn one from the other*). I see rather clearly what might be said on this subject, which really, I believe, can give, in *all orthodoxy*, a great unity and a great "physiceity" ["physicéité"] to the sanctification of souls and bodies in Christ.— . . . .—That which you tell me concerning the great horizons opened up by the idea of a Eucharist understood as an essential *mechanism* of spiritual transformation (and not simply as a work of love) is exactly the case: and it is this which startles me, that so few men perceive them (i.e. these ideas), whereas the great majority of us, I believe, are convinced (and preach) that the Eucharist is not an *optional* means of salvation (ex natura entis supernaturalis—from the nature of supernatural being). (Besides, how can it be said otherwise, following St. John and St. Paul?)[26]

The problem still remains, however, in any such attempt to push back the limits of the Incarnation to embrace such pleromic dimensions without at the same time destroying the distinctions that must neces-

24. *C&E*, pp. 17-18; *Oeuvres*, 10:24. Cf. chap. 4, §A; 4 above.
25. *C&E*, p. 20; *Oeuvres*, 10:26.
26. Unpublished, *T.A.*, Correspondence Teilhard-Valensin (my translation); cf. Appendix D, §2, d, i, for French original.

sarily stand—those between the "hypostatic union" effected in the Incarnation, the "transubstantiation" that occurs in the Eucharist, the
"incorporation" of the faithful in the building up of the "mystical" Body
of Christ, and finally, any means by which the limits of the Incarnation
are somehow extended to include "la nature inférieure." That Teilhard
recognized that there must be such distinctions seems readily recognizable in many of his more general statements.[27] But just how or in what
metaphysical terms the evolutionary workings of the cosmos can properly be included within the concept of the divine pleroma is something
else again. In plain words, how can it be possibly said (as Teilhard was
convinced) that Christ possesses a "cosmic body"?

Perhaps at least part of the answer can be found in two other short
essays that followed in the year 1920 (although the first of the two is
undated). In his essay "On the Notion of Creative Transformation"
Teilhard complained that Scholastic thought has provided us with no
adequate categories of thought to express God's creative activity other
than those of pure creation ("Productio entis *ex nihilo* sui et *subjecti*")
and pure transformation ("Productio entis ex nihilo sui et *potentia
subjecti*").[28] For Teilhard, these categories must be completed by a
new notion, that of "la Transformation créatrice," which he described,
rather than defined, as "an act *sui generis* which *makes use* of a preexistent created being and builds it up into a *completely* new being."[29]
Again:

> This *act is really creative*, because it calls for renewed interven-
> tion on the part of the First Cause.[30]

In consequence of this new approach to God's activity, he asserted:

> Understood in this way, creation is not a periodic intrusion of the
> First Cause: it is an act co-extensive with the whole duration of the
> universe.[31]

What effect does this view have on the notion of the pleroma?
Teilhard did not say at this point, but the following words are significant, even if taken in a broader context:

> This notion of "creative transformation" (or creation by
> transformation) . . . brings real "emancipation": it puts an end to the

27. Typical would be this passage from the 1918 "Note sur l'Elément universel," where
    Teilhard distinguishes his concept of Christ's influx as "Forma mundi" from the un-
    differentiated union of classic pantheism: "A l'inverse de l'Elément universel
    panthéiste, il se pose, dans les êtres, *proportionellement* à leur differentiation,
    spiritualisation, sanctification." (*Ecrits*, p. 362; *WTW*, p. 275.)
28. *C&E*, p. 21; *Oeuvres*, 10:29.
29. *C&E*, p. 22; *Oeuvres*, 10:31.
30. *Ibid.*
31. *C&E*, p. 23; *Oeuvres*, 10:31.

paradox and the stumbling-block of matter (i.e. our bewilderment when we consider the part played by the brain in thought and by passion— ἔρως—in mysticism); and it transforms them both into a noble and illuminated cult of that same matter.[32]

In the second essay addressed to this subject, dated January 1920 and entitled "Note on the Modes of Divine Action in the Universe," the following statements are found:

> We cannot pin down the point at which the hand of God is apparent. It acts upon the whole body of causes without making itself evident at any point: thus, externally, there is nothing so like the action of the Prime Mover as the action of a soul of the world, so much like the divine wisdom as destiny or fate. It would be beside the point to wonder whether such an arrangement suits us or not: *it is there*, and that is all about it.[33]

> Thus, sometimes by *excess of extension*, sometimes by *excess of depth*, the point at which the divine force is applied is essentially extra-phenomenal. The First Cause is not involved in effects; it acts upon individual *natures* and on the movement of *the whole*. Properly speaking, God *does not make*: He *makes things make themselves*.[34]

While the application of this line of thought may not be immediately apparent in regard to the pleroma, let another look be taken at a paragraph quoted only in part in the previous chapter:

> First of all, it appears contradictory (to the nature of participated being) to imagine God creating an *isolated* thing. Only one being can exist in isolation: *Ens a se* (Being which exists only in itself). Everything which is not God is essentially multitude—multitude organized in itself, and multitude organizing around itself. If God, then, is to *make a soul*, there is only one way open to his power: *to create a world*.[35] In consequence, man includes among his fully realized conditions of possibility more than just "animality and rationality"; the notion of man implies also "mankind, earth, universe. . . ." This takes us a long way from the facile "possibility" which the logicians imagine for things. But at the same time it adds to our stature—and, most of all, when applied to our Lord, it suggests the idea of an astonishing unity in creation. For now at last we can see that if God wishes to have Christ, to launch a complete uni-

32. *C&E*, pp. 23-24; *Oeuvres*, p. 32.
33. *C&E*, pp. 26-27; *Oeuvres*, 10:37.
34. *C&E*, pp. 27-28; *Oeuvres*, 10:38.
35. At this point, Teilhard added the following note:

> A *world*, i.e. not only a *whole*, but a *progressive* whole. We are inclined to conceive the power of God as supremely uninhibited in the face of "non-being." In this we are mistaken. *"Non-being" offers God only an infinitestimal purchase-point* (obediential potentiality); God, therefore, can overcome it only *gradatim* (gradually), by producing participated being which is progressively more capable of supporting the creative effort. This is what makes itself apparent to us as an evolution. (*C&E*, p. 32; *Oeuvres*, 10:42, n.4.)

verse and scatter life with a lavish hand was no more than he was obliged to do. Strictly speaking, then, is there, in all that moves outside God, anything else *in act* today, other than the actualizing of Jesus Christ, for which each fragment of the world is, proximately or distantly, necessary (*ex necessitate medii*—as a necessary means)? We need have no hesitation in saying that there is not.[36]

Whether or not these passages actually cleared up the question in Teilhard's mind as to *how* the pleroma is to include all created being (to some degree), there is no doubt as to *why*, in his mind, the pleroma must incorporate all reality.

Two passages in Teilhard's December 17, 1922, letter to Auguste Valensin (cf. chap. 1, §D above) stand out in this regard.

1) You have been wrong to scorn the pantheism of the poets. This pantheism is the mysticism by which Spinoza and Hegel have become theologians. It represents a psychological force, and it contains considerable living truth. It is a living pantheism. You are like a man who, within Christianity, scorns St. Therese for not being a St. Thomas or a Cajetan.
2) You leave the reader with the impression that the Spinozian position, for example, is simply bad or false,—How is it that you have not allowed yourself to see that between the Spinozian "incarnation" where All is hypostatically divine, and the "incarnation" of extrinsicist and timid theologians where the Pleroma is nothing but a social aggregation, there is a place for an Incarnation terminating itself in the edification of an organic Whole, where (there is) the physical union to the Divine *by degrees*?—You oppose Christian morality to Spinozian morality by saying that the first only says that we become "similar to God." I do not accept this opposition. For the Christian, to be (? ?) is to participate, as by a channel ["sous la similitude de conduite"], in a common being:—it is really "to become Christ," "to become God."[37]

While the note "On the Notion of Creative Transformation" goes on to the problem of evil, something that Teilhard would have later to reconcile with his pleromic ideas, for the time being he remained confident that in the end "Credenti omnia convertuntur in bonum," and that in the context of the pleroma, the sum total of all God's creative action on the universe will be

36. *C&E*, p. 32; *Oeuvres*, 10:42-43. Karl Rahner, in his essay "On the Theology of the Incarnation," speaks in much the same vein as Teilhard, but fails to draw the correlative conclusion about the necessity of the rest of the created universe when he says: ". . . the Logos made man has been called the abbreviated Word of God. This abbreviation, this code-word for God is man, that is, the Son of Man and men, who exist ultimately because the Son of Man was to exist. If God wills to become non-God, man comes to be, that and nothing else, we might say." Cf. *Word and Mystery*, ed. Leo J. O'Donovan, S.J. (New York: Newman, 1968), p. 286.
37. *TA*: Correspondence Teilhard-Valensin, #17. See Appendix D, §2, d, ii for original French. (? ?) designates a missing or illegible word, although the context would most likely call for "sanctified," or possibly "graced," in this case. (My translation.)

an infallible synthesis of the whole, operated by combined internal
and external influences; such, in brief, would appear to be (apart
from the exceptional amplifications we meet in miracles) the most
general and most perfected form of God's action upon the world: respecting all, "forced into" many roundabout ways and obliged to tol-
erate many things which shock us at first—but ultimately integrating
and transforming all.[38]

In addition to this hint that not only all facets of created being will
be included in the pleroma, and this in some mysterious way including
both the good and the bad, there appears in another essay of this very
same month (Jan. 1920), Teilhard's "Note on the Universal Christ,"
something equally daring in its implication regarding the universality of
Christ. Although the word *plérôme* does not appear in this essay, its
insistence on the development of an understanding of Christ who is
truly an *"Organic centre—of the entire universe"*[39] and on that
universe's being understood as one that possesses a certain "coherence
[cohésion] 'in unitatae materiae et in unitate spiritus.' "[40] This demands
that the pleromic universality must be understood in a way that involves a certain mutual interdependence of Christ and the universe.

> If Christ is universal (if, in other words, he is gradually consum-
> mated from all created being) it follows that his kingdom, in its es-
> sence, goes beyond the domain of the life that is, in a strict sense,
> called supernatural. Human action can be related to Christ, and can
> co-operate in the fulfilment of Christ, not only by the intention, the
> fidelity, and the obedience in which—as an addition—it is clothed,
> but also by the actual *material content* of the work done. All pro-
> gress, whether in organic life or in scientific knowledge, in aesthetic
> faculties or in social consciousness, can therefore be made Christian
> even in its object (since all progress, *in se* is organically integral with
> spirit, and spirit depends on Christ).[41]

While the above passage in many ways anticipates the theme of *The
Divine Milieu*, it also subtly anticipates a much more difficult problem
that was eventually to face Teilhard: that of the active versus the
strictly passive interpretation of the pleroma—the question whether
Christ completes his pleroma, or whether the pleroma completes
Christ.

Meanwhile, a curious thing should be called to attention. During all
these years of development of the concept of the pleroma, Teilhard
never once tied the term to any particular text of St. Paul. True, the
text of Ephesians 4:9-10 was occasionally used ("Descendit-
ascendit . . . ut impleret omnia"), but without any direct reference

38. *C&E*, p. 35; *Oeuvres*, 10:45.
39. *S&C*, p. 14; *Oeuvres*, 9:39.
40. *S&C*, p. 16; *Oeuvres*, 9:41.
41. *S&C*, pp. 16-17; *Oeuvres*, 9:41-42.

to the *plérôme* or even "plenitude." Only after his first mention of this "plénitude du Christ" in the 1918 "Mon Univers" does he appear to have been quoting even part of a text closely associated with this term in St. Paul: the place where he spoke of "ma vision fondamentale *du Christ en toutes choses*" (Eph. 4:23).[42]

This situation seems suddenly to change in 1921. In the essay 'Science and Christ" appeared a whole battery of scriptural phrases centering on what obviously were Teilhard's convictions concerning the pleromic Christ:

> Turn to the most weighty and most unmistakable passages in the Scriptures. Question the Church about her most essential beliefs; and this is what you will learn: Christ is not something added to the world as an extra, he is not an embellishment, a king as we now crown kings, the owner of a great estate. . . . *He is the alpha and the omega, the principle and the end, the foundation stone and the keystone, the Plenitude and the Plenifier. He is the one who consummates all things and gives them their consistence. It is towards him and through him*, the inner life and *light of the world*, that the universal convergence of all created spirit is effected in sweat and tears. He is the single centre, precious and consistent, who glitters at the summit that is to crown the world, at the opposite pole from those dim and eternally shrinking regions into which our science ventures when it descends the road of matter and the past.[43]

If the above passage marked the emergence of a new return to biblical terminology on this subject, still, the underlying preoccupations were the same. In fact, in Teilhard's "Pantheism and Christianity," written two years later, is found (as the title boldly indicates) a venturesome new excursion into this perennial "cosmic sense." But this time he not only did not hesitate conceptually to associate Christianity with his "pantheistic" leanings, but emphasized this conviction even more with the use of Scripture. The pleroma as a developed concept in Teilhard's thought was finally coming to birth. True, in the five times that the *plérôme* is mentioned explicitly in this essay, the first three instances indicate little or no distinction between the mystical body of Christ and the pleroma. In each instance, however, he was posing essentially the same question:

> what sort of bonds hold together the members of Christ's mystical body, the elements of the pleroma. How are we to understand the consistence of this mysterious organism?[44]

But in his answer does there not appear the beginning of a careful distinction?

42. *Ecrits*, p. 273.
43. *S&C*, pp. 34-35; *Oeuvres*, 9:60-61. (Emphasis added.) Cf. Rev. 1:8; Luke 19:17; Col. 1:19 (Eph. 1:23); Eph. 1:10; Col. 1:17; Col. 1:16; and John 11:25, 8:12 (9:5).
44. *C&E*, p. 67; *Oeuvres*, 10:84.

We should not do what could be read into the language censured in some mystics (Eckhart, for example) and try to make of the consummated Christ a being so unique that his subsistence, his person, his "I," takes the place of the subsistence, the personality, of all the elements incorporated in his mystical body. This concept of a hypostatic union extended to the whole universe (which, incidentally, is simply Spinoza's pantheism) is not in itself either contradictory or absurd; but it conflicts with the whole Christian view of individual freedom and personal salvation. There is, however, no difficulty in avoiding the exaggerated "physicism" introduced by this attempt to express the unification of the world in Jesus Christ. Without having to fall back on monism, there are, in fact, plenty of ways of conceiving a "graduated" type of union for the pleroma (modified by the very excess of its physical perfection), such that, without losing anything of their subsistence or personality, the elect would be *physically* incorporated in the organic and "natural" whole of the consummated Christ. . . . Thinking along those lines we can arrive at an idea of the mystical body of Christ which indeed appears both to satisfy the legitimate "pantheist" aspirations of our minds and hearts, and to allow Christian dogma and mysticism the only environment in which they can develop freely.[45]

And to top this bold stroke, in the succeeding pages seven biblical citations follow to stress his point. Beginning with the "in eo omnia constant" of Colossians 1:17,[46] these direct quotations include Ephesians 4:9-10,[47] Romans 8:22,[48] and Colossians 3:17.[49] The fifth citation extends the "hoc est corpus meum" formula to "the whole of nature . . . slowly and irresistibly undergoing the supreme consecration," to the point where Teilhard envisions that "fundamentally—since all time and for ever—but one single thing is being made in creation: the body of Christ."[50]

However, lest the pleromic aspect of all this be lost or overlooked, the final paragraph of the essay, which contains the final two scriptural quotations, should be read in its entirety:

Already, at this very moment, by everything we do, we all share in all, through and in him whom we might think distant from us, but in whom, quite literally, "*vivimus, movemur et sumus.*" A little while yet—what hope could be grander?—creation, totally dominated by Christ, will be lost in him and through him within the final and permanent unity, where (in St Paul's very words, the most clear-cut assertion we have of Christian "pantheism") "ἔσται ὁ Θεὸς πάντα ἐν πᾶσιν."[51]

45. *C&E*, pp. 69-70; *Oeuvres*, 10:86-87.
46. *C&E*, p. 71; *Oeuvres*, 10:87.
47. *C&E*, p. 71; *Oeuvres*, 10:88.
48. *C&E*, pp. 71-72; *Oeuvres*, 10:88.
49. *C&E*, pp. 72-73; *Oeuvres*, 10:89. The final phrase in this passage is paralleled by that of the preceding paragraph, which ends with the words: "l'édification du Plérôme."
50. *C&E*, pp. 73-74; *Oeuvres*, 10:90.
51. *C&E*, p. 75; *Oeuvres*, 10:91 (Acts 17:28, 1 Cor. 15:28).

What is to be made of all of this? Despite the use of the word *dominated* (*dominée*) in the last paragraph, this first use of 1 Corinthians 15:28 (in a slightly modified form—*estai* [will be] rather than *hina hēi* [in order that . . . might be] signaled the definitive birth of the *plérôme* as understood by Teilhard. It was in his mind a veritable "panthéisme chrétien," which is a prolongation or extension of the Eucharistic and "mystical" (i.e., ecclesial) Body of Christ—in truth, nothing less than what he had already termed in earlier essays the "corps cosmique du Christ."

What remained to be done (a sort of cutting of the umbilical cord, so to speak) took place a year later in the 1924 "Mon Univers." Teilhard expressed his having given up trying to convince the juridicists (". . . je renonce à convertir mes contradicteurs"[52]) on the basis of his "physical" understanding of the Body of Christ. Without renouncing his own convictions, his approach had noticeably changed. Whereas the former approach had more or less concentrated on the *present* state of affairs under the image of the "mystical Body" (pushed to its extreme limits of interpretation), his new one appears to concentrate on the *future*, the Omegic-Christ who possesses "that energy 'qua sibi omnia possit subjicere' (Phil. 3:21), which we must unhesitatingly attribute to the Incarnate Word"[53] and which brings everything to its universal term.

But just what is this "energy"?

> The vital, organising, influence of the universe, of which we are speaking, is essentially grace. We can see, however, from the point of view of creative union, that this wonderful reality of grace must be understood with a much greater intensity and width of meaning than is normally attributed to it. Theologians, in order to make it clear that grace does not make us cease to be ourselves, include it in the humble category of "accidents," along with sonority, colours, or good spiritual qualities. Enslaved to their philosophical categories they make it (in contrast with the universal practice of the mystics) into something infra-substantial. This, we say, is because they cannot bring themselves to accept the existence of incomplete substances, hierarchically ordered, in other words, Substances-of-Substance. We, on the other hand, take this new class of beings as the foundation of our explanation of the world, and in consequence will say that grace is no less intimate to ourselves, no less substantial, than humanity.[54]

Understood in this manner, Teilhard saw grace as simply the classic term for what he understood as the "influence 'morphogénique' " of Christ-Omega:

52. *S&C*, p. 55; *Oeuvres*, 9:83.
53. *S&C*, p. 57; *Oeuvres*, 9:85.
54. *S&C*, pp. 57-58; *Oeuvres*, 9:86. Teilhard did not go into the classic argument here concerning the existence of "uncreated grace." The editor of "Oeuvres," however, does correct Teilhard's overstatement by a reference to *S.T.* I, II, q. 110, a. 4, where St. Thomas speaks of grace as giving man a "new nature."

In consequence, his directing and informing influence runs through the whole range of human works, of material determinisms and cosmic evolutions. By convention, we call these lower processes in the universe "natural." In reality, by virtue of Christ's establishment as head of the cosmos, they are steeped in final purpose, in supernatural life, even to what is most palpable in their reality. Everything around us is physically "Christified," and everything, as we shall see, can become progressively more fully so.[55]

It is this "Christification" (later to be termed "Christogenesis") that brings about what he now dared call *pan*christism as distinguished from false pantheisms. The reason this is possible is that, while false pantheisms would dissolve individuality in a universal fusion of identity and unconsciousness, in this "Christification," the Christ-Omega "is placed at the upper term of conscious spiritualization; his universal influence, far from dissociating, consolidates; far from confusing, differentiates."[56]

And so he went on to describe this "Christification" as a twofold movement that affects the pleroma:

All around us, Christ is physically active in order to control all things. From the ultimate vibration of the atom to the loftiest mystical contemplation; from the lightest breeze that ruffles the air to the broadest currents of life and thought, he ceaselessly animates, without disturbing, all the earth's processes. And in return Christ gains physically from every one of them. Everything that is good in the universe (that is, everything that goes towards unification through effort) is gathered up by the Incarnate Word as a nourishment that it assimilates, transforms and divinises. In the consciousness of this vast two-way movement, of ascent and descent, by which the development of the Pleroma (that is, the bringing of the universe to maturity) is being effected, the believer can find astonishing illumination and strength for the direction and maintenance of his effort.[57]

In the remaining sections of the essay, Teilhard went on to draw out the implications of this pleromic view of the universe in a manner well known to all who have read his mystical-ascetical treatise *The Divine Milieu*. Many of the same scriptural quotations appear in very similar contexts, but others are different, as the following:

Not only "in ordine intentionis" but "in ordine naturae," "omnia in eo condita sunt"—"all things are contained in him," not only "in the order of intention" but also "in the order of nature."[58]

55. *S&C*, pp. 58-59; *Oeuvres*, 9:87.
56. *S&C*, p. 59; *Oeuvres*, 9:87.
57. *S&C*, pp. 59-60; *Oeuvres*, 9:87-88.
58. *S&C*, p. 61; *Oeuvres*, 9:89. The reference is apparently to Col 1:16, which reads in the Vg. "quonium in ipso condita sunt universa in coelis et in terra. . . ."

Further on he again utilized Ephesians 4:10 ("Descendit et ascendit ut impleret omnia"), but, he stated in the subsequent paragraphs, the incarnation takes place as a continuing act.

> Like the Creation (of which it is the visible aspect) the Incarnation is an act co-extensive with the duration of the world. How, then, here and now, is the influence of the universal Christ transmitted to us? Through the Eucharist; but by the Eucharist understood, once again, in its universal power and realism.[59]

> The Host, it is true, is in the first place, and primarily, the fragment of matter to which, through transubstantiation, the Presence of the Incarnate Word attaches itself among us, that is to say in the human zone of the universe. The centre of Christ's personal energy is really situated in the Host. And, just as we rightly give the name of "our body" to the local centre of our spiritual radiation (though that does not perhaps necessarily mean that our flesh is more ours than is any other matter) we must say that the initial Body of Christ, his *primary Body*, is confined to the species of bread and wine. Can Christ, however, remain contained in this primary Body? Clearly, he cannot. Since hs is above all omega, that is, the universal "form" of the world, he can attain his organic balance and plenitude only by mystically assimilating (and we have already explained the hyper-physical sense to be attached to that word) all that surrounds him.[60]

Note the term *hyper-physical*. This essay marks Teilhard's first use of this most important term in his writings, especially in his more theological essays. To read into this word a developed meaning along the lines of his *The Phenomenon of Man* of some fifteen years later would be somewhat premature. Earlier in this essay the word is followed simply by a parenthesized "super-substantial."[61] But certainly he did not mean this in the sense of "spiritual" and definitely it means more than the "mystical" he found so restricting. May there not be seen here instead something of a connecting link between the early intuitions of the two undated essays "What Exactly Is the Human Body"[62] and "Note on the Physical Union. . . ,"[63] on the one hand, and on the other the general theory of energy proposed in *The Phenomenon of Man*? The occurrence of the word *coextensive* at the beginning of the paragraph quoted above, as well as the clear statement of the unity of matter-spirit toward the beginning of this 1924 "Mon Univers," would make such a connection highly probable.[64]

If this be true, then the connection between the Eucharist, the Mystical Body, and the pleroma as understood by Teilhard was not simply

59. *S&C*, p. 64; *Oeuvres*, 9:92.
60. *S&C*, p. 65; *Oeuvres*, 9:93.
61. *S&C*, p. 55; *Oeuvres*, 9:84.
62. *S&C*, pp. 11f; *Oeuvres*, 9:31f.
63. *C&E*, pp. 19f; *Oeuvres*, 10:19f.
64. "Matter and Spirit are not opposed as two separate things, as two natures, but as two directions of evolution within the world." *S&C*, p. 51; *Oeuvres*, 9:79.

a theological complement to the general outlines of his "phenomenolog-ical" world view, but might be, at the same time, expressible in terms of his "energetics," that is, in terms of his more developed "hyper-physical" theory of two forms of energy: "tangential" and "radial."[65]

Whatever may have been the direction of Teilhard's speculations, it is nevertheless clear that by 1924 the pleroma had fully emerged as a distinct concept in his thought and that despite its origins in the earlier formulation of the Body of Christ as he understood it, this pleroma now existed in its own right and even with its own distinctive scriptural foundation, which in Teilhard's estimation was to be 1 Corinthians 15:28. Thus, he closed the 1924 "Mon Univers" with these words:

> At that moment, St Paul tells us (1 Cor. 15. 23 ff), when Christ has emptied all created forces (rejecting in them everything that is a factor of dissociation and superanimating all that is a force of unity), he will consummate universal unification by giving himself, in his complete and adult Body, with a finally satisfied capacity for union, to the embrace of the Godhead.
>
> Thus will be constituted the organic complex of God and world —the Pleroma— . . .
>
> Like a vast tide, Being will have engulfed the shifting sands of be-ings. Within a now tranquil ocean, each drop of which, neverthe-less, will be conscious of remaining itself, the astonishing adventure of the world will have ended. The dream of every mystic, the eter-nal pantheist ideal, will have found their full and legitimate satisfac-tion. "Erit in omnibus Deus."[66]

The particular significance of the 1924 "Mon Univers" as a summary of Teilhard's views at the close of this initial period of development cannot be overstressed. It represents, along with the "The Mass on the World" (written in the Ordos Desert of China during this first trip to the Orient, April through September, 1923), the first of his nonpaleon-tological writings to come out of China, which was soon to become his place of "exile" early in 1925 after the storm broke over his "Note on

65. According to Teilhard's theory, as stated in *The Phenomenon of Man*, all energy (which is basically "psychic" in nature) (cf. *PM*, p. 64; *Oeuvres*, 1:62) can be under-stood as being manifested in either of two manners: either *tangentially* (that which links an element to others on the same level of existence), or *radially* (that which draws something forward to greater levels of complexity and centreity). (*PM*, p. 62; *Oeuvres*, 1:65.) If this be the case, then would not the Eucharist by its "tangential" presence, (esp. in its sacramental reception) be such that at the same time it "ra-dially" reaches out to all the universe in a manner proportionate (i.e., "graduated") to the potential of the being that is reached? Teilhard never went so far as to offer such a "hyper-physical" explanation of the Eucharist, perhaps because his theory of energetics never quite reached a finished form in his mind (the later "Journals" have many references of a self-questioning nature about his energetics). Neverthe-less, his ideas on "coextension" seem to be to some extent explained and developed by his theory of energetics.

66. *S&C*, p. 85; *Oeuvres*, 9:113-14. While the intention seems obviously to be that of quoting 1 Cor. 15:28, grammatically (as noted before) its structure is closer to the Vulgate rendition of Col. 3:11: ". . . sed omnia et in omnibus Christus." This will prove to be an interesting combination in view of his further thought on the sub-ject.

Some Possible Historical Representations of Original Sin" of 1922. His imminent return to China would mark a severe spiritual crisis in his life, and the 1924 "Mon Univers" is a summary of all he held by way of conviction up to that period, much as "Cosmic Life" of 1916 was a testament on the eve of his entrance into the Great War. The similarity of circumstances and themes, as well as the changes that had taken place in this thought, cannot be overestimated. This "Mon Univers" was, for that period, his "Apologia pro vita sua."

2. The Years of Research and Reflection in China (1925-1944)

The 1924 "Mon Univers" brought the first period of his thought to a close and initiated the beginning of a new phase, of which the first major product was Le Milieu divin. Yet, in many ways, The Divine Milieu is a second recapitulation, much the same as "Mon Univers." But there are differences. First of all, The Divine Milieu was written not so much as a testament to Teilhard's overall world view as addressed to a particular problem: the Christian ascetical-mystical view of the relationship to God and the universe. To the degree that it involved Teilhard's world view, as expressed in the more generally philosophical-theological "Mon Univers," The Divine Milieu repeats much of the former. Also, Teilhard consciously wrote this new work not so much for himself or his close friends as with the intent to publish for a more general reading audience, presenting his vision under the aspect of an appeal to the more widely accepted norms and themes of traditional Christian spirituality. In other words, The Divine Milieu, for all its innovations (from an outsider's point of view), was meant to be a defense of his orthodoxy. For all this, the book seems to represent a new stage in Teilhard's thought, in that despite its careful efforts to confine itself within the bounds of accepted orthodoxy, at least two points are raised which, if not entirely new in Teilhard's thought, now reach a new stage of expression. The first is the relationship between the pleroma and evil in its concrete and ultimate expression in the Christian concept of hell; the second concerns the relationship of the pleroma to the Parousia. Lurking under both of these questions, despite Teilhard's most careful qualifications, is a third, less explicit, but much more basic question.

In all, there are nine explicit references to the pleroma in The Divine Milieu. On page 25 (43 in the French edition[67]) the pleroma is described as being first of all "the consummation of the world"—which is "a communion of persons (the Communion of Saints). On pages 30 and 31 (pp. 49, 50) the word is associated with quotations from Psalm 103

---

67. DM, p. 25; Oeuvres, 4:43. The pagination of the English is that of the Harper & Row hardbound ed. of 1961.

(104):2 ("Amictus mundo"), Colossians 1:17 ("in quo omnia constant"),
Ephesians 4:10 ("Quid est quod ascendit, nisi quod prius descendit, ut
repleret omnia"), and Romans 8:22 ("Omnis creatura adhuc ingemiscit
et parturit"). On page 100 (pp. 148-49 in the French) where the
pleroma is mentioned twice, the following description is given from
Teilhard's theory of creative union:

> The action by which God maintains us in the field of His presence is
> *a unitive transformation*.
>   Let us go further still. What is the supreme and complex reality
> for which the divine operation moulds us? It is revealed to us by St.
> Paul and St. John. It is the quantitative repletion and the qualitative
> consummation of all things: it is the mysterious Pleroma, in which
> the substantial *One* and the created *many* fuse without confusion in
> a *whole* which, without adding anything essential to God, will
> nevertheless be a sort of triumph and generalisation of being.[68]

He then went on to describe "the active centre, the living link" ("La
Lien vivant, L'Ame organisatrice") of the pleroma as being that very
Christ "dead and risen *qui replet omnia, in quo omnia constant*."[69]

But not until the end of this slim volume does the real development
take place. After speaking of our own efforts to build up the pleroma
by means of the divine milieu—"The divine milieu which will ultimately be one in the Pleroma"—[70] the question must be broached
about those who fail to take their place, through their own selfishness
and ill-will, in this great vocation. The answer, in response to an earlier inquiry, is nothing less than surprising:

> *I know, too, that considered from the point of view of the void
> created by their defection from the Mystical Body, the fallen spirits
> cannot detract from the perfection of the Pleroma. Each soul that is
> lost in spite of the call of grace ought to spoil the perfection of the
> final and general union; but instead, O God, You offset it by one of
> those recastings which restore the universe at every moment to a new
> freshness and a new purity. The damned are not excluded from the
> Pleroma, but only from its luminous aspect, and from its beatifica-
> tion. They lose it, but they are not lost to it.*[71]

The distinction between the Body of Christ in its mystical aspect (here
Teilhard concedes to use the word, but in a more grace-oriented than
ecclesiastical sense) and the pleroma can be seen here in its greatest
possible contrast. It not only embraces all that is capable of being
joined in the great movement of *aggregation*, but to some extent even

68. *DM*, p. 100; *Oeuvres*, 4:149. The texts loosely quoted are from Eph. 4:10 and Col.
    1:17.
69. *DM*, pp. 100-101; *Oeuvres*, 4:149.
70. *DM*, p. 124; *Oeuvres*, 4:182.
71. *DM*, p. 130; *Oeuvres*, 4:190. (Emphasis added.) In the 1919 "The Priest" Teilhard
    asked if this "immortal loss" might not still add some "mysterious complement to
    the Body of Christ." Cf. *WTW*, p. 214; *Ecrits*, p. 293.

takes within its comprehension the results of the inevitable and corresponding *segregation.*[72]

In light of all that Teilhard had said in the past about the inevitability of evil ("Necessarium est ut scandala eveniant") and its ultimate
vindication ("omnia cooperuntur," even "convertuntur in bonum"), his
conclusion is not illogical, yet pressed this far, it is surely startling.

But certain confusions remain. If this pleroma adds nothing to God,
at least essentially, and if the tragedy of damnation does not detract
from the perfection of the pleroma, why then the insistence that we
engage ourselves unreservedly in its building up? Is it not perhaps
even more paradoxical if, while we may build up the world in preparation for the pleromic transformation, that transformation itself is a consummation that will reach its definitive state only at the Parousia or
Second Coming? Still, the moment of this consummation is destined to
take place when man collectively desires this to come about.

> Expectation—anxious, collective and operative expectation of an
> end of the world, that is to say of an issue for the world—that is
> perhaps the supreme Christian function and the most distinctive
> characteristic of our religion.[73]

Why is this so? Teilhard firmly believed that the Parousia of Christ
would not be an event the date of which is arbitrarily fixed by God,
but rather that "it is an accumulation of desires that should cause the
Pleroma to burst upon us."[74]

Although both the aforementioned problems are formidable enough
in their own right, the underlying one is still more so. For if man's
personal defection does not detract from the pleroma (at least as a manifestation of God's supreme dominion), and yet man's failure to work as
he should in this world can in some way delay its fulfillment, the real
problem comes back, in the end, to the ontological relationship between the pleroma and God. Did Teilhard recognize this? Perhaps he
did. But he did not attempt to solve the problem directly, at least not
quite yet. In *The Divine Milieu*, as has been seen, he was careful to
qualify his statement about the pleroma as a *"totality"* wherein "the
created *Multiple* rejoined without confusion to the substantial *One,
without adding anything essential to God*, will be nevertheless a kind
of *triumph and generalization of being."*[75]

Can this problem, or the implications raised by it, be so easily con-
jured away? This is the question that implicitly or explicitly, continued
to vex Teilhard for the rest of his life; and it will be the central concern
of the remainder of this section. Furthermore, because of this ques-

72. See the use of these terms on p. 128 of *The Divine Milieu; Oeuvres*, 4:187.
73. *DM*, pp. 134-35; *Oeuvres*, 4:196-97.
74. *Ibid.*, see chap. 2, §E, above.
75. My translation and emphasis. Cf. *DM*, p. 100, also *Oeuvres*, 4:149.

tion, two ideas must dominate this investigation: Teilhard's continued and intensified insistence on a "véritable panthéisme chrétien," and his almost equally constant appeals to 1 Corinthians 15:28.

Teilhard's first resumption of these themes took place not in China, but during a short trip back to France in 1930. On Wednesday, December 10, Teilhard delivered the fourth of a series of talks, entitled "Essai d'intégration de l'homme dans l'univers," to the Groupe Marcel Legaut gathered at Chadefaud.

In the course of that talk[76] he seems to have somewhat combined 1 Corinthians 15:28 with Ephesians 1:23 to stress the role of Christ, as well as to speak critically of pantheism in general. But in an essay written two years later, he showed himself more exact in his quotation of Scripture and more careful in discerning various forms of pantheism. Speaking of its monistic form in particular, he wrote in the essay entitled "La Route de l'Ouest: Vers une mystique nouvelle" (continuing a passage already quoted in part):

> ". . . God will become all in all: *en pasi panta Theos.*" For Christianity to remain faithful to itself in becoming Westernized, it is necessary and sufficient to maintain that, in addition to the primacy of the spiritual over the material (which makes, as we have seen, for the renouncement of possession), the primacy of the *personal* within the spiritual, combining the maximum distinction of elements with their maximum of union. But this second primacy, like the first, is it not precisely the nature and mechanism of "convergence"? How can the Multiple *lose itself* in the Unity (which characterizes false pantheism), except by the ontological movement of convergence which reunites the elements among themselves being exactly that which makes each one of them, to a lesser degree, incommunicably itself![77]

In this general adoption of 1 Corinthians 15:28 in terms of an incarnationally understood "pantheism," it is obvious that it is not God, theistically understood as such, who is the center of this convergence; rather it is: "Christ in his role as the Center 'in whom all things have their consistence.'" For, as he went on to say:

> Christ is forever the only element in the cosmos which, if illuminism and its trap is to be avoided, gives a body to modern hopes of a spiritual organisation of the World.—All the more reason then for the Church, reviving the visions passionately described by St. Paul, to commit itself to recognizing and proclaiming them finally, *in their*

76. Unpublished. *T.A.* #92, IV, p. 10. See chap. 2, §4, E, above; Appendix D, §1, 6, for the French. While the talk appears to have been recorded rather than taken from a manuscript of Teilhard, notice that Teilhard's translation of St. Paul's words as "tout en tout" varied from his usual translation of the "en pasin" as "en tous." Hence it is not simply a personalistic union that Teilhard emphasized but also a union that encompasses the entire cosmos.

77. *Oeuvres*, 11:59. See chap. 2, §D, 5, above (my translation). Cf. *TF*, p. 54.

entirety and such as they are, as meeting universal hopes and energies.[78]

Teilhard still continued to maintain that distinction between God's being (which remains an unqualified absolute) and "Universal Being" (the "triumph and generalization of being").[79] But in "La Route de l'Ouest" this distinction is expressed thus:

> From this point of view, the idea that we tend to hold today concerning the structure and function of the Multiple leads directly to the Christian views concerning the final consummation of the Universe. On the one hand, in virtue of the Incarnation, God can no longer (at least *hic et nunc*—here and now—or ever) dispense with the Multiple in which he has immerged himself; and, on the other hand, the reality "God + Multiple", in Christo Jesu, seems, in Christian practice and Pauline mysticism, to represent a perfection completely extrinsic respecting God, bringing with it a real completion in the equilibrium of Universal Being."[80]

It may be asked if Teilhard found it necessary to further clarify these notions, unsatisfactory as they may seem to some. Apparently not, for at least for the time being he seems to have been content only to repeat them, and then, for the most part, from different points of view and through slightly varying formulas. Thus, in his 1933 "Occident et Orient: La Mystique de la Personnalité" (again a study of comparative mysticisms) Teilhard said, according to notes taken by one Jean Bousquet:

> The attitude of Western mysticism has all the strength of Oriental pantheism without its drawback; thus reunion with God is not accomplished through (self-) elimination, but through a purification and refining of whatever is most personal and accomplished [clair] in things: the strength of pantheism is realized: God is all in all things, and it is even more so as they are unified in their purest essence.[81]

Again, in the same year (1933), Teilhard repeated himself in "Christologie et Evolution," this time in terms of the doctrine of creation:

> To create, even when we use the word omnipotence, must no longer be understood as an instantaneous act but as a process or controlled movement of synthesis. Pure act and "non-being" are diametrically opposed in the same way as are perfected unity and pure multiple. This means that in spite of (or rather because of) his perfections, the Creator cannot communicate himself immediately to his creature, but must make the creature capable of receiving him.

---

78. *Oeuvres*, 11:60. (*TF*, p. 55.)
79. As in *The Divine Milieu* (*DM*, p. 100; *Oeuvres*, 4:149).
80. *Oeuvres*, 11:63. (*TF*, p. 58)
81. Unpublished, *T.A.* #118, p. 2. See chap. 2, §4, D above for remainder of passage, also French original in Appendix D, §1, c.

If God is to be able to give himself to the plural, he must unify it to his own measure. In consequence, the constitution of the pleroma, from the origins of the world until God, must necessarily make itself apparent to our minds by a progressive advance of spirit.[82]

In the 1934 "How I Believe," his expression was more directly Christological, and at the same time more daring in its clear statement of the mutual interdependence of Christ and evolution for a complete understanding of both:

> The Universal-Christ, such as I understand, is a synthesis of Christ and the Universe. By no means a new Divinity,—but the inevitable development of the Mystery in which is summed up Christianity: the Incarnation.[83]

> Thus is defined, in front of us, *a Universal Cosmic Center*, where all meets, where all is explained, where all is understood, where all is ruled. It is precisely at this physical pole of Universal Evolution that it is necessary, I feel, to place the plenitude of Christ. Because in *no other type of Cosmos*, and *from no other place*, no being, *however divine he be*, could exercise the function of universal consolidation and of universal animation which the Christian dogma recognizes in Jesus. Evolution in discovering a summit to the World, makes Christ possible,—just as Christ, in giving a meaning to the World, makes Evolution possible.[84]

In 1936 Teilhard again returned to his preoccupation with pantheism, this time in his "Sketch of a Personalistic Universe." In this essay, after a painstaking analysis of the laws that govern the growth of personality, he went on to discuss their ultimate convergence in a personal God. From this point of view

> God can only be defined as a *centre of centres*. In this complexity lies the perfection of His unity—the only final goal logically attributable to the developments of spirit-matter.[85]

In order that the reader might not miss the startling word, Teilhard repeated it immediately and expanded it: *"complexité de Dieu."*[86] How can this be possible? It is possible only on condition that the habitual association of complexity with "mutual exclusiveness" and "eventual disaggregation of parts" be eliminated. These two weaknesses of "inner opposition" and "fragility" (i.e., corruptibility) are, according to Teilhard, only temporary imperfections of composite being in the present stages of evolution. In the end, things will be different:

82. *C&E*, pp. 82-83; *Oeuvres*, 10:101-2.
83. "Comment je crois" in *Oeuvres*, 10:146 (*C&E*, p. 126). The translation above, which varies somewhat from that of René Hague in *C&E*, is taken from a private printing in English made in Peiping (Peking) in 1936 (p. 41 of the latter ed.). The translation may be Teilhard's own.
84. *Ibid.*, pp. 42-43. Cf. *Oeuvres*, 10:147-48; *C&E*, pp. 127-28.
85. *HE*, p. 68; *Oeuvres*, 6:86.
86. *Ibid.* (My emphasis.)

We must imagine for ourselves thinking molecules interiorized on one another when they reach their perfection conjunction. A perfect mutual transparency in a perfect self-possession, this is the only pantheistic fusion logically conceivable for souls in the divine milieu.[87]

Was Teilhard saying here that God is, after all, still in the process of formation? It appears so, that is, until he insisted that such a consummation is possible only if this center of convergence is already *real*:

Since by definition we are "reality," and multiply our race in reality, the apex of the world clearly cannot be conceived as simply a "virtual" point of convergence. It must be *real* also. But to what extent is it already *realized*? The one does not seem to follow immediately from the other.[88]

Here then reappears Teilhard's distinction between the Omega-point at the hypothetical culmination of evolution, and the Omega-God, along with a recognition of the possibly Anselmic nature of his argument. And although his solution of this problem should already be familiar —Teilhard always tended to repeat his earlier thought in each subsequent essay—his answer to this recurring question in this particular essay has particular relevance to the problem of the ultimate distinction between the pleroma and God.

In the extra-temporal metaphysics of being this question may seem lacking in respect. Before all creation, proclaim the scholastics, the absolute existed in its fullness. For us who are simply trying to construct a sort of ultra-physics, by combining the sum of our experiments in the most harmonious way, the answer to the problem is not so positive. From the empirical point of view there is no pure act but only a final term to which the serial bundle that envelops us is converging. What kind of actuality must we recognize in this term in order that it may be real?

I should not be surprised if a more profound analysis of the conditions imposed on the world by the laws of union were to lead us one day to recognize in the God of evolution an exact equivalent of the attributes accorded to the *"Ens a se"* by mediaeval philosophy. But if I have not yet reached this point in my thought, there are at least two things which I consider gained and which seemed to me sufficient provisionally to guide our march forward.[89]

While thus marking the limit of his "ultraphysics" or "hyperphysics," the two things he was certain of are: first, that the future center of the Universe must be considered to have "*from the beginning*, by something in itself, emerged into the Absolute";[90] and, second, that this

87. *HE*, pp. 68-69; *Oeuvres*, 6:86-87.
88. *HE*, p. 69; *Oeuvres*, 6:87.
89. *HE*, p. 70; *Oeuvres*, 6:88.
90. *HE*, p. 70; *Oeuvres*, 6:88.

center must be already "a personality superior to the one it evokes."[91] Thus, even within the limits of his "ultraphysics," Teilhard's Omega-God is *absolute*, at least to the extent that it must have within itself "its own principle of consistence" ("il faut qu'il trouve en soi-même sa propre consistance"),[92] and that it is already some "super-personality" ("Supra-personnel déjà actuelisé").[93]

It would seem clear from the above statements, contrasted to those which have gone before, that Teilhard affirmed the dogmatic tradition of the immutable absoluteness of God as against his concept of a yet-to-be-achieved pleroma. Nevertheless, on the level of his "hyper-physical" reasoning ("hyperphysical" in the sense of a metaphysics propounded as strictly "phenomenological" or "empirical" in origin), Teilhard was forced to admit that God, while in some sense absolute ontologically and as a person, is nevertheless destined to have His being "increased" in relation to "Universal Being." Despite his hope that his future speculations in "hyperphysics" might uncover reasons for someday being able to arrive at a notion of God that is the equivalent of the "ens a se" of medieval philosophy, Teilhard was never able to reach a very convincing conclusion in this direction, at least on the level of his "hyperphysics." In this more or less philosophical aspect of his thought, Teilhard's reasoning appears to resemble to some extent A. N. Whitehead's convictions about the "antecedent" and "consequent" natures of God.[94]

91. *HE*, pp. 70-71; *Oeuvres*, 6:89.
92. *Oeuvres*, 6:88. The English (*HE*, p. 70) is J. M. Cohen's translation.
93. *Oevures*, 6:89; *HE*, p. 71. In a letter to P. d'Ouince, dated Nov. 15, 1936, concerning this essay on a "Personalistic Universe" ("Esquisse d'un Univers Personnel"), he was considerably more definite on this point: "Mais je suis convaincu que, par un chemin différent, j'arrive bien aux mêmes attributs de l'Etre que ceux defendus par la Philo. traditionnelle. Plus j'y pense, plus je me vois amené à regarder l'Unité comme une synthèse descendant d'en haut (et non créant sur terre) et donc comme associée à de la Pluralité (ceci n'est-il pas le fond même de l'idée Trinitaire? . . .) (Unpublished, *T.A.*, Correspondence N-O-P, #105).
94. Cf. A. N. Whitehead, *Process and Reality* (New York, Harper, 1960), pp. 519-23. Teilhard apparently never read Whitehead at firsthand, and mentioned him only once by way of a quotation concerning education that he copied from a book of Julian Huxley's. But in this matter the differences as well as similarities are evident in the following excerpts from *Process and Reality*:

> So long as the temporal world is conceived as a self-sufficient completion of the creative act, explicable by its derivation from an ultimate principle which at once is eminently real and the unmoved mover, from this conclusion there is no escape: the best we can say of the turmoil is, "For so he giveth his beloved —sleep." This is the message of the religions of the Buddhistic type, and in some sense it is true. . . . The notion of God as the "unmoved mover" is derived from Aristotle, at least so far as Western thought is concerned. The notion of God as "eminently real" is a favorite doctrine of Christian theology." (p. 519)
> In the first place, God is not to be treated as an exception to all metaphysical principles, invoked to save their collapse. He is their chief exemplification.
> Viewed as primordial, he is the unlimited conceptual realization of the absolute wealth of potentiality. In this aspect, he is not before all creation, but with all creation. (*Ibid.*, p. 521)
> But God, as well as being primordial, is also consequent. He is the beginning and the end. He is not the beginning in the sense of being in the past of all members. He is the presupposed actuality of conceptual operation in unison of

Teilhard's most accessible escape from these apparent contradictions was, of course, in his understanding of Christ as the coextensive center of the converging universe and as the personal increase of universal being. And so, in the conclusion of his "Sketch of a Personalistic Universe," in the section entitled "The Religion of Personality," he stated that

> The essence of Christianity is neither more nor less than a belief in the unification of the world in God by the Incarnation. All the rest is only secondary explanation or illustration. In view of this, so long as human society had not emerged from the "neolithic," family phase of its development (that is to say until the dawn of the modern scientific-industrial phase) clearly the Incarnation could only find symbols of a juridical nature to express it. But since our modern discovery of the great unities and vast energies of the cosmos, the ancient words begin to assume a new and more satisfying meaning. To be the alpha and omega, Christ must, without losing his precise humanity, become co-extensive with the physical expanse of time and space. In order to reign on earth, He must "super-animate" the world. In Him henceforth, by the whole logic of Christianity, personality expands (or rather centres itself) till it becomes universal. Is this not exactly the God we are waiting for?[95]

Gathering all these ideas into one total vision, whatever their underlying contradictions, Teilhard was not hesitant to express essentially the same themes again and again. Even in his *The Phenomenon of Man*, the major work of all these years of exile, a book that he addressed to all men of science, he concluded in his epilogue:

> As early as in St. Paul and St. John we read that to create, to fulfil and to purify the world is, for God, to unify it by uniting it organically with himself. (Following Greek thought—following all thought in fact—are not "to be" and "to be one" identical?) How does he unify it? By partially immersing himself in things, by becoming "element," and then, from this point of vantage in the heart of matter, assuming the control and leadership of what we now call evolution. Christ, principle of universal vitality because sprung up as man among men, put himself in the position (maintained ever since) to subdue under himself, to purify, to direct and superanimate the general ascent of consciousnesses into which he inserted himself. By a perennial act of communion and sublimation, he aggregates to himself the total psychism of the earth. And when he has gathered everything together and transformed everything, he will close in upon himself and his conquests, thereby rejoining, in a final gesture, the divine focus he has never left. Then, as St. Paul tells us, *God shall be all in all*. This is indeed a superior form of "pantheism" (*"En pasi panta Theos"*) without trace of the poison of adulteration or annihilation: the expectation of perfect unity, steeped in which

> becoming with every other creative act. Thus by the relativity of all things, there is a reaction of the world in God. (*Ibid.*, p. 523)

95. *HE*, p. 91; *Oeuvres*, 6:113.

each element will reach its consummation at the same time as the universe.[96]

But again, fearing that he may not have made himself clear enough, Teilhard added a "résumé" or "post-face" (undated) to this same work in which he hastened to put all fears of a falsely understood "pantheism" to rest. The universal center is not one that comes to be out of "fusion" or "confusion," but is to be conceived as "préexistent" and "transcendent". It is to be understood as

> a very real "pantheism" if you like (in the etymological meaning of the word) but an absolutely legitimate pantheism—for if, in the last resort, the reflective centres of the world are effectively "one with God," this state is obtained not by identification (God becoming all) but by the differentiating and communicating action of love (God all *in everyone*). And that is essentially orthodox and Christian.[97]

During the years that remained of his exile in China, Teilhard's recurring expression of the pleroma continued to find varied expression. In his 1939 "Some General Views on the Essence of Christianity" (written during his past prewar visit to Paris), the word *plérôme* is not mentioned, nor are there any direct appeals to Scripture, but there is (as in the "Esquisse d'un Univers Personnel" of 1936) what amounts to a description of the pleroma in personalistic terms: " 'A supreme I (or Me),' a hyper-personal God, incorporates in itself, without destroying their identity, the human 'I's,' in and through the 'Christic I.' "[98] In the discussion that followed, Teilhard remarked that precisely because of a statically conceived metaphysics there has been a problem concerning persons and natures in God and in Christ. On the other hand, when conceived dynamically,

> the multiple (created) converges gradually towards unity (in God), the apex of the cone being formed by Christ, in whom the unified plural (the organized sum total of created centres of consciousness) meets the active centre of unification.[99]

From this perspective, he went on to say, the creation of man, the birth of Christ, and his redemptive death as historic facts take on a new dimension: "[They] are only a specially heightened expression of a process which is "cosmic" in its dimensions."[100]

Although Teilhard failed to explain just how this dynamic scheme of union of personal centers solves the problem of persons and nature in

96. *PM*, pp. 293-94; *Oeuvres*, 1:327-28.
97. *PM*, p. 310; *Oeuvres*, 1:344.
98. "Quelques Vues générales sur l'Essence du Christianisme" in *Oeuvres*, 10:155; *C&E*, p. 133.
99. *C&E*, p. 133; *Oeuvres*, 10:156. Cf. accompanying diagram, *idem*.
100. *C&E*, p. 135; *Oeuvres*, 10:157.

God, he did defend, near the end of this short note, "a true pantheism" in which "the elements *are fulfilled* by entering a deeper centre which dominates them and supercentres them in itself."[101]

In the 1940 "La Parole attendue," Teilhard moved back from this personalistic type of expression to one centered on the theme of the completion of the universe. It amounted to a new definition of the pleroma.

> The Pleroma: the mysterious synthesis of the Uncreated and the Created,—the grand completion (both quantitative and qualitative) of the Universe in God.[102]

Much the same approach was taken in his 1942 "Note sur la notion de Perfection chrétienne," which, although it deals more expressly with the problem of sanctification in this world, also has four accompanying diagrams. Concerning the third, the one that portrays the "classical Christian attitude" toward reconciliation of personal perfection and worldly progress, he wrote:

> God, in this diagram, truly gathers souls in a one to one relationship. But he does not complete in himself the collective development of the world "as a whole." He incorporates individuals: but the Universe and Humanity escape him. From this viewpoint, there are *two* distinct spiritual poles in the Universe: the one natural (K); and the other supernatural (D). In this perspective of a "bicephalous" Spirit, the Incarnation is in a "parasitical" relationship to the World: it does not recast it in a "monocephalous" Pleroma in Christ. What would St. Paul and the chorus of Greek Fathers have said about this?[103]

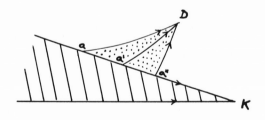

Fig. 3. The classic formula of "detachment" literally transferred to a World in the course on its on-going natural growth.

101. *C&E*, pp. 136-37; *Oeuvres*, 10:158.
102. *Oeuvres*, 11:106 and *Cahiers de Teilhard de Chardin*, #4, p. 26. On the following page, pursuing this theme, he also included his usual paraphrased quotation of Eph. 4:9-10: ("Descendit, ascendit *ut repleret omnia*"). My translation (cf. *TF*, p. 97).
103. *Oeuvres*, 11:115-16. My translation (cf. *TF*, pp. 103-4).

After rejecting this "bicephalous" vision for a "monocephalous" one
(pictured by converging cones with a common apex "K-D"), Teilhard
again cited Ephesians 4:9-10 as being "the same economy as that of the
Incarnation."[104]

There are two final references to 1 Corinthians 15:28 and two more
to the *plérôme* in Teilhard's writings of his years in China, mostly in
that work alternatively titled "Introduction à la vie chrétienne" and
"Introduction au Christianisme." Almost immediately upon beginning,
with a section he styled "L'essence du Christianisme: A 'Personalistic
Universe' " (he had already used this English subtitle in explaining his
1934 essay by that name), he quoted 1 Corinthians 15:28 to buttress
three points:

> From the realistic and biological point of view which is eminently
> that of Catholic dogma, the universe represents: (1) The arduous,
> personalizing unification in God of a tenuous mass of souls, distinct
> from God, but in subordinate dependence on him, (2) by incorpora-
> tion in Christ (incarnate God), (3) through the building up of collec-
> tive humano-Christian unity (Church).
>   'When all things are subjected to him, then the Son himself will
> also be subjected to him who put all things under him, that God
> may be everything to every one' (1 Cor. 15:28).[105]

The unique thing about this essay, at least up to this time in his
writings, was Teilhard's treatment of the Church within the context of
the pleroma. Prior to this period, the Church had in his writings been
more or less subsumed under the concept of the Body of Christ, or to
be more exact, was seen as simply the "mystical" extension of the
Eucharistic Body in the life of the believer.[106] In this later essay, however, he not only spoke of Christianity in general as "the phylum of
love" in this world, but more specifically of Catholicism as an ecclesial
Body within Christianity. In a passage that prefaces one already
quoted, he stated:

---

104. *Oeuvres*, 11:117. The fourth diagram (*ibid.*, p. 116) is as follows, with the accompanying notes:

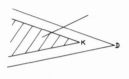

Fig. 4. Diagram expressing the incorporation of natural progress in the
spiritualization and the Christian detachment (K), which is not achieved except in D (God)—D incorporating K
("from the very need of K") for the realization of the pleroma.

(Cf. also *TF*, p. 104.)

105. *C&E*, p. 151; *Oeuvres*, 10:179-80.
106. E.g., "Note sur l'Union physique. . . ," *Oeuvres*, 10:19f.; *C&E*, pp. 15f.

After what has been said earlier about the living and evolutive nature of the Christian faith it is easy to understand that this privilege claimed by the Church of Rome of being the only authentic expression of Christianity is not an unjustified pretension but meets an inevitable organic need.[107]

Nevertheless, having made his act of faith in the central authority of the Church that viewed with askance so many of his ideas, Teilhard closed this apologetical essay with a reaffirmation of his insistence that Christianity be understood as a true pantheism. Again he appealed to 1 Corinthians 15:28:

Ultimately, God is not alone in the totalized Christian universe (in the pleroma, to use St Paul's word); but he is all in all of us ("*en pasi panta theos*"): unity in plurality.[108]

Teilhard's final theological essay from China was his "Christianity and Evolution," dated November 11, 1945. In it, Creation, Incarnation, and Redemption are characterized as "the three aspects of one and the same fundamental process: they are aspects of a *fourth* mystery. . . : the mystery of the creative union of the world in God, or Pleromization."[109] On the surface, it would seem that Teilhard was simply playing with terminology, or combining old ideas of his ("The Struggle Against the Multitude" and "Creative Union"—1917) with his newer concepts. Perhaps; but notes from his Journal of this period indicate that he was probing into this "Fourth Mystery" of pleromization with a great deal of daring speculation.[110]

3. The Final Years (1946-1955)

Teilhard's postwar arrival in Paris was on May 3, 1946. His first theological essay of this period was an article, "Catholicisme et Science," written in August of that same year for the review *Esprit*.[111] It

---

107. *C&E*, p. 167; *Oeuvres*, 10:195. See chap. 2, §F above, for preceding section.
108. *C&E*, 171; *Oeuvres*, 10:199-200.
109. *C&E*, p. 183; *Oeuvres*, 10:213.
110. A Journal note of July 25, 1945 ("Journal" 13 (1): 146), which remains very difficult to decipher, makes clear reference to "the problem of the coincidence of the Maximum" in a way that appears to link a God who is seen as metaphysically absolute as nevertheless being seen in conjunction with a universe in the process of maximum interiorization. The possible answers to this riddle, as mentioned in this note, would seem to include a new metaphysics of creative union wherein evolution creates that object of union without which the Omega accomplishes nothing in its unitive efforts. Plenitude would thus form a kind of supplemental element to unification. The concept of "Aseity" would have to give way before the concept of a fullness of union.
    Whatever this note was meant to convey, the latter part speaks of creatures being "necessary" to the pleroma in such a way that without adding to the Omega of absolute being as such, they nevertheless are born integrally out of union with the Omega. Thus creation can be said to be a necessary threshold by which absolute being is "complemented." But this threshold remains *within God* alone.
111. Republished in *Oeuvres*, 9:235-41; *S&C*, pp. 187-91.

evidences a certain ecumenical concern and hope that "Christogenesis" will become the key to the reconciliation of mankind's intellectual strivings, just as it was his hope, later on, for a point of future agreement among Christians.[112] Of particular note, however, in his writings of that year, in which the concept of the pleroma figures, is his "Outline of a Dialectic of Spirit" (dated Nov. 25, 1946). His concern to incorporate the Church more consciously in the pleroma is shown in the section subtitled "The Living Church and the Christ-Omega":

> This takes us in conclusion, by a final ascent to the less known, to a last and supreme definition of Omega point: the centre, at once one and complex, in which, bound together by the person of Christ, may be seen *enclosed one within the other* (one might say) *three* progressively deeper *centres*: on the outside, the immanent ('natural') apex of the humano-cosmic cone; further in, at the middle, the immanent ('supernatural') apex of the 'ecclesial' or Christic cone; and finally, at the innermost heart, the transcendent, triune, and divine centre: The complete Pleroma coming together under the mediating action of Christ-Omega.

To the accompanying illustration is attached the following explanation:

> Note. In this combination it is arguable whether the humano-cosmic apex "demands" a Christic apex. It is clear, however, that the Christic apex could not come into being without the existence of a humano-cosmic apex.[113]

This little note contains a very important admission for Teilhard, but as he explained in a final note, the dialectic that he had been outlining was, like most of his writings, first of all written for nonbelievers, while for believers he tended to "jump" directly to the level of revealed truth.

On June 1, 1947, shortly before his intended departure for South Africa to survey the paleontological findings that had taken place during his long absence, Teilhard suffered a rather severe heart attack. During his convalescence, as his biographers have pointed out, his thoughts turned rather naturally to the limited number of years that awaited him and, accordingly, to the more eschatological aspects of his thought. But everything was to be considered always within the context of the problem of the pleroma.[114]

As for the Parousia and its relationship to the pleroma, Teilhard's

112. Cf. "Oecuménisme," Dec. 15, 1946, in *Oeuvres*, 9:253-54; S&C, pp. 197-98.
113. "Esquisse d'une Dialectique de l'Esprit" in *Oeuvres*, 7:156; AE, p. 149.
114. A Journal note of July 25, 1947 ("Journal" 15 [3]: 18 bis.) speaks of the problem faced by all mystics on how to incorporate the "all" within the "all." The whole Christian solution, according to Teilhard, is contained within the concept of the pleroma. But the essential condition for understanding this pleroma is that the cosmos that is in evolution be allowed to engender a mysticism that is not only that of maximum unification but also of activation.

position remained intractable. His insistence on the Divine intention in the "Cosmologie et Théologie" debate with Père Dubarle (see chap. 2, §A, above) and his equally strong insistence that man's contribution to the pleroma had a determinative influence on the occurrence of the Parousia remained unshaken. In 1948, following the lecture "Foi humaine–Foi spirituelle,"[115] where the Parousia was ultimately identified with the pleroma, two more affirmations of this cooperation of divine and human activity toward the achievement of the Parousia are found. In "Trois choses que je vois (ou: une Weltanschauung en trois points)" of February 1948, the three points are listed as follows:

> 1. First judgment of value. Evolutively, Humanity is engaged in a collective movement towards a future Point of Maturation.
> 2. Second judgment ov value. In the concrete, the Point of human Maturation, as given before, coincides with the point called "The Christic Parousia."
> 3. Third point, or Corollary. A new psychic energy is at the service of Noogenesis: The problem and the synthesis of two Faiths.[116]

Finally, in his summary essay "Comment je vois" (Aug. 26, 1948), section 24, he described the convergence of his metaphysical views and his religious beliefs:

> From a phenomenal point of view we observe that only here that the relation appears between what I called the human "critical point of maturation" on the one hand, and, on the other, the point of the Parousia (or the second, triumphal coming of Christ) by which the Christian horizon is closed at the end of time. Inevitably, by their very structure, the two points coincide,—in the sense that the achievement of Hominization through ultra-reflection appears as a necessary precondition of its "divinization".

But this footnote is attached to the word "nécessaire":

> "Necessary," but not sufficient. There is no "millenarism" in this, because the point of human ultra-reflection (corresponding to the point of the Parousia) does not mark a phase of repose, but of maximum tension.[117]

How explain all this, except in the light of the pleromic understanding of the world's destiny? For the same reason Teilhard was to decry

---

115. *Parousie* = apparition − retour du Christ
    attende d'un évent humain =
    monde phenomenal doit rejoindre monde céleste
        +
    opérer unification de l'humanité sur elle-même
    = plérôme de St Paul
    (Jan. 1948, *T.A.* #117. Notes taken by Solange Lemaître and L. Rionet.)
116. *Oeuvres*, 11:164, 168, 170. (My translation; italics follow the underlining of *T.A.* #65, pp. 2, 5, 7.) (cf. *TF*, pp. 149, 153, 156.)
117. *Oeuvres*, 11:206. (cf. *TF*, p. 191.)

abberrant ideas of the "Néoparousie" in a note of May 28 1950, as being a "Néo-primitivisme."[118]

Again, as he said in a letter only some two months before his death: "—The accomplishment of the Earth is not a simple addition, but an essential co-condition of the Parousia."[119]

To return to the year 1947, however, in his "Reflections on Original Sin," pleromization was again stressed as being a single three-fold operation (as against the two distinct operations of creation as contrasted to the Incarnation-Redemption viewed in an "Alexandrian" type of universe):

> it is not precisely either Creation, or Incarnation, or Redemption, in their mechanism, but "pleromization": I mean the mysterious "repletive" (if not "completive") relationship which links the first being with participated being.[120]

Shortly before this, on August 27, 1947, Teilhard had entered a note in his Journal that showed his intention of writing a new "Mon Univers," the outline of which was to consist of sections entitled "Physique," "Dialectique," "Métaphysique," and "Mystique," respectively.[121] Apparently, this intention was carried out in his "Comment je vois" of August, 1948, except that the section to be called "Dialectique" was absorbed into the "Physique," which itself became divided into two major sections: "Le Phénomène Humain" and "Le Phénomène Chrétien." In the section entitled "Métaphysique" (Teilhard's first use of this term in any favorable sense in his essays since the World War I period!), the following description of pleromization is found:

> a) Before all, we discover that, if creation can include a limitless number of phases, accordingly (and a little similar to Trinitization) it can not be accomplished but a single time—if one may so speak—in the "life of God." And in effect, once the reduction of the Multiple has taken place, no form of unresolved opposition (neither interior, nor exterior) can subsist in "pleromized" being. All imaginable pos-

118. "Journal" 17 (5): 104.
119. "L'achèvement de la Terre n'est pas un simple surcroît, mais une co-condition essentielle de la Parousie." Letter to Felix Soignon, Feb. 16, 1955, unpublished, T.A., vol. S-T.
120. C&E, p. 198; Oeuvres, 10:230. (Emphasis added.) N.B. The editor of Oeuvres comments on Teilhard's position as expressed here with a note (cf. ibid., p. 225 [259] n.1) comparing Teilhard's use of "réplétive" with certain ideas of Card. de Bérulle, especially the latter's idea of creation's participation in the Trinitarian life. It should be noted that an entry of Teilhard's Journal parallels in another way another thought of Card. de Bérulle's: that of the Spirit producing the Word-Incarnate, who himself returns creation to its "fontal source of the deity in the Father."
    A Journal note of Teilhard's from Oct. 26-27, 1945 ("Journal" 14 [2]: 1) seems to confirm that the notion of the Christ-Omega is inconceivable without the Father as its "ontological focus." The note then goes on to speak of the "Four great mysteries" in which there is a kind of trinity of the mysteries of Creation, Incarnation, and Redemption summarized in one great mystery of "Pleromization."
121. Journal 15 (3): 31.

sibilities of union (both active and passive) are found to be exhausted; "being," having arrived at this level, is completely saturated.*

b) Accordingly, we are aware that in order to create (because, again, to create is to unite), God is inevitably led to immerse himself in the Multiple, finally "incorporating" himself in it.[122]

And again, in the final section of this part called "Métaphysique," there appears this detailed explanation of the above, with even more detailed footnotes:

And so it is that, sooner or later, a series of notions, for a long-time considered independent, show themselves to be organically related. No more God (up to a certain point . . .) without creative union. No more creation without incarnational immersion. No more Incarnation without redemptive compensation. [n.1, see below] In a Metaphysics of Union, the three fundamental "mysteries" of Christianity [n.2, below] do not appear as being more than three faces of the one same mystery of mysteries, that of Pleromization (or the unifying reduction of the Multiple). And, by that stroke, it is a renovated Christology which finds itself as the axis, not simply historical or juridical, but structural, of all Theology. Between the Word on the one hand, and the Man-Jesus on the other, a kind of Christic "third nature" (if I may so speak! ! ! .) is unleashed (se dégage),—everywhere to be read in the writings of St. Paul: that of the Christ who is total and totalizing, in whom, through the transforming effect of the Resurrection, the individual human element born of Mary is taken into a state not only of being a cosmic Element (or Milieu, or Encompassment [Courbure], but also the ultimate psychic center of a universal gathering. [n. 3, below.][123]

Without a doubt, "Comment je vois" was the third major milestone in Teilhard's long series of essays (along with "La vie cosmique" in 1916 and the "Mon Univers" of 1924). In it was gathered into one all

---

122. *Oeuvres*, 11:211 (my translation).* Teilhard's footnote reads as follows: "There is evidently an infinite number of conceivable *modalities* within the *single Universe* as the object of Creation: but these diverse modalities, like the diverse paths traced upon the side of a mountain, lead inevitably to the same summit." (cf. *TF*, p. 196).
123. *Oeuvres*, 11:213-14. (My translation.) (cf. *TF*, pp. 198-99.)

[n. 1] Truly, in the "creative penalty" expressed in the idea of Redemption, *two* elements should probably be distinguished: a) to begin with, without doubt, compensation for statistical disorders; b) but also a specific effort of unification, overcoming a kind of ontological declivity (or inertia) because of which participated being constantly tends to fall back into Multiplicity.
[n 2] Up to now, I repeat, they have been commonly presented as entirely separable from each other. In popular teaching, it is still currently admitted that: 1) God is able *absolutely* (simpliciter) to create or not to create; 2) if he creates, he is able to do so either with or without an Incarnation; and 3) if he does incarnate himself, he is able to do so with or without the ability to suffer. It is this conceptual pluralism, in whatever system is proposed, which, it appears to me, it is essential to correct.
[n. 3] In the Universe each element is (physically as well as metaphysically) an elementary center in relation to the totality of time and space. But, in the case of Christ, this co-extension of coexistence becomes a co-extension of domination.

the fruits of his speculation up to this period, and here surfaced for the first time his ideas about a "Third Nature" of Christ. What surfaced here was the result of the dialectic between his metaphysics (for so long hidden under the concept of *hyperphysics*) and his cosmic Christology. As to what he actually meant by this "Third Nature," two notes from 1945 may help shed some light on the subject, indicating that his choice of the word *nature* was dictated more by lack of sufficient vocabulary than by any desire to invent heterodox formulas. More speculation on this matter was to appear in the final two years of his life.[124]

In the meantime, Teilhard's thoughts turned back to a final attempt to clarify what he stubbornly insisted on calling his "Christian Pantheism." In July of 1950 he was to write "A Clarification: Reflections on Two Converse Forms of Spirit." While the *plérôme* is not explicitly mentioned in this essay, there is a considerable play on the words of 1 Corinthians 15:28. Summing up his two "isotopes" (i.e., two forms of what is basically the same element) of the spirit, he categorized them as:

> Pantheism of identification, at the opposite pole from love: "God is all." And pantheism of unification, beyond love: "God all in all."[125]

The formulation centered on "tout-tous" (all-everything) is carried one step further in his footnote on the same page, where he further categorized the various "pantheisms" as follows:

1. *To become all beings* (erroneous, and impossible to effect): para-pantheism.
2. *To become all* ("eastern" monism): pseudo-pantheism.
3. *To become one with all beings* ("western" monism): eu-pantheism.[126]

The key elements in Teilhard's thinking on this matter were two-fold: the reality of the material universe and the evolution of that universe into distinct personalities. "True pantheism" can ignore neither, nor

124. A note in the 26th.-27th. of October 1945 Journal entry ("Journal" 14 [2]: 1) indicates that for Christ to be the evolutive center of consistence and amorization, his "Ego" must be in some way triple or trinitarian, for the pleroma is the Trinity and the cosmos combined. (Teilhard's reasoning seems to be that if Christ is the focus of the cosmos, the trinitarian structure must in some way be reflected within Christ himself. A simple diagram accompanies the note, with a line, representing the evolving cosmos, converging on a tripartite center designated as the Omega.)

This trinitarian aspect of Christ seems to be distinct from Teilhard's speculation on a "third" or cosmic "nature" in Christ, although in a Journal note of Nov. 24, 1945 ("Journal" 14 [2]: 9), Teilhard denies that the triple or third aspect of Christ involves a third nature but is rather the edge of interaction ("frange d'interférence") between the divine word and the cosmic dimension of all human nature (assumed by Christ in the Incarnation).

125. "Pour y voir clair: Réflexions sur deux formes inverses d'esprit." *Oeuvres*, 7:231-32; *AE*, p. 223.

126. *Ibid.*

suppress neither, for the two are the two faces or "pôles" of what is ultimately one and the same "Weltstoff." Thus, in the end Teilhard envisions God as

> finally becoming *all in all* within an atmosphere of pure charity ("*sola caritas*"); in that magnificent definition of the pantheism of differentiation is expressed in unmistakable terms the very essence of Christ's message.[127]

In October 1950, Teilhard wrote another long essay of an unusually autobiographical cast entitled "Le Coeur de la Matière." In it he explored the development of his "sens plérômique" from its earliest beginnings in his boyhood passion for rocks (the symbol of what is solid and lasting), through his early attraction to pantheism to his final understanding, by means of evolution, of the truly irreversible nature of spirit, and its final integration with God through the cosmic Christ. Toward the end of this long essay, he made two statements concerning the pleroma, both bearing on the "completion" of God:

> Concerning the World as an object of "Creation," classical metaphysics had accustomed us to seeing a sort of extrinsic production, issuing from, out of an overflowing kindness, the supreme *efficacious causality* [*efficience*] of God. Invincibly,—and in all justice enabling [us] to both act and love fully—I am led at the same time (conforming to the spirit of St. Paul) to see a mysterious product of *completion and achievement* for Absolute Being itself. No longer *Being participated through extra-position and divergence*, but *Being participated through pleromization and convergence. It is an effect, not so much of causality, but of creative union!*[128]

There is evidence that Teilhard later softened the force of the words "de complétion et d'achèvement" by substituting a simple "de satisfaction" in their place.[129] If so, it was done more out of considerations of prudence than from a change of conviction.[130] As late as January 1952, Teilhard remarked in a letter to François Richaud:

---

127. *AE*, p. 225; *Oeuvres*, 7:234. Teilhard repeated himself in slightly different words in a short paper of the winter of 1951 entitled "Quelques remarques 'POUR Y VOIR CLAIR' sur l'Essence du sentiment mystique":

> Dans le premier cas, Dieu (un Dieu "impersonnel") était *Tout*. Dans le second cas, Dieu (un Dieu ultra-personnel) parce que "centrique" est *Tout en Tous* (formule même de St Paul). (Cf. *Oeuvres*, 11:228.) *TF*, p. 210.

128. *Oeuvres*, 13: 65-66. (My translation.)
129. Cf. Tresmontant's article "Le Père Teilhard de Chardin et la Théologie" in *Lettre* (publ. of the Dept. of Philosophy, #49-50, Univ. of Paris, Sept.-Oct., 1962), p. 33; also Claude Tresmontant, *Pierre Teilhard de Chardin: His Thought* (Baltimore: Helicon, 1959), p. 93.
130. The change in question seems to have occurred in a mimeographed copy of the essay sent by Teilhard to George B. Barbour; however, the version published in *Oeuvres* 13 contains the original wording. Cf. *Oeuvres*, 13:65 n.12.

In that which touches God and the World, contemporary intellectual systems (e.g. Scholastic, Vedic . . .) are always caught in a dilemma: either to divinize or to minimize [annihilate] the World. And
yet the truth may very well be in the notion of the "Pleroma" of St.
Paul: Creation in some way "completing" God. There is, in other
words, some kind of absolute perfection in the Synthesis of the One
"a se" and of the Multiple. Pleromization in addition to [*en outre*]
Trinitization.[131]

Whatever emendations may have been made to the sentence of "Le
Coeur de la Matière" in question, there still remain other phrases in
the conclusion ("Prayer to the Ever-greater Christ") of the same essay
that betray his real thought on the subject:

All this seems frightening to the man who is still hesitant to launch
himself into the great tide of matter, fearing to see his God burst in
the acquisition of one more dimension. . . .
    But for my intelligence and soul, could anything precisely make
you more lovable, alone lovable, O Lord, than perceiving that, as *a
Center ever open in your inmost self, you continue to intensify
yourself—deepening your hue—ever more gathering in and subduing
the Universe in the depth of your heart ("until the moment when
You and the World in You reenter the bosom of the One from whom
you sprang") you pleromize yourself?*[132]

In the spring of 1953, Teilhard again returned to this problem of the
"completion" of God, but this time in slightly different language in his
"The Contingence of the Universe and Man's Zest for Survival," which
is described in a subtitle as: "or How Can One Rethink the Christian
Notion of Creation to Conform with the Laws of Energetics?"[133] Here
he tied the problem of the complementary nature of the pleroma for
the last time with what he considered the root problem—the inadequacy of the scholastic categories of thought to cope with an evolutionary
view of reality. It has been seen how, as far back as his early essay on
the notion of creation, Teilhard expressed this criticism of classical
thought. All along he was convinced, even if he could not express himself as adequately as he wished, that an exaggerated concept of the
"self-sufficiency" of God, and the equally exaggerated notion of the

131. Unpublished, *T.A.*, Correspondence "R", #118 (Jan. 18, 1952). (My translation.)
    Two drafts of this letter are in existence, the first stating, "La Création complète en
    quelque façon Dieu," while the second substitutes *"complétant"* (including quota-
    tion marks) for the *complète* in the first draft. See Appendix D, §2, c, for the French
    transcript.
132. Pp. 31-32 (my translation). The editor of *Oeuvres* (see 10:213, *C&E*, p. 183) has
    contributed the following excerpt from a letter of Teilhard's to Père J. M. Le Blond
    (April 1953):

        The pleroma *is more* (in absolute value) than "God alone" before Christ has
    entered into it "with the world incorporated in himself." The pleromization of
    being must one day be linked to "trinitization in some generalized ontology."

133. See *C&E*, pp. 221f.; *Oeuvres*, 10:236f.

complete "contingency" of creation, had, at its root, an overemphasis on the notion of "efficient causality" at the expense of "formal causality" in the understanding of the creative act, with the result that God's transcendence was identified wrongly with a completely "extrinsicist" formulation of participation of being.[134] In this new essay he tied the inadequacy of the scholastic views with his line of "apologetics" based on what he called "energetics," that is, the laws governing the development of the noosphere and the necessary conditions for its fulfillment in the Omega.

> And it is just at this point, in fact, that without our being sufficiently prepared for it, the apparently completely theoretical and innocent problem of *participated being* suddenly enters a vitally concrete sphere—that of man's zest for action.
> It is sound Scholastic philosophy, as everyone knows, that being, in the form of *Ens a se* [Being in itself] is posited exhaustively and repletively, and instantaneously, at the ontological origin of all things. Following this in a second phase, all the rest (i.e. "the world") appears in turn only as an entirely gratuitous supplement or addition: the guests at the divine banquet.
> Strictly deduced from a particular metaphysics of potency and act, this thesis of creation's complete gratuitousness was acceptable in the Thomistic framework of a static universe in which all the creature had to do was to accept his existence and effect his own salvation. By contrast, it becomes dangerous and virulent (because disheartening) as soon as, in a system of cosmogenesis, the "participated being" we all are begins to wonder whether the radically contingent condition to which the theologians reduce it really justifies the pain and labour required for evolution. For, unless only individual happiness is to be sought at the term of existence (a form of happiness we have definitively rejected), how could man *fail to be robbed of his zest for action* by this alleged revelation of his radical uselessness?[135]

Such extrinsicism, in Teilhard's mind, had to be counteracted by a new concept of God's transcendence, one that is associated not with a splendid isolation of God from his universe but in a convergence of that God with that same universe. It would call for an uncompromising change of perspective, one that in this same essay he entitled: "Un cor-

---

134. An interesting Journal note of Dec. 16, 1946 ("Journal" 14 [2]: 131) speaks of a conversation with P. Lebreton touching on the subject of the "formal cause" of creation and the question as to whether the pleroma (as such a formal cause) doesn't really compromise the doctrine of the pure spirituality of God through introducing some notion of "composition." Here, Teilhard notes, we can see the insufficiency of scholastic categories (as in the problem of grace). There are no categories allowing for something between identity and unity.

135. *C&E*, pp. 224-25; *Oeuvres*, 10:268-9. In a two-line note of May 20, 1954 ("Journal" 20 [8]: 52), Teilhard excoriates the "puerility" of the aristotelian-thomistic metaphysics, comparing its potency-act concepts to the Chinese concepts of the Yin-Yang. For a more serious statement on Teilhard's ideas on causality, especially his concept of "création-informante," see his letter of Feb. 15, 1955 to Claude Cuénot (Appendix D, §2, a).

rectif à la contingence: la notion du Plérôme." In this final section Teilhard went on to say:

> Let us, in fact, forget about *"Ens a se"* and *"Ens ab alio"* ["Being existing by another"] and go back to the most authentic and most concrete expressions of Christian revelation and mysticism. At the heart of what we can learn or drink in from those, what do we find but the affirmation and the expression of a strictly bilateral and complementary relationship between the world and God? "God creates by love," the Scholastics say, quite rightly. But what is this love, at once inexplicable in its subject and degrading for its object, which *is based on no need* (except the pleasure of giving for the sake of giving)? If we reread St John and St Paul . . . what a sense we find of the absolute value of a cosmic drama in which God would indeed appear to have been ontologically involved even before his incarnation. And, in consequence, what emphasis on the pleroma and pleromization!
>
> In truth, it is not the sense of contingence of the created but the sense of the mutual completion of the world and God which gives life to Christianity. And, that being so, if it is just this soul of "complementarity" which Aristotelian ontology fails to get hold of, then we must do what the physicists do when mathematics is found wanting—change our geometry.[136]

But where exactly is this "complementarity" to be consummated, if not in Christ? It is on this final point that Teilhard's flirtation with the idea of a third nature of Christ must be put in perspective. The concept appeared some years earlier in Teilhard's notes than in his writings. The formulation varies, sometimes being that of two subdivisions of the "cosmic" Christ, elsewhere a quasi-distinct "Third Nature."[137]

A slightly later note gives the key to one of the sources of Teilhard's concern in this matter—the possibility if not the outright probability, of other "thinking planets."[138] And it is precisely in the face of this possibility (recognized before under the problem posed by the doctrine of original sin) that Teilhard's first mention of a third nature of Christ appears in one of his essays, "A Sequel to the Problem of Human Origins: The Plurality of Inhabited Worlds," written in June, 1953. He maintained that by necessity of our expanded world view we must come to grips with two notions, namely:

136. *C&E*, pp. 226-27; *Oeuvres*, 10:270-71.
137. According to the August 30, 1946 Journal entry ("Journal" 14 [2]: 106), a neo-Christianity would save and exalt three Christs: the historical Christ (a sort of nuclear seed); the Cosmic Christ of hominization; and the Transcendent Christ, who gives irreversibility to the Universe. But another note, written soon after (Oct. 7, 1946), although it also speaks of three natures, this time the first nature being divine, seems to indicate that the human nature of Christ is but a "sector" of his cosmic nature. (*Ibid.*, p. 115).
138. The Journal note of Feb. 7, 1948 ("Journal" 15 [3]: 97), speaks of the "three natures" of Christ as divine, human, and that of the "cosmic-leader." A curious little diagram, however, seems to indicate that the "third nature" is but an extension of Christ's human nature, multiplied or subdivided "n" number of times to correspond to "n" number of planets in the universe having thinking life.

both of *universe* psychically convergent on itself, through the whole of itself (as a result of the evolutive process known as "complexification-consciousness"); and of *Christ universalized* in his operation, in virtue of, and by virtue of, his resurrection.[139]

Accordingly, faced with these disconcerting probabilities, there is only one really necessary fact that remains solidly established: "the dogma that sums up all dogmas: '*In Eo Omnia constant.*' "[140]

All this implies but one solution, which he clarifies in a postscript:

The only solution: in the two combined ideas:
a. of convergent universe (= centred)
b. of Christ (3rd nature) centre of the universe.[141]

Given this necessity of greatly expanded vision of the "cosmic" Christ, Teilhard was caught between the Divine nature (which is truly universalized but of itself is not that of the "Panconsummator") and the human nature of Christ (which traditional theology assigns a mediating Lordship in respect to humanity).[142] For this reason, among others, Teilhard wrote the March 1955 "Le Christique," which he sensed might turn out to be his last will and testament. Here, in the section entitled "L'Univers Christifié," where he delineated a double perspective of "La Consommation de l'Univers par le Christ" and "La Consommation du Christ par l'Univers," he stated his final questions in this regard:

In the total Christ (on this point Christian tradition is unanimous) there is not simply Man and God. There is also the One who, in his "theandric" being gathers in all Creation: "in quo omnia constant."

Up to now and in spite of the dominating place that St. Paul gives it in his vision of the World, this third aspect or function—or even, in a true sense, this third "nature" of Christ (a nature which is neither human, nor divine, but "cosmic") has not yet attracted much of the explicit attention of the faithful or of the theologians. . . .

But there are difficulties; for how can we, ultimately, conceive of a Christ who "immensifies himself" according to the needs of our

139. *C&E*, p. 234; *Oeuvres*, 10:280.
140. *C&E*, p. 235; *Oeuvres*, 10:281.
141. *C&E*, p. 236; *Oeuvres*, 10:281-82. This final note was added to the above essay by Teilhard in reference to the "Hypothèse J.M." The editor of *Oeuvres* describes this thesis, as reformulated and completed since 1953, as advocating the totally cosmic repercussions of the Incarnation of the Word (as well of his passion and death) both in time and in space. The thesis appears to be that of J. Maréchal.
142. In two notes of late 1950, Teilhard seems to have had in mind this same problem as interpreted in reference to 1 Cor. 15:28. The first (Oct. 12, 1950; "Journal" 17 [5]: 159) speaks of "the two faces of Christ" corresponding to the two phases of Christic evolution: thus, in addition to his function as mediator, we have the double function of "consummator" and "irreversibilitator."
    The second note (Dec. 29, 1950; "Journal" 18 [6]: 16), again referring to the "en pasi panta Theos" of 1 Cor. 15, interprets it as the pre-pleromic (pleromizing) and assimilating operation of Christ and designates it in the context of cosmogenesis as being "ultra-humanizing" rather than supernaturalizing in the strict sense.

understanding of Space-Time, without, by the same count, losing his divine personality and, in some way, causing himself to vanish?

But if . . . our Universe* really does form a kind of biological "vortex" dynamically centered upon itself, then how can it not be seen that a unique, singular position is discovered at the temporo-spatial summit of the system, where Christ, without any deformation of effort, becomes literally, with an extraordinary realism, the *Pantocrator?*[143]

In what turned out to be his final statement on this matter,[144] Teilhard formulated his answer to this question of a lifetime. In it are gathered the thoughts of all of his research, meditation, and prayer:

From the supposition of an evolutive Omega, it becomes not only possible to conceive that Christ radiates physically over the bewildering totality of things; but that also this radiation inevitably attains a maximum of penetration and activation.

Set up as the Prime Mover of the evolution of complexity-consciousness, the cosmic Christ becomes cosmologically possible. And at the same time, *ipso facto*, he acquires and develops, in all fullness, a veritable *omnipresence of transformation*. All energy, every happening, for each one of us, becomes superanimated with his influence and his attraction. In the final analysis, Cosmogenesis, after its discovery, according to its principal axis, Biogenesis, then Noogenesis, culminates in that Christogenesis which all Christians reverence.[145]

In this passage can be seen every major theme of Teilhard's synthesis, including the Pauline pleroma (fullness—*plénitude*), and in the passage that follows, his continued fidelity to his initial insights of World War I:

And then behold how, to the marvel of the believer, it is the eucharistic mystery itself which is infinitely extended in a veritable universal "transubstantiation," wherein not only the words of Consecration fall upon the sacrificial bread and wine, but also upon all the joys and pains engendered in its progress, by the Convergence of the World,

—and there descends likewise the possibility of a universal Communion.[146]

143. *Oeuvres*, 13:107-8. (My translation). The footnote reads: "Et probablement (dans la mesure ou créer, c'est unifier), *tout* Univers possible."

144. The notes on the final page of his "Journal" ("Journal" 21 [9]: 35) seem to indicate that Teilhard was planning two new essays, the first to be called "Le Troisième Infini" and the second to be called "Ce que je crois." While this latter phrase appears as the heading of a personal statement of faith in the April 6, 1955 note (see *Oeuvres*, 5:404-5; *FM*, p. 309, for a simplified transcription of part of these notes), a final section sets the phrase off in quotation marks and associates the "third infinite" theme with the first section of the proposed essay.

145. *Oeuvres*, 13:108-9.

146. *Oeuvres*, 13:109.

B. THE "PLEROMA" IN NEW TESTAMENT EXEGESIS

Compared to the great amount of material on the *plérôme* in Teilhard's writings, the amount of material available among the exegetes is comparatively modest, at least in proportion to that on "the Body of Christ," a subject to which the pleroma is often appended. This in itself is a situation upon which Teilhard often looked upon with askance.[147]

1. Earlier Commentators

In the commentary of Cornelius a Lapide, for example, little is said on the subject other than to comment on the various types of "plenitudinem" that the Fathers assigned to Colossians 1:19 ("divinitatis," "omnis perfectio," and, in the estimation of Theodoretus, "Ecclesia").[148] However, there appears a diversity of meaning in his exposition of Ephesians 1:23, where *plērōma* is rendered as "complementum" and is identified with the Church as a body, following the interpretations of Chrysostom, Ambrose, Anselm, and Aquinas.[149] It is accompanied by a note that associated the "Adimplebo" of Colossians 1:24 with the "implet" of Ephesians 1:23, an association that Teilhard appeared to take for granted, but that later authors, like Feuillet, will call into question. The 1 Corinthians 15:28 text, which Teilhard so constantly associated with his concept of the pleroma, is explained by a series of literary images, or else by the concept of all the perfections of God becoming united in a single vision or consummation. Any suggestion of conversion of created being into uncreated being (the Gerson-Ruisbrochius controversy) is vigorously put down as heretical.[150]

The *Cursus Scripturae Sacrae*, however, has substantially more to say, especially from a philological point of view. While Knabenbauer's analysis of Colossians 1:19 repeats the opinions listed by Lapide, it calls attention to the opinion of Theodore of Mopsuesta who, according to Knabenbauer, interpreted the pleroma as meaning "omnem creaturam quae ab eo repleta est probavit (Deus) illi conjungere." This substantive meaning of the term is seen to be "praeter rem et extra contextum," and Knabenbauer adopted the more unanimously traditional "plenitudinem gratiae."[151]

In his treatment of the pleroma in Ephesians, however, Knaben-

---

147. Teilhard in an Oct. 6, 1950 Journal note ("Journal" 17 [5]: 157), scores the lack of even a brief quotation of 1 Cor. 15:28 in the Roman Breviary of that time and the lack of any theological studies on the pleroma as being "two scandals."
148. See Cornelius a Lapide, *Commentarius in Scripturas Sacras* (Paris: Vivès, 1868) 19: 77-78.
149. See *ibid.*, 18: 598.
150. *Ibid.*, 18: 405.
151. See Knabenbauer, Jos., *Cursus Scripturae Sacrae* (Paris: Lethielleux, 1898), 9:301-2.

bauer took a more analytical approach to the precise possibilities of meaning. *Plērōma* can be taken in either an active or passive sense, translated as "complementum" (active—that which fulfills), or a "plenitudinem" (passive—that which is fulfilled). He at first appears to have approved the active meaning when applied to the Church in the Epistle to the Ephesians, but only on condition that the expressly active sense of the transitive participle *plēroumenou* be admitted, hence the meaning of the pleroma itself is to be understood as being passive (in accordance with Lightfoot's rule about words ending in -*ma* always to be understood as indicating a passive concept).[152] Hence, the pleromas of Ephesians 3:19 and 4:10 must also be understood as referring to the graces of God.[153]

Regarding the "ut sit Deus omnia in omnibus" of 1 Corinthians 15:28, Corneley in the same commentary[154] did not connect the text directly with the later concept of the pleroma, but instead, while allowing for the various patristic interpretations, favored the expression's being interpreted in the light of the distinction between the Church militant (in which Christ reigns as King) and the Church triumphant (in which this kingdom has been delivered over to the Father), a solution with which he credited Cajetan.[155]

It should be noted with perhaps more than just casual interest in this review of the opinions of exegetes and biblical theologians of the nineteenth century and earlier, that Matthias Scheeben associated in one chapter of his *Dogmatik* some of the same texts that appear to have fascinated Teilhard in their relationship to the pleroma. They are 1 Corinthians 15:28, John 17:22 ("ut sint unum, sicut et nos unum sumus") and Ephesians 1:23, which in the French translation of Scheeben's *Dogmatik* is referred to as "la plénitude (*plērōma*) de celui qui [per] *omnia in omnibus impletur.*"[156]

F. Prat, unlike the earlier commentaries, treats the question of the pleroma with a great deal more precision. He drew his analysis from what he judged to be the five most important occurrences of the word in St. Paul (out of a total of 12 in the Pauline works) taken from Colossians and Ephesians. Admitting that the word can be understood generally in three senses: as "a) plenitude, b) complement or supplement, c) accomplishment" he restates the rule about -*ma* endings denoting a

152. *Ibid.*, 9:65.
153. *Ibid.*, 9:106, 118.
154. *Ibid.*, 7:479-81.
155. P. José M. Bover, S.J. in his *Teologia de San Pablo* (Madrid: B.A.C., 1946), p. 918, credits Suarez as being the innovator of this solution. Interestingly, Suarez no less than rejects the opinions of Origin, Cyril, Chrysostom, the two Cappadocian Gregories, and Theodoretus that it is Christ in his mystical Body and not in his proper person who becomes subject to the Father. This same opinion, which is but a modification of that of Epiphanius and the others mentioned above, according to Bover, is followed by Cornely and Guistiani (with less precision), and by many moderns, including Prat. (Cf. *ibid.*, pp. 920-22.)
156. Cf. J. M. Scheeben, *La Dogmatique*, translated by L'Abbé P. Bélet (Paris: V. Palmé, 1881), §§ 997, 1004, and 1005, pp. 473 and 778 respectively.

generally passive sense.[157] The five passages in question he then pro-
ceeds to interpret within four separate applications: first, Colossians
1:19 ("In ipso complacuit omnem plenitudinem inhabitare")—"the
plenitude of divinity is divinity itself . . . 'the sum total of divine Being' "; second, Colossians 2:9 ("In ipso inhabitat plenitudo divinitatis
corporaliter")—"the *plenitude of God* is the union [l'ensemble] of
supernatural blessings which he loves to bestow upon his friends
. . . and of which he has made Jesus Christ the universal deposi-
tary."[158] The third is *"the plenitude of Christ"* (taken from Eph. 4:13,
"in mensuram aetatis plenitudinis Christi")—"the superabundant measure of graces which the Savior receives from his Father, that he may
pour them out upon the Church, which is his body, and upon the faithful who are his members."[159]

The fourth sense, however, bearing on Ephesians 1:23, is unique:

> In an entirely different sense, the Church is the *plenitude of
> Christ*, because it completes and perfects him in the plan of re-
> demption, the nourishment of grace being able to go from the
> Head to the members only through the medium of the body.[160]

In explaining this exception, Prat was forced to refer directly to the
Greek (not simply cite it in a footnote as in the case with Eph. 4:13).
With his citation he is forced to admit the active cast given to the word
by the accompanying participle:

> Finally, when the Church, the mystical body of Christ, is desig-
> nated under the mysterious appellation: τὸ πλήρωμα τοῦ τὰ πάντα
> ἐν πᾶσιν πληρουμένου, without dealing further in subtle distinc-
> tions, and taking the *pleroma* in its most ordinary meaning, we un-
> derstand that Christ is completed by the Church as the head is
> completed by the members.[161]

157. F. Prat, *Théologie de St Paul* (Paris: Beauchesne, 1908), pp. 410, 414, n. 8; 1912
    ed., 1:352-53; *The Theology of St. Paul* (Westminster, Md.: Newman Press, 1952),
    1:294-95.
158. Given in the order in which they appear in Prat's résumé, cf. *ibid.* (1908), p. 414;
    (1912) 1:357 (Eng. ed., 1:299). In the development in the pages before, the order is
    reversed. In the 1908 ed. both of these first two usages are considered together as
    the "Plérome de Dieu" corresponding to Eph. 3:19, ". . . selon la mesure (eis) de
    tout le plérome de Dieu" (p. 412), while the corresponding passage in the 1912 ed.
    changes "plérome" to *"plénitude"* (1:355).
159. *Ibid.* (Eng. ed.), 1:299.
160. *Ibid.* (1908), p. 414; (1912) 1:357-58 (Eng. 1:298-99). The end of the sentence is
    changed somewhat in the 1912 ed. to read: ". . . arriver de la tête aux membres
    que par l'intermédiaire du corps," from "arriver aux membres que par l'influx du
    corps mystique" in the 1908 edition.
161. *Ibid.* (1909), pp. 413-14; (1912) 1:357 (Eng. 1:299). The footnote along with the
    above (*) is expanded in the 1912 ed. to include the suggestion that the participle
    plēroumenou be possibly understood in the middle reflex rather than passive voice
    to yield the sense "qui se complète." (Ibid., 1:357-58; Eng. 1:298.) A note on the
    same verse in Vol. 2 (p. 341 [p. 283] of the 1912 ed.) suggests two other translations,
    giving a total of four possible readings:
    1) ". . . le complément de celui qui complète toutes choses,"
    2) ". . . le complément de celui qui est complété" (en toutes choses?).
    3) ". . . le complément de celui qui se complète en tous de toute manière."
    4) ". . . celui qui parfait tout, qui amène tout à sa perfection."

But as has been seen in dealing with Prat's treatment of the Mystical Body, this active sense of the word *pleroma* is modified somewhat by the further interpretation that Prat gives it; that despite the fact that Christ fills everything with his plenitude,

> he none the less needs to be completed, in order to exercise his redemptive work; and the Church does complete him, as a passive power which he endows with his virtue, or as a receptacle which he fills with his graces. It is, therefore, justly called "the complement of him who fills all in every way," or, no doubt better, "the complement of him who is wholly completed in all" his members.[162]

Be this as it may, it is still apparent from this different and exceptional meaning that Prat admitted for the pleroma of Christ, no matter how qualified it be, that not only does this conform solidly with Christian tradition[163] but that it added a solid exegetical foundation to that position which Teilhard was continually to maintain in one way or another, that "The Christ is he in whom all becomes all."[164] True, this "Plénitude of Christ" was for Prat synonymous with the Church, the "Mystical Body," and considering what Prat had to say about the absence of any idea of a physical restoration of the universe within the scope of a Pauline eschatology (cf. chap. 4, §B, 2 above), it must be admitted that Prat's understanding of the pleroma was far removed from Teilhard's. Nevertheless, Prat's admission of something more than a purely passive meaning for the pleroma in at least one context was a carefully considered judgment that could have assured Teilhard that he stood on firm ground.

2. More Contemporary Exegesis

In the light of this somewhat favorable exegesis on Prat's part, perhaps the rather disappointed remarks of Teilhard concerning Cerfaux's treatment of the pleroma can be better understood. For despite the fact that Cerfaux's exegesis favors the physical realism of the Body of Christ, this same corporality does not extend, in his opinion, to the concept of the pleroma. Thus, while Cerfaux traces his understanding of the Body of Christ as being dependent on the broader concept of the pleroma, the pleroma has no real existence apart from God except in a purely passive sense. In his treatment of the Colossians Hymn in his earliest work, *Christ in the Theology of St. Paul*, after

---

162. *Ibid.* (1908), pp. 413-14; (1912) 1:357 (Eng. 1:299).
163. Prat cited J. Armitage Robinson's referral to Origen and Chrysostom, as well as the first Syriac and the Coptic texts, as to the legitimacy of this more active meaning of the Pleroma, hence yet another translation is defended, that of the Old Latin: ". . . supplementum ejus qui omnia et in omnia impletur." Cf. *ibid.* (1908), pp. 413-14; (1912) 1:358 (Eng. 1:298-99).
164. "Essai d'Intégration de l'Homme dans l'Univers," unpublished, *T.A.* #92, p. 10.

making a strict division between the two major "strophes" of the hymn, Cerfaux remarks concerning the relationship of the pleroma to the Body of Christ:

> It is also of the Church that we think when reading that Christ has the primacy over all things and that the pleroma, the fullness of God, dwells within him. This pleroma is the power of sanctification in the Godhead, which dwells in the body of the risen Christ. The efficaciousness of Christ's death is naturally linked with that of his resurrection and is one with it. God, through the death of Christ, has reconciled all things to himself (here it is a question of the Church in which gentiles and Jews form only one people, the people reconciled to God). But on the other hand, pacification concerns the Powers, for they are pacified and subjected to Christ by force.[165]

This judgment is entirely consistent with what he had deduced from his analysis of Colossians 2:9-10 in his earlier work La Théologie de l'Eglise suivant S. Paul, where he commented particularly on the meaning of the participle peplērōmenoi:

> The verb plēroō is used in this context (2:10) as an explanation of the noun: Christ receives the fullness of the godhead, and you in your turn are "filled" in him. Obviously the verb here has the meaning of "to fill," to complete in holiness: see Col. 1:9: "that you may be filled with the perfect knowledge of his will." And in this context the verb entails that plērōma will have the meaning of sanctifying fullness, which is an active meaning of the word.[166]

But while thus admitting a certain active meaning to the pleroma (what Prat called the "Plénitude de Dieu"), the "plérôme du Christ" found in Ephesians 1:22f. must be interpreted, according to Cerfaux, in a sense entirely consistent with the judgment given above:

> And so we can say that Christ is the sanctifying fullness of Christians. In keeping with this formula, but taking plērōma in the passive and concrete sense to mean the entirety of those who receive life and sanctification from Christ, Paul writes that the Church is the body of Christ, his pleroma, that is to say, the sphere in which is exercised the power of life and sanctification of him who "fulfils" holiness completely in all (Eph. 1:23).[167]

Understood in this concrete sense as the passive recipient of Christ's sanctifying action, the pleroma extends beyond the Church, but can only be indirectly understood as extending to a realm beyond that of

165. Christ in the Theology of St. Paul (New York: Herder & Herder, 1959), p. 401; Le Christ dans le théologie de S. Paul (Paris: Editions du Cerf, 1951), 1951), pp. 300-302.
166. The Christian in the Theology of St. Paul (New York: Herder & Herder, 1959), p. 223; La Théologie de l'Eglise suivant S. Paul (Paris: Editions du Cerf, 1948), p. 274.
167. Ibid.

sanctification of men.[168] It is no wonder that Teilhard saw his pleroma as being "diminished by Cerfaux's scholarship."[169]

Somewhat differently from Cerfaux, Pierre Benoît understands the Body of Christ not as a particular manifestation of the divine pleroma, but quite the opposite. The pleroma is taken to be, in a less direct manner, an extension of the Body of Christ. Understanding the Body of Christ in the most realistic sense he deems possible, Benoît says of the transhistorical Christ:

> Henceforth he gathers all those who are united to him, by their bodies in the rite of baptism, and have become "his members," he extends himself, constructs himself, develops himself to the point of embracing the whole Church, and ultimately, in an indirect manner, the whole Cosmos.[170]

What then is the pleroma? While admitting a certain development in Ephesians that tends to identify it with the Church, Benoît denies that the cosmic and angelic powers (which do accrue to the pleroma) can properly be considered part of the Body of Christ.[171] On the other hand, to speak of the pleroma as the divine essence dwelling "corporaliter" in Christ (along the lines of Cerfaux's as well as Prat's interpretation of Col. 2:9) strikes Benoît as tainted with Nestorianism.[172] Here Benoît likewise denies any strict division of the Colossians hymn into two strophes based on a supposed contrast between the divine and human natures of Christ; rather, the subject of the hymn is the "Person of Jesus."[173] Caught between these two unacceptable explanations

168. The building up of the body of Christ (the growth of the Church) will come about when each one as a particular individual comes to the unity of faith (all uniting together in this unity) and to the perfect knowledge of the Son of God when we reach the perfect state of man, to the age which corresponds with the fullness of holiness which is enjoyed is Christ (*eis metron helikias tou plērōmatos tou Christō* Eph. 4:12 et seq.). Christ's fullness of holiness, moreover, works upon the whole of creation, above which he is set, since he has gone up above the heavens (Eph. 4:10).

   If we go into this passage at greater depth, we reach the fact that the sanctifying fullness of Christ reaches as far as the Principalities. But immediately (v. 11) Paul applies the influence of Christ to the one Church—the apostles, prophets, evangelists, etc. And it is always in this way that he thinks of things: Christ has conquered the powers, he is above them, and that was done on behalf of the Church. (*Ibid.*, pp. 324-25; Fr. ed., p. 275).

169. Nevertheless, Cerfaux in his later work (*Christ in the Theology of St. Paul*) does admit a certain tendency toward a broader notion of the Pleroma, but it still remains entirely passive:

   > Thus we notice in the captivity epistles a tendency to extend Christ's pleroma, that is, the sphere in which his spiritual power spreads, to the whole of the cosmos, including the heavenly Powers. This runs counter to the doctrine of the redemption which is strictly limited to men. Some good exegetes interpret Eph. 1:10 and 1:22 et seq. in this sense, and they go so far as to consider the Church as a spiritual organism which includes the angels.
   > We would be disinclined to go as far as this. (Pp. 428-29; Fr. ed., p. 322.)

170. Benoît, "Corps, Tête, et Plérôme," in *Exégèse et théologie* (Paris: Editions du Cerf, 1961), 2:115. (My translation.)

171. Cf. *ibid.*, 2:137.

172. Cf. *ibid.*, 2:141.

173. *Ibid.*

of the pleroma, Benoît sees St. Paul as having understood the pleroma in a certain "substantive" sense borrowed from Stoic thought in the manner evidenced in Ecclesiasticus (Sirach) 43:27 and Wisdom 8:11:

> St. Paul then comes upon the idea of the universe as a "Plenitude" where God is present to all things, not only under the form of an immanentistic pantheism in the Stoic vocabulary, but now already adapted to the transcendence of biblical monotheism in the books of Scripture. . . . I understand the Plenitude of being as not simply that of divinity according to that interpretation which we have refuted, but again as that of the Cosmos; and not simply the plenitude of the Cosmos, as seems to be the understanding in the exegesis of Theodore of Mopsuestra, but also that of the Divinity. It is all this which is found to be gathered in Christ. He is God and, through his redeeming work, he brings about in himself a New Creation, not only regenerated Humanity which is his body, but again, the whole new world which constitutes the setting of this Body.[174]

Likewise, regarding the problem as to whether this pleroma is to be understood in a strictly passive sense or not, Benoît, while favoring the passive meaning adopted by the majority of the ancient translations and accepted by the majority of Church Fathers, nevertheless has to admit in the case of Ephesians 1:23 a certain active meaning that allows one to see that God " 'remplit' le monde et 'est rempli' par le monde": and, as applied to the case of Christ,

> he himself "fills" the new world and takes possession of it through his recreative influence as extended to the cosmos; but he also "is filled" by the world to the extent that he is progressively completed, achieved in his total Plenitude by the growth of the Church and of the world which it brings in itself to Christ.[175]

But then, if this be the case, what is the relationship of this doubly active-passive pleroma to God himself? Benoît notes that these final words of Ephesians 1:23 were understood by ancient commentators as applicable to God more or less directly, and as thus tied closely to Co-

174. *Ibid.*, pp. 144-45. Two other opinions concerning the origin and nature of this *Pleroma* as a substantiative term in the NT are of interest here.

Kittel's *Theological Dictionary of the NT* traces the Pauline Pleroma to early Christian Gnosticism, an opinion that Benoît rejects because of its strongly implied dualism. However, the *TDNT* admits of its more biblical adaptation along the lines of late OT times. (Cf. *TDNT* 5:300-303.) Fred B. Craddock, in a note on Col. 1:15-20 in *NTS* 12 (Oct. 1965): 78-80, holds for the stoic character of the passage, but opts for H. Hagermann's strong emphasis on its modification through the Logos concept, where in NT thought the Logos is a preexistent principle, while in Stoicism the Logos is diaexistent. (*Die Vorstellung vom Schöpfungsmittler im hellenistischen Judentum und Urchristentum* [Berlin: Akademie Verlag, 1961].) Should Hegermann's point be correct, this would imply a substantial difference in the corresponding idea of the Pleroma, from being the fulness of being that exists through the action of the Logos, to the fulness of the Logos, which preexists all.

175. *Ibid.*, p. 151.

lossians 1:19, should be given the widest possible interpretation, as applied to both God and the Cosmos.[176]

While Benoît's judgment in this matter bears directly on the pleroma as it appears in the epistles of the captivity, there is no doubt that what he says, and even the way he says it, bears a striking resemblance to what Teilhard claimed for the pleroma—it was to be primarily understood not simply in the order of grace and domination, but, in terms of its ultimate meaning, phrased in the words of 1 Corinthians 15:28 that Teilhard so often used.[177]

3. The Position of André Feuillet

The opinions of André Feuillet are now treated separately, inasmuch as his major exegetical study, Le Christ: Sagesse de Dieu,[178] has been, by the author's own admission, in part inspired by the pioneering speculations of Teilhard. Not that Feuillet approaches his task as an apologist for the Teilhardian synthesis as such, or, even less, as a defender of the latter's somewhat singular type of biblical exegesis. On the contrary; and particularly on the question of the meaning of the pleroma, Feuillet's positions are more reminiscent of Cerfaux than of Benoît, and correspondingly would have proved a disappointment to Teilhard.

To begin with, Feuillet calls into question Benoît's strong reliance on a supposed Stoic origin for the concept of the pleroma as a substantive expressing the "fullness of being."[179] In his treatment of Colossians 1:15-20, Feuillet makes a strong case for the more distinctively Alexandrine-Sapiential origin of the concept, especially the influence of Philo, and sees a strong resemblance between the first part of the Colossians hymn (verses 15-17) and the prologue of St. John's Gospel. To be included in this line of thinking is the anakephalaiōsasthai of Ephesians 1:10 as well.[180] Not that he totally rejects the Stoic influence on this late OT mode of thought, but, rather, he judges it to be so highly modified that it hardly merits the adjective.[181]

---

176. C'est donc en Lui, en sa Totale Plénitude, que s'achève le salut: elle est le terme dernier (eis) auquel parviennent les sauvés en étant comblés d'une plénitude (hina plērōthēte) qui les intègre à toute la Plénitude de Dieu (eis pan to plērōma tou Theou). En ce texte qui vise lui-même à une plénitude aussi vaste que possible, il faut prendre les expressions dans leur ampleur maxima. C'est toute la plénitude, non seulement du cosmos mais de la vie divine, non seulement du Christ mais de Dieu, qui est au terme de tout; c'est en continuant cette plénitude, comme en étant remplis par elle, que les chrétiens y sont consommés. (Ibid., p. 152.)

177. See n. 108 above. Benoit, in a later article printed in the same series, appears to tie Eph. 3:11 (in which the ta panta-pasin phrase again appears) with J. A. T. Robinson's use of 1 Cor. 15 in stressing the corporate (hence "pleromic") dimensions of the resurrection. (Cf. Benoît, "Le Corps chez S. Paul selon J. A. T. Robinson," 2:169-70.)

178. (Paris: Gabalda, 1966).

179. Cf. ibid., pp. 229-31; cf. above.

180. Cf. ibid., p. 212.

181. Feuillet, for example, appears to reject J. Weiss's (Earliest Christianity. A History

Having thus disposed of this exaggerated substantive meaning of the pleroma that he finds in Benoît, Feuillet approves more of Cerfaux's definition of it as "the divine sanctifying power."[182] In this he finds Théodore of Bèze and St. Thomas Aquinas also more precise than F. Prat.[183]

Feuillet goes on to question Prat's admission of something of an active sense to the term *pleroma* in Ephesians 1:23, despite the mysterious "completion" implied by Colossians 1:24 and 2 Corinthians 4:10-12. Holding fast to Lightfoot's rule about "*-ma*" endings, Feuillet first stresses the completely passive sense of the verb and noun combination of Ephesians 3:19 (*hina plērōthēte eis pan to plērōma tou Theou*) and the noun in 4:13 (*eis metron hēlikias tou plērōmatos tou Christou*) and concludes that Ephesians 1:23 must therefore also be understood in a completely passive sense: "the Church does not complete Christ, but it is rather the place where he pours out his riches."[184]

However, and this should be stressed, Feuillet admits that in some sense Christ nevertheless is completed, despite what he maintains is the completely passive sense of the *plērōma—plēroumenou* combination. How? Feuillet reasons thus: if the phrase *ta panta en pasin* is taken adverbially (which he claims it should be, being the NT equivalent of the classical *pantapasin*), then it fits logically with a passive understanding of *plēroumenou* as referring to Christ's being completed in

of the Period AD 30-150, [New York: 1937], 2:465) linking of the *ta panta en autoi sunestēken* of Col. 1:17 with the stoic concept of "the Soul of the World." Curiously, although this verse (in the form of "in quo omnia constant") remained as one of Teilhard's favorite Christological quotations, he himself did not use this verse in his 1918 "L'Âme du monde" or its sequel, "Forma Christi," of the same year. The quotation first appears in Teilhard's "Le Prêtre," however, which did appear the same year. Feuillet, in contrast to Weiss, sees Col. 1:17 as being parallel to the function of "Wisdom" as described in Sirach 43:26 and similar texts. Cf. Feuillet, p. 215.

James M. Robinson, in "A Formal Analysis of Colossians 1:15-20" (*JBL* 76 [1957]: 270-87) holds similar opinions concerning the origin of the Colossian hymn: "The concept of the creation and recreation of the pleroma 'in him' fits into this context of Anthropos speculation, cf. Hippolytus. . . . The closely related Jewish Sophia is mediator of creation. . . . Thus we have to do with a series of concepts which had already found a crystallization point in Judaism, and could consequently be applied *en bloc* to Jesus." *Ibid.*, p. 278.

"The liturgical unit employed in the Prologue of John also makes use of the same group of Logos concepts as in Col. 1:15-20. . . ." *Ibid.*, p. 279.

Bruce Vawter, on the other hand, in his recent "The Colossians Hymn and the Principle of Redaction" (*C.B.Q.* 33 [1971]: 62-81) refuses to assign the hymn either a strictly stoic or even Alexandrine-Sapiential origin, but suggests that the syncretistic nature of Mediterranean thought of the New Testament era made it quite possible that a number of currents of thought, including those of Gnosticism and Platonism, may have influenced the vocabulary and perhaps, to a lesser extent, the theology of the hymn. *Ibid.*, pp. 71-73.

182. Cerfaux, *Le Christ*, pp. 320-21.
183. Cf. Feuillet, p. 235. Feuillet also faults Benoît, and even to some extent Cerfaux, with an overemphasis on the sacramental-corporeal concept of the Body of Christ, and stresses Andriessen's emphasis of the bride-bridegroom theme. He also quotes T. Torrance's approval of the point raised by J. Muirhead, that Christ finds in his Church not a *prolongation* of himself but rather an *encountering* of himself ("rencontre") much as Adam did in Eve. *Idem*, p. 225.
184. *Ibid.*, p. 285. (My translation.)

his Church *by* God. This idea he ties in with his exposition of Colossians 1:20 as expressing the theme of "la réconciliation universelle"[185] and which he finds altogether harmonious with his principal thesis, that of the "Wisdom-Logos" theme underlying both John and Paul's Christology.[186]

These connections with the thought of Philo account, in Feuillet's estimation, for the fact that St. Paul's thought is so totally theocentric as always to place his Christology and Ecclesiology in an equal and parallel relationship when it comes to the relationship existing between God and mankind.[187] Thus Feuillet insists that "the idea of Christ 'filled' by God" agrees entirely with the immediate context of Ephesians 1:23, but goes on to draw a parallel that would truly have elicited Teilhard's interest:

> The First Epistle to the Corinthians teaches us that in the end of time it is God who will be *ta panta en pasin*, but that, in the interval that elapses between the Resurrection and the Parousia, the universal sovereignty must be exercised by Christ, for "God has placed all things beneath his feet." Eph. 1:21-23 does not say anything else and has in common with I Cor. 15:25-28 the citation of Ps. 8:7 and the formula *(ta) panta en pasin.* The difference between the two texts is that the absolute primacy of Christ, presented in I Cor. as the end which is still to come of the actual development of history, is celebrated in Eph. as an already accomplished fact. For Paul had already written in Co. 3:11: *alla panta kai en pasin Christos.*[188]

In the face of all of this, may it not be asked if Feuillet is being entirely consistent? For if Christ is in some way "completed" or 'fulfilled" (albeit by his Father, if not by himself, as according to Prat), and this action is essentially the same described by 1 Corinthians 15:28, then cannot it be said that in some way God "completes" himself in Christ (even if this completion is restricted to some sort of "souveraineté")? In his "Note sur Teilhard de Chardin" in the conclusion of his book, Feuillet even approves Teilhard's occasional substitu-

---

185. Cf. *ibid.*, pp. 238-46, esp. its "cosmic" character, p. 241.
186. Concerning this view in respect to Paul, Feuillet says: Nous ne prétendons pas que la doctrine de l'Apôtre des Gentils soit véritablement dépendante de Philon. Mais, on l'a fait remarquer maintes fois, en dépit de toutes les concessions du philosophe alexandrin au monde grec, son Dieu demeure essentiellement celui de la Bible. Il n'est donc pas sans signification pour nous qu'il conçoive son Logos comme étant essentiellement rempli par Dieu et qu'il contemple comme une sorte de descente de l'action transcendante de Dieu dans le Logos, puis du Logos dans l'univers. Philon reproche aux Stoïciens de s'être figuré que le monde 'ou bien était Dieu ou bien renfermait Dieu en lui' (*De Migratione Abrahami*, p. 179). A ses yeux, Dieu est absolument transcendant au monde: il contient tout et n'est lui-même contenu par rien. . . . Mais ce Dieu, qui n'est rempli que par lui-même, *remplit son Logos* de puissances incorporelles . . . grâce auxquelles il dirige l'univers. (*Ibid.*, p. 290.)
187. la pensée de l'Apôtre est toujours foncièrement théocentrique et que de plus, chez lui, ecclésiologie et christologie sont unies par les liens les plus étroits: ce qui caractérise également, toutes proportions gardées, les rapports qui existent entre Dieu et les hommes. (*Ibid.*, p. 290.)
188. *Ibid.*, pp. 291-92. (My translation.)

tion of "Christ" for "God" in relation to the 1 Corinthians text.[189] But
if St. Paul could do this, speaking of Christ as a *person*,[190] then what is
to prevent Teilhard from doing likewise, and conversely considering
that in some way God, as a person, somehow finds Himself "completed" in the same way? And if one must be more precise, lest the
champions of absolute divine transcendence be offended, who can fault
Teilhard with locating this completion within Christ and then speculat-
ing on the possibility that this growth is to be understood as accruing
not to the divine nature as such, nor to the human nature of Christ as
commonly understood, but to a quasi-third nature, located in the cosmic dimensions of his Incarnation, but centered not on the static concept of nature but on the consummation of all things in Christ?[191]

4. Conclusion on the Teilhardian Pleroma

In the course of this study of the pleroma as understood by Teilhard
and the somewhat shorter evaluation of this understanding in the light
of the exegesis of his day and our own, it has become evident that this
theme served as a locus for the recapitulation of all the other elements
incorporated within his doctrine of Christogenesis. Seen in the light of
his earlier emphases on the expectation of all creation and on the Body
of Christ, the theme of the pleroma became the heir not only to the
brilliance of his insights expressed in these earlier themes, but also to
the problems that were inherent within them. Within this process of
incorporation and refinement, not only were the previous insights
transposed into a new level of understanding, but their radical departure from previous traditions of theological understanding became
transformed into problems involving successive levels of abstraction.

The insights provided by Teilhard on St. Paul's Epistle to the Ro-

189. Aux yeux de saint Paul, de même que Dieu le Père est à l'origine de toutes choses
    (l'Apôtre, nous l'avons dit, lui réserve la préposition *ek*), de même il doit être un
    jour "tout en tous" ou "en toutes choses" (1 Cor. XV, 28). Ce texte est cher à
    Teilhard, qui aime d'ailleurs substituer le Christ au Père: *Christus omnia in
    omnibus*. Une telle substitution est légitime: le même saint Paul, qui dans la
    Première Epître aux Corinthiens annonce que Dieu sera tout en toutes choses lors
    de la Parousie (*Deus omnia in omnibus*), proclame dans l'Epître aux Colossiens
    (III.11) que le Christ est tout et en tout (*omnia et in omnibus Christus*). (*Ibid.*, p.
    379.)
190. Although Feuillet distinguishes the two parts of the Colossians hymn, he stresses
    that in both parts "*c'est toujours le même Christ qui est premier; il l'est en tout et
    sous tous les rapports.*" *Ibid.*, p. 202.
191. Two notes from Teilhard's Journals about the time that speculation on a "Third Na-
    ture" appeared seem to be concerned with seeking a solution to this problem. The
    first (Feb. 5, 1946) refers directly to Eph. 1:23, "qui omnia in omnibus adimpletur,"
    and draws a parallel between this verse and the "Deus erit omnia in omnibus" of 1
    Cor. 15:28, suggesting a distinction between the function designated by the verb
    "plerousthai" in the Greek verb of the first and the "being" (esse) in the second of
    the quotations. ("Journal" 14 [2]: 39.)
       The second note (Nov. 12, 1946) simply suggests that the "sole mystery" is that
    pleromization in which God can be said to "sur-center" himself. ("Journal" 15 [3]:
    62.)

mans proved at a very early date to be unassimilable as long as they remained tied to the Pauline cosmology in general and to the Pauline doctrine of original sin in particular. Consequently, when the Pauline vision concerning the future of all creation in Christ was translated into Teilhard's doctrine of a "cosmic" Body of Christ, the exegetical problems highlighted in this earlier theme became transformed into the "hyper-physical" realm of the relation of spirit to matter and its ramifications into the theological doctrine of the relationship of the natural to the supernatural. The discovery of the pleroma appeared to Teilhard to provide the answers to the overly restrictive elements of these earlier themes, both regarding the origin and problem of evil and the dualistic elements implied in the traditional understanding of the Body of Christ, but the apparent advantages offered by the assimilation of his earlier insights into a broader doctrine of "pleromization" at the same time brought with them not only the old problems but new expressions of the same. Teilhard's exegetical difficulties over the Pauline cosmology and his reservations over the theological interpretation of the Pauline doctrine of nature and grace were now transformed to the metaphysical realm as it applies to the understanding of the creative act and the transcendent nature of God. In this way Teilhard's earlier explorations into the question of the nature of creative causality (e.g., "Sur la Notion de Transformation créatrice" and "Note sur les Modes de l'Action divine dans l'Univers"[192]) became in the end concentrated into the final problem as to whether "pleromization" in some way "completes" God. Half-expressed though this final question remained in Teilhard's writings—in terms of God in himself or even Christologically expressed in speculation about a "Third Nature of Christ"—this major development can be ignored only at the cost of underestimating, the originality (its "revolutionary" impact as well as its evolutionary framework) of his synthesis.

From all these developments a rather paradoxical situation came about. Teilhard clearly rejected what he knew to be St. Paul's cosmology and doctrine of original sin as it appears in Romans and as established by solid exegetical opinion. He just as sharply rejected the common understanding of the Body of Christ that was also backed up by the exegesis of his day. Nevertheless, appealing to what he considered to be long-ignored traditions of ancient patristic theology, Teilhard remained convinced that the principal and ultimately most important teaching of St. Paul was of the cosmic Christ in whom God becomes "all in all." This was the single and far-reaching culmination of the Pauline theology that Teilhard chose to reinterpret in terms of a Christogenic evolution that would result in the pleromization of the universe in God.

192. Cf. *Oeuvres*, 10:27f., 33f.; *C&E*, pp. 21f., 25f.

6

*The Johannine Element
in the Synthesis
of Teilhard de Chardin*

Teilhard's reinterpretation of the Fall and his rejection of Pauline cosmology indicate that despite constant appeals to the inspiration Paul so obviously provided, there was a certain metaphysical presupposition that overruled all exegetical considerations. The present chapter will show that this was also the case in Teilhard's understanding of St. John.

The final matter to which attention must be given in this second part, which has dealt with the major Pauline themes in Teilhard's works, is the relationship of these themes to the thought of St. John. Many of Teilhard's earliest appeals to Sacred Scripture were to St. John. During the World War I period these are almost as numerous as the citations of Pauline material. And although Johannine quotations gradually decreased in proportion to the Pauline as the years went on, Teilhard still made occasional reference to St. John by name when he spoke of St. Paul.[1] Sometimes there is additional mention of "the Greek Fathers" along with the double reference to John and Paul. It will be the task of this chapter to investigate what specifically Johannine elements Teilhard had in mind and to point out how they differ from or agree with the Pauline themes.

1. There are some seventy-five references to St. Paul by name in Teilhard's various essays and works, excluding his notes and correspondence. Sixteen of these references include St. John by name, usually mentioned before Paul. One other reference to John does not mention Paul, but instead compares John to the synoptics. (Cf. "Sur le Règne de Dieu," *T.A.*, 1946, p. 12. For a listing of those references cited in this study, see Appendix C below.)

A. THE "JOHANNINE" CHARACTERISTICS
OF TEILHARDIAN THOUGHT

That Teilhard continued throughout his life frequently to link together the names of Saints John and Paul would seem to indicate that
he saw a deep complementarity between their theologies, even if there
is not always an exact parallelism between the two.[2] Two major Johannine elements appear to have influenced Teilhard's thought: the
preeminently "Incarnational" and "unitive" themes that are evidenced
in Teilhard's works from a very early date and that even seem to have
colored his understanding of St. Paul.

1. The Preeminence of the Incarnation

Of all the theological aspects of the Teilhardian synthesis, the one
that most frequently comes to mind in both Teilhard's admirers and
critics is the heavy stress laid on the Incarnation as the central point of
salvation history. This is generally considered to be a distinctively
Johannine characteristic in contrast to St. Paul's more soteriological
concerns, which appear to emphasize the redemptive passion, death,
and Resurrection of Jesus. If this should actually be the case, which
some may dispute,[3] then one must conclude that Teilhard was more
Johannine than Pauline in his overall Christological orientation, inasmuch as there is little doubt that Teilhard considered the "soteriological" aspect of Christology to be ontologically secondary in importance
to the fact of the Incarnation itself—so much so that his position on this
matter can be accurately described as being Scotist.[4]

Teilhard's position on this matter of supposed contrast between John
and Paul was similarly mild; in fact, for him no such contrast appeared
to exist; rather, it is more the contrast between the immediate existential concerns of fallen mankind in Paul's theology and his more "cosmic
Christ" of the captivity epistles that gave Teilhard pause.

Instead, Teilhard appears to have stressed the similarity of Johannine
and Pauline thought, and in this he for once reflected the influence of
his seminary teachers. A. Durand, who taught Sacred Scripture at

2. On this matter see T. W. Manson *On John and Paul* (London: SCM Press, 1963).
3. Bruce Vawter, C. M., in his treatment of "Johannine Theology" in *The Jerome Biblical Commentary* (pp. 828-39), speaking a bit more cautiously of this supposed difference, admits that "the propitiatory conception of Christ's work of salvation, one
of the cornerstones of Pauline theology, is not . . . given a place of prominence by
John" (p. 830). Nevertheless, despite John's emphasis on the fact that "above all, it
is in him that the meeting of God and man takes place" (*idem*, p. 831), "the idea of
the Word is eminently a soteriological one" (*idem*, p. 832). Schnackenburg, in his
Das Johannesevangelium (Freiburg: Herder, 1965) seems to take a similar position
when he speaks of "the fundamental affirmation of the Incarnation" in which "For
John, Christ in the flesh is not the representative of Adamite man, as in Paul (cf.
Rom. 8:3), but the leader who brings earth-bound man home to the heavenly world
of life and glory (cf. John 6:62f.; 14:6; 17:24)." (Eng. trans., Montreal: Palm Publ.,
pp. 268-69.)
4. G. M. Allegra, *My Conversations with Teilhard de Chardin on the Primacy of
Christ* (Chicago: Franciscan Herald Press, 1971). See esp. pp. 92-107.

Hastings, was later to write a popular study of St. John that was first published in Paris in 1927.[5] While Durand naturally had to take cognizance of the varying emphases between the two sacred authors, his underlining of the common elements between the Johannine prologue and the hymn of Colossians 1 cannot have but impressed Teilhard.[6] While it is true that Teilhard did not put a similar emphasis on the preexistent Word, Durand's continued pointing up of the parallels between John and Paul in this case may have had a telling effect on his thought. Concerning the Incarnation in particular, Durand stressed the Johannine concept as a continuing and to some extent "increasing" event:

> The Incarnate Word *has dwelt among us* in a permanent fashion and not in passing, as in the case of the days of his fleeting manifestation. Under the pen of St. John, the word of the text which we translate as *"to dwell"* ("habiter") has lost the primitive sense of a temporary stop-over as suggested by its etymology. If we have here a biblical allusion, one thinks most easily of the presence of the divine glory in the Tabernacle during the time of Moses. Whatever be the case, the symbolic name of Emmanuel, given by Isaiah (8:14) to the Christ to come, is fully realized in the Incarnation. In all truth, Jesus Christ is "God with us."[7]

Durand also linked verse 16 of the prologue with the pleroma of Colossians and similarly with the "incorporation" of Colossians 1:18-20 and Ephesians 1:23,[8] a connection that Lagrange and others were less ready to admit.[9]

Whatever Teilhard's impression of the opinions of these scholars, or of those who were to follow, there is no doubt that he continued to see both John and Paul as complementary sources of what he understood as the altogether overwhelming reality of the Incarnation and its universal function in the universe.[10]

5. Alfred Durand, S.J., *Evangile selon Saint Jean* 6th ed. (Paris: Gabriel Beauchesne, 1930).

6. *et sans lui rien n'a été fait de ce qui été fait.* Cette insistance, qui est tout à fait dans la manière hébraïque, met en relief l'universalité de l'action créatrice du Fils de Dieu. C'est, du reste, ce que saint Paul avait déjà fait: "Il est l'image du Dieu invisible, né avant toute créature, car c'est en lui que toutes choses ont été créées, celles (qui sont) sur la terre, les choses visibles et les choses invisibles. . . ; tout a été créé par lui." (Col. 1:16) (*Ibid.*, pp. 11-12.)

7. *Ibid.*, pp. 23-24. (My translation.)

8. *Ibid.*, p. 27.

9. Cf. M.-J. Lagrange, *Evangile selon saint Jean* (Paris: Libraire Lecoffre, 1945), p. 25. (First published in 1925.)

10. Paul Henry, S.J., in a study entitled *Compléments de Christologie*, published in the theological series issued by the "Institute Catholique de Paris" (#7) makes the following observations concerning the relationship between the christology of John and Paul.

> Si l'Evangile de Paul est celui d'un Christ selon l'esprit, celui de Jean, l'évangéliste spirituel, est celui d'un Christ selon la chair. . . . Tout le récit de l'Evangile est une réfutation directe du docétisme" (p. 31). However, despite the similarity (due to its eye-witness origin) of the figure of the Johannine Christ to that of the synoptics, John "paraît vouloir marquer comme Paul que dans l'individualité personnelle du Christ il y a une *fonction universelle*. (*Idem*, p. 33)

2. The "Unitive" Theme of St. John
in Teilhard

Teilhard once described his whole philosophy in terms of John 17:21 ("That they may be one . . .") and of the Pauline doctrine of the Body of Christ.[11] True, this was a very early statement in terms of the development of his thought, but there is good reason to argue that this intuition of the classical problem of the one and the many remained the central, if not always conscious, concern of his thought to the very end.[12] If nothing else, his theory of "creative union," if not entirely original in formulation, did achieve a new and comprehensive interpretation in the light of evolutionary science.

But, by any stretch of the imagination, can this all-pervasive theme be termed Johannine? Is not the Johannine spirit the very epitome of dualistic expression: of light vs. darkness, good vs. evil, of "this world" vs. the "next world," of "matter" vs. "spirit"? Vawter ascribes this characteristic of John not directly to any metaphysical dualism, but as an adaptation to the religious-philosophical genre of the time.[13] It is in the face of a prevailing tendency toward a metaphysical dualism and a consequent distortion of its moral counterpart that John's Gospel uses this dualistic language as a tool, paradoxically enough, to affirm the great theme of universal reconciliation, atonement in the original sense of that word.

The older scriptural authorities, although generally brief on this subject, are positive on this theme of unity in John 17:21. Cornelius a Lapide approvingly spoke of a unity not of identification, but of similitude, and quoted Augustine and St. Bernard on love as the force that achieves this unity.[14] Likewise, he cited St. Denis [Pseudo-Dionysius] and his parallel understanding of Ephesians 4:4-6 ("unum corpus et unum spiritus . . . Unus Deus et pater omnium").[15] Knabenbauer connected the theme similarly with Romans 15:5 and 1 Corinthians 1:10 and with what he considered to be "in primordiis rei christianae (Acts 2:46; 5:12)."[16] Teilhard's former professor Durand also connected this Johannine theme with 1 Corinthians 3:22-23 in a more cosmic sense:

11. Cf. *Ecrits*, p. 113; *WTW*, p. 94.
12. This position is the central thesis of Donald P. Gray's *The One and the Many: Teilhard de Chardin's Vision of Unity* (New York: Herder & Herder, 1969). See chap. 2 above, n. 42.
13. Vawter terms John's "dualism" a component of *Heilsgeschichte* and cites R. Bultmann's *Kerygma and Myth* as to the complete absence of any real matter-spirit dualism in the NT. Cf. "Johannine Theology" in *The Jerome Biblical Commentary* (Englewood Cliffs, N.J.: Prentice-Hall, 1968), p. 831.
14. Cf. "Commentarium in Johannem," *Commentarius in Scripturas Sacras* (Paris: L. Vives, 1868), 16:600.
15. Cf. *ibid.*, 16:602.
16. Cf. Knabenbauer, *Cursus Scripturae Sacrae* (Paris: Lethielleux, 1898), 7:500.

It is through his Christ that God so extends himself to attach himself to "the world" which grows in him. In the formula which he has given to this divine hierarchy, St. Paul highlights this character of subordination: "All is for you, but you, you are Christ's, and Christ's is God's".[17]

M.-J. Lagrange, it is true, contested this interpretation of Durand, particularly as it tends to interpret the difficult word [in this context] *doxan* of John 17:22 as a share of something that cannot be shared by God (the old problem again of what Teilhard considered the "extrinsicity" of grace in traditional theologies). Lagrange stated concerning John 17:22:

> It appears, to speak precisely, too much to call this the adoption of the sons of God, for the texts of Eph. 1:6, 12, 14 are not an explication of the same thought: the adoption that is spoken of here is rather for the praise of the glory of Christ (as against the positions of *Schanz, Durand, Till.*). Another exaggerated specification would be "by this communion of divine life which is symbolized and nourished in the Eucharist" (as in *Loisy*, p. 449).[18]

Teilhard's overall attention to this text, however, was not to be deterred by controversy over the meaning of the *doxan* in the subsequent verse (22), although Teilhard was not afraid to push its meaning to the most ontologically radical position possible.[19] Curiously, verse 21, which Teilhard called "the definitive formula that gives us the key to the Gospel and to the World," was never used again by Teilhard in any explicit sense again after he first used it these two times in this 1917 "The Struggle Against the Multitude."[20] The possibility has been mentioned that Teilhard may have been criticized even then for his overenthusiastic application of Scripture. But that this insight did continue to serve as a basic guideline for his thought there seems little doubt. If St. John was speaking more immediately of the life of grace and the unity of the Christian community, still, in Teilhard's understanding of the convergent and consistent nature of all reality, it would appear perfectly natural and logical to see in this Gospel verse the whole "key" to understanding and reconciling the classic philosophic problem of the "one and the many" and the evolutionary movement of the universe.

17. A. Durand, p. 454. Teilhard made use, as has been noted, of this same Pauline progression of thought in *The Divine Milieu*, p. 25; *Oeuvres*, 4:41-42. Cf. chap. 2, n. 5, above.
18. Lagrange, p. 451.
19. M. N. Wildiers, in his footnote p. 155 of *HE* (*Oeuvres*, 6:192, n. 1), quotes this same verse in relation to Teilhard's statement in the text that the individual "in some way completes God." Teilhard was perhaps a bit more restrained in his attribution of scriptural backing to his ideas than are some of his admirers. A similar overly-specific attribution of scriptural backing occurs in the footnote application of John 11:51-52 to Teilhard's thoughts in "La Lutte contre la multitude," *Ecrits*, p. 124 (*WTW*, p. 106), n. 12.
20. Cf. *WTW*, pp. 94, 113; *Ecrits*, pp. 113, 131.

While Teilhard's particular application or extension of this text of St. John may or may not have been exaggerated in the opinion of certain exegetes, there appears to be no doubt that, in his early choice of this text as an expression of his earliest and most lasting intuition, he had also singled out one of the most certainly common Pauline-Johannine themes: the consummation of all things in God through Christ.

B. DEPARTURES FROM THE JOHANNINE PATTERN BY TEILHARD

It is evident that the unitive theme that dominates St. John's thought and its expression in a theology that is eminently incarnational continued to inspire Teilhard's general outlook—and his interpretation of St. Paul as well—despite the difficulties presented by the dualistic manner of expression that characterizes the fourth Gospel. It is also evident that beneath this surface difficulty lay two others of a more basic nature. The first, bearing on an "emanationist" concept of the Incarnation, was never expressed publicly by Teilhard; the second, bearing on the "realized" view of the Parousia, appears to have remained somewhat outside of Teilhard's eschatological concerns.

1. The Alexandrian "Logos" and Teilhardian Christology

That Teilhard did not show much enthusiasm with regard to the development of the theme of the preexistent *Logos* as found in St. John, or even to interpretations of Colossians 1:15-19 that see a similar starting point in Paul's Christology, is understandable enough in a thinker whose primary interest was not trinitarian theology but the characteristics of the personal Omega-point who awaits the evolutionary process "above and beyond." For Teilhard the creative act was not considered in terms of a beginning (the *archēi* of John 1:1), but rather as "un processus ou geste de synthèse"[21] animated by that Omega-God who draws it from "ahead." Perhaps the closest Teilhard ever came to a concept somewhat parallel to that of the sapientially based notion of the *Logos* would have been in his somewhat tentative rejection of expressing the idea of God in terms of efficient causality and in his emphasis on the "formal causality" of God. Nowhere, however, did Teilhard consciously connect this revised notion of causality to the preexistent Logos;[22] consideration of the Logos as an integral element of the creative act of God seems to have remained unspecified in

21. "Christologie et Evolution," *Oeuvres*, 10:101; *C&E*, p. 83.
22. In a note of Jan. 26, 1952 ("Journal" 18 [6]: 132), Teilhard definitely states that he believes that, to effectively demonstrate the existence of God, we must not search for quasi-efficient causality in the past but rather a quasi-formal causality in the future; God as the condition of the achievement and the survival of a higher form of life.

trinitarian terms. In a "Journal" note of January 3, 1946, Teilhard had already stated that creation is "an organic continuation and completion of the Trinity" (in a sense exterior to its own being), the Trinity being a sort of "cleavege of the One upon itself," while Creation is characterized as both "a projection of its [the Trinity's] Shadow" into the absolute multiple and a reduction of this multiple toward unity.[23] It is easy to see how Teilhard might have had reservations about the suitability of Johannine theology for an evolutionary synthesis, not in terms of his own personal belief in the preexistent divinity of the Word, but because of John's own emphasis on this point.

In a hitherto unnoticed passage in one of Teilhard's "Carnets de Retrait," some of these reservations were explicitly stated. In the retreat notebook of 1942 (pp. 13 and 14) are a number of passages from St. John's Gospel copied on the right-hand page in Latin, while opposite them, on the left-hand page, appear Teilhard's comments. Concerning verses 16 and 17 of chapter 1 ("De plenitudine ejus . . . omnes accepimus" and "Deum nemo videt umquam: unigenitus filius . . . ipse enarravit"), Teilhard remarked that these verses speak more of a theme of emanation and descent than anything understandable in terms of evolution, and again, after quoting from chapter 3, verse 13 ("Nemo ascendit in coelum nisi qui descendit de coelo, Filius hominis, qui est in coelo"), Teilhard expanded his comments concerning what he saw to be a "descent of condescendence" more than a theme of "emersion" through emergence (something he saw to be present in the "descendit . . . ascendit" of Eph. 4:9-10). He also saw the same verse as reflecting an idea that he found even less evolutive, that of "illumination by revelation." Concerning verses 27 and 32 of chapter 3 ("Non potest homo accipere quidquam nisi fuerit ei datum de coelo" and "Qui de coelo venit super omnes est"), Teilhard here saw that the essential element in belief is not merely an intellectual recognition but rather an adherence to a "universal charity," like that expressed in verses 16 and 35 of the same chapter of the Gospel of John, which were underlined as follows: "Sic Deus dilexit mundum ut Filium suum unigenitum daret . . ." and "Pater diliget Filium et omnia dedit in manu ejus . . . qui credit in Filium habet vitam aeternam." Yet despite his recognition of those phrases (those underlined above) which seem to best fit in with his cosmic vision of Christ, Teilhard still had to admit that he found in the Johannine mode more the idea of "the descent of Being through priority" than the "consummation of itself" or anything

Again, in a note of July 20, 1952 ("Journal" 19 [7]: 16), Teilhard remarks that the five classical proofs of God's existence, as we generally understand them, do not have much validity except in a static universe, while in terms of "Cosmogenesis" God is not strictly demonstrable except as the principle of the irreversibility (and activation) of the evolutionary movement toward a cosmos that is reflectively convergent.

23. Journal 14 (2): 22. Cf. also p. 213n of Oeuvres, 10 (C&E, p. 183) relative to "Pleromization" in terms of "Trinitization."

resembling "Omegalization." Teilhard concluded his remarks on these two verses with the singling out of the task of reconciling the idea of preexisting being with the concept of the pleroma, a task that he cryptically suggested can be depicted in terms of two gifts existing in a reciprocal relationship—the Son given to the world, and the world given to the Son.

While this set of retreat notes also cites John 3:31, and in addition contains some underlining of certain words in John 4:34, no more comments appear until verses 34-44 are cited in an abbreviated form and bracketed together in such a way as to distinguish what he calls (in the accompanying comments) the "divinizing functions" of the Father (to "send" Christ and to "draw" humanity to him) from those of Christ (to "not reject," to "give life," and to "raise up").

Teilhard's 1942 retreat remarks on John close with the partial citation of John 7:38-39. While the comment on the verse 38 is not entirely clear, it seems to be directed toward seeking a link between this verse ("Si quis sitit veniat ad me et bibat . . .") and the idea of an infinite consummation in the "Christ-Omega." As for verse 39 ("Nondum enim erat Spiritus datus quia Jesus nondum erat glorificatus"), Teilhard's comment suggests that there is a direct relationship between the glorification of Christ and the "transfiguration" of the cosmos.

From all this it can be deduced that Teilhard saw possibilities of further incorporation of Johannine themes into his synthesis, but only on condition that the somewhat Alexandrian conceptualization of creation be excised from the Johannine mode of thought. Just as Teilhard had finally to part from the Pauline cosmology while affirming Paul's cosmic Christology, so he found himself in a similar predicament with the Johannine genre. Stripped of its dualistic expressions, John's thought contains much that exercised a metaphysical fascination over Teilhard, but at the same time, there is a certain concept of "the eternal return" that John used rather liberally. Feuillet, in tracing both the Logos of St. John and the preexistent Christ of Colossians 1:15-17 to the Alexandrian mode of modified Platonism found in Philo and the sapiential authors, seems to have confirmed Teilhard's suspicions that there is something unassimilable in John's mode of thought in this matter. At the same time Feuillet would seem to have provided biblical backing, however slight, for Teilhard's stressing the formal over the efficient causality of God's creative act.[24]

2. Eschatology: Johannine, Pauline, and Teilhardian

The final comment of Teilhard's little meditation on John, that on 7:39 shows a divergence from the Johannine mode of thought—that

24. See A. Feuillet, "La Création de l'univers 'dans le Christ' d'après l'Epitre aux Colossiens (1:16a)", NTS, 12 #1 (Oct. 1965) pp. 1-9. Cf. Le Christ sagesse de Dieu (Paris: Gabalda, 1966), pp. 202-17.

concerning eschatology. As is generally conceded, St. John's is almost totally that of a "realized" nature, and as such is intimately connected with his well-developed theology of the Holy Spirit.[25] Teilhard's theology of the Holy Spirit, unless his speculations about Christ as "the soul of the world" are considered to be such, is practically nonexistent. Typically, the words of John 7:39 were taken from their pre-resurrection context by Teilhard and given an evolutive-eschatological meaning in which the "glorification of Christ" (on whom the sending of the Spirit depends) is associated with, if not quite identified with, the transfiguration of the Cosmos. In this, at least regarding its postponed fulfillment, Teilhard's eschatology would seem to resemble more that of St. Paul, or at least that of 1 Corinthians and Colossians, without the apocalyptic elements of Thessalonians. In this regard, Feuillet again points out the difference between the Pauline notion of the "fullness of time," in both the cases of the Incarnation and of the Parousia, as being more or less God's own fixed "Kairos" as contrasted to Teilhard's conviction that these times necessarily correspond to the world's appropriate development for these events to have their maximum effect.[26] In no way can Teilhard's concept be related directly to that of St. John. At best, ecclesially speaking, the "realized" element is that of the Epistle to the Ephesians.

While Teilhard's understanding of the Church, as well as insistence on the Incarnation as the definitive entry of God into the world of matter, would have allowed for a more explicit use of St. John's "realized" eschatology within his theological synthesis, it is evident that the relative absence of the element of postponed eschatology in the fourth Gospel inclined Teilhard to bypass the eschatological possibilities of St. John's thought—except to the degree that it appears in the Apocalypse. Only to the extent that Teilhard spoke of beatitude in terms of the consummation of the Eucharistic union does there appear to be a connection between his eschatology and that of the Gospel of St. John.[27]

C. THE APOCALYPSE IN TEILHARD'S WRITINGS

On no occasion did Teilhard associate the Book of Revelation with the Gospel of St. John. All his allusions to it are instead simply in the context of the Christological vision that it shares with the Pauline cosmic Christ. Nevertheless, it would be a mistake to see Teilhard's use of

---

25. Cf. Vawter, *J.B.C.*, p. 837.
26. Feuillet, *Le Christ sagesse de Dieu*, p. 381.
27. "L'état de béatitude doit se comprendre, en définitive, comme un état *d'union eucharistique permanente*, où nous serons élevés et maintenus *en corps* (c'est-à-dire tous "per modum unius") et "*in corpore Christi*." ("Note sur l'Union physique . . ." in *Oeuvres*, 10:23; *C&E*, pp. 16-17.) While the above statement appears to have been inspired by the theology of 1 Cor. 10:14-22, the note of personal union in view of beatitude parallels that of John 6:48-59.

the Apocalypse as simply nothing more than a literary borrowing of the
Alpha-Omega theme. Vawter,[28] despite the perennial problem of the
book's authorship, does not hesitate to point out certain Johannine
traits that find their complement in the fourth Gospel, and that are also
reflected in Teilhard's Christology. Foremost among these traits is the
glorification of Christ, but not without a careful connection of the
glorified Christ with the historical Jesus, a trait that is found in almost
identical proportions in Teilhard. Likewise, while the Alpha-Omega
image is prominent in the beginning and the end of the book, the very
structure and preoccupation of the book are those of an interpretation
of the present in the light of the final victory of Christ. In this regard,
Teilhard's nearly complete preoccupation with the Omega rather than
the Alpha resembled that of the Apocalypse; only the rather dualistic
language of the latter, found also in the Gospel of John, was missing.
Vawter[29] characterizes the Apocalypse as having the same incarnationally stressed Christology as that of the fourth Gospel, to which the
soteriological element, so predominant in the Pauline Christology, is
given a strong, but nevertheless subservient, place. This too is a typically Teilhardian trait. Finally, hardly of minor importance, the nearly
totally "realized" eschatology of St. John's Gospel becomes in the
Apocalypse more one of tension between the elements of "ecclesial
realization" and "end-time" fulfillment.

Feuillet, speaking of this same eschatological tension that permeates
the Apocalypse, characterizes the place of Christ in terms that emphasize the tension as being already synthesized in Christ, and he does
so in language strangely reminiscent of Teilhard. As Feuillet puts it:

> In consequence [of the unfolding of the divine plan of salvation
> history] the summit, the function of which is to organize all history
> as leading to God—the omega which accounts for the alpha—is no
> longer to be awaited; it exists already in Jesus Christ.[30]

If Feuillet finds this tension already resolved in the Apocalypse in
the Christ who has already come, Teilhard found this to be a still-
continuing process, one still being revealed, one that, despite the inevitable setbacks and disasters, finds its guarantee in Christ who is yet
to come in his full glory. The source of Teilhard's almost incredible optimism was not a naive myth of inevitable progress! In his "The Directions and Conditions of the Future" (June 1948) he made himself clear:

> For a Christian, provided his Christology accepts the fact that the
> collective consummation of earthly Mankind is not a meaningless
> and still less a hostile event, but a pre-condition of the final,

28. Cf. *J.B.C.*, p. 839.
29. *Ibid.*
30. A. Feuillet, *L'Apocalypse* (Paris-Bruges: Desclée de Brouwer, 1963), p. 66. (My
     translation.)

"parousiac" establishment of the Kingdom of God—for such a Christian the eventual biological success of Man on Earth is not merely a probability but a certainty: since Christ (and in Him virtually the World) is already risen. But this certainty, born as it is of a "supernatural" act of faith, is of its nature supra-phenomenal: which means, in one sense, that it leaves all the anxieties attendant upon the human condition, on their own level, still alive in the heart of the believer.[31]

It is evident from this that the world will inevitably "progress" in its slow evolution of complexity and consciousness, but this is at the same time a process that leads to a "paroxysm"—an intensification of the powers of good and evil. Despite the assured victory of Christ, the final outcome, at least for each thinking and choosing being, is not yet assured.[32]

In any case, whether Teilhard's views toward the end of his life tended to modify or even contradict his much celebrated optimism for the future of the world, it remains clear that for him it was ultimately the Christ-Omega who stands as the end of cosmic evolution and of human history.[33]

D. CONCLUSION

The Johannine element in Teilhard's thought and its relationship to his reinterpretation of the Pauline themes discussed in the preceding chapters has brought us back to some of the questions posed at the conclusion of Part I. One question was this: to what extent could

---

31. *FM*, p. 237; *Oeuvres*, 5:305.
32. Joseph Pieper, in his *Hope and History (Hoffnung und Geschichte* (New York: Herder, 1967) faults Teilhard with a general confusion of history with evolution (p. 32), but also claims that Teilhard entertained two views of the "Omega-point": an earlier view that tended to support a theory of inevitable progress in the optimistic sense of the word, and a later corrective view that allows for a tragic outcome as well (pp. 55f.). If this be the case concerning his views on the general outcome of human history as some of his later essays in *The Future of Man (Oeuvres*, 5, cf. esp. "La Grande Option" (1939), pp. 37f.) would seem to indicate, this must be distinguished from his constant conviction of the inescapable possibility of the frustration of the destiny of the individual. Cf. *DM*, pp. 128f.; *Oeuvres*, 4:187f. on this latter point.
33. Mathias Rissi, in his 1966 work *Alpha und Omega* (Basel: F. Reinhardt Verlag) sees this tension resolved in much the same progressive sense as did Teilhard, in contrast to Feuillet's emphasis on an already-realized eschatology. Rissi writes:

> Der letzte Grund der Gewissheit liegt in Gott selbst, denn er ist "das A und O." Der erste und der letzte Buchstabe im griechischem Alphabet, *Alpha* und *Omega*, bezeichnen ihn als den Grund aller Dinge (der am Anfang steht, der die Welt geschaffen, der seine Rettungsgeschichte der Menschheit in Israel begonnen) und zugleich als Vollender (der, was er angefangen, in Jesus erfüllt hat und am Ende aller Dinge allen offenbaren wird). Kein anderer wird der Letzte sein, der Gott noch überholen könnte, kein Engel, kein Teufel oder Mensch. Sein Kommen ist das Kommen des Durchstochenen, des Erlösers. Darum wird zuletzt kein Raum auserspart bleiben von der Gegenwart des Kommenden, sondern Gott wird sein "alles in allem" (1 Kor. 15, 28) (pp. 26-27).

Teilhard's interpretation of SS. John and Paul be claimed as an authentic restoration of the cosmic dimensions of ancient Greek patristic theology? This question rightly belongs to the field of positive theology as distinct from the more strictly exegetical question pursued in Part II. But the two fields are obviously related. For all its scientific method, modern exegesis—at least as far as the Catholic theologian is concerned—can only serve as an aid toward a deeper and more accurate understanding of that theological enterprise in which he is engaged as a living member of the Church.

In this context of the vital relationship between scriptural interpretation and positive theology as depository of traditions of reflection upon revelation, several questions must be asked about Teilhard's understanding of Scripture. Despite the brilliance of his adaptation of these Pauline themes, does not his reluctance to endorse certain Johannine ones (beyond the unitive and incarnational emphasis that the fourth Gospel provided) confirm the fact that, in contrast to his appeals to ancient patristic traditions, he was offering instead a radically different interpretation of Sacred Scripture, one that is in many ways at odds with any previous tradition in the history of theology? In other words, despite his insistence on the centrality of the cosmic Christ within his synthesis, something that he could legitimately claim recaptured the thrust of an all-but-forgotten tradition, did not his recasting of this theme in terms of a Christogenic evolution noticeably depart from the "pantocratic" Christ of the ancients in nearly every way except in their common desire to see Christ as the consummator of all things?

Specifically, while Teilhard indeed revived the ancient desire to see the total universe in both its physical and spiritual reality find a place in the final parousial consummation, did not his practical rejection of the doctrine of original sin (in its historical-Adamite as well as pre-cosmic-"Alexandrian" formulations) preclude anything like the restitutive *apokatastasis* as taught by Origen and Gregory of Nyssa? Likewise, while Teilhard shared with some of the ancient Fathers a more integral notion of grace as constitutive of human nature (at least as it achieves its God-given destiny), can his evolutionary approach to this problem be in any way equated with the "recapitulation" (*anakephalaiōsis*) as understood by Irenaeus? Furthermore, while Teilhard's vision of the pleroma shared a truly universal, almost pantheistic, vision of the Parousia, can this almost "completed" as well as "completing" concept of God be in any way equivalent to the universal reestablishment of all things in God proposed by Origen?[34]

34. So then, when the end has been restored to the beginning, and the termination of
    things compared to their commencement, that condition of things will be reestab-
    lished in which rational nature was placed, when it had no need to eat of the tree of
    the knowledge of good and evil; so that when all feeling of wickedness has been
    removed, and the individual has been purified and cleansed, he who alone is the
    one good God becomes to him "all," and that not in the case of a few individuals, or

It may be maintained, as many have said, that Teilhard continues a tradition of a cosmic vision of Christ that extends from St. Paul through these Greek Fathers and shares with them an incarnational emphasis that begins in St. John and can even be found in John Duns Scotus and the Franciscan school even to our own day. But that he shared with them, or even with Ss. John and Paul, their adaptation of a Logos theory of emanation and descent as the driving force behind his Christology (despite his occasional speculations about creation understood as "Trinitization") would be hard to support. On the contrary, it may be argued that Teilhard's synthesis, for all its Christological emphasis, was essentially a theological interpretation of evolution, and as such began with a cosmological supposition. In contrast, the theologies of the Fathers were precisely theology, and only secondarily drew upon the cosmology of their day; and even these were interpreted along the line of a Platonic and Plotinistic mode of thought that could hardly have less in common with Teilhard's "phenomenology."

This brings a final question into focus, one that is neither strictly exegetical nor theological but more broadly "hermeneutical" in the modern sense of the word. In the context of this more basic problem of the process of human understanding, Teilhard's reinterpretation of Scripture and his understanding of Revelation will be examined in Part III.

of a considerable number, but He Himself is "all in all." *De princ.* 3, 6, 3 (*ANF*) as quoted by Johannes Quasten, *Patrology* (Westminster, Md. Utrecht, Antwerp: Newman Spectrum, 1963) 2:89.

PART III

The Teilhardian Hermeneutic

7

The Interpretive Methodology of Teilhard de Chardin

Hermeneutics is generally understood to refer to the science of rules for understanding, whereas *hermeneutic* is reserved for the basic task of understanding how God's word becomes clear to men. The singular form is the more applicable here, since, far from Teilhard's attempting to elaborate specific rules for biblical interpretation, his concern was simply to make God's word, particularly in its Pauline expression, take on a new and vital meaning for modern man.

The foregoing sections have delineated the slow evolution and refinement of Teilhard's original insights into the meaning of St. Paul's message concerning the destiny of creation, the Body of Christ, and the pleroma. Now we shall explore the hermeneutical orientation—the steps contained, explicitly or implicitly, in Teilhard's reasoning process. If Teilhard really has presented a new and bold interpretation, as is indicated by the volume of commentary devoted to his synthesis, then it is vitally important to uncover the content of his interpretation, and, further, to examine critically the scriptural and theological methodology that informs it.

The present chapter will attempt to evaluate Teilhard's methodology by comparing his approach to the speculations of modern hermeneutics. The final chapter will hope to expose his unique understanding of the revelatory process itself, which, because it is so completely bound up with his theory of the convergence of human reflection, merits consideration as part of a more general process of evolutionary awareness, a generalized hermeneutic in the broadest sense of the word.

André Feuillet's recent work, *Le Christ sagesse de Dieu*,[1] while ac-

1. (Paris: Gabalda, 1966).

knowledging the great interest Teilhard's speculation has engendered, takes little notice of Teilhard's method of interpretation. Similarly, G. A. Vögtle, who in his recent work *Das Neue Testament und die Zukunft des Kosmos* acknowledges Feuillet's substantial interest in the subject, explains the general dearth of any substantial study of Teilhard's scriptural methodology as the normal reaction of exegetes to a man who did not himself seem to take traditional exegetical study very seriously.[2] Teilhard's more positive admirers and expositors, such as Tresmontant, Mooney, and DeLubac, have concentrated on his insights in the light of Scripture.

One notable exception is Leo Scheffczyk, who published a long article in 1963 entitled "Die 'Christogenesis' Teilhard de Chardins und der Kosmische Christus bei Paulus." Scheffczyk's remarks are on the whole very critical of Teilhard's scriptural interpretation.[3] In particular, he scores the apparent incompatibility of Teilhard's understanding of evil with the Pauline concept of original sin, for he considers it the source of a displacement, on Teilhard's part, of the whole relationship of the Redemptive Act to the destiny of the cosmos. He also considers the source of the apparent distortion by Teilhard of the Pauline idea of the Parousia. Scheffczyk's conclusion is that while it is certain that St. Paul's thought had greatly influenced Teilhard, Teilhard's interpretations can in no way be construed as compatible with the "literal sense" of the passages he claims for inspiration. What Scheffczyk allows Teilhard is a brilliant use of "the so-called 'accommodated sense' " (the meaning of which Scheffczyk fails to specify), which may be useful in channeling man's "mystical" aspirations in the direction of integration with the cosmic process. But, according to Scheffczyk, Teilhard's appeals to St. Paul are without value to dogmatic theology.[4]

1. (Paris: Gabalda, 1966).
2. A part of "Kommentare und Beiträge zum AT und NT" (Düsseldorf, 1970). Cf. p. 12.
3. In *Theologische Quartalschrift* 143 (1963): 137-74.

> Es ist nicht zu übersehen, dass die Unterschiede zwischen der paulischen Heilslehre und dem Denken T.s [Teilhard's] auch bezüglich der Gesamtkonzeption und der ganzen Lehrgestalt gross und so geartet sind, dass eine Zurückführung der einen Gestalt auf die andere und eine Deckung beider nicht möglich erscheint. Weil man andererseits nicht bestreichen kann, dass T. hier von biblischen Vorstellungen inspiriert ist und aus ihnen Schlussfolgerungen ableitet, wird man auch ein bestimmtes positives Verhältnis seiner theologischen Gedanken zur Schrift zugeben müssen. Die Verhältnisbestimmung dürfte m. E. (mit Evolution) in der Weise getroffen werden, dass man T. für die versuchte biblische Begründung seiner christologischen Konzeptionen den sog. *akkomodierten Schriftsinn* zubilligt. Es ist jener Sinn, der vom ursprünglichen Wortgehalt abgeht, aber doch nicht direkt zum Fremdsinn wird, weil er in der Übertragung und Anpassung des ursprünglichen Sinnes an einen neuen Sachverhalt eine gewisse Ähnlichkeit mit dem ursprünglichen Inhalt bewahrt. Es handelt sich um eine in einem neuen Bereich (hier in dem mystischem Bereich) ausgreifende Anwendung des ursprünglichen Wortes. Dieser Schriftsinn hat aber für den dogmatischen Beweis aus der Schrift keine Kraft." (Pp. 172-73)

4. "Es sagt aber nicht, dass diese mystiche und visionäre Schau des kosmischen Christus *theologisch* ohne Bedeutung wäre; denn die Naturwirklichkeit und -geschichte

While Teilhard was mistaken in his underevaluation of modern ex-egesis and its possible contribution to his synthesis (and by this token contradicted his own theory of convergent knowledge, although his somewhat harsh judgment was based more on what he thought to be the failure of modern biblical scholarship than on what he hoped would some day issue from it), the question remains as to just what he was attempting to do by his frequent appeals to Scripture, with his special emphasis on St. Paul. Despite his insistence that he was only expound-ing "littéralement et physiquement"[5] what he read in St. Paul, in no way did he approach the texts in the manner of a professional exegete, nor did he quote any exegetes to support his interpretations. On the other hand, neither did he claim to be writing as a professional theologian or even philosopher; for despite his frequent forays into these subjects, he made a general disclaimer in the Preface and Foreword to *The Phenomenon of Man* that could well be extended to all of his work. The disclaimer says that first and foremost he consid-ered himself an articulator of the *phenomena*, a "seer" compelled to share with others his vision of the totality of the universe on all levels. As we learn from the epilogue of this same work, this totality includes the revelation of Christ.[6]

What then? Was Teilhard a man who read the Bible purely for its inspirational value? Were his insights governed strictly by his own per-sonal needs? Or was he a devotee of the "spiritual sense" of Scripture, whose appeals to the "literal" sense were limited to the aesthetical lure of words and phrases such as *the Body of Christ* and the *pleroma*, but who, not content to use them simply by way of devotional inspiration, turned about and forced their meanings to cinch his arguments?

If, as our comparative study (Part II above) indicates, Teilhard truly intended to *re*interpret St. Paul, still, in his own eyes, he remained entirely faithful to the spirit of the Apostle. But the double question remains as to just how he managed to do this, and, in so doing, whether his effort can be taken as a serious contribution to theology or merely an *ersatz* attempt to synthesize the altogether distinct (if not conflicting) areas of revealed truth and evolutionary science.

The tasks here, then, are, first, to attempt to categorize, in terms of

kann zur Keilswirklichkeit und Heilsgeschichte nicht ohne Beziehung sein. Das vermochte T. als gläubiger Naturwissenschaftler deutlicher zu sehen als viele an-dere. Aber die genauere Fixierung des Verhältnisses zwischen Natur- und Heilsge-schichte, die abgewogene Bestimmung der Bedeutung der Evolution für das Heil in Christus und die theologische Erklärung der Realität, die dem kosmischen Christus zukommt, ist T. nicht gelungen. Das sind Aufgaben, die die Theologie in leben-digem Kontakt mit dem ganzen, auf die Schrift fundierten Heilsehre und der mo-dernen Naturerkenntnis noch zu lösen hat." (*Ibid.*, p. 173) Cf. also Christopher Mooney's remark on Scheffczyk's article in *Teilhard de Chardin and the Mystery of Christ* (New York: Harper & Row, 1964), p. 233, n.43.

5. "Super-Humanité, Super-Christ, Super-Charité" (1943) in *Oeuvres*, 9:211; *S&C*, p. 166.

6. *PM*, pp. 29-36, 291-99; *Oeuvres*, 1:21-29, 324-32.

contemporary hermeneutics, the type of hermeneutical process that best characterizes Teilhard's approach; second, to explicate more fully the existential presupposition that underlies this approach; and third, to evaluate the legitimacy of this approach in terms of the accepted sense or meaning of Sacred Scripture.

A. TEILHARD'S SCRIPTURAL APPROACH: THE "MODUS OPERANDI"

Teilhard seems to have paid little if any attention to the whole movement known as *hermeneutics*; indeed, there are no references to this term in his works, notes, or correspondence. But the problems that sparked the awakening of this great modern concern are reflected in Teilhard's whole approach to Scripture, which is that of relating the data of revelation as they appear in Scripture to the world view of modern man, a world view that Teilhard deemed inescapably evolutionary. As long as Western Man clung to a world view that was, rightly or wrongly, deemed to be compatible with what was taken to be a "biblical" cosmology, exegetes—with perhaps the exception of those infected with the excesses of nineteenth-century historicism and its rationalistic predecessors—generally remained undisturbed within their traditional service to theology. While it was within the safe confines of this more or less undisturbed tradition of biblical exegesis that Teilhard had received his own training, it was amply evident to anyone who looked beyond the seminary walls, or who even read the newly imposed "Oath Against Modernism," that this smug security was coming apart at the seams.[7]

There is ample evidence that Teilhard foresaw early in his career the need for a radical reinterpretation that transcends the immediate concerns of historical exegesis. In his early "Notes et esquisses" under the date of August 15, 1917, he posed the problem (which still concerned him greatly in 1952[8]) of "Le Sens de la Croix." The first two subdivi-

---

7.   Karl Lehmann, in his article on Hermeneutics in *Sacramentum Mundi*, 3:23-27 (also in *Encyclopedia of Theology* ed. Karl Rahner [New York, Seabury, 1975] pp. 611-15).

   As long as "tradition" is accepted and transmitted without question—prescinding for the moment the re-interpretations possibly concealed therein—individual "misunderstandings" and many "errors" arise, rather than fundamental difficulties of interpretation. But the sense of the passage of time, changes in vocabulary, concepts and thought-forms can bring about a break with tradition, which will now appear as "strange" and questionable. (*SM*, p. 25; *ET*, p. 611.)

   Within such a tradition, Lehmann indicates, there is likewise a traditional hermeneutics, i.e., a set of practical rules that insure the maintenance of exegetical orthodoxy. Modern hermeneutics, on the other hand, has been born from the very rupture of a once-unified synthesis of man's world view, his self-understanding, and its assumed congruence with the scriptural word.

8.   Cf. *Oeuvres*, 10:251-62; *C&E*, pp. 212-20.

sions are enough to convey the nature of the conflict as he saw it:
"1.—Point de vue primitif, (Paulinien)" and "2.—Point de vue
Evolutif." Concerning the contrast of this second point of view with the
background of the first, he remarked:

> Historically, the paradisiac conception (earthly paradise) seems to
> be *extra-historical*, incompatible with the geological world, which
> has always been a world of suffering and death. Death and concupis-
> cence are *evolutive stigmata* of natural (not secondary or intrusive)
> realities.[9]

In the face of these natural realities, he went on to this early date to
propose a "Conciliation," which he considered possible on two counts:
(1) "The *altogether human* and psychological *origin* of the dogma of the
Redemption (—interpretation of death . . .)"; and (2) "to demonstrate
the substantial evolution of Dogma."

These two sweeping admissions, the first traceable to a misunderstanding by St. Paul himself and the second based (as Teilhard believed)
on a misreading of St. Paul's intent, led Teilhard to a double conclusion regarding the status of the redemption dogma itself and its future
meaning for man.

> It remains that, historically, the Paulinian view, based on a histor-
> ical and tangible fall, remains "up in the air"—*true*, but
> *undemonstrable* (and this merely from the fact of the most classical
> theology, as soon as one admits that death and concupiscence are
> natural, thus not intrusive, as St Paul humanly thought) (the concep-
> tion of nudatum and of spoliatum is very skillful, but frankly, ought
> not to be in the spirit of St. Paul. (*It reconciles a primitive dualism*)
> in a secondary synthesis.
> This, which must be *considered frankly* and loyally, leads to re-
> garding the evolution of the dogma in a very profound way not only
> in the transformation of formulas, but in the birth of dogmas. There
> is a great part of psychology in that. The theory of Redemption was
> born from a "wrong" interpretation of the problem of Evil . . . (In
> the sense that St Paul subjectivized [subjectivé], considered death as
> intrusive essentialiter (non solum historically).
> And meanwhile we love the same Christ as St. Paul, and that
> Christ is in the plenitude of the 20th century of Life and love![10]

In addition to calling to mind the perennial problem that the doctrine of original sin presented to Teilhard's attempts at synthesis, the
above passages bring two other very important elements to the fore:
the interrelation of Teilhard's hermeneutical approach to Scripture with
the question of the development of dogma, and the particular order of

9. Unpublished, *T.A.*, Cahier 3, p. 20. (My translation. See Appendix D, §1, a, for
French text.)
10. *Ibid.*, p. 21 (see Appendix D, §1, a). The above passages contain many abbreviations; however, the full spellings have been given according to the transcription
provided by the Foundation Teilhard de Chardin, Paris.

dialectic that engages him in his approach to the whole subject.

Just how did Teilhard proceed as a thinker? From the above quotation we see that his concern was with the cosmic or historic (or what he occasionally called the *existential*[11]) situation of man. In this case it is the situation of the Christian thinker who finds himself posed between the literal meaning of St. Paul's concept of the Fall (coupled with its traditional interpretation along the lines of a dogmatic theory of redemption) on the one hand, and the seeming incompatibility of this account with evolutionary science on the other. If his predicament may be analyzed in the terms proposed by R. Lapointe's study of hermeneutics,[12] Teilhard was faced with an apparent conflict between the ontological (or literal-exegetical) meaning of St. Paul's writing (further complicated by the theological elaboration of this exegetical meaning into the position of a dogma of redemption) and the seeming existential impossibility of making this literal meaning square with a scientific-evolutionary world view. While it is true that in this case Teilhard attempted to resolve the dilemma by appealing to an "essential" or meta-historical meaning conveyed by Paul's account (which he believed theology had misunderstood), he still had to admit that the basis for the misunderstanding of this as being a historically localized fall (apart from a broader ontological context) is traceable to Paul's own humanly explainable but mistaken view of the origin and place of death in the universe.

At first glance it would appear (and perhaps many of Teilhard's critics would agree) that Teilhard was simply engaging in his own private style of Bible reading, beginning with his own existential questioning (and preformed answer) and arriving at his own *sui generis* interpretation of Paul's words by forcing them to conform to an evolutionary pattern of thought. This is what many of his critics accuse him of doing.[13]

From another angle, which is perhaps more common among his sci-

---

11. That Teilhard did not, however, equate his existential concern with what is currently known as "existentialism" is clear in a Journal note of 1953 (June—date unmarked; "Journal" 19 [7]: 77). Commenting on *The Christian Philosophy* by Prof. Longmead Casserley (Exeter College), Teilhard speaks of the "existential" tendencies of the Augustinian tradition as throwing light on the science vs. religion conflict in such a way that "the psychological discontinuity" between the transcendent goal of man and the natural goals of creation are seen in a disjunctive relationship, a tendency that explains the uneasiness with this view as it was inherited by the Thomists. Teilhard suggests that his version of the "Neo-God" is one that must embrace both goals,—"a combination that is absolutely strange to the 'existentialists.' "

12. Roger Lapointe, D.E.S., *Les trois dimensions de l'Hermeneutique* (Paris: Gabalda, 1967). The three dimensions elaborated in this book are measured in terms of three "parameters," which are closely interrelated: the *aesthetic* (or strictly literary element), the *ontological* (embracing the historical and actual substrata of the content) and the *existential* (which embodies the meaning in regard to the interpreter's present life-situation).

13. While Maritain's criticisms are more pointedly philosophical, the eminent Christian philosopher believed that Teilhard was ultimately unfaithful (in his thought) to the priorities that Maritain felt should mark the believer, i.e., that Teilhard was guilty "of kneeling before the World." Cf. *The Peasant of the Garonne* (New York: Holt, Rinehart, Winston, 1968), p. 116.

entific and theological critics, Teilhard appears to be engaging in a species of "apologetics" or religious philosophy where, beginning again with his own *existential* situation (the conflict between science and religion as experienced by him from his student days), he simply proceeded, by way of the inspiration he found in his own literary interpretation of Scripture, to a directly ontological conclusion, namely, that, historically speaking, St. Paul has in fact an Omega-Point personified in the Cosmic Christ.[14]

A third possibility, but one that Teilhard certainly did not intend, would be that he was actually engaging in a species of biblical theology, for despite the existential nature of his questioning, Teilhard himself claims that his vision is inspired not so much by the exigencies of scientific theory as from Scripture itself. Unlikely as this first appears, this is exactly what he did claim in his essay "Creative Union" of November 1917:

> *With* knowledge of Christ, this almost delirious dream becomes to some degree a Reality known by faith. As the reader must have seen for some time, the philosophy of creative union is simply the development—generalization, extension to the universe—of what the Church teaches us about the growth of Christ. *It is the philosophy of the universe expressed in terms of the notion of the mystical body.* It was primarily as such that I myself came to grasp it, and it is only so that it can be understood: by striving to love and hold Christ in all things.[15]

Even at this early date, Teilhard was approaching Scripture as a person torn between the claims of science and his loyalty to the faith, but what he found to be the answer to his dilemma is an answer inspired by faith, an answer that he first of all found articulated in the revealed Word of God. It is precisely this revealed element, this "extrapolation" based on faith, that even in his mature thought others find difficult if not impossible to grasp, unless they are believers.[16] But that Teilhard's "modus operandi" is that characterized by biblical or "positive" theol-

---

14. Here the analysis of hermeneutical procedure suggested by Lapointe's chapter, "The Circularity of Parameters," is followed. (Cf. pp. 121-38.) While there are twelve possible combinations employing all three parameters (the aesthetic, ontological, and existential) there are four possibilities that apply most directly in this case:

Existential → Ontological → Aesthetic $\Longrightarrow$ Private Interpretation
Existential → Aesthetic → Ontological $\Longrightarrow$ Apologetics and/or Religious Philosophy
Aesthetic → Existential → Ontological $\Longrightarrow$ Biblical Theology
Aesthetic → Ontological → Existential $\Longrightarrow$ Systematic Theology

15. *WTW*, p. 174; *Ecrits*, p. 196.   —
16. Sir Julian Huxley, for example, writes in his introduction to the English edition of *The Phenomenon of Man*: "Though many scientists may, as I do, find it impossible to follow him all the way in his gallant attempt to reconcile the supernatural elements in Christianity with the facts and implications of evolution, this in no way detracts from the positive value of his naturalistic general approach." (*PM*, p. 19)

ogy hardly seems the case. Biblical theology, according to Lapointe, moves from the aesthetic or literary meaning of Scripture through the mediation of the existential "sitz-im-leben" toward an ontological objectivity of historical judgment. Teilhard, on the contrary, with an obviously existential question in mind and seeking an existential answer, usually appears when dealing with scriptural meanings to be beginning from an aesthetic (perhaps even naive reading of Scripture, i.e., one that takes little account of scientific exegesis) and going on to seek an existential meaning by means of rigorous subjection or reinterpretation of the biblical word according to the thought forms imposed by evolutionary science. Astounding as this may be, what Teilhard seems to have been doing, at least in the best moments of his hermeneutical method, is something that at least vaguely resembles the methodology of systematic theology. Many theologians will no doubt protest such a comparison, but the resemblance is striking, even to the extent that systematic theology has had much the same criticism leveled against it by exegetes and biblical theologians as that leveled against Teilhard —the tendency to use Scripture by taking words and phrases out of context and reading into them historically conditioned thought forms (one aspect of the "ontological" element) in the attempt to achieve an existential understanding meeting the specifications of the theologian's own "system." This in turn engenders a kind of pseudo-apologetic in which the biblical sources, taken originally in a freely inspirational function, end up as being considered proofs of the theological systematization that has been erected. If Teilhard displayed serious weakness in his theological methodology, it might be because he was suffering from some of the same weaknesses all too evident in that Thomistic theology which he criticized so freely.[17]

Yet Teilhard himself had no ambition to become a systematic theologian. In fact, in one rather surprising passage of a letter to a friend, a passage perhaps a bit overdrawn, he even disclaimed that his intention was primarily to erect any system of thought: theological, scientific, or otherwise. It was rather to elucidate what was, upon final analysis, an intuition, or even a mystical insight into the total nature of reality:

> fundamentally, what I desire so greatly to propagate is not exactly a theory, a system, a *Weltanschauung*, but a certain taste, a certain perception of the beauty, the pathos, and the unity of *being*. This may even account for the incomprehension I encounter. I try to translate the species of calm intoxication produced in me by an awareness of the profound substance of things into theories (how I wish I could translate it into music!), but these theories really matter to me only by their vibrations in a province of the soul which is not that of intellectualism. Those who do not hear the fundamental har-

17. As at the conclusion of "Pour y voir clair"; cf. *Oeuvres*, 7:234f.; *AE*, p. 225.

mony of the Universe which I try to transcribe (fortunately, many do) look in what I write for some kind of narrowly logical system, and are confused or angry. Fundamentally, it is not possible to transmit directly by words the perception of a quality, a taste. Once again, it would be more to my purpose to be a shadow of Wagner than a shadow of Darwin. Taking myself as I am, I see no better course than to strive by all means to reveal Humanity to Men.[18]

While stated in humanistic terms to an apparently unbelieving friend, Teilhard's intentions are clear. He was trying to be neither a systematic theologian, nor a systematic philosopher, but simply a scientist who "sees." As a human he asked "existential" questions. As a believer he searched revelation for clues to an answer. And as a scientist, he submitted both his questions as a human and his inspirations as a believer to the process of systematization through evolutionary science. But this discursive process ever remained subordinate to the *intuition* he had first experienced and the vision that remained. If his essays and works sometimes resembled theological tracts, philosophical essays, or scientific treatises, they must all be understood on this discursive level—a level on which each makes its contribution to the total insight yet in the end remains subservient to the mysticism that informs them.

In terms of Lapointe's hermeneutical parameters, it appears that Teilhard's methodology, while somewhat resembling that of apologetics and biblical theology, in the end gravitated toward the structure of systematic theology. While he began with an existential question (which indeed forms the background of all inquiry, not merely that of apologetics) that is particularly apologetical in concern (the reconciliation of faith with scientific theory), his use of the aesthetic or literary parameter as manifested in Scripture did not proceed to immediate ontological conclusions (as would be the case in pure apologetics) but rather returned to begin again from the existential point of view, this time in terms of an adaptation of historical methodology as generally utilized by biblical or "positive" theology insofar as it traces the development of a doctrine within Scripture. However, while this resulted in a historical judgment, as is generally the case with biblical theology, in Teilhard's case this judgment did not stand as a conclusion concerning the validity of Scripture in its own right, but simply as a confirmation of the congruence of his own interpretations with that of Christian exegetical tradition as manifested in the cosmic interpretation of the Pauline-Johannine Christology found in the early Greek fathers. In the conviction that he stood squarely within this tradition rather than on any ontological judgment based on his aesthetic reading of Scripture or on the results of historical methodology, Teilhard finally returned a third time

18. *Letters to Two Friends*, trans. Helen Weaver (New York: New American Library, 1968), pp. 58-59; *Accomplir l'Homme* (Lettres inédites 1926-1952) par Ruth Nada Anshen (Paris: Editions Bernard Grasset, 1968), pp. 74-75. (From a letter of Feb. 14, 1927.)

to the existential parameter, much in the manner of a systematic theologian. However, even in this case he was not content with a merely "existential" conclusion, but instead resubmitted the conclusion to a thoroughly evolutionary presupposition, that of the universal applicability of evolutionary process to all reality. From this he arrived at an extraordinary new ontological conclusion, one that transformed the existential interpretation of traditional Christology into the ontological discovery of "Christogenesis."

In any attempt further to simplify this immensely complex dialogue within Teilhard's mind, it must be concluded that what is witnessed here is not a movement that falls neatly under the category of apologetics, biblical theology, or systematic theology. Rather, what appears is a triple descent from a parameter that is first and last existential in character, centered on Teilhard's conviction of the validity of the evolutionary paradigm. While his first effort attempted to interpret Scripture apologetically in terms of this evolutionary presupposition, the second phase used this existential presupposition as the starting point of a historical methodology understood in terms of the development of doctrine. The third and final application of this existential parameter resulted not in a simple reinterpretation of doctrine for the sake of its actualization in Christian life (along the lines of Bultmann's "existential interpretation"), but went on to extract from this reinterpretation a new ontological conclusion, one that Teilhard believed revealed a hitherto obscured aspect of the revelation of Christ and a new dimension of the very concept of revelation as well.[19]

In the light of this analysis, insofar as it helps clarify the processes that characterize Teilhard's thought, it must be concluded that his hermeneutical approach, while it does resemble traditional systematic theology, nevertheless goes beyond it in its fresh ontological affirmations, and goes beyond it to the same degree that traditional systematic theology goes beyond positive-biblical theology in its existentially motivated attempt at synthesis. To this degree, Teilhard's "theology" in the

19. In my attempt to plot this triple descent from the existential parameter in terms of Lapointe's three dimensions of hermeneutics, the following diagram is submitted:

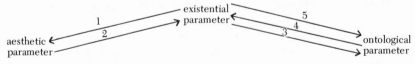

Hermeneutical Movements:
1-2 *First movement*: (apologetic in motivation—but incomplete); no ontological conclusions claimed other than a tentative convergence with forgotten Eastern Patristic Theology.
3 *Second movement*: application of a historical methodology (biblical-positive theology) to affirm in ontological terms the insights of the first movement.
4-5 *Third movement*: reinterpretation of the ontological-dogmatic traditions of patristic "cosmic" theology in the light of an existentially universal parameter of evolution, leading in turn to new ontological conclusions.

end would seem to fit into what merits the name *existential analysis* in its most comprehensive sense.[20] It is the elucidation in dogmatic terms of the ontological content of Christian belief as it applies not only to man's present existence, but—even beyond that, given his evolutionary perspective—to a projection of the meaning of these same ontological affirmations in respect to the "existential exigencies" of man's continued hope of the future and his belief in what Teilhard called "The God of Evolution."[21]

Because of the preponderance of what may be termed *existential analysis*, understood in the context of a cosmological dimension that embraces the totality of space and time, and even more particularly as projected into the realm of the future, it is necessary that this subject not be passed over lightly or taken for granted. For if Teilhard's concern was eminently existential, it still was not limited in its deductions to merely establishing a suitably "scientific" backdrop onto which the eternal verities of Christianity can be reprojected and rearranged so as to become humanistically relevant to man's cosmic situation. Much more is at stake. Indeed, the very concept of Christ and the subsequent relationship between the doctrines of the Incarnation, redemption, and parousia (along with the scriptural passages that have established these doctrines) will, in time, demand radical reinterpretation, a fact of which Teilhard himself only slowly became aware. But once the fact of evolution is accepted, there is no escaping the necessity of the attempt at such a radical reinterpretation. Regardless of what one may think of the attempts of Teilhard in this direction, it is impossible for the Christian theologian to avoid applying himself to the task unless he wishes to abdicate his responsibility toward the science of theology and the Christian faith.

No attempt to assess the validity of Teilhard's synthesis can presume to rest its argument on questions of hermeneutical or theological methodology, valid as these may be in evaluating the results of his ef-

---

20. Piet Fransen, in his chapter "Three Ways of Dogmatic Thought" (*Intelligent Theology*, vol. 1 [Chicago: Franciscan Herald Press, 1969]) characterizes most theology as being one of or a combination of three modes of thought. The way of *Psychological Description*, Platonic in origin and typified by Augustine and Anselm in the West, was succeeded by *Essential Analysis*, which was Aristotelian in origin and typified in the Scholastics. This latter he characterizes as being an inquiry "into the 'necessary and universal a priori conditions of a given fact or truth.' It is a kind of transcendental analysis, not of a formal kind, as in Kant, but of a truly metaphysical nature" (p. 24). He notes that it has proved itself incapable of dealing with a dynamic world view (p. 26) and proposes a third way, which he terms *existential analysis* (German "Existentielle Analyse" vs. "Existential Analyse" of Bultmann) and defines as "the systematic exposition of the necessary a priori conditions of the possibility of a given real existence in the wholeness of the human situation" (p. 29). If it be true, as Fransen claims, that such a theology is concerned "with our existence as a whole [as against a thology of essences], in its dialectical tension between the spiritual unity of our personal liberty and the multiplicity of our existence in time and space" (p. 27), then Teilhard's approach would eminently merit this definition of "existential theology," particularly if this "existential" element is seen as being concerned with the preconditions of the future.
21. *Oeuvres*, 10:283; *C&E*, p. 237.

fort. To criticize the answer proposed by Teilhard does not excuse one from addressing himself to the question. The question in this situation (the existential starting point of all theological inquiry) concerns the evolutionary presupposition.

Thus, if the challenge posed by Teilhard is to be faced, and his efforts criticized, further examination must be focused on what amounts to the all-embracing and all-conditioning "evolutionary presupposition." Such an existential presupposition cannot be wished away. If it at first looms as an apologetical hurdle, and in the process of confrontation suggests epistomological considerations, it will eventually, as it did for Teilhard, necessitate certain ontological accommodations. The presupposition, once admitted, leaves little room for escape.

B. THE EVOLUTIONARY PRESUPPOSITION: FROM APOLOGETICS TO SYNTHESIS

Teilhard's first formal confrontation with the theory of evolution was to take place unmistakably in the field of Christian apologetics. Because of his developing competence in paleontology as well as his scholastic acumen during his studies, Teilhard was asked to contribute to the long article on "Man" in the *Dictionnaire Apologétique de la Foi Catholique*, published under the editorship of A. D'Alès in the years just before the outbreak of the First World War. Teilhard's contribution was the section entitled "L'homme devant les enseignements de l'Eglise et devant la philosophie spiritualiste."[22] In that section, devoted primarily to the defense of Catholic doctrine on the origin of the soul and its relationship to the body in terms of its unique and permanent individuality, Teilhard, while basing his arguments primarily on psychological analysis in the scholastic sense of the word, showed keen awareness of the implications that biological transformism and philosophical evolutionism would have for traditional Christian doctrine. Admitting the provisional character of all philosophies in relationship to theological expression of dogma, Teilhard nevertheless based his arguments on the inescapable acceptance of the dual nature of man as understood by the church in terms of the rational soul as "per se et essentialiter" the "forma corporis humani" (C. of Vienne, Denz. #481 [409]). Taking this affirmation as his starting point, Teilhard went on to say categorically that

> this most particular dualism is no doubt one of the easiest notions to distort in a philosophical construction. (All) can easily see the radical opposition of dogma with materialism or determinism, or an evolutionism that would render the soul perpetually unstable and unfinished in its substance.[23]

22. *Dictionnaire Apologétique de la Foi Catholique* (Paris: G. Beauchesne, 1911), 2:502-14.
23. *Ibid.*, p. 502. (My translation.)

Acknowledging that ideas concerning the nature of human corporality were changing, even within the scope of Christian philosophy, he reaffirmed, on the philosophical level, the primacy of the individual over species and the "fixity" of the "individual type." On the dogmatic level, he maintained both the "apartness" and the "centrality of dignity and finality" of the human species, and the necessity of maintaining the immediate and monogenetic creation of the first man. Speaking of the revealed data, Teilhard held that:

> a Christian is not free to imagine absolutely to his liking the historical origins of humanity. On this subject, undoubtedly, light has been half brought. Genesis is such a special kind of story that for a long time doubts will remain as to the precise meaning of many a detail that it keeps in store for us.[24]

Having already listed the necessity of holding the idea of special and monogenetic creation of the first man, and because of its connection with the doctrine of original sin, Teilhard concluded that

> for all these reasons, we see that it is necessary to reject an evolutionism that, by joining man in the depth of his being to the inferior forms of life and matter, would only make him the product of a transformation,—whether it be [through the joining of] like to like, through the recasting of primitive combinations,—or whether it be of lesser to greater, through the increase (even if they be taken from a divine source) that does not end in a sudden and profound recasting, a breaking away from the common current, placing humanity in a region of transcendence in stability.[25]

In pondering these challenges, which he apparently accepted with utmost gravity, Teilhard was convinced that "the opposition between science and philosophy [i.e., the philosophic principles maintained by Catholic theology] is illusory."[26] Is not, he asked, a science of appearances more or less incomplete? But he had to admit when speaking of that philosophy which is not determined by the demands of dogmatic truth:

> From a strictly philosophical point of view the appearances (whatever they may be) of an evolution including man are not distasteful. Only biblical data could be an obstacle, because they impose on human history certain limits that can theoretically be verified:—some insisting upon a certain degree of visible discontinuity between the first man and animals; others even, like monogenism, implying the "quasi-artificial" intervention of a free activity.—Practically, the always remaining difficulty in making precise the concrete and scientific form of the facts stated by Genesis,

24. *Ibid.*, pp. 504-5.
25. *Ibid.*, p. 505.
26. *Ibid.*, p. 512.

together with the great part of uncertainty and approximation of which paleontology and prehistory will never be rid, all this makes a conjunction of dogma and sciences very unlikely.[27]

It can be seen from this that Teilhard had begun to essay the question that would occupy his entire life. Similarly, a few passages later, the emergence can already be seen on the train of thought that could no longer be confined to the "science-faith" conflict as he then experienced it—a mere invitation to further and more refined apologetics. Instead it beckoned him to develop a whole new synthesis of human evolution and theology. On the primacy or "la royauté" of man, Teilhard now wrote:

Already, from a merely experimental point of view, one could hold that nothing more perfect, more accomplished, more "qualitatively" central than intelligence exists in the world. By bringing light to the unsuspected riches of the sanctified soul, revelation especially discloses that it is precisely with a view to collecting humanity that God started the current of visible things.[28]

Taking this primacy of the human intellect as his cue, Teilhard was willing to try to understand that intoxication of the human intelligence which evolutionary theory has produced and the profound distaste that modern man feels for the apparently extrinsic and contingent view of creation that Catholic doctrine seems to offer as a poor substitute for a faith in the absolute and necessary development of the universe. This alienation of religious faith from faith in the world Teilhard countered with a view of the universe that would find its ultimate coherence in Christ.

Therefrom, without a tearing of all the sails of determinism, or a replacement of intimate and organic relationships by a most artificial network of conventions, they [i.e., believers] will see the fragmentary irregularities that shock their minds coordinate themselves into a varied flexible whole, enlightened by a God's love, invested by supernatural extensions,—in a word, centered on Jesus Christ. The Universe will harmonize before their eyes into a unity far superior to the one that formerly charmed them. Then, perhaps, they will begin to appreciate the beauty of man's physiognomy, such as the Church protects with a holy jealousy.[29]

If this essay—the first of Teilhard's on this subject and one of the few to be published with an imprimatur during his lifetime—shows a certain hesitation about the evolutionary presupposition as a fact, it leaves no doubt about Teilhard's having seen it as a factor to be reck-

27. *Ibid.*, pp. 512-13.
28. *Ibid.*, p. 513.
29. *Ibid.*, p. 514.

oned with. During the next decade and a half he was to elaborate more and more the general lines of this synthesis and to fill in the details of his personal intuitions. However, while his own thought evolved further in this direction, and his convictions grew more and more ontologically secure, there remained a certain hesitation to admit, beyond the question of a certain evolution or development of dogma, that the evolutionary presupposition might apply to the process of revelation itself. This hesitation was understandable in view of the problem that his speculations on the question of Original Sin were to produce.

When did this concept begin to clarify itself in his mind? Notes to this effect can be found dated as early as 1945;[30] but, as will be seen, the question of such an epistomologically related application of the presupposition begins, in somewhat different terms, as early as 1916. Due to the loss of the 1926-1943 notes, what was actually occurring in his speculations can only be conjectured, but it is evident from a "Journal" note of May 16, 1951, that he had been pondering the question for some time.

The note in question[31] distinguishes between the historical "core" or nucleus in all religions and the "envelope of myth" and speaks of the difficult task of keeping a proper balance between the two. But what is at stake is more than just the question of the "ontological value" of the historic core. According to Teilhard it is a question of grasping the whole evolutionary nature of both the historical and literary elements of the religious phenomenon, that is to say, its "phyletic" character. But such an approach was hardly new for Teilhard, who as far back as the 1930s spoke of Christianity in this genre.[32] Here, however, the application is extended to include all religion in both its ontological reality and its psychological expression. We are therefore dealing with a universal presupposition that demands a radical reassessment of the whole gnoseological frame of reference. As early as 1933, he had begun more intensely to explore the implications of this altered world view for our theological systematization:

> The quite recent (and still continuing) transformation which has taken the universe from a state of static reality to one of evolutive reality, has all the characteristics of a deep-rooted and definitive event. All that could be said in criticism of it is that we are still a long way from completely appreciating the extent of the changes logically entailed by perception of this new cosmic dimension: Duration. The universe is no longer endless in space alone. In all its strands, it now unfolds interminably into the past, governed by a constantly active cosmogenesis. It would be superfluous to analyse

30. In a short but very important Journal note of Jan. 5, 1945 ("Journal" 13 [1]: 71), Teilhard speaks of the "emergence in history" as the root problem in biblical criticism inasmuch as Christianity in its totality must be studied as a "process." Teilhard judged Loisy's approach to be only "un morcelage."
31. "Journal" 18 (6): 59-60.
32. Cf. *The Phenomenon of Man*, pp. 291f.; *Oeuvres*, 1:324f.

the breadth or the forward drive—both irresistible—of this new outlook, which is basically characteristic of what we call "the modern
spirit." I need do no more than note that at the present moment
human knowledge is developing exclusively under the aegis of
evolution, recognized as a prime property of experiential reality. So
true is this that *nothing can any longer find place in our construc-
tions which does not first satisfy the conditions* of a universe in process of transformation. A Christ whose features do not adapt themselves to the requirements of a world that is evolutive in structure
will tend more and more to be eliminated out of hand.[33]

What is typified as "the modern spirit" in the above passage Teilhard
explored more thoroughly in terms of its general effect on all facets of
human thought in an essay of 1942 entitled "The New Spirit." In it he
described in terms of general human perception this revolution as involving a transformation of our whole notion of time as related to
space, and also contrasted the ancient and hitherto traditional view of
time with that imposed by evolutionary thought.[34] The outmoded view
was that of a merely homogeneous chronological sequence within
which one element is interchangeable with another and to a large extent independent of another; for example, our imagining "Socrates
being born in the place of Descartes" or, it might be added from implication, the concept that Christ might have appeared at some other
point in history.

In contrast to what might be called this "chronological nominalism"
Teilhard expounded a newer, organic concept of time involving three
great differences from the old: a point in time is understood to be
causally dependent on its antecedents, totally unique (and thus nonin-
terchangeable), and structurally interrelated with all other elements existing within the same time segment. This last characteristic is closely
tied to the notion of the *spatial* coextensivity of each existing element
in the universe, which plays an important part in Teilhard's earliest
theological speculation (see chap. 4, §1, D, esp. n. 52).

The effects of this organically altered notion of time and space should
be emphasized. Teilhard went on to speak of the revolution that this
altered concept of time has brought to human thought:

> We believed that we did not change; but now, like newborn infants
> whose eyes are opening to the light, we are becoming aware of a
> world in which neo-Time, organising and conferring a dynamic upon
> Space, is endowing the totality of our knowledge and beliefs with a
> new structure and a new direction.[35]

However, if the movement of this radically new concept of space-
time is seen to be basically convergent in nature, a notion that those

33. "Christology and Evolution," *C&E*, pp. 77-78; *Oeuvres*, 10:96-97.
34. Cf. *FM*, pp. 83-84; *Oeuvres*, 5:111-12.
35. *FM*, p. 85; *Oeuvres*, 5:113.

familiar with Teilhard's thought will recognize as permeating all of his synthesis, then this convergence is not simply a biophysical phenomenon but a universally applicable fact that involves the evolution of human thought processes and their lasting achievements:

> To accept that Space-Time is convergent in its nature is equally to admit that Thought on earth has not achieved the ultimate point of its evolution.[36]

But if this be true, what about Christianity, which for Teilhard represents the highest achievement of human consciousness thus far?

> As recently as yesterday Christianity represented the highest point attained by the consciousness of Mankind in its striving to humanise itself. But does it still hold this position, or at the best can it continue to hold it for long?[37]

This is the challenge that Teilhard spent his life in meeting, and as he believed, successfully. But that success hinged not on a simplistic accommodation of Christian belief to a "theory" of human origins, or a facile concordism between The Book of Genesis and the college texts of geology and biology. It involved, instead, a total recasting of the human approach to arriving at the truth. In his 1946 essay "Degrees of Scientific Certainty in the Idea of Evolution," even the "first degree" makes this amply clear:

> 1. At a first and completely general degree, the scientific idea of evolution implies no more than the affirmation of this fact: that every object and every event in the world has an antecedent which conditions its appearance among other phenomena. Nothing, we say, appears in history except by way of birth: so that each element in the universe is, by something in itself, a link in an unbreakable chain that stretches behind and in front of it until it is lost to view. This does not, of course, rule out the interpolation between two successive links, of a mutation, a jump, a critical point of emergence. . . .
> At this degree of generality, at which evolution simply means the *organicity* of the stuff of the universe (a temporal, combined with a spatial, organicity) it is not enough, I must emphasize, to speak of certainty. What we should say is "evidential fact." For our age, to have become conscious of evolution means something very different from and much more than having discovered one further fact, however massive and important that fact may be. It means (as happens with a child when he acquires the sense of spatial depth) that we have become alive to a new *dimension*. The idea of evolution: not, as is still sometimes said, a mere hypothesis, but a condition of all experience—or again, if you prefer the expression, the universal

---

36. *FM*, p. 89; *Oeuvres*, 5:118.
37. *FM*, p. 93; *Oeuvres*, 5:122.

curve to which all our present and future ways of constructing the universe must henceforth conform, if they are to be scientifically valid or even thinkable.[38]

Is this not too much? Would it not imply an unwarranted intrusion (if extended beyond conceptions of the universe as such to the realm of universal truth, which would be the case in "Christology and Evolution") of human thought into the area of absolute revealed truth? So it would be, if he were talking of a Truth that existed in an altogether transcendent order apart from human formulation, a pure theology in which the Logos had no human existence. Teilhard seems to have been well aware of this objection and the consequent protests that an altered view of creation, Incarnation, and redemption would raise in his critics. A year earlier he had already prepared his answer in his "Christianity and Evolution: Suggestions for a New Theology." To the first, more general claim that he was subverting the transcendent message of the Gospels, he answered:

> In the first century of the Church, Christianity made its definitive entry into human thought by boldly identifying the Christ of the gospel with the Alexandrian Logos. The logical continuation of the same tactics and the prelude to the same success must be found in the instinct which is now urging the faithful, after two thousand years, to return to the same policy; but this time it must not be with the ordinating principle of the stable Greek kosmos but with the neo-Logos of modern philosophy—the evolutive principle of a universe in movement.[39]

And to the claim that this recasting of the Gospel message dissolves the Christ of the Gospels into a mere abstraction, Teilhard answered even more fully:

> Objections have, I know, been raised to this generalization of Christ-the-Redeemer in a true "Christ-the Evolver" (he who, with the sins, bears the whole weight of the world in progress); to this elevation of the historic Christ to a universal physical function; to this final identification of cosmogenesis with a Christogenesis. It has been said that all this may well mean that the human reality of Jesus Christ is lost in the super-human and vanishes in the cosmic. Nothing, I believe, is more baseless than such doubts. The more, indeed, we think about the profound laws of evolution, the more convinced we must be that the universal Christ could not appear at the end of time at the peak of the world, if he had not previously entered it during its development, *through the medium of birth*, in the form of an *element*. If it is indeed true that it is through Christ-Omega that the universe in movement holds together, then, corres-

38. "Sur les degrés de certitude scientifique de l'idée d'Evolution," in *Oeuvres*, 9:245-46; *S&C*, pp. 192-93.
39. *C&E*, pp. 180-81; *Oeuvres*, 10:211. Note that the final sentence of this paragraph in the French is stated more tentatively, in question form.

pondingly, it is from his concrete germ, the Man of Nazareth, that Christ-Omega (both theoretically and historically) derives his whole consistence, as a hard experiential fact. The two terms are intrinsically one whole, and they cannot vary, in a truly total Christ, except simultaneously.[40]

Having thus attempted to disarm his critics, Teilhard was deadly serious about this total reinterpretation of Christ in terms of the evolutionary presupposition. There was for him no escaping this, for in a universe that must now be understood in light of the Incarnation, theology is by necessity centered in Christology, and as such cannot escape expression in conjunction with a "cosmology," be it for good or ill. In the essay quoted immediately before the two passages above, the following reassertion of his claim is found:

> I said earlier that Christian dogma, as it first emerged, had necessarily adapted itself to a cosmos of the static type. It could not do otherwise, because at that time human reason could not conceive the world in any other form. But consider what would happen if an attempt were made, following a line already suggested by the Greek Fathers long ago, to transpose the evidence of Revelation into a universe of the non-static type. . . . Experience shows that traditional Christology can accept an evolutionary world-structure; but, what is even more, and what contradicts all predictions, it is within this new organic and unitary ambience, and by reason of this particular curve of linked Space-Time, that it can develop most freely and fully.[41]

Teilhard proclaims here that not only is Christology as a theological reflection capable of being accommodated to an evolutionary world view, but now, by virtue of this evolutionary world view, Scripture itself yields its more valid interpretation:

> It is there that Christology takes on its true form. The great cosmic attributes of Christ, those (more particularly in St Paul and St John) which accord to him a universal and final primacy over Creation —these had without difficulty been susceptible of a moral and juridical explanation. But it is only in the setting of an evolution that they take on their full dimensions: always subject to a condition which science itself in fact suggests in so far as it makes up its mind to allow man his rightful place in Nature—that this evolution be of the type that is both spiritual and convergent. With that reservation nothing is simpler or more tempting than to look to revealed Christogenesis for an ultimate explanation of the Cosmogenesis of the scientists and to set the final seal upon it. Christianity and evolution: not two irreconcilable points of view, but two ways of looking at things that are designed to dovetail together, each completing the other. After all, has not this alliance for long been deeply enshrined in the instinctive felicity of the spoken language? Creation, Incarna-

40. C&E, p. 181; Oeuvres, 10:211.
41. "Catholicism and Science" (1946), in S&C, p. 189; Oeuvres, 9:239.

tion, Redemption—do not these very words, in their grammatical form, evoke the idea of a process rather than a local or instantaneous act?[42]

A "revealed Christogenesis" in which cosmogenesis finds its completion! How can this be? What is implied here is more than just a development of dogma—that is, a development of theological reflection based on a revelation that is fixed in its literal meaning; it is that the meaning of Scripture itself is dependent not just on a narrow exegetical analysis, but on the convergent interaction of human knowledge with the deposit of the revealed word. What this amounts to is the concept of a developing or continuing revelation. But before this concept of Teilhard's can be explored in its entirety, there must be some discussion of what has been called in the debates of modern hermeneutical circles the "sensus plenior" of Sacred Scripture.

C. THE *SENSUS PLENIOR* AND TEILHARD'S UNDERSTANDING OF SCRIPTURE

As with the technical but still flexible terms *hermeneutics* and *hermeneutic*, the term *sensus plenior* does not appear in any of Teilhard's works, nor is it mentioned in his correspondence or notes. The absence of a so-highly debated term is fortunate, for had he attempted to ascribe his understanding of the "literal and physical" sense of St. Paul to what has been called a *sensus plenior* by a number of hermeneutical experts, he would certainly have blundered his way into a subject that is highly complex and abounding in disagreement. For all that, the attempt to sum up Teilhard's approach to understanding the Scriptures can hardly be made without drawing at least a rather sketchy comparison between his thought and that which has become, for better or worse, the theory of a *sensus plenior* of Scripture. In the comparison are found areas of similarity, and, perhaps less markedly, areas of contrast.

The trouble with all such discussions of biblical "senses" is the ambiguity of the word *sense*. Even though Raymond Brown admits that the literal sense should be considered that "which the human author directly intended and which his words convey,"[43] he writes in an earlier article that the medieval understanding of *literal sense* was whatever sense the words will bear, more or less independently of the intent of the author.[44] Such a shift back to the medieval understanding

---

42. *C&E*, pp. 189-90; *Oeuvres*, 10:239-40.
43. "Hermeneutics" in *JBC*, p. 607.
44. In many ways it would be a better use of the term "literal." From some discussions of the literal sense we might get the impression that, first, one knows what the human author meant and that, therefore, one knows what a text means. Actually the process of exegesis is the reverse: one discovers first what the text says, and then the attempts to draw from this the outlook and meaning of the author.
    "The 'Sensus Plenior' Ten Years After," in *CBQ* 25 (1963): 263ff. (This important

would make appeals to a *sensus plenior* unnecessary. However, since Brown now appears willing to go along with the majority opinion, which is also that apparently held in the encyclical "Divino Afflantu Spiritu," he has to admit the existence of authentic "more-than-literal" senses among which he asserts the existence of a *sensus plenior*.[45] This last sense he first defined simply as "a deeper meaning intended by God, but not clearly intended by the human author."[46] And in the *Jerome Biblical Commentary* article of five years later he expands this definition:

> The SPlen (sensus plenior) is the deeper meaning, intended by God but not clearly intended by the human author, that is seen to exist in the words of Scripture when they are studied in the light of further revelation or of development in the understanding of revelation.[47]

Clearly some development in Brown's understanding is reflected in this altered definition. His expanded definition seems to be passing judgment on two (not just one, as in the earlier statement) controversial questions concerning the existence and nature of any *sensus plenior*. The first concerns the debate whether or not the human author may in any manner have intended a deeper meaning beyond that which the words themselves obviously convey.[48] The second question bears on the problem of what criteria should be admitted as authenticating the de facto existence of any such deeper or fuller sense in the case of any particular scriptural passage. While at first glance it would seem that these two questions are completely unrelated, they are in fact very much interdependent when the problem is faced whether a presumed sense of Scripture is indeed a meaning of the passage itself (i.e., so intended by the human author or by God) or rather a new understanding in the mind of the reader. Aside from the bearing that such an interrelationship would have on distinguishing an "authentic" *sensus plenior* from equally authentic typology, analogy, or even accommodation (as in the New Testament's use of certain Old Testament passages), this double question calls into question the whole under-

---

article was written approximately ten years after Raymond Brown's noted thesis, *The "Sensus Plenior" of Sacred Scripture* (St. Mary's, Baltimore, 1955).

45. Cf. *JBC*, p. 610.
46. Cf. *CBQ*, 25:263.
47. *JBC*, p. 616.
48. According to Brown, Benoît stands at one extreme in holding that the "secondary sense" (i.e., "sensus plenior") is that intended by God but unbeknown to the human author. John J. O'Rourke, on the other hand, would insist that the human author must have had at least a vague awareness of this fuller sense. Brown would appear to be, as his later definition and earlier discussion indicates, straddling this question somewhat, but leaning toward Benoît's more liberal view, while not ruling out the possibility of the human author's awareness of a deeper sense. Cf. *CBQ*, 25:264.

standing of the concept of revelation, which would be at the root of the whole debate, and as such takes the discussion beyond any debate over the ambiguity of the word *sense*.[49]

Keeping in mind these two questions posed by Brown's definition, let us go as far back as Teilhard's initial comprehensive essay, "Cosmic Life" of 1916.

> The mystical Body of Christ should, in fact, be conceived as a physical Reality, *in the strongest sense the words can bear*. Only so can the great mysteries and the great virtues of religion, only so can Christ's role as mediator, the importance of Communion, and the immense value of charity, *assume their full significance*; only so can the Person of the Saviour retain its full hold on our minds and continue to provide the driving force our destinies demand.[50]

Along with this same call for a literal reading of the Scriptures, Teilhard issued this challenge:

> If we read Scripture with openness and breadth of mind, if we reject the timid interpretations of the narrow common-sense that is ready to take the words of Consecration literally (because faith obliges us to do so) but in all other contexts looks for the meaning with the least impact, we shall find that it speaks in categorical terms.[51]

In the 1917 essay "Creative Union" he spoke again of understanding the words of St. John and St. Paul "sans atténuation et sans glose" so that one will arrive at the point where one sees "that Christ has not only a *mystical*, but a *cosmic body*, the most impressive description of whose chief attributes we owe to St. Paul—even if he never uses the actual term."[52]

However, despite this call to take the Scriptures in their most literal sense, Teilhard indicated that the source of understanding them in this way is not determined entirely by the texts themselves. Another ele-

---

49. Another possible approach to the question is that of Fr. Charles H. Giblin. According to Brown

> One of Giblin's main objections to the SP is that the theory implies a univocal use of "Scriptural sense," i.e., suggests that the SP is different from the literal sense only in degree. For him [Giblin] the real solution to the hermeneutical problem lies in an analogical use of "sense" or "meaning." He speaks of one analogate as the "theological meaning" . . . and the other analogate as the literal sense. These two senses are really distinct (not in degree but in kind), but both are senses of Scripture. We think that he means that in a given text we may encounter two factors: what the author *intended* (literal sense) and what a later stage in God's plan came to understand (theological meaning). If we use the term "sense" to cover both the intention and the understanding, we are using it analogically." *CBQ*, 25:277.

50. *WTW*, p. 51; *Ecrits*, p. 41.
51. *WTW*, p. 58; *Ecrits*, p. 48.
52. *WTW*, p. 175; *Ecrits*, pp. 196-97.

ment enters the picture, as is seen in "The Universal Element" of 1919:

> Once we have understood the nature of this *"cosmic composition" of created being*, and have appreciated the closeness and universality of the ties it forms with the Multiple, Christ's features take on an extraordinary sharpness and immediacy—and the meaning of Scripture is given incomparable clarity and depth. [53]

This other element, then, involves the advancing consciousness of mankind, which is not necessarily to be found through further revelation. Instead, as Teilhard had noted some pages before:

> This element can be glimpsed (by minds that are sufficiently receptive or informed) as *a common fringe* on the outskirts of each of the great operative processes or main directing energies of our life. [54]

Nevertheless, despite the presence of this mysterious "universal element" (or "cosmic sense") Teilhard still insisted in his 1924 "Mon Univers":

> Once we make up our minds to take the words of Revelation literally—and to do so is the ideal of all true religion—then the whole mass of the universe is gradually bathed in light. [55]

Still, what Teilhard appeared to have taken to be the literal (or "à le lettre") sense of the Scriptures was not necessarily to be taken for reality as such. After his struggles with the problem of original sin, especially during the 1920s, he was forced to admit in 1933, in his essay "Christology and Evolution" that

> "through sin comes death." In order to get away from evidence that is only too clear, an attempt is now being made to weaken this illuminating phrase. "Death, it is agreed, most certainly existed for animals before man's transgression; and, had man been faithful, even in his case it could not have been averted except by a sort of permanent miracle." However, now only do these distinctions still leave the problem of evil intact, they *contradict the obvious meaning of the biblical text*. For St Paul, we must remember, the world was only a week old when Adam sinned. Nothing in paradise, accordingly, had yet had time to perish. In the mind of the apostle, it was that transgression which ruined everything for the whole of creation. [56]

A distinction now seems at least implicit in Teilhard's thought. To be understood "littéralement" or "à la lettre" was not necessarily the same

53. *WTW*, p. 297; *Ecrits*, p. 408.
54. *WTW*, 290; *Ecrits*, p. 401.
55. *S&C*, p. 74; *Oeuvres*, 9:102.
56. *C&E*, p. 81; *Oeuvres*, 10:100. (Emphasis added.)

for Teilhard as "le sens obvie." In fact, the literal sense, according to the 1943 essay "Super-humanity, Super-Christ, Super-charity," is acquired only after the reader assumes a certain frame of mind! In speaking of the attenuation of the role of the cosmic Christ at the hands of Western theologians (which increased in the face of the disclosure of the size of the universe by modern science and the resulting contradictions and inconsistencies that ensued), Teilhard remarked:

> All these improbabilities disappear and St Paul's boldest sayings readily *take on a literal meaning* as soon as the world is seen to be suspended, by its conscious side, from an Omega Point of convergence, and Christ, in virtue of his Incarnation, is recognised as carrying out precisely the functions of Omega.[57]

From this context and from the preceding quotations, it must be concluded that for Teilhard the phrase *physiquement et littéralement* (used three times in the succeeding paragraphs of the same essay) meant the fullest and most concrete interpretation that a text will bear given the state of understanding possible for mankind. While retaining the phrase *literal sense*, Teilhard was apparently talking about something that in some manner resembles what is understood by some as a *sensus plenior*. However, there are also differences.

Brown and Benoît, as do most others, demand that two criteria be met before any reading of Scripture be considered a truly *sensus plenior* of Sacred Scripture rather than a simple accommodation on the one hand, or a theological conclusion of some sort on the other. The first condition is "homogeneity," that is, a certain compatibility with the literal sense (which most accommodations lack): the second is a kind of legitimacy based on revelation (or based on development in our understanding of revelation, Brown would add) that would amount to "evidence" that God intended that the text be understood in a fuller sense.[58]

There is no doubt that Teilhard's interpretations of Scripture generally displayed a strong homogeneity with the literal sense. It is probably this element that Teilhard was stressing when he spoke of taking Scripture "littéralement," something he believed that he was most faithfully doing when using Pauline words such as *Corps du Christ* and *plérôme*. Significantly, it is Benoît who, quite independently of Teilhard, insists on this same realism in understanding the Pauline use of the terms *sōma* and *"plērōma*, which Teilhard claimed to be their meaning "à la lettre." On the other hand, although he remained convinced that all creation was truly "awaiting in expectation" its redemption in Christ (Rom. 8:22), Teilhard greatly curtailed his reference to that text as the years went by; he seems to have accepted the verdict of the exegetes that the meaning of that

57. *S&C*, p. 166; *Oeuvres*, 9:211. (Emphasis added.)
58. *CBQ*, 25:274.

verse was intimately bound up with Paul's concept of the servitude of the world as dependent upon the original sin. This is to say that Teilhard found his own interpretation to lack sufficient homogeneity with the author's "obvious" or intended meaning.

The second criterion, that of the *sensus plenior* as somehow established in each particular case through subsequent revelation, presents particular difficulties for Brown, for according to Benoît, we can only speak of a *sensus plenior* of Old Testament texts, and then only when the fuller meaning has been established by the New Testament! Brown finds this much too confining, and marshalls as evidence the rather obvious *sensus plenior* that the OT wisdom books find in material derived from the Pentateuch. Similarly, he doubts whether we can confine all the meanings now seen in many NT texts as being thus understood during the NT period.[59] For Brown, the *sensus plenior* can continue to unfold within the general development of dogma, and this unfolding is, in his opinion, to be classified as neither "illative consequent sense" (syllogistic reasoning with a nonrevealed minor proposition) nor mere "consequent explicative sense" (i.e., explanation of the text by application of general rules of logic).[60]

When put into this more liberal classification of what it means to have a *sensus plenior* established within the framework of revelation or doctrinal development, Teilhard's interpretations would, for the most part, appear not to be based on a supposed *sensus plenior* but rather derived as an "illative consequent sense." But even here, without crediting Teilhard with an intuitive knowledge of such technicalities, attention might be called to his correlative but changing use of the terms *Corps du Christ* and *plérôme*. In this case, while remaining convinced that Christ possesses a "cosmic" body as well as an ecclesial-sacramental body, he nevertheless gradually relinquished the former terminology in favor of the expanded use of the word *plérôme*. Why? Simply because the reasoning that led him to his insistence on the "cosmic body" was derived in part from his own conclusions based on the nature of "spirit-matter" and the "coextensivity" of being, rather than on any parallel development of doctrine within the Church. Let us reread the passage in *The Divine Milieu*, and compare it with the earlier passage of the 1924 "Mon Univers":

> In spite of the strength of St. Paul's expressions (formulated, it should be remembered, for the *ordinary run* of the first Christians) some readers may feel that we have been led to strain, in too realist a direction, the meaning of "Mystical Body"—or at least that we have allowed ourselves to seek esoteric perspectives in it.[61]

59. *CBQ*, 25:271.
60. *CBQ*, 25:264; see n. 16.
61. *DM*, pp. 101-2; *Oeuvres*, 4:150.

the context, . . . is categorical: even in Col. 1. 15 ff, St Paul quite obviously has in mind the theandric Christ; it was in the Incarnate Christ that the universe was pre-formed. As regards the weakened interpretation of the Apostle's words, I dismiss it simply because it is less in conformity with the spirit of St Paul as it animates the body of his Epistles, and less, too, in conformity with my general view of the world. However, I have given up hope of converting those who reject my version.[62]

Teilhard made no such concession, even verbally (much less conceptually) with the term *pleroma*. In Teilhard's mind there could be no escape by way of appeal to metaphor or analogy from the literal meaning of this word, and he was ready to exploit its fullest meaning, taken literally, to the very end. For Teilhard, the pleroma was to remain, whatever elaborations his thought was to take, essentially as he defined it in 1940:

> The Pleroma: the mysterious synthesis of the Uncreated and the Created,—the grand completion (both quantitative and qualitative) of the Universe in God.[63]

Teilhard's insistence on the literal meaning of *pleroma*, in its active as well as passive sense, best illustrates the ultimate problem in his hermeneutics, for if the literal sense is taken as that conveyed by the words (in this case, by the word itself)—as Benoît took it in his acceptance of the active as well as passive meanings of *pleroma* as being faithful to St. Paul's thought—the conclusion can be reached that, for Teilhard, any fuller understanding of Sacred Scripture is but the fullest literal meaning that the text will bear, given the current stage of human understanding. On the other hand, if Teilhard's understanding of the pleroma is rejected, especially in its active sense (i.e., that which *completes* Christ), as not being consistent with the thought of St. Paul (such are Cerfaux's and Feuillet's opinions) then the credit, or discredit, must be given Teilhard for having sought to uncover a "fuller sense" that goes far beyond the usual understanding of literal meaning.[64]

62. *S&C*, pp. 54-55; *Oeuvres*, 9:83.
63. "La Parole atténue," *Oeuvres*, 11:106 and *Cahiers de Teilhard de Chardin*, #4, p. 26. A short note of March 23, 1950 ("Journal" 17 [5]: 85), repeated this same literal meaning of the pleroma, a meaning that encompasses both its active and passive senses. Thus Teilhard remarks that the pleroma can be said to be both "containing" and "contained," but here, somewhat paradoxically, it involves both God's being filled by the world and the world being filled by God. (Cf. also *TF*, p. 97.)
64. In one of Teilhard's first tentative remarks concerning this active meaning of the pleroma, that found in *Le Milieu divin*, he seems to have reached this meaning by way of an "illative consequent conclusion" in that he appealed to "l'interliaison Matière-Ame-Christ" as the basis for concluding that "*quoi que nous fassions*, nous ramenons à Dieu une parcelle de l'être qu'il désire." But this statement comes immediately after one in which he claimed:

> Par notre collaboration qu'il suscite, le Christ se consomme, atteint sa plénitude, à partir de *toute* créature. *C'est saint Paul qui nous le dit. (Oeuvres*, 4:50; *DM*, pp. 30-31. Final emphasis added.)

Although the foregoing comparison of a theory of a *sensus plenior* to the Teilhardian approach to Scripture may be instructive, it proves, in the end, inadequate, not only because it clashes with Teilhard's own terminology but also because initially it places an impossible burden on the exegete: that of trying to second-guess the human author's possible foresight of deeper meanings beyond the supposed literal meaning. On the contrary, Teilhard wisely decided that the best we can do in the matter of second-guessing is to try to extrapolate the author's overall intention (from the obvious sense of his words) by trying to adapt the apparent literal meanings of these words as best we can to the present situation of man with his greatly altered world view.[65]

The language theory proposed by I. A. Richards in his *Philosophy of Rhetoric*[66] has interesting overtones for this presumed conflict between the literal and fuller sense of Scripture. If meaning is primarily contextual in nature and not a simple construct of words, each with its own proper meaning and usage (what Richards calls the "Proper-Meaning Superstition"[67]), then it would seem that the attempt to deduce a direct literal meaning of a passage prior to or even outside of its overall scriptural context (which can be presumed to be theological) may be not only backwards but futile. Individual words, rather than possessing fixed meanings, are but symbols representing "the missing parts of the contexts from which [they draw their] delegated efficacy."[68]

Without reducing language to pure form without content—something that many fear would result from such a fluid concept of *meaning*—Richards suggests that metaphor, far from being relegated to the mere category of figure of speech, constitutes the "omnipresent principle of language."[69] As such, as has ever been the case in the interpretation of the Bible, belief itself appears equally capable of adherence to either of the disparate elements of any statement (the "tenor" or its "vehicle") as analyzed in its metaphorical structure, or in the totality of the impression resulting from the interaction of the two. Either element may be apprehended by the believing subject as an ob-

---

65. Two quotations by R. Lapointe in his *Les trois dimensions de l'herméneutique* (pp. 105-6) may be appropriate to this approach.

    H. Bouillard—"L'exégèse elle-même, à son sommet, ne se contente pas de reproduire les idées de l'Ecriture; elle doit les repenser sous sa responsabilité propre."

    Kierkegaard—"It is only through the higher force of the present that we are able to interpret the past."

66. (New York: Oxford University Press, 1965.)
67. *Ibid.*, p. 11.
68. *Ibid.*, p. 35.
69. *Ibid.*, p. 92.

ject or both may be combined insofar as the meaning itself (God's Word) grips us (the believing Church).[70]

Applied to Teilhard's approach to Scripture, Richards's analysis of verbal communication would expedite an understanding of Teilhard's insistence on what he called the "physical" and "literal" meaning of Scripture. Freed from the narrowness and occasional arbitrariness of the literal sense as understood and depreciated by the medieval commentators, the reader must likewise be delivered from the often-impossible task of exactly determining the original author's intent and the correlative appeal to a "fuller sense" in the attempt to biblically justify consequent doctrinal developments.[71] Rather than trying to guess exactly what St. Paul intended when he used such phrases as *the Body of Christ* or the *pleroma*, or trying to ascribe a "fuller meaning" probably unknown to the author but intended by God, Teilhard was content to explore the possible understandings of these phrases as far as their metaphorical (or vehicular) content lends itself to fuller comprehension and application by modern man, with his developing comprehension of the cosmos. While the theological tenor of St. Paul's writing is presupposed (a presupposition inherent in its acceptance as part of revelation), its Christological applications are seen to be fluid and capable of indefinite expansion. This expansion of meaning is in part due to the ever-increasing ability of man to apprehend the implications of *tenor* and *vehicle* as working together in a way capable of transcending the "obvious" sense that captured the immediate attention of St. Paul. The theme of the "second Adam," with its metaphorical base in the Old Testament, would thus still retain its continuity with the tenor, but with a greatly altered understanding of the vehicle of expression.

As might be expected, such an operation, when analyzed in the

---

70. See *ibid.*, pp. 134-35. By *tenor* Richards understands the "underlying idea or principal subject which the vehicle or figure means," as opposed to more misleading designations, such as "the original idea," or "the meaning," etc., which generally imply that the metaphorical expression is a mere literary embellishment or at best a descriptive device, rather than an essential although flexible element of the message itself. Cf. *idem*, pp. 96-97. My acceptance of the insight Richards provides on this question does not imply my total agreement with all the elements of his theory of language, which seems to be built upon a generally behavioristic understanding of human psychology. D. G. James, in his 1937 criticism of Richards, judges his psychology to lead inevitably to a "materialistic-associationism." See *Critiques and Essays in Criticism*, ed. Robert Wooster Stallman (New York: Ronald Press, 1949), p. 485.

71. In this same line of thought, one note (from Easter 1949; "Journal" 16 [4]: 47), which is not entirely legible, comments on this tension between the literal and the mythical in Scripture, which Teilhard saw, as usual, in terms of convergence. In it, Teilhard's understanding of myth as what he appears to characterize as the "formal" component seems to agree with I. A. Richards's ideas about the essential function of metaphor in speech. Teilhard seems also (in a parenthesis in the same note) to speak of the convergence of the two elements of literal and mythical expression on "a real axis"—something that reminds us of the "real" sense of Sacred Scripture as understood by the medieval commentators.

categories suggested by Richards, meets with varying degrees of success in the case of the three separate but interrelated Pauline themes of the "expectatio creationis," the "Body of Christ," and the "pleroma," if by success is meant Teilhard's claim that his understanding is to be considered as being in line with the Pauline meanings taken "physiquement et littéralement" and "sans atténuation." What Teilhard understood to be the literal sense rules out any dichotomy between a literal sense and a supposed *sensus plenior*. Instead, following the lead suggested by Charles Giblin, it must be concluded that for Teilhard the literal sense includes both the "obvious sense" and its "theological meaning"; and where these two seemingly contradict each other (as in the case of the "par le péché, la mort" in Romans 5:12 when transposed into the modern world view), it is the theological meaning that must take precedence. Implied in such an approach is the conviction that whatever be the obvious, or literal, or "real" sense as understood by the medievals, the true meaning, the literal sense as understood by most modern commentators, or the "spiritual sense" in medieval terminology, is first and last the theological meaning contained therein.

Yet, it may be objected, does not this theological meaning acquire deeper or fuller dimensions "in the light of further revelation or in the development in the understanding of revelation" (to quote in part Brown's definition of the *sensus plenior*)? Teilhard would surely have acknowledged this insight; but, while these additional dimensions could reflect a continuing process of revelation, they must be allowable as the apparent theological intention (but not a presumed foreknowledge) of the human author within the literal sense of his words or they are not properly speaking a "sense" of Scripture as written. The deeper and fuller dimensions of this literal sense may be lost or regained, or even discovered for the first time, but either they flow from the literal sense of Scripture or they do not belong to it at all. This is not to say that subsequent theological development beyond the literal sense cannot be authenticated by an appeal to the theological meaning that has been deduced from this literal sense. But in most instances Teilhard was convinced that his own interpretations, reflecting the situation of modern man, were authentic and true to the literal sense.[72]

72. Christopher Mooney's critical remark about Teilhard's thinking in this matter is well made:

> in speaking of St. Paul, Teilhard almost always neglects to state explicitly one of the steps of his reasoning process. For example, he will say that what is important for him is Paul's assertion of "the universal domination of the Incarnate Word over the cosmos," then add that such supremacy corresponds exactly to the function of Omega in his own system of thought. But since this system is founded upon the key concept of cosmogenesis, he is naturally led to discuss Christ's domination over evolution and to use such expressions as "the Christogenesis of St. Paul." At this point, however, he usually neglects to inform the reader that what he is now dealing with is no longer the thought of St. Paul, but the thought of St. Paul incorporated into his own hypothesis of a converging universe" (*Teilhard de Chardin and the Mystery of Christ*, p. 88).

Understood in this way, Teilhard's appeals to the literal yet fullest meanings of Scripture were entirely consistent, if not always well articulated. Despite the incomprehension of his critics, his insistence that the *Body of Christ* be understood literally and organically was not, in his mind, a *sensus plenior* beyond the literal sense, much less a mere theological development, legitimate though that might be. But blocked by his critics' incomprehension, Teilhard, instead of taking the easier route of feigning a more modest claim to "theological development," only reintensified his claim to find this organically cosmic Christ literally revealed in Scripture, this time under the Pauline terminology of the *pleroma*, a word whose basically abstract meaning tended to bypass all appeals to metaphorical interpretation. In the light of this term, taken first in its literally passive meaning of "that which is completed" and then later in its equally literal active meaning of "that which completes," Teilhard was convinced that he had discovered the deepest and fullest meaning of what remains the equally literal sense of the phrase *en pasi panta Theos*.

D. CONCLUSION: TEILHARD'S METHODOLOGY SUMMARIZED

Despite his denial that his overall approach was to construct a phenomenologically based synthesis or *Weltanschauung* with evolution as its key of intelligibility, Christian doctrine (with its sources in divine revelation, thus unique in its origin and degree of certainty) was what Teilhard, as a committed believer, took to be the one phenomenon among all the others that must be incorporated in a total world view. This was no pious afterthought or "apologetical" self-justification out of a preformed universal theory of evolution, extrapolated to include his Christian faith (as is so often deemed to be the case, especially by those familiar only with the later published writings of Teilhard—*Le Phénomène humain* and *Le Milieu divin* in particular). His Christian belief instead has been revealed to be, particularly in respect to his most early and copious use of scriptural themes, the guiding influence behind his initial approach, both philosophical and phenomenological, to the scientific world in which he was soon to be immersed. Far from

This remark, while accurately outlining the apparent gap in Teilhard's exposition of the Pauline themes that have been the subject of this study, also puts into relief, perhaps inadvertently, the difference between what is the Teilhardian understanding of the "literal sense" of St. Paul (or as he put it in one place, the "obvious sense") and what is, in terms of theological reflection, the sense that most "littéralement et physiquement" expounds the meaning of St. Paul's revelation for our own day and age. What Mooney characterizes as a flaw in Teilhard's approach, the "making simultaneous use of two sources of knowledge, one from phenomena and the other from revelation, without bothering to distinguish between them" (*ibid.*), which is also one of Maritain's criticisms (pp. 116f.), may be indicative instead of an altered concept of revelation itself, seen as a "process" rather than as a given "fact" that exists in the past.

revealing Teilhard to have been forcing a reinterpretation of Christian doctrine to conform with the findings of science, the writings of his early period give some credence to the claim, made by critics having a more "scientific" orientation, that the case was exactly the opposite: Teilhard was a Christian mystic who from the very beginning of his career was attempting to reinterpret scientific theory in the light of Christian doctrine.

Teilhard, as we have seen, drew much of his inspiration from certain scriptural passages in much the same (and criticizable) manner as did most dogmatic theologians of his period, in which discipline he, as a Jesuit, had been given a more-than-standard seminary training. Drawing from various quotations that appeared appropriate (taken at their face value in terms of their literary and broadly literal meaning, and filtered through his own understanding of their meaning in the light of Christian belief and his own growing appreciation for the evolutionary world of science), Teilhard was able to arrive at his own existential understanding of these texts. The texts became "actualized" or rendered meaningful in the context in which the modern believer finds himself: immersed in the positivism of an almost infinitely expanded world of science whose cosmic dimensions all but dwarf and altogether isolate the all-too-limited stage on which the drama of man's redemption has hitherto been presented.

But the evolutionary vision that Teilhard first sought to reconcile with his Christian belief became slowly but certainly a universal paradigm, something that he understood in the light of Christian revelation, and also that could itself light up, in fullest relief, certain "cosmic" aspects of ancient Christian belief in such a way that these seminal statements concerning the universal Christ, those of Paul in particular, could now be understood as perhaps never before, in their fullest and at the same time most literal sense. In this way, evolution as a universal phenomenon applies to the process of revelation itself. Scripturally speaking, while the data of revelation call for an ever deeper and fuller penetration of human understanding, this is not some mysterious *sensus plenior* half-apprehended by the writer, but is a new extension by the reader of what is already literally contained within the text itself, which must itself be apprehended not alone in the context of the peculiar thought forms of the author's day and age, but in the light of the exigencies of our own day as well. Although Teilhard insisted that Scripture be understood in its most literal and physical sense, this is not always the sense that is most obvious. It may be that which is discerned only after human reflection, by virtue of its own advancement in awareness of the universe in which it finds itself, in which it is able to find in the ancient data of revelation its fullest and most extensive meaning.

What is more than implied here is a theory of revelation that is itself evolutionary in character. Beyond being an exegete (in the wide sense of an "actualizer" of scriptural meaning) or thinker whose passion for synthesis brings him close to the methodology of systematic theology, Teilhard was also a theological theorist—one not content to systematize or even structurally synthesize Christian doctrine with a new cosmology, but one whose evolutionary presupposition would lead him eventually to examine and rethink the whole concept of revelation itself.

8
Teilhard's Theory of Revelation in Process

If this study of Teilhard's hermeneutical presuppositions and its applications in his theological speculations has led to any conclusions, they should be obvious by now. We are no longer dealing with a man who saw Christianity in terms of a confrontation with an evolutionary cosmos, but one who saw it—and the revelation that affirms its dogmatic foundations—as encompassed within the evolutionary process. Such a sweeping reevaluation—not just of man's external world view, that is, of ontological structures viewed objectively as extrinsic to man, but also of his epistemological stance in relation to his apprehension of reality—did not occur to Teilhard as a flash of inspiration. Nor did he, finding his Christian faith challenged by Darwinian transformism, resolve the conflict by having scientific theory absorb belief. Quite the contrary; evolution, as a universal paradigm of reality, had for him all the earmarks of an idea very much "in the air," one of those seminal but hitherto-unthinkable ideas whose time has finally come.

A. THE DEVELOPMENT OF DOCTRINE:
TEILHARD AND THE THOUGHT OF JOHN HENRY NEWMAN

Much has been made of Teilhard's early fascination with the thought of Henri Bergson. Bergson's *"L'évolution créatrice"* was without doubt one of the major factors in affecting Teilhard's world view. But his departure from Bergson's line of thought, even while he continued to owe much to it, soon became evident[1] at a comparatively early date in his career.

A strong similarity also exists between the extent of Teilhard's evolutionary synthesis and that of Herbert Spencer, although one of the few times Teilhard makes reference to Spencer is by way of disagreement.[2] Despite the similarity of their incursions into moral and ethical evolution, the English philosopher provided the French one with little inspiration for theological development.

Also, while there was undoubtedly some affinity between Teilhard and Blondel, and there are many references to the latter by Teilhard,[3] their differences became obvious in their correspondence.[4] Although there was certainly a striking resemblance in their concern for a certain apologetic "intrinsicism,"[5] the major influence on Teilhard's views of the evolutive nature of the revelatory process in itself must be traced to the writings of John Henry Newman.

Despite his sojourn in England during his days in the theologate, Teilhard only really "discovered" Newman during the early days of World War I. In his first notebook of this period, he recorded that he had been reading Newman's *Essay on the Development of Christian Doctrine* and *Essay on Matter*.[6]

1. See *Bergson et Teilhard*, Madeleine Barthélemy-Madaule (Paris: Editions du Seuil, 1963). Teilhard tried (unsuccessfully to the mind of some critics) to disassociate himself from the vitalism of Bergson's "élan vital," and even more markedly, from Bergson's model of a "diffusive" universe with its own understanding of the evolutive process as ultimately convergent. Cf. "Mon Univers" (1924), in *S&C*, p. 48; *Oeuvres*, 9:76.
2. Cf. "Centrology," in *AE*, p. 103; *Oeuvres*, 7:109.
3. See the collection of Teilhard's World War I letters, *The Making of a Mind* (New York: Harper & Row, 1965); *Genèse d'une pensée* (Paris: Grasset, 1961).
4. *Blondel et Teilhard de Chardin*, ed. Henri de Lubac (Paris: Beauchesne, 1965); *Correspondence, P. Teilhard de Chardin—M. Blondel* (New York: Herder & Herder, 1967).
5. Cf. text and accompanying footnote in the 1924 "Mon Univers," *Oeuvres*, 9:86; *S&C*, p. 58.

6. 28 Fevr. [1916]—Suivre le forme sous laquelle, à mes yeux, se divinise la M. [Matière] = métal inaltérable, énergie, *éther*: tout ce qui est partant, inaltérable, *consistant. . . .*
    —L' "essay on Development" de Newman est né des besoins mêmes de sa vie intime, il représente la solution du problème religieux (et total) tel qu'il s'est présenté à sa vie. . . . Il me semble que j'ai à écrire (au moins pour moi) q.qch [quelque chose] d'analogue, non plus sur le terrain de l'Eglise (*Antiquité* à concilier avec "*nouveautés*"), mais sur celui du Devenir cosmique (Détacht [Détachement] à concilier avec amour légitime de la η μήτηρ) . . . "Essay on Matter," "Attitude(s) en face de la Matière."
    —Newman p. 116 "It never could be that so large a portion of Christendom (Anglicans . . .) should have split off from the Communion of Rome, and kept up a protest for 300 years for *nothing*. . . . All aberrations are *founded on*, and *have their life in*. . . ." (1841)
    —Nous ne somme *pas* dans la matière comme *ds*/dans/ *un bourbier* dont nous dépêtrer, *mais* comme *dans une matrice* dont *qqch*./quelque chose/ (doit suivre
    (passe en nous.
    et dont l'ensemble mérite d'être chéri. (Cahier 1:20)

In a letter to his cousin he remarked that he was also reading Newman's *Apologia*;[7] several months later he had begun Thureau-Dangin's study *Newman Catholique*, and noted: "The more I read Newman, the more I sense a common source . . . of his spirit and mine."[8] Writing again to his cousin on July 22, 1916, he devoted a long passage to Newman, tracing in particular those elements of the Cardinal's thought which most appealed to him:

> I feel more than ever in sympathy with the great Cardinal, so un-daunted, so firm of faith, so full, as he says himself, "of life and thought,"—and at the same time, so thwarted. And once again, I was conscious within myself of the inspiration that calls me to the great work of reconciling the supreme and absolute love of God with the lower (but still legitimate and necessary) love of life embraced under its natural forms.—A host of Newman's ideas: That it is more important to fight against fundamental errors of thought than to make a few conversions or confine oneself to sectarian disputes; that the intellectual function of the Church consists primarily in eliminat-ing, in choosing, in selecting from within, the positive dogmatic de-velopment expressed primarily in the body of the faithful.— Those who try to win the day for a truth, *before its time*, run the risk of ending as heretics . . . these and other similar ideas, so far-reaching, so open, and hence realistic, have entered into my mind as into a dwelling long familiar to them. And what has made it all the more heartening to me to find this community of inclination and apprecia-tion, is that the man who felt them so deeply had bitterly experi-enced, without being scandalized, the bitter temptation of being born before the due hour or season for his thought.[9]

These remarkable passages not only indicate the general affinity that Teilhard saw between himself and Newman in terms of their intellec-tual vocations (and the dangers contained therein), but show a certain assimilation of Newman's ideas, particularly on the development of doctrine and attitude to the material world.

Beyond the agreement with Newman's thought stated in the letters, a number of other parallels impress themselves upon the reader of both men. All reinforce the impression that these two great minds en-tertained a strikingly similar approach to the phenomenon of doctrinal development, and suggest a real dependence of Teilhard upon New-man. Although the product of dissimilar cultural and theological back-grounds and representing very different concerns (Teilhard addressed himself to the growing secularity of the twentieth century while New-man seemed most concerned with the religious sectarianism and the aggressive atheism of the nineteenth), both seem to have been imbued with the notion of organic development as extrapolated to the doctrinal

7. Feb. 2, 1916; cf. *Genèse d'une pensée*, p. 118; *The Making of a Mind*, pp. 93-94.
8. "Plus je lis Newman, plus je sens une parenté . . . entre son esprit et le mien." Cahier 1:56-57.
9. *The Making of a Mind*, p. 114; *Genèse d'une pensée*, p. 145.

development of Christianity. There are, in fact, some interesting anticipations of Teilhard's approach in Newman's expressions in this regard.

Newman, like Teilhard, saw special significance, at least by implication, in Matthew 5:17: "Think not that I have come to destroy the Law and the prophets; I have not come to destroy but to fulfill."[10]

In the section immediately before this quotation from Matthew, Newman dared to speak of the revelation of the Old Testament prophets as not simply a matter of accumulation, but as "a process of development."[11] Shortly after, he made it clear that he, along with Bishop Butler (whose *Analogue* he quoted), understood this phenomenon in terms of a "general analogy of the world, physical and moral," which "confirms this conclusion."[12]

Concerning the interpretation of Scripture in particular, Newman expressed the same impatience as did Teilhard concerning overrestrictive exegesis, especially that which refuses to admit of understanding in the light of further doctrinal development.[13]

Equally arresting, by way of comparison with certain of Teilhard's ideas in this matter, is Newman's assertion that the conservative norm of orthodoxy, derived from Vincent of Lerins, is not the only one, but must share responsibility with a norm of "converging evidence." Drawing on an analogy taken from the physical sciences, Newman concluded that:

> a converging evidence in favour of certain doctrines may, under circumstance, be as clear a proof of their Apostolical origin as can be

10. Cf. *An Essay on the Development of Christian Doctrine* (New York: Doubleday Image Books, 1960), p. 86. Newman's attachment of a developmental meaning to this verse is even more explicit than Teilhard's (cf. "L'incroyance moderne. Cause profonde et remède", *Oeuvres*, 9:152; *S&C*, p. 116, and "Le sens humain" (March 1929), *Oeuvres*, 11:43; *TF*, p. 37. In a retreat ("Carnet de Retraite") note of Aug. 20, 1946, Teilhard quoted the Gospel verse "non veni solvere sed adimplere," underlining the last word and identifying it with the pleroma. Again, on Sept. 24, 1948, he identified this verse as pointing to the "Dogma" [*sic*] of the Christ "Panconsummator." ("Journal" 14 [3]: 158.)
11. Newman, *Development of Doctrine*, p. 85.
12. *Ibid.*, p. 93.
13. Newman wrote that it is

> but a parallel exercise of reasoning to interpret the previous history of a doctrine by its later development, and to consider that it contains the later *in posse* and in the divine intention; and the grudging and jealous temper which refuses to enlarge a sacred text for the fulfilment of prophecy is the very same that will occupy itself with carping at the Antenicene testimonies for Nicene or medieval doctrines and usages. When "I and my Father are One" is urged in proof of our Lord's unity with the Father, heretical disputants do not see why the words must be taken to denote more than a unity of will. When "This is My Body" is alleged as a warrant for the change of the Bread into the Body of Christ, they explain away the words into a figure, because such is their most obvious interpretation. (*Ibid.*, p. 121)

> It is noteworthy that Newman, like Teilhard, implied a distinction between the literal and "obvious" meanings of a text (but what is literally possible, by way of interpretation, appears to depend on doctrinal development of some sort).

reached practically from the *Quod semper, quod ubique, quod ab omnibus.*[14]

To confirm this idea of converging evidence on doctrinal development, Teilhard cited the development of Marian doctrine, but not without some criticism of the manner of expression of the developments that have taken place. In a letter to Jeanne Mortier on August 25, 1950, Teilhard comments at length on the recently defined dogma of the Assumption:

> Of course, regarding the Encyclical and the Assumption, I think essentially as you do, but it is something of a "scandal" for those who are educated and of good will. . . . I think that I understand well what Rome has in view: to advance Mariology in a manner that is parallel to Christology, and to prevent a certain evaporation of dogma into abstract symbols. But "realism" is not necessarily "literalism"; and it is not irenism and conciliation to adjust (through expansion and reenforcement) dogmatic representations to a Universe which has acquired a new dimension (the "genetic") (a Cosmogenesis in place of a Cosmos). From this point of view, I greatly fear that the affirmations of "an individual Adam" (despite the recognized symbolic character of Genesis on this point!) and of the literal incorruption of the body of Mary (implying an evasion, by a group of proteins, from the cosmic cycle, maintained beyond time and space) appears to the great majority of Christians or thinking gentiles [i.e. non-Christians] as an affront to that which is most essential and most definitive in modern science. . . . Recall that article by Cardinal Ruffini in the *Osservatore Romano* concerning evolution as extended to man: [this is] exactly the position of the Encyclical . . . (there are only the integralists to make themselves the gadflies or alarmists of irenism!) But this is what reassures me. Integralism, like Stalinism, tends to force man to inactivity: but he will not remain sterile and ends up by making a leap.—Something else. . . : to define the Assumption is (by the very act itself) to affirm that "revelation continues," which is to say that dogma grows (that it lives): There is not more magnificent proof that Christianity (like whatever is living and human) evolves (in the correct, "genetic" sense of the word).[15]

Of special interest in this matter is Newman's discussion of those notes or qualities which characterize true doctrinal development.[16] Re-

14. *Ibid.*, p. 136.
15. *T.A.*, Correspondance à J. Mortier. (See Appendix D, §2, b. for French text.) The very same day, Teilhard affixed this postscript to a letter to Mme Pesson-Depret: ". . . J'ajoute un point: ce qui est *très* important dans le geste de définir l'Assomption (vérité certainement pas contenue dans la lettre de l'Ecriture!!) c'est que ipso facto,—et sans s'en douter peut-être l'Eglise affirme que 'La Révélation' dure encore: ce qui est éminemment biologique et 'évolutif.'" Teilhard Correspondence "N-O-P", *T.A.*, Paris.
16. Newman's seven "notes" are, briefly put:
   1) Preservation of Type
   2) Continuity of Principles
   3) Power of Assimilation

ferring to the second "note" (i.e., "continuity of its principles"), he made a careful distinction between the "principles" of Christianity on the one hand, and its "dogmas" on the other.[17] While Newman listed nine such principles, three that feature in Teilhard's theological synthesis in particular should be noticed: the Incarnational-Sacramental principle (#4) and its logical corollary, the sanctifiability of matter (#9). But the third, most striking of all, is Newman's insistence that one outstanding mark or "principle" (#5) of Catholic Orthodoxy is its constant and considered use of a second or "mystical" sense of Scripture "as a medium of thought and deduction"[18] as against the overly restrictive "mere literal interpretation of Scripture," which has often marked the beginnings of heterodoxy.[19] Such a "mystical" sense, according to Newman (who quoted Lengerke) does exclude the purely "allegorical."[20]

Whether such opinions about literalism vs. "mystical" interpretation actually influenced Teilhard's views remains problematic, because of his apparently different understanding from Newman's of the connotation of the word *literal*. But the fact that Newman understood that a freer use of Scripture was the hallmark of Patristic Theology can hardly have failed to have influenced Teilhard, at least subconsciously, in his conviction that his scriptural appeals to a Cosmic Christ were valid within a solid tradition stemming from the Greek Fathers of antiquity.[21] While Teilhard does not seem to have explored further the thought of the Greek Fathers through any personal first-hand study, certainly Newman's conviction that the incarnational principle stood at the very core of patristic theology and that its corollary in the sacramental view of matter found its natural complement in the Athanasian theme of the divinization of man through grace[22] could not but have helped convince Teilhard that he stood on solid and traditional ground in his own realistic interpretation of these doctrines.

4) Logical Sequence
5) Anticipation of the Future
6) Conservation of the Past
7) Chronic Vigor
Teilhard's own phrasing of some of these properties is found most clearly in his "Introduction à la Vie chrétienne" (1944). Among them, he spoke of ". . . un système cohérent et progressif d'éléments spirituels collectivement associés. . . . c'est dans le Catholicisme seul que continuent à germer les dogmes nouveaux . . . ne saurait être que par l'axe vivant et organisé de son Catholicisme romain qu'il peut espérer se mesurer avec les grands courants humanitaires modernes, et les assimiler." *Oeuvres*, 10:196-97; *C&E*, pp. 167-68.
17. *Development of Doctrine*, p. 311.
18. *Ibid.*, p. 329.
19. *Ibid.*, pp. 326-27.
20. *Ibid.*, p. 328. In giving examples of heretical "literalism," Newman touched on both exaggerated and restrictive literalism, like Millenarianism, drawn from a too literally extravagant interpretation of the Apocalypse, and a restrictively scientific literalism, as practiced by the School of Antioch, and which in large part gave rise to Arianism and, later on, to Nestorianism. Newman concluded from all of this that "it may be almost laid down as a historical fact, that the mystical interpretation and orthodoxy will stand or fall together." *Idem*, pp. 327, 323.
21. Cf. *S&C*, pp. 122, 165, and 189; *Oeuvres*, 9:161, 210, and 239.
22. *Development of Doctrine*, pp. 151-52.

An attempt must now be made to account for Teilhard's strong conviction that an undeniable development of Christian doctrine does in fact imply a continuing process of revelation in itself. As for Newman's influence on Teilhard on this point, although Newman made the traditional distinction between the cessation of the "developments of Revelation" itself and the continuing development of doctrine drawn from this revelation, he professed to be "unable to fix a historical point at which the growth of doctrine ceased and the rule of faith was once for all settled."[23] Further, he seemed to imply that there was a certain overlapping of the process of revelation and the development of doctrine during the lifetime of the Apostles. But this took place after the Ascension of Christ.

But assuming that the "rule of faith" in its scriptural expression be considered completed during the Apostles' lifetime, Newman stated that this Scripture

> to the end of our lives and to the end of the Church . . . must be an unexplored and unsubdued land. . . . Of no doctrine whatever, which does not actually contradict what has been delivered, can it be peremptorily asserted that it is not in Scripture.[24]

Interestingly, Newman gave a long quotation from Bishop Butler concerning this point, which sees the understanding of revelation as a continuous development. By the very nature of man's learning process, it goes on till the end of time.[25]

Whether this particular passage did catch Teilhard's eye in the trenches of the Western Front, remains problematic. But the striking resemblance of the words of this Anglican theologian, whom Newman quoted so often, to what Teilhard was later to insist was his under-

---

23. *Ibid.*, p. 88.
24. *Ibid.*, p. 91.
25. The more distinct and particular knowledge of those things, the study of which the Apostle calls "going on unto perfection," and of the prophetic parts of revelation, like many parts of natural and even civil knowledge, may require very exact thought and careful consideration. The hindrances too of natural and of supernatural light and knowledge have been of the same kind. And if it is owned the whole scheme of Scripture is not yet understood, so, if it ever comes to be understood, before the "restitution of all things," and without miraculous interpositions, it must be in the same way as natural knowledge is come at, by the continuance and process of learning and liberty, and by particular persons attending to, comparing, and pursuing intimations scattered up and down it, which are overlooked and disregarded by the generality of the world. For this is the way in which all improvements are made, by thoughtful men tracing on obscure hints, as it were, dropped us by nature accidentally, or which seem to come into our minds by chance. Nor is it at all incredible that a book, which has been so long in the possession of mankind, should contain many truths as yet undiscovered. For all the same phenomena, and the same faculties of investigation, from which such great discoveries in natural knowledge have been made in the present and last age, were equally in the possession of mankind several thousand years before. And possibly it might be intended that events, as they come to pass, should open and ascertain the meaning of several parts of Scripture. (Bishop Butler's *Anal*, ii, 3, as cited by Newman in *Development of Doctrine*, p. 91.)

standing of revelation as the "Third Reflection," must not escape attention, despite its differences from Teilhard's later attempts to develop a
similar theory.

B. THE TEILHARDIAN THEORY OF REVELATION:
"THE THIRD REFLECTION"

During the later years of his life, Teilhard was gradually transforming
the concept of doctrinal development along the lines of his growing
convictions about the development of the "noosphere" or the ever-
thickening "envelope" of interdependent thought. This noosphere is
formed from the myriad of thinking beings who find themselves drawn
ever closer together on the limited surface of this planet. This convergence of historical context with his phenomenological overview of
evolutionary progress was a result of his characteristic tendency toward
synthetic systematization as facilitated through a series of extrapola-
tions. By these, conclusions drawn from one order of thought are transferred to another, thus yielding a certain amount of "coherence," which
for Teilhard characterizes truth.[26] However, such a transposition, particularly from a development of doctrine to a development of revelation, was to remain highly tentative in his thought, and for the most
part unexpressed, except in his later Journal notes. Nevertheless, there
were strong indications of this development in his writings during
World War II.

*1. The Early Stages of a New Theory of Revelation: Revelation Seen in
the Light of Doctrinal Development*

Around the beginning of the 1940s, Teilhard began to give more explicit attention to the phenomenon of process of development within revelation itself. Drawing on his own insights on this matter, which he
judged to be confirmed on the plane of liturgical-doctrinal development
in the Church, he spoke of the relationship between the devotion to
the "Heart of Jesus" (which in his own childhood had dominated his
family's piety) and the official establishment of the Feast of "Christ the
King," which had taken place in 1925. Between the two there seemed
to exist a certain organic relationship that suggested a true evolution of
doctrine. From this context Teilhard stated in his essay "La Parole attendue" of October 31, 1940, that the elaboration of doctrine indicated

---

26. "Plus j'y pense, et moins je vois d'autre critère pour la vérité que d'établir un max-
    imum croissant de cohérence universelle. Un tel succès a quelque chose *d'objectif*,
    dépassant les effet de *tempérament*." (*Oeuvres*, 10:150, n. 1; *C&E*, p. 130, n. 12.
    For Teilhard's application of this same criterion in more strictly scientific matters,
    cf. *Oeuvres*, 6:118; *HE*, p. 94.)

by the growth of the cult of the Heart of Jesus and the establishment of the feast of Christ the King both evidenced a deepening awareness of the organic ties that exist between Christ and the Universe.[27]

Whether or not Teilhard was reading his own interpretation into what he believed to be the motives for this "elaboration of dogma" is for the reader to decide, but there is no mistaking the fact that he judged that this is not simply an elaboration of piety, but a true example of an unfolding of the meaning of revelation. He went on to say:

> My idea and dream would be that, by a logical extension of the same movement, the Church make clear and present to the world, as St Paul already did to his converts, the great figure of the One in whom the Pleroma finds its physical principle, its expression and consistence: Christ-Omega, Christ-Universal. "Descendit, ascendit, *ut repleret omnia.*" For the Romans, Corinthians, Ephesians, Colossians, this image undoubtedly had but a confused meaning, because then the "World," the "Whole" (with the meaning of something organically definite these words today convey for us) did not yet exist in human consciousness. But for us, who are fascinated by the newly uncovered grandeur of the Universe, it exactly expresses the aspect of the God expected by our adoration.[28]

In his "Christ the Evolver" of 1942 Teilhard was a little more restrained, admitting that the salvational aspects of the Gospel message had for a long time necessarily left uncovered the cosmic implications of Christ's position in regard to the universe. This unrealized aspect required the growing understanding of the phenomenon of evolutionary "humanization" (the present advance wave of the evolutionary process) before the Christological dimension of this phenomenon could begin to be understood. In contrast to the era in which the natural sciences stood apart in a field quite removed from human concern, stated Teilhard,

> when we come to "humanization" it is a very different story. Here we have a new compartment or rather an additional dimension; and suddenly this compartment and dimension, of which *there is no explicit mention in the gospel,* intervenes and enlarges man's destiny almost limitlessly. Hitherto the Christian had been taught to think, to act, to fear and to worship, *on the scale of his own individual life and death.*[29]

However, this situation changes radically when the projected summit of this "humanization," the "Omega Point," is foreseen. This new dimension demands a new Christology:

---

27. *Oeuvres*, 11:106-7; also in *Cahiers de Teilhard de Chardin*, #4, p. 27. Cf. *TF*, pp. 97-98 for translation of the passage.
28. *Oeuvres*, 11:107. (My translation.) Cf. *TF*, pp. 98-99.
29. *C&E*, p. 142; *Oeuvres*, 10:167.

Surely this "Omega Point" (as I call it) is the ideal place from which to make the Christ we worship radiate—a Christ whose supernatural domination, we know, is matched by a physical power which rules the natural spheres of the world. *"In quo omnia constant."* We have here an extraordinary confluence, indeed, of what is given to us by faith and what is arrived at by reason.[30]

The above passages approach this question of revelation from more or less phenomenological viewpoints. But the 1944 essay "Introduction to the Christian Life" approaches it from a standpoint more openly apologetic. After introductory sections describing the "essence" and "credibility" in evolutionary terms, Teilhard went on to examine nine points that he considered the "points forte et points apparemment faibles du christianisme." Among them, after the doctrine of the Trinity and the divinity of the historical Christ, appears the whole claim to special revelation. This claim, as he saw it, follows as a logical possibility from the existence of a personal God; indeed, it becomes a theoretical probability when understood as "une réflexion de Dieu sur notre conscience," inasmuch it is entirely within the structure of reality that

> in the universe, relations between elements are in all cases in proportion to the nature of those elements: they are material when between material objects, living between living beings, personal between reflective beings.[31]

But even when the question of the problem of the disproportion between the transcendent and the created is bypassed (as it is here) the passage from theory to fact remains problematic.

> It is not quite so simple (1) to establish the historical reality of this influence and this "word," and (2) to explain their psychological mechanism.[32]

While both problems must be given attention, Teilhard was obviously more interested in the second; in fact, he seems to have taken his approach to the second from analogy to the first.

> Those who are concerned with the theory of Christianity are still far from reaching agreement on these two points. One thing at least appears certain, that (even in the case of Christ, who *had* to make himself man to be able to speak to us) God never reveals himself to us from outside, by intrusion, but *from within*, by stimulation, elevation and enrichment of the human psychic current, the sound of his voice being recognizable primarily by the fullness and coherence it contributes to our individual and collective being.[33]

30. *C&E*, p. 143; *Oeuvres*, 10:168.
31. *C&E*, pp. 159; *Oeuvres*, 10:188.
32. *C&E*, p. 160; *Oeuvres*, 10:188.
33. *Ibid.*

He expounded this same immanental viewpoint again in a more highly philosophical essay of 1946, in which he traced his "phenomenology" in terms of "The Outline of a Dialectic of Spirit." Here he posited the concept of revelation as "the reflection, in the living thought of the Church, adapted to our evolutionary state, of the thought of God." This concept rests on the prior hypothesis that

if the universe is rising progressively higher towards unity, it is therefore not only under the influence of some external force, but because in that unity the transcendent has made itself to some degree immanent. This is the lesson of revelation.[34]

When revelation is thus seen to be in terms of a divine response to man's quest for a higher degree and certainty of consciousness, then this immanental view of revelation takes on the character of a dialogue, of divine-human conversation:

Hitherto, in our anticipations of fuller-being we had proceeded entirely by the way of reason, our successive intuitions remaining within the scientific framework of "hypothesis." As soon, however, as we admit the reality of a *reply* coming from on high, we in some way enter the order of certainty. This, however, comes about only through a mechanism not of mere subject-to-object confrontation but of contact between two centres of consciousness: it is an act no longer of *cognition* but of *recognition*: the whole complex interaction of two beings who freely open themselves to one another and give themselves—the emergence, under the influence of grace, of theological faith.[35]

That revelation occurs thus (in respect to his earlier question about its psychological mechanism) was in no way a denial of the divine initiative on the ontological level. As Teilhard had already indicated in his discussion of miracles, which followed the question of revelation in his "Introduction to the Christian Life" two years before, it is the question of "a special sensitizing of the eyes and ears and of our soul (grace)," which grace Teilhard went on to describe, in terms designed to contradict all "extrinsicist" formulations, as

a special sort of sense or super-sense, whose existence, we should note (if union with God does indeed correspond to a higher degree of life), is perfectly in harmony with the laws of biology.[36]

Understood in this manner, the "phyletic" character of Christianity described near the conclusion of that same 1944 essay seems not to have been intended by Teilhard as simply an extrapolation in terms of Christianity as a historical phenomenon, nor simplistically as an application

34. *AE*, p. 148; *Oeuvres*, 7:154-55.
35. *Ibid.*
36. *C&E*, pp. 161-62; *Oeuvres*, 10:190.

of biological laws to the "organic" reality of the Body of Christ, but as a direct extension of these same laws in the realm where evolution is now most active on this planet—in the collective convergence of reflective human consciousness, that is, the "noosphere," and particularly in its leading phyletic "shoot," Christianity. Thus he was to state:

> in virtue of its essence, Christianity is much more than a fixed system, presented to us once and for all, of truths which have to be accepted and preserved literally. For all its resting on a core of "revelation," it represents in fact a spiritual attitude which is continually developing; it is the development of a Christic consciousness in step with, and to meet the needs of, the growing consciousness of mankind. Biologically, it behaves as a "phylum"; and by biological necessity it must, therefore, have the structure of a phylum; in other words, it must form a coherent and progressive system of collectively associated spiritual elements.[37]

Although the development of doctrine plays an important part in this "phyletic" growth, it appears from the above passages that such development goes beyond a mere reflective elaboration on dogmas that remain fixed in their formulation for all time. It is the formulation of new "attitudes" expressed in "new dogmas" (a phenomenon that Teilhard found uniquely present in Catholicism[38]) that suggests that in the years that marked the end of World War II he was beginning to see that revelation itself is still in process.

It remains, however, to understand why any such development of doctrine, or even of dogma, was sooner or later to appear to Teilhard as tantamount to considering revelation an ongoing process not restricted to a particular era in the past (i.e., the period closing with the death of the last Apostle). Part of the answer lies in his analysis of the process of human reflection in general, exemplified and culminating in the phenomenon of mysticism in particular.[39]

2. Reflection and Revelation

Central to this discussion of revelation is the Teilhardian notion of "Reflection" as the dominating theme of his law of "Complexity-

---

37. *C&E*, pp. 167-68; *Oeuvres*, 10:198.
38. Cf. *ibid*.
39. A Journal note ("Journal" 14 [2]: 3) from this period (Nov. 15, 1945) appears to have been directly addressed to this problem, even though revelation is not explicitly mentioned. In it Teilhard probed the relation between metaphysics (taken as a "Weltanschauung") and mysticism. Each variety of mysticism draws on a metaphysical phylum or tradition and within them Teilhard (like Bergson) distinguished a fixed element that is summarized in approved formulas from a moving element inasmuch as it engages in further reflection. This reflection, however, also involves a double aspect, since it is both a limitation of the intuitive current or potential and yet is something that is seized upon and taken up through a complexifying organization. If so, mysticism, as Bergson alleged, forms the heart of an "open" religion and Teilhard's association of mysticism with the revelatory process would also imply an "open" revelation.

Consciousness." Mere consciousness must not be confused with reflection. As his *Phenomenon of Man* makes clear, all energy is basically psychic in nature;[40] consequently, all material elements, even the inorganic, possess a rudimentary "consciousness." However, even the truly recognizable consciousness that exists in animals is but a building block for the "central phenomenon" of evolution, which is reflection.

> From our experimental point of view, reflection is, as the word indicates, the power acquired by a consciousness to turn in upon itself, to take possession of itself *as of an object* endowed with its own particular consistence and value: no longer merely to know, but to know oneself; no longer merely to know, but to know that one knows.[41]

While Teilhard hoped to explain this great evolutionary leap in terms of the complexity-convergence, the "hyper-physical" underpinnings of this process remained a matter of speculation to him throughout his lifetime.[42] The approach suggested in the *Phenomenon of Man*, based on a division of energy into its "radial" and "tangential" aspects, again found a place in his highly abstract essay "Centrology," written in 1944. In this essay he reaffirmed his contention that

> consciousness is a universal molecular property; and the molecular state of the world is a manifestation of the pluralized state of some potentiality of universal consciousness.[43]

Taking this as his basic premise, Teilhard maintained against Spencer (and it would also seem Bergson) that evolution does not consist merely in a transition from the homogeneous to the heterogeneous state of matter, but also in

> a transition from a dispersed heterogeneous (lacking unity) to an organic (unified) heterogeneous—or, to put it still more clearly, *to a transition from a lower to a higher state of centro-complexity.*[44]

In the same essay, he went on to describe this process in terms that are perhaps overly geometrical for such an abstract approach.

40. A point that has been occasionally misunderstood, particularly because of a mistranslation in the first English trans. of *Le Phénomène humain*; cf. Mooney, *Teilhard de Chardin and the Mystery of Christ* (New York: Harper & Row, 1964), p. 38 and p. 223, n. 8.
41. *PM*, p. 165; *Oeuvres*, 1:181. This same definition is repeated many times in the course of Teilhard's essays, along with further variations. Noteworthy among these is a footnote in his 1951 "Un problème majeur pour l'Anthropologie" where he stated: "Réflexion: état d'une conscience devenue capable de se voir et de se prévoir elle-même. *Penser* c'est non seulement *savoir*, mais *savoir qu'on sait.*" (*Oeuvres*, 7:330; *AE*, p. 316.)
42. Much of Journal 17 (5) (Aug. 10, 1949-Oct. 31, 1950), is taken up with notes reexamining this tentative division of energy into "radical" and "tangential" forms, a division that never intended to be taken as two different "kinds" of energy, but simply as two manifestations or vectors of one and the same force.
43. *AE*, p. 101; *Oeuvres*, 7:107.
44. *AE*, p. 103; *Oeuvres*, 7:109.

Nevertheless he advanced an elaborate foundation for his continued position: what happens in the case of the phenomenon of reflection is but a repetition on a higher and more complex scale of the transition in the passage of matter from nonlife to life. This for him is basically a movement from a "fragmentary centreity" through "phyletic centreity" toward "eu-centrism." It is not entirely clear, on this abstract level, exactly how Teilhard connected his notion of "fragmentary centreity"[45] to individual human beings, but as it related to the "phyletic" level he was working toward an understanding that would apply to the noosphere or the general complex of interacting human consciousnesses. Finally it would apply to their "eu-centric" convergence in an Omega, which he posited as being "personal-individual," "already partially actual" (i.e., present), and "partially transcendent."[46]

Teilhard's writings during the rest of the 1940s frequently mentioned this phenomenon of recurring levels in terms of "higher" or "new stage of" human reflection.[47] This higher stage of reflection manifests itself in a new "sense of species," a true "hominization" involving a "collective faith" that manifests itself in terms of "a concerted reflection of all the elementary human reflections, now mutually interreflective."[48]

While Teilhard was thus developing his thought in the area of collective human consciousness and applying it to topics such as "The Psychological Conditions of the Unification of Man"[49] or "The Evolution of Responsibility in the World,"[50] another more directly theological application of the phenomenon of reflection was taking shape in his mind. The first sign of the new mode of expression that linked this progression of human reflection to revelation can be found in a long summarizing note in his Journal entry of June 2, 1946. In it Teilhard alleged that the essence of his world view in terms of his theory of complexity-consciousness or "interiorization" through complexification

45. While Teilhard seems by this term to have been first describing the threshold of life from nonlife, he spoke of this process ("the closing-up on itself of a chain of segments") as being reduplicated on a higher level in the case of reflection. Cf. *AE*, p. 106; *Oeuvres*, 7:112.
46. *AE*, p. 112; *Oeuvres*, 7:118.
47. In his "The Place of Technology in a General Biology of Mankind" (Jan. 1947), Teilhard spoke of the place of technology as being an adjunct to man who is seen not just as an "aggregate" but as "a structural whole." Accordingly, Teilhard states that

> general technology is not merely a sum of commercial enterprises, a mechanical dead-weight on our shoulders, but rather the sum of processes combined reflectively in such a way as to preserve in men the state of consciousness which corresponds to our state of aggregation and conjunction. *AE*, pp. 157, 159; *Oeuvres*, 7:157, 165-66.

48. Cf. "The Sense of the Species in Man" (May 1949), *AE*, p. 203; *Oeuvres*, 7:209, n. 3.
49. "Les Conditions psychologiques de l'Unification humain" (Jan. 1949) in *Oeuvres*, 7:175-85; *AE*, pp. 169-80.
50. "L'Evolution de la Responsabilité dans le Monde" (June 1950) in *Oeuvres*, 7:211-22; *AE*, pp. 205-14.

is a synthesis of three laws: the law of recurrence which here is equated with knowledge; the law of action or activation (on which he does not here comment); and contemplation, which he here termed "the principle of reality." These three "laws" or elements appear in the note to roughly parallel his ideas on "the triple reflection" (individual hominization, planetary hominization, and, finally, revelation as the response of God to the first two). Then Teilhard asked how essential the maturity of individual reflection is to the collective reflection of humanity. The same question is repeated in a marginal note.[51]

At first glance this note seems to be summing up, and to some degree clarifying, what was to be contained in the "Outline of a Dialectic of Spirit" a few months later. Rather, building on the same foundation, it extends the implications of the same "Weltanschauung" over a much broader field, applying this *"triple"* sequence of reflection (the triple aspect is here for the first time explicit) to the totality of human cognitive activity, *including mysticism*. Of particular interest is the classification of revelation as the third level of reflection, a reflection of God himself upon the dual level of 1) individual human reflection ("le Réfléchi h") and 2) collective human reflection ("le Réfléchi H," "H" to be understood as "Humanité").

This newly expressed triple reflection and its close association with the problem of mysticism was not to be mentioned in any essays until some years later. The subject, however, continued to occupy Teilhard's mind during the period of intense activity that followed his return from China and during the long convalescence imposed by his heart attack of autumn 1947. Various aspects of the subject are scattered through his notes of this period.[52]

Closely associated with his interest in the cognitive aspects of triple reflection is also a growing concern for the affective aspects of mysticism, especially in regard to how it might account for the truly valid contributions of Far-Eastern and other mysticisms that lie outside the mainstream of Judeo-Christian revelation.

Hence a note of July 20, 1946, suggests that love is the dynamic source of consciousness or that consciousness is but the first vague

---

51. "Journal" 14 (2): 82.
52. A Journal note of Aug. 17, 1946 ("Journal" 14 [2]: 100), comments on the contradictory claims of what is taken to be revelation by various cultures and, moreover, the predictability of this phenomenon. Teilhard suggested that coherence must be sought in terms of general directions.

   In a note three days later, Teilhard spoke of these apparently conflicting but ultimately converging strains of mankind's religious quest as a kind of "stereogenesis" (*ibid.*, p. 101).

   A third note (from Sept. 25, 1946), which may be related to the above, speaks of the persistence of the terrestrial within the noosphere in the form of phyletic determinations as evidenced by "two laws," the first being that whatever may be occurring in one person's consciousness is recognizable to the rest of humanity, and the second being that whatever appears in one consciousness that is truly progressive is inevitably destined to be taken up some day by the total noosphere (*ibid.*, p. 109).

wave of love and that as a consequence the noosphere will be fully activated only to the extent that its affective unification is "dynamized" or transformed through "Christification."[53] Following this line of thought, an interesting "definition" of revelation is found in the conclusion of a note of September 25, 1946, which says that revelation is a supreme emergence ("center-to-center")—all such "emergences" being creative reflections of the Omega "sur le Christ." Thus revelation is termed "Centric Creation."[54]

Again, in a long note of October 31, 1946 ("Journal" 14 [2]: 118), can be found a fascinating critique of Aldous Huxley's understanding of mysticism, a mysticism that Teilhard saw related to objective revelation. But in it Teilhard made a careful distinction based on the exigencies of the evolutionary view of human reflection and other ideas he had begun to review on the nature of man's ultimate union with the Omega.

More particularly, Teilhard quoted with some interest a passage of Aldous Huxley's concerning certain individuals who achieved "direct awareness of the 'eternally complete consciousness' which is the ground of the material world," this independently of their own personal stage of development or at any stage of history. This Teilhard felt was "subtly inexact," and instead suggested that while the divine presence may be sensed from time to time, this is not so much an advance as such as an individual realization of what could be possible for all if the Omega ahead were truly seen. The problem really is that while most mystics seem to *return* to a *divine ground*, the real focus of divinity is ahead. God really is not to be found in the immobility of a ground but in the movement of centration. This loss of sense of time and direction is what, according to Teilhard, stands behind the paradoxical concepts of a divine emptiness or void beneath the personhood of God as seen in the godhead-god distinction of Hindu and Eckhardian types of mysticism.[55] At the same time, however, Teilhard continued to probe the subject of mysticism for the keys it might provide for the understanding of revelation as a process. A single-line note from the following spring gives evidence of his concern with this aspect, speaking of revelation as involving "not so much a fact as *a curve*."[56]

53. "Journal" 14 (2): 93.
54. *Ibid*., p. 110. The note described above is prefaced by a remark to the effect that while the Gospels are literarily hetereogeneous (literally and symbolically fragmented), still each element more or less fits into an overall homogeneity. But with the case of Original Sin (as found in the Epistles) the situation is different. Here a certain mythological heterogeneity intrudes on the theological content. But here Teilhard also made an objection to his own argument: regarding the words of Eucharistic consecration, do we not have to seek a synoptic-Johannine synthesis? In any case, Teilhard went on to state that he believed that theological adjustments of this type do not result in mere syncretism but rather in a deepening of essential axes of thought. He then quoted someone who once said: "When one falls off his feet, then one finds he has wings."
55. *Ibid*., p. 118.
56. "Journal" 15 (3) (April 26, 1947): 7.

Over a year later Teilhard again commented in his Journal on the process that appears to tie mysticism (characterized as noospheric inter-reflection) with revelation (designated as interiorization of a mutually "com-penetrating" sort).[57] The second of two notes, following a marginal remark in parentheses, scores William James's *Varieties of Religious Experience* with more or less the same errors as those criticized in Aldous Huxley's *Perennial Philosophy*—the errors of an extra-evolutive view of mysticism that holds that all ways of arriving at the Ineffable are equally valid and that the religious problem is strictly an individual one, existing outside the context of evolving humanity.[58]

While it may appear from these notes that Teilhard was becoming more interested in the individual mystical elements involved in the third reflection, which he had already indicated or characterized as being his understanding of revelation, what seems most to have bothered him was the "fixist" view of revelation, which had to his way of thinking stifled the growth of Christianity and imposed certain categorical thought forms that would continue to thwart its message unless radically revised.

3. Basic Obstacles to His Theory: "Fixism" and the Objectivity of Revelation, and the Problem of the "Supernatural Evolutive"

In two notes in December 1948, Teilhard ennumerated rather sarcastically in psychological terms what he considered to be the basic problems of Christianity; in both cases the then-current concept of revelation is first on the list. The first note, dated December 8, brackets fixation on the past (revelation as behind us) with a fixation on the supernatural conceived as pertaining to "heaven," with the result of pharisaism and human insensibility.[59] The second note, that of December 17, lists, along with revelation in this fixist sense, three other Christian "complexes": the spirit as opposed to the flesh, the supernatural, and Original Sin.[60]

But far from Teilhard's implying here that revelation as such constitutes a barrier to the continued growth of religion, he sees its part as absolutely indispensable to man, particularly in his latter stages of evolution, faced as he is with the "existential exigency" of finding a continuing motive for prolonging the evolutionary process in the face of his "existential fear" of a cosmic purposelessness.[61] In the spring of

57. *Ibid.* (Nov. 17, 1948), p. 167.
58. *Ibid.* (Nov. 18, 1948), p. 167.
59. *Ibid.*, p. 175.
60. *Ibid.*, p. 176.
61. Cf. "A Phenomenon of Counter-Evolution in Human Biology" (Jan. 1949) in *AE*, p. 181f.: "Un phénomène de Contre-Evolution ou la Peur de l'Existence," *Oeuvres*, 7:187f.

1949 a note criticized Julian Huxley's *Religion without Revelation* as symptomatic of the lack of stability, "permanence," or "irreversibility" that a dearth of revelation entails.

Teilhard faulted Huxley with the untenable presupposition that a strictly "human credo" can be founded on "permanence." On the contrary, from what science tells us, such a "Religion without Revelation" would be without hope, for it avoids the issue of irreversibility, and similarly would be without love (lacking a center for the field of human consciousness).[62]

Leaving aside this defense of the objectivity of revelation, there still remains the question of the development of Teilhard's understanding of the process that is nevertheless involved. Taking as his starting point that all truth is of a piece, his speculation on the reflective process involved in revelation necessitates a return to his ideas on the "second reflection"—that of the human collectivity. In this context he had begun to ponder in his notes of November and December of 1948 what he called "the circle of 'Orthodoxy.'"

One note, which is illustrated by a segmented circle, the segments being labeled philosophy, theology, physics, biology, etc., asserts that in view of the three criteria of truth (coherence, fecundity, and psychological dynamism) no change can take place in one field without in some way affecting the others.[63]

But in addition to this Teilhard noted on Christmas day of that same year that, in virtue of this interaction of the segments of the noosphere, we can even speak of a "Néo-sphere," inasmuch as there is something "ontologically new" created in the Christic center of the sphere due to the constant modification of human awareness.[64]

This Christmas Day note then speaks of two theories of centrism, the first analogous to the segmented circle concept, while the second apparently is recast along the lines of Teilhard's more usual concept of human convergence, visualized in terms of a south-to-northward movement on the surface of the globe, a conceptualization that appears most notably in *The Phenomenon of Man* and that is utilized to express the initial expansion-diffusion movement of human evolution with its

---

62. "Journal" 16 (4) (Mar. 6-Apr. 9, 1949): 44-45 (pages 42-5 have no specific dates). In a letter to the same Huxley, with whom he had in the meantime become personally acquainted, he was to imply this same lack of a revealed center to man's aspirations as they are described in Huxley's "Evolutionary Humanism" and other essays, Teilhard wrote:

> Tant que ce pas ne sera pas fait, il est *inutile* (à mon avis) de chercher à faire apparaître une Idéologie humaine,—ni d'écrire une Histoire humaine. Idéologie et Histoire présupposent un centre de perspective et un dynamisme de fond. Autrement, on ne peut éviter l' 'abstraction' ou le 'catalogue.' (Teilhard Correspondence "G-K" Apr. 1, 1952).

63. *Ibid*. (Nov. 1, 1948), p. 22.
64. "Journal" 15 (3): 179.

later phase of compression-convergence, resulting in a certain "infold-ing" of culture and thought.[65]

Despite the highly tentative character of these rather complex notes, and their apparent reversion to the immanental side of the reflection-revelation concept, Teilhard did not fail to ponder the transcendental side of this mystery. But the question remained: is this transcendental factor to be encountered as a beginning or as an end? This is the ques-tion that forms what Teilhard called "the Heart of the Matter" (an En-glish phrase that Teilhard had adopted from the novel of Graham Greene) in a note of January 12, 1949, where he singled out "The Supernatural-Evolutive" as being the theological node of the question.[66] If the supernatural is indeed to be conceived in evolution-ary terms, then mankind has been looking in the wrong direction for the revelation of God in thinking that this transcendental truth has been revealed primarily as a fixed "point" in the past rather than as an "axis" that points toward the future. Thus Teilhard again scored (in a note of April 9, 1950) what he considered to be one of the weakest points of Christianity: its tendency always to look to the past for the truth, to think that somehow the ancients always knew best. This is a case of confusion again, opposing the truth seen as a "point" (in the past) to that truth seen as an "axis" (leading toward the future). Rather, it should be seen as a convergence of both.[67]

From this point of view, a single line in Teilhard's notes, which ap-pears to be a quip about the "God is Dead" theology (long before it became popular in the United States), is perhaps meant to be taken seriously—that instead God has "changed."[68] And similarly, in answer to the position of Huxley[69] that the notion of God can no longer serve effectively as a noetic integrator, having proved itself long ago to gen-erate only intolerance, Teilhard responded that Huxley's "God-ground" (this is actually more akin to Aldous Huxley's position) is inert. Instead, a "God-as-goal" would first engender an "orthogenesis of humanity" (humanity progressing toward a common goal), followed by an "Ortho-doxy," and as such produce convergence rather than intolerance.[70]

These notes throw a strong light on a changed view of revelation, which Teilhard suggested was really the result of a changed view of God: thus another note pairs a change in the "Face" of God with a change in the Word of God—that the appearance of the Logos ("le verbe") instantaneously changes the appearance of the Word ("La Parole")—a change in the concept of revelation (designated here as

65. Cf. *Oeuvres*, 1:263f.; *PM*, pp. 237f. This same concept is illustrated in an earlier note of Dec. 3, 1948 ("Journal" 15[3]:173).
66. "Journal" 16 (4): 33.
67. "Journal" 17 (5): 90.
68. *Ibid.* (May 26, 1950), p. 104.
69. Julian Huxley, *Knowledge, Morality and Destiny* (New York: Mentor Books, 1957), pp. 53-54.
70. "Journal" 17 (5) (June 16, 1950), p. 110.

"F3") necessitating a reassessment of the relationship of both collective and individual human thought ("F2" and "F1") to revelation as well.[71]

This correlation of three "reflections" with three "F"s was made explicit again in a note appended to the November 1950 manuscript entitled "The Zest for Living," where a second conclusion for this essay is proposed in the following terms:

> A different ending?
> Religious "contact" = Initiation of the 3rd. *reflection* (F^2/F^3) = *neozest made explicit*: Love (higher form of zest!!).[72]

Be this as it may, the explication of this third level of reflection as the key to man's continued will to live in terms of a divine-human contact consummated in revelation is clear from the text of the essay itself:

> What is carried along by the various currents of faith that are still active on the earth, working in their incommunicable core, is no longer only the irreplaceable elements of a certain complete image of the universe. Very much more even than *fragments of vision*, it is *experiences of contact* with a supreme Inexpressible which they preserve and pass on. It is as though, from the final issue which evolution demands and towards which it hastens, a certain influx came down to illuminate and give warmth to our lives: a true "trans-cosmic" radiation for which the organisms that have appeared in succession throughout the course of history would seem to be precisely the naturally provided receivers.[73]

But, as he again makes clear in a passage that follows shortly, this current of mysticism is not the result of human striving alone, rather:

> We now find another condition of cosmic animation and another possibility in it. It is that sustained and guided by the tradition of the great human mystical systems, along the road of contemplation and prayer, we succeed in entering directly into receptive communication with the very source of all interior drive.
>
> The vital charge of the world, maintained not simply by physiological artifices or by rational discovery of some objective or ideal, bringing with it—but poured directly into the depths of our being, in its higher, immediate, and most heightened form—love, as an effect of "grace" and "revelation."[74]

Teilhard, for all his insistence on the convergent development of human mysticism, saw the divine initiative as altogether indispensable.

In another note, written the same day as the one previously cited

71. *Ibid.* (Aug. 29, 1950), p. 145. The use of the symbol "F" (*threshold* ["foyer"]) in place of R (reflection) is also seen in the Nov. 5, 1949 entry. (*Ibid.*, p. 36.)
72. "Le Goût de vivre," *AE*, p. 243; *Oeuvres*, 7:251.
73. *AE*, pp. 241-42; *Oeuvres*, 7:250.
74. *AE*, p. 242; *Oeuvres*, 7:250-51.

(Aug. 29, 1950), occurs an expansion of this linking of the concept of God and the concept of revelation into a third dimension, that of God's "action." It would appear that, along with the two preceding dimensions of God's "face" and God's "word," God's "action" is intimately affected by its relationship to the growth and intensification of the noosphere, here expressed as a higher communion which nevertheless implies a kind of self-reduction involved in the anthropomorphic manifestation of God within the phenomenon of revelation.[75] Whether he had in mind the Pauline "kenosis" is not clear; however, a note that returns to the question of the "Evolution of Dogma" written a week or so later appears to suggest that the idea of the evolution of dogma has been retroactively discovered by the Church as a necessary reaction to the psychological development of humanity.[76]

The major difficulties with which Teilhard contended in the course of his speculations about revelation, manifested principally in the Journal notes of December 1948 through October 1950, could be reduced to the old conflict between a static view of reality and the evolutionary view. That this conflict in relation to revelation came to a head at this time may have been the natural result of all Teilhard's speculations concerning the pleroma during the same period, particularly those which had already led him to the brink of admitting a more than purely passive concept of the pleroma, of suggesting the possibility that God Himself is yet to be completed.[77] Is it any wonder then that Teilhard was perplexed by the seeming rigidity of Catholic doctrine of the completeness of revelation, and this in the face of an admitted evolution of the same up through apostolic time and an equally admitted evolution of doctrine based on the same revelation in the ages that have followed?[78] In the face of such apparent and self-contradictory

75. "Journal" 17 (5): 145.
76. *Ibid.* (Sept. 7, 1950), p. 150.
77. "Le Coeur de la Matière" (Oct. 30, 1950), *Oeuvres*, 13:65. Cf. chap. 5, §A,3 above.
78. A Journal note of May 8, 1950 ("Journal" 17 [5]: 96) contains the following quote from the breviary reading for the following day: "Sacras Scripturas interpretantes non ex proprio ingenio, sed ex majorum ratione et auctoritate interpretantes. . . ," and then comments on this as being an example of "fixism" on the phylum rather than on the "phyletic."
   In respect to this problem of an apparent "fixism" in the notion of revelation, Jürgen Moltmann makes an interesting distinction between two concepts of tradition, namely, the "classical" vs. biblical concept. He remarks, that "in this (first) conception of tradition, revelation stands at the beginning" (*Theology of Hope* [New York: Harper & Row, 1967], p. 296). Having tied such a classical idea of tradition (and its neo-Romanticist counterparts) to a cyclical view of nature and a mythical view of history, he goes on to quote Josef Pieper's remark about Plato's opinion that "the ancients are near the beginning" and "are better than we and dwell nearer the gods" (*Philebus* 16 c 5-9). "The most important thing," says Pieper, "is that this remark of Plato's is largely identical with the answer which Christian theology for its part supplies to the same question . . . then we must surely ask whether there is any essential difference between Plato's description of the ancients on the one hand, and on the other hand the definition which Christian theology applies to the writer who is 'inspired' in the strict sense of the word, the author of the holy book" (J. Pieper, *Über den Begriff der Tradition* [1957], pp. 23f.). Moltmann answers this question by insisting that the biblical idea of tradition is distinctively different,

"fixism," Teilhard was to draw the conclusion that, while it did not explicitly deny the distinction between revelation and doctrinal development, it did place them both within the same evolutionary process. "Orthodoxie: est une *Orthogénèse!*"[79]

4. Reflection and Revelation:
Later Summaries and an Open Question

If all these notes and jottings of Teilhard reveal anything of substance (and there is a virtually unmined lode of them in these notebooks), one thing in particular stands out as perhaps more than any other summing up the direction of his speculation on revelation. It is a simple, largely unadorned diagram inspired by the giant Mount Palomar telescope, which Teilhard must have seen on one of his visits to California (Aug.-Sept. 1933; July 1939; July-Aug. 1952):

The diagram simply arranges the individual centers of reflection (designated as "r") in a convex configuration to form a cross-section view of a mirror similar to that contained in the base of a reflector type of telescope. This convex surface, as a whole, is designated "R" (and involves the element of "ω", i.e., human co-consciousness as united on the plain of human goals). But it is at the same time focused on a center point designated as "Ω" (and this with a double halo, forming a triple-layer omega).[80]

The meaning of this diagram becomes clear, at least in its humanistic dimensions, in the July 1951 essay "The Convergence of the Universe." Speaking of "the human biological revolution," explained in "The organo-psychic threshold of reflection," he added that now, as a result of the countless forces of socialization freely and continuously rising to the surface of the earth;

> it is no longer the simple isolated reflection of an individual upon himself, but the conjugate and combined reflection of innumerable elements, adjusting and mutually reinforcing their activities, and so gradually forming one vast mirror—a mirror in which the universe might one day reflect itself and so fall into shape.[81]

In the conclusion to the essay, he speaks of this mirror as ". . . the new Palomar about which we dream."[82]

being a concept of historically founded promise, which "turns our eyes not toward some primaeval, original event, but toward the future and finally toward an *eschaton* of fulfilment" (Moltmann, p. 298).

79. "Journal" 18 (6) (Jan. 10, 1951): 18.
80. "Journal" 18 (6) (Nov. 12, 1950): 5. Assuming that Teilhard's understanding of reflector telescopes was correct, the Omega-point in this diagram is meant not to indicate the transcendent object of observation in itself but rather the upward and forward position of the image of the goal (as well as its viewing point).
81. *AE*, p. 288; "La Convergence de l'Univers," *Oeuvres*, 7:300-301.
82. *AE*, p. 295; *Oeuvres*, 7:308.

Lest the directly theological implications of this model be overlooked by mistaking the "R" of combined human reflection ("r") in terms of an immanentally conceived goal, a quick glance must be taken at some of the successive notes of that year. One of them translates part of this image into Christocentric terms, suggesting that God (Christ) is conscious of each and all of the cells of his Body-pleroma, for he himself is the supreme consciousness and they (his cells) are the personified reflections of this consciousness.[83] Another graphically illustrates a divine-human interaction, as the relationship between an ascending consciousness and a "descending" revelation, which cannot be encountered except through the ascending movement, the one presupposing the other.[84]

Accordingly, in a summary note written at the end of May of that year, the specifically Christic element of revelation is postulated, for the centrically directed human sense of the "All," which gives impulse to the highest form of love, is seen as the essential cause of revelation—a revelation consummated in a personal-corporate union in Christ, the essence of which is a "polar effect", that is, the "intercentric" result of the anticipation of a "Eu-super-Ego." The "secret" of this revelation is to be found in the soul of Christ, in a contact not only of love but also a kind of "co-ego."[85]

Unfortunately, there is no distinctively theological summary of this whole question of reflection and revelation in the course of Teilhard's essays, but only several hypothetical schemas in two rather abstract essays written during the years that remained, plus one short "phenomenological" summary in which he did venture to make a slightly theological application. The first is to be found in "The Reflection of Energy" (April 1952), which stands as the most elaborately schematized exposition of this line of thought. In it the whole subject is still stated in somewhat hypothetical form, but the "three reflections" are clearly delineated.

Speaking of the first reflection, Teilhard states:

> Taken in its origin in each human element, reflection (or the transition, for a being, *from the conscious to the self-conscious state*) corresponds to a critical point separating the two species of life from one another.[86]

This level is that spoken of as R^1 or "r" in the Palomar diagram. It is reached through the "critical point" F^1, the "threshold" that distinguishes human life from that of plants and animals.

Regarding the second reflection, he says:

83. "Journal" 18 (6) (Jan. 15, 1951): 20.
84. *Ibid.* (Apr. [sic] May 10, 1951), p. 44.
85. *Ibid.* (May 28, 1951), p. 65.
86. *AE*, p. 336; "La Réflexion de l'Energie," *Oeuvres*, 7:352.

Once reflective life has been initiated elementarily within individuals (continuing the movement of non-reflective life and transposing it into a new domain) it never ceases to diversity and intensify, following a collective process which is closely linked to the technico-cultural convergence of man.[87]

This second level is that of R^2 (or simply "R" in the Palomar diagram), and while it begins at almost the same point as F^1, the really critical point F^2 is reached when mankind has begun to experience its new stage of global "compression" after the many millennia of global "expansion".

Finally, regarding the third reflection, Teilhard writes:

> At the term of this process of ultra-reflection (operating on a limited planetary "quantum") a pole of maximum convergence can be distinguished. As a result of the demands for irreversibility which are inherent in reflective life, this pole cannot be regarded as a transitory state (or "flash"), but must be seen as a higher critical point (of reflection) beyond which the evolutionary curve of complexity-consciousness emerges, so far as our experience is concerned, from space and time.[88]

This third level of reflection, R^3 (which does not appear in the Palomar diagram, but is suggested by the convergent direction of the radii from "R" focusing on "Ω"), is not fully reached as soon as man begins to reflect on the problem of "irreversibility" (i.e., immortality) in individualistic terms, but only when his collective reflection upon this problem is recognized in terms of the survival of the total universe; only then will the final threshold ("F^3", as explained above; cf. also n. 71) be confronted and the issue resolved. This problem, centering upon the specter of the ultimate transitoriness of intelligent life in the universe, is crucial. Speaking of this "point critique," Teilhard had stated:

> From this point of view, it is now absolutely impossible to regard reflective psychism, within the cosmos, as a mere transitory *superstructure*. When life has become self-conscious, it manifests itself to our experience as self-evolving: but, further, it must necessarily be self-consistent, this essential self-consistence itself being, in its turn, explicable in two ways:
> a. either because it is born *exclusively from the confluence* of reflective particles reflecting on one another,
> b. or (and more probably) because it calls for and discloses the existence of a supreme centre—not simply potential, but *real*—of cosmic convergence.[89]

87. *AE*, p. 336-37; *Oeuvres*, 7:352.
88. *AE*, p. 337; *Oeuvres*, 7:352.
89. *AE*, p. 336; *Oeuvres*, 7:351.

The same division of reflection appears in a much shorter form (one in which the theological dimension is unquestioningly included) in "The Stuff of the Universe" in July 1953; in it the old Teilhardian categories of energy appear, but in a new form of successive "zones":

> The secret and the mainspring of my spiritual drive will have been to see that, underlying this outer envelope of the phenomenon (and yet in genetic continuity with it) there stretched another domain. In this, which was no longer a domain of the *tangential* but of the *centric*, a second species of energy (not electro-thermodynamic but spiritual) radiated from a starting point in the first: and this could be divided, in ascending order, into three successive zones of increasing interiorization.
> —First, the zone of the *human* (or of the *reflective*).
> —Secondly, the zone of the *ultra-human* (or of the *co-reflective*).
> —Finally, the zone of the *Christic* (or of the *pan-reflective*).[90]

It is this final, this "Christic" zone of Reflection, that he identified as being constituted by

> the astonishing energetic properties of the *divine Milieu* which is generated in the utmost depths of human consciousness by this truly "implosive" meeting between a rising flood of co-reflection and a second, descending, flood of revelation.[91]

Finally, this same viewpoint is repeated for the last time (at least, in a schematized form), but in its most theological application in Teilhard's "A Summary of My Phenomenological View of the World," which he wrote and sent to Claude Tresmontant in January 1954. In it he postulated a final convergence between human "co-reflection," revelation, and the "Christian Phenomenon":

> The more we consider the indispensability of an Omega to maintain and animate the continued progress of hominized Evolution, the more clearly can we see two things.
> The first is that a purely conjectural Omega—one that was arrived at simply by "calculation"—would be powerless to keep active in man's heart a passion strong enough to make him continue the process of hominization to the very end.
> The second is that if Omega does really exist, it is difficult not to accept that its supreme "Ego" in some way makes itself felt as such by all the imperfect Egos (that is to say all the reflective elements) of the Universe.
> From this point of view the ancient and traditional idea of "Revelation" reappears and again finds a place in Cosmogenesis—entering it, this time, through biology and the energetics of evolution.[92]

90. *AE*, pp. 375-76; "L'Etoffe de l'Univers," *Oeuvres*, 7:398.
91. *AE*, p. 381; *Oeuvres*, 7:404.
92. Cf. *Oeuvres*, 11:235-36; also "Un Sommaire de ma Perspective Phénoménologique du Monde," published by J.-P. Demoulin in *Je m'explique* (Paris: Editions du Seuil, 1966), p. 103; *Let me Explain* (New York: Harper & Row, 1970), pp. 73-74. Cf. also *TF*, p. 215.

Yet, in comparing these later, somewhat scattered summaries with the Journal entries that preceded them, the undeveloped character of the theological dimensions of this theory of revelation-reflection remains evident. On the one hand, judging from the Journal notes of the final years, much of Teilhard's thought was occupied with the basic rethinking of this hypothesis concerning the nature of energy and its ramifications in the general field of what he termed "energetics." On the other hand, theologically speaking, his thought had become almost exclusively centered on the pleroma. A note of June 24, 1952, expresses this tension, as well as a resolution (apparently never fulfilled) to write an essay on the Third Reflection, one that would seek a final synthesis of energetics and pleromization in terms of a universal theory of spirit-matter or transformation of energy. The note implies that pleromization in some way results in a "neo-divinity" (or "neo-trinity"?) or an extension of the divine beyond the "Christic" (i.e., beyond the present concept of the Incarnation).[93]

Underlying the concerns evidenced here is the problem raised by the question whether, in terms of a universe conceived as being evolutionarily convergent, there is not the inescapable conclusion that both the evolution of the universe and its final "Omega-point"—and thus the religious attitude imposed by it—become somehow "closed" rather than "open," that is, posit a final, irresistible end of all further development.

Thus the Journal notes of both December 14 and 16 (1951) ask whether we must in some way envision the final stage of religion as either "open" or "closed." Teilhard suggested that the answer lies in how we conceive the omega-summit in a universe that is psychologically convergent, thus implying a certain closing in on itself.[94]

Teilhard's concern seems to have predated an exception taken to his thought by modern "process theologians" who, in following their mentor, A. N. Whitehead, see evolution as a completely open-ended process, with God's "consequent nature" in no way ever reaching a culmination or completion. Thus, no such thing as the "Parousia" is admitted by this school in the sense of a definitive "end of time."[95]

93. "Journal" 19 (7): 5.
94. Journal 18 (6): 123-24. The first of these notes was apparently prompted by Teilhard's having read some of the philosophical reflections of Percy Williams Bridgman, American physicist and philosopher of science, winner of the Nobel Prize in Physics in 1946. One of his last books, Reflections of a Physicist, was published in New York in 1950. Noted as the founder of a school of scientific philosophy known as "Operationalism" (cf. Encyclopedia of Philosophy, vol. 5), Bridgman was also interested particularly in the question of entropy, on which Teilhard based much of his own prognostications concerning evolution. Bridgman published The Logic of Modern Physics in 1927, The Nature of Physical Theory in 1936, and The Nature of Thermodynamics in 1941, among other works.
95. One "process theologian," Lewis S. Ford of Pennsylvania State University, suggested in the course of his talk at the "Hope and the Future of Man" Conference (held at the Riverside Memorial Church, New York, Oct. 8-10, 1971) that the Christian "Parousia" be not understood as the ultimate end, but rather as a "penul-

Understood in terms of this concern over a "closed" vs. "open" another note of Teilhard's takes on added significance, one that rejects the common solution of "pseudo-supernaturalization," that is, a solution that seeks evolutionary fulfillment in a course in which the term of the process "escapes" entirely from the realm of the material side of creation into a world of "pure" spirit.

In his note the effect of "pseudo-supernaturalization" is likened to a reflection bouncing back from the surface of a liquid. The resultant breaking of the "cone of convergence" (i.e., the direct plane of our vision) causes the object as viewed to become mislocated, while the true transcendent object of our vision lies within the original plane of our vision, at the end of the unbroken cone of convergence or "ultra-convergence."[96] Here Teilhard seems simply to have been trying to account for classical Christianity's conceptualization of the supernatural as being in a world entirely removed from the universe as we know it—the world of spirit as opposed to and entirely removed from the world of matter. Nevertheless, some have suggested that this issue of spirit-matter remains ultimately unresolved in Teilhard's thought.[97] Perhaps this is true in the long run, but it seems hardly likely. That Teilhard wished to discount the place of matter once evolution had run its course seems untenable in view of the existence of notations such as the one that indicates that the "Neo-Spirit" (also designated by a capital "phi") definitely includes the physical (designated by a lower case "phi") and is therefore "nonmetaphysical."[98]

Instead of pursuing the question of an open vs. closed universe any further in these terms (although he continued, by way of his speculations on "energetics," to try to clarify the spirit-matter relationship in terms of variations on his "radial-tangential" theory of energy), Teilhard opted for a universe and an Omega which, although they meet in parousial consummation, by no means terminate in the stultification of

timate" end marking the termination of this "eon" of cosmic evolution, to be succeeded, in all probability, by others yet to come. (This talk has been subsequently published by the Garnstone Press, London, as part of #5 in the Teilhard Study Series.)

96. "Journal" 19 (7) (June 27, 1952): 6.
97. Émile Rideau judges that "Teilhard even considers that at the end of history the two tendencies of energy will not be reconciled: matter has played its part if it has succeeded in producing the right conditions for the development of person and the emergence of spirit. After that, it walks off the stage and loses all interest, it seems to have no share in the final success of the world" (*Teilhard de Chardin: A Guide to His Thought* [London: Collins, 1967], p. 399). Piet Smulders seems to suggest that Teilhard's difficulties with this whole matter (as well as his perhaps oversimplified solution) stems from a possibly insufficient understanding of classical metaphysics. (Cf. *The Design of Teilhard de Chardin* [Westminster, Md.: Newman, 1967], pp. 67f.) On the other hand, Oliver Rabut, O.P. (cf. *Teilhard de Chardin: A Critical Study* [New York: Sheed & Ward, 1961], esp. Part I, §§ 4 & 5) questions Teilhard's dynamic viewpoint on matter and spirit on the basis of other, often contradicting, scientific evidence.
98. "Journal" 17 (7): 23. The above remark appears at the conclusion of a note of Aug. 28, 1952, that speaks of the task of arriving at a definition of the spirit that would include both the "structural" and the "genetic."

dynamic personal relationship, but rather become intensified in a continuing process of "amorization" corresponding to the highest degree of reflection. Thus in a July 15, 1952, Journal note, Teilhard paralleled the "R_1, R_2, R_3" series of degrees of reflection with a series of degrees of "amorization," A_1, A_2, A_3, remarking that at the same time as reflection grows in the universe, there is a parallel and conjoined growth of love in the form of "unanimity," evidenced by the gradual replacement of reproduction by "union."[99] Later the same year he sketched the effects of this "amorization" in more detail, distinguishing two principal movements within the process: one "active," proceeding along the two vectors of "vision" and "co-reflection," the other "saving" the elementary "egos" or personalities. He then suggested that this whole process is capable of being intensified without limit. Regarding the matter of vision, the only question remaining is whether the intensification is accomplished *by means of* ("par") or *along with* ("avec") this first vector.[100]

Whether any "process theologian" would find this answer satisfactory, Teilhard seemed to find the "amorization" inherent in the process of reflection sufficiently open to unlimited intensification as to satisfy all worries about a convergent universe leading to a static or closed end. Yet this end, this culmination of the process of total reflection —structured as it is by the very materiality of the universe in evolution—issues in a total, but never completely totalized, dimension of amorization. This is by virtue of the fully personalized potentialities of matter in which it *continues* to have its matrix.

This completion of reflection in terms of amorization does not mean, however, that revelation as a process today is simply to be identified with mysticism in this life or with the enjoyment of a "beatific vision" in the next. Such a "transcendentalization" of the process of reflection-revelation in terms of "exstasis" or "heavenly beatitude" would be to betray the whole dynamic thrust of Teilhard's thought. Rather, if revelation, from the human side of the encounter, is dependent on a continuing process of reflection, both in the individual and the collective realm, then the present process of reflection-revelation will necessarily continue as long as the evolution of the cosmos does. Prescinding from whatever form of pure amorization might constitute the continuation of this process after the Parousia, it would seem that, according to Teilhard's approach, the process of reflection-revelation can hardly come to a halt as long as man is still caught up in the process of understanding the meaning of his own existence and of discovering the secrets of the cosmos within which he takes his origin. Nor can a continuing revelation be conceived as being simply a matter of theological reflection and elaboration of revealed data given in the past, for such an

99. *Ibid.*, p. 14.
100. *Ibid.* (Dec. 20, 1952), p. 53.

intellectualization would betray the element of personal encounter between God and man, which itself is also partially dependent on man's
personalization in relation to other human beings.

Such a view of the process of revelation in terms of reflection, dependent as it is on Teilhard's dynamic view of the interrelationship of
spirit and matter (or rather their being but two aspects of the single
"Weltstoff") does nothing by itself to solve the apparent problem presented by the Church's "fixist" view of revelation as essentially complete at the end of the apostolic era. On the contrary, Teilhard's concept of revelation seems only to deepen the gulf. If there is any room
for a period in which revelation will stand as complete, this era would
have to begin with the final Parousia, in which reflection would no
longer be dependent on a continuing material development of the cosmos but, resting in the "fixed" product of that development, would
begin a new stage of timeless intensification characterized by an infinitely developing union of persons in the Omega.

Is there a way out of this conflict between Teilhard's views of revelation in process and the more traditional formulations of the Church?
Do Teilhard's views on the identity of spirit and matter ultimately lead
to a denial of the uniqueness and sufficiency of the revelation of
Christ? This is the decisive problem that comes to bear on the final
legitimacy of Teilhard's insights—at least from the point of view of the
Catholic theologian—and with it the viability of Teilhard's Christogenic
synthesis insofar as it depends on any reinterpretation of the scriptural
evidence. Teilhard himself did not directly solve this problem in terms
of his understanding of the process of reflection-revelation. However,
in terms of his overall view of the essence of Christianity as one vast
process of pleromization, there is evidence of a final touch—one that
links his thought on revelation not so much to his more abstract and
"hyperphysical" views of spirit-matter, as, without departing from these
views, to the more concrete evidence of Christian revelation. This final
argument of Teilhard was constituted in nothing but an appeal to a
total understanding of revelation in the light of the Incarnation.

C. REVELATION AND THE INCARNATION:
TOWARD A FINAL SYNTHESIS

If pleromization is to remain, as suggested by Teilhard, the final
term of evolution, a final synthesis of matter and spirit, then it seems
inevitable that the Incarnation and revelation do not simply coexist as
two separate manifestations of God, but interpenetrate each other as
two aspects of God's relationship to the evolution of this same matter-
spirit. There should be no surprise to find tucked into the notes already examined another note, dated June 25, 1952, which designates

"The Third Reflection" as being not only "The Revelation" but also "The Incarnation" of the Word.[101]

The core of this insight is hardly new in the history of theology. A recurring theme from the time of St. John's Gospel onward, this association of God's Word and the "Word of God," the divine Logos, is not original. What is new here, however, even in comparison to the other expressions of Teilhard, is the typification of the Incarnation itself as a manifestation of the "third reflection." Teilhard had always considered the Incarnation primarily as the "point of insertion" of the Divine Omega into the process of cosmic-human evolution, the historical moment that marks "the plunging of the divine Unity into the ultimate depths of the Multiple,"[102] and from this point of view it was seen to initiate a three-fold movement in which:

A. The revealed Christ is identical with omega.

B. It is inasmuch as he is omega that he is seen to be attainable and inevitably present in all things.

C. And finally it was in order that he might become omega that it was necessary for him, through the travail of his Incarnation, to conquer and animate the universe.[103]

Nothing that Teilhard ever had to say, whether about the Resurrection, the Eucharist, or the Parousia, departed from this basic view of the Incarnation. The so-called Third Nature of Christ and Pleromic Christ were but extensions of this same idea, as evidenced by speculations in a Journal note of September 28, 1953, where Teilhard admitted that he had not decided whether the historical Jesus was "the real Christ" or more or less a projection of the "Trans-Christ" in such a way that it can be said that Jesus has released or unleashed ("declanché") the (true) Christ.[104] But if Teilhard so questioned this relationship between the Christ revealed in Jesus and the "Trans-Christ" who exists in (perhaps even preexists?) this revelation, he had also already questioned in notes of July 23 and July 25, 1952, the relationship of this revelation and its continuing place, understood as a "dogma," to the continuing process of reflection.

The first of these Journal notes asks whether or not the " 'Revelation' of Christ" is really any different from "the 'Discovery' " (of the same) by human collective religious thought. His own suggestion is that the answer is to be found in the "Necessity of the Third Reflection" (which, he has already indicated, includes the Incarnation).

The second of these two Journal notes scores the error and illusion of placing or imagining that dogma remains "living, winning, and opera-

101. *Ibid.*, p. 5. Cf. June 24 and June 27, 1952, nn. 93 and 96, above.
102. "Mon Univers" (1924), *Oeuvres*, 9:89; *S&C*, p. 60.
103. *S&C*, p. 54; *Oeuvres*, 9:82.
104. Journal 20 (8): 23.

tive" whatever might be the form taken by the cosmos under the activation of this reflection.[105]

From these questionings and their implied answers it can be seen that for Teilhard neither revelation, the development of dogma, nor the Incarnation itself can be conceived outside his concept of the "third reflection" understood as the culmination of the collective human reflection and its divine response. If the divine Omega has become incarnate in Christ Jesus it is nevertheless still in process of becoming "Omega" in relation to mankind, a process in which both the Incarnation and redemption, as well as creation, continue to take place and be revealed in relation to mankind's reflective growth. Thus, in a note of September 29, 1953, Teilhard defined the final essence and function of Christianity as being "The Amorization of Evolution." Then he lists the four mysteries of creation, Incarnation, redemption, and revelation (adding the latter to his previous list) as aspects or "functions" of pleromization.[106]

What is most striking about this note is the placement and full capitalization of *Revelation* at the end of this series of pleromizing "functions." In this context, revelation takes its place alongside the three other mysteries, which together form a fourth (now fifth) greater, all-embracing mystery, that of pleromization as was expressed in "Christianity and Evolution" back in 1945:

> Creation, Incarnation, Redemption: seen in this light, the three mysteries become in reality no more, for the new Christology, than the three aspects of one and the same fundamental process: they are aspects of a *fourth* mystery, which alone, when finally examined by thought, is absolutely justifiable and valid. To distinguish this mystery from the other three we must have a name for it: it is the mystery of the creative union of the world in God, or Pleromization.[107]

That "revelation" should take its place in this general movement of "pleromization" is altogether logical, but should it not be placed (from the normal Christian standpoint, including as it does, the Old Testament) between the mysteries of creation and Incarnation? If the language Teilhard used as far back as his 1924 "Mon Univers" is carefully noted, the word *phase*, as well as *"act,"*[108] is used to describe the Incarnation and redemption, which like creation are continuing processes, but which, from the historical point of view, received their definitive expression in the Christ-event only two thousand years ago. However, there is good evidence that Teilhard was not speaking primarily of a chronological sequence, but of a logical one, a view he first came

---

105. *Ibid.*, pp. 1, 2.
106. *Ibid.*, p. 23.
107. *C&E*, p. 183; "Christianisme et Evolution: Suggestions pour servir à une théologie nouvelle," cf. *Oeuvres*, 10:213.
108. *S&C*, pp. 61-63; *Oeuvres*, 9:88-91.

to by way of some of his early reflections on Original Sin. Let another look again be taken at his "Note on Some Possible Historical Representations of Original Sin" of 1922, in which he stated:

> Creation, Fall, Incarnation, Redemption, those vast universal events no longer appear as fleeting accidents occurring sporadically in time—a grossly immature view which is a perpetual offence to our reason and a contradiction of our experience. All four of those events become co-extensive with the duration and totality of the world; they are, in some way, aspects (distinct in reality but physically linked) of one and the same divine operation. The incarnation of the Word (which is in process of continual and universal consummation) is simply the final term of a creation which is still continuing everywhere and does so through our imperfections ("omnis creatura adhuc ingemiscit et parturit").[109]

That this "timeless" view continued, albeit paradoxically, in Teilhard's evolutionary synthesis seems borne out by such comments as these in his 1953 essay "The Contingence of the Universe and Man's Zest for Survival":

> If we reread St John and St Paul, we shall find that for them the existence of the world is accepted from the outset (too summarily, perhaps, for our taste) as an inevitable fact, or in any case as an accomplished fact. In both of them, on the other hand, what a sense we find of the absolute value of a cosmic drama in which God would indeed appear to have been ontologically involved even before his incarnation. And, in consequence, what emphasis on the pleroma and pleromization![110]

That this ontological view was ultimately the same for Teilhard is certain, but he recast it into a "dynamic" mold:

> For example, we see that from a dynamic point of view* what comes first in the world for our thought, is not "being" but "the union which produces this being." Let us, therefore, try to replace a metaphysics of Esse by a metaphysics of Unire (or of Uniri).[111]

If an attempt be made to extrapolate in a Teilhardian way from this view of a dynamic ontology, it might be concluded from his placing revelation as a final ontological link in the process of pleromization that, even if revelation chronologically preceded, in part, the Incarnation, and even if it received its definitively unique historical expression in the Incarnation, it is no more completed by that fact than is the Incar-

---

109. *C&E*, p. 53; *Oeuvres*, 10:69.
110. *C&E*, p. 227; *Oeuvres*, 10:271.
111. *Ibid.* *The following note was added by Teilhard:

> And by analogy with what happens in physics, where, as we now know, acceleration creates mass: which means that the moving object is posterior to motion. (*Ibid.*, n. 7)

nation complete. Just as the Incarnation remains a continuing process (along with creation and redemption) toward the goal of final unity, so too does revelation. For if the "Body of Christ," the great pleroma of God's universe in God, is itself not to be complete until all that is salvable in this universe is incorporated into Christ, in order that through Christ "God may be all in all," so must revelation itself be in no sense complete until all the fragments of human science and mysticism —indeed, all the reflective elements of the universe—be unified in a common vision.

Furthermore, if Teilhard's view of the nature of the "Weltstoff" is correct—if matter is but the "matrix" of spirit, and spirit but the most refined expression of matter—then revelation, under the form of "amorization," remains the highest, never-exhausted goal of all evolutionary movement. Reflection indeed remains forever grounded in the material side of the universe in which it has its matrix. But in its highest form, expanded in the parousial breakthrough, reflection will transcend its present limitations and, transformed in the final revelation, will move into the realm of infinite intensification or "amorization." Awareness, the "parameter" of all evolutionary development, becomes the eternal reflection of God in the pleromic Christ.

Understood in the more concrete terms of the Incarnation, Teilhard's view of revelation as the ultimate stage of pleromization would explain to a large extent his continued aversion to a "fixist" view of revelation as already "completed" in Christ. Despite the uniqueness and quality of "being for all time" in the historical manifestation of Christ, the revelation of the incarnate Son of God remains incomplete, not simply in the sense that doctrinal reflection on the meaning of past events remains an unfinished task, but also in the sense that the Incarnation itself is still unfinished. Teilhard's speculations about a Third (or Cosmic) Nature of Christ, if tentative, were not meant to be a mere theological corollary, nor simply thoughts that might some day lead to a new dogma concerning Christ. As incautious as Teilhard's language sometimes appears to have been, there is a certain element of careful consideration (and personal agony) in a short note written during that tumultuous period which marked Teilhard's return to France after his long years of exile and reflection in China, in which he stated that it is his vocation to "reveal" the Christic energy as the complete evolutive energy.[112] Whether such a qualified use of the term *revelation* is to be taken as indicative of Teilhard's actual understanding of his own part in the continuous discovery of Christian truth, may be open to question. Perhaps he occasionally took himself too seriously. But this is not the point. The real question, granted the definitive and, to this extent "fixed" nature of God's self-revelation in Jesus of Nazareth, is whether

112. Journal 15 (3) (Sept. 13, 1947): 37.

the living Christ does not continue ever to reveal himself within the ever-expanding dimensions of the Universe.[113]

From all indications, it must be concluded that the answer to this question is in the affirmative. Revelation is indeed a continuing process, and in an eminently progressive sense. Revelation as the supreme manifestation of pleromization continues, despite all fluctuations and apparent setbacks within human history, toward its fullest expression in the "ever-greater Christ," and toward its infinite intensification within the depths of the "Omega-God."

D. CONCLUSION TO PART III

In view of the unfinished nature of much of the material quoted in this chapter and its correlative relationship to those elements of Teilhard's thought which did receive a more nearly final form, it may be well to summarize in a way that directly relates these ideas to the hermeneutical questions discussed in the previous chapter. This will lead to an outline of the final synthesis that was germinating in Teilhard's mind. Reduced to bare essentials, the conclusions are three in number:

First, in the context of scriptural interpretation it has been seen that Teilhard understood his own insights—and what he confidently predicted would be those of the Church of the Future—to be of a fuller and more universal understanding of Christology in the light of a more fully appreciated *literal* understanding of Scripture itself. But rather than attribute this understanding to the product of some mysterious *sensus plenior* intended by God but not necessarily grasped by the human author of Scripture, he believed that the key lay in a fuller understanding of the text itself. Although his use of the term *literal* is not to be confused with what Newman called the "merely literal sense," Teilhard seems to have understood his own approach to be in harmony with a theory of development of doctrine not unlike that proposed by Newman.

However, and this is the second conclusion, Teilhard did not understand this process to be one of simple deduction from revealed propositions (again he follows Newman, as well as Butler, as opposed to the strictly syllogistic development advocated by later scholastics), but

---

113. Another note (Oct. 18, 1947; "Journal" 15 [3]: 53) from the same period (not entirely legible) adds to this same line of thought. In it (quoting St. Paul's "Christ lives in me") he singled out the error of that esotericism which sees special revelation as an initiation that can be transmitted through a long-term human effort of teaching and expounding, with the result that its object is more to be "believed" than "sought." Even more, we should distinguish the difference between the supposed meeting of a consciousness with a hardened object of thought ("un 'objet' granitée") and the meeting of two consciousnesses in mystical union. Here Teilhard seems to have been criticizing the excessive "reification" of revelation.

rather in terms of a convergent reflection. Teilhard judged this to be the result of a growing human consciousness that is mediated both by man's increasing awareness of his cosmos and his own self and by his mystical search for a unified world view. (This also explains Teilhard's insistence on the pantheistic nature of all religious aspiration.) And at the same time this reflection is animated by the attraction of the divine Omega, which is the object of man's quest for meaning and his striving for unity: the "amorization" of evolution. It is this vastly expanded and processive view of man's continual and culminant efforts to reach union with Omega, and of the ever-increasing attraction of Omega upon man in the course of his evolution, that impelled Teilhard to see this movement as much more than a "development of doctrine." He saw it as a continuing process of revelation within which development of doctrine is but a restricted part. In this context, the development of doctrine is a necessary and eminently vital manifestation of the organic growth of the Christian "phylum" in its unifying function; yet it remains an essentially limited process in contrast to the greater process of God's continuing and growing self-revelation to an ever-more-convergent humanity.

Third, Teilhard saw the continuing process of revelation as analogous to that of the Incarnation; indeed, given his views of the ultimate spiritualization of matter (in a metaphoric rather than dualistic sense), revelation, in the fullest sense of "amorization," appears to be the ultimate purpose of the Incarnation, to some extent transcending it by its capacity to remain a continuing process.

Given these three interrelated and basic positional affirmations, the weakness they present must be surveyed, particularly in relation to contemporary reflection on Catholic doctrine. In reverse order (that is, beginning with that in greatest doctrinal conflict), it must be admitted that Teilhard seems to have taken with insufficient seriousness the insistence of the Church that revelation as such has in fact ceased with the death of the Apostles (Denz. 2021, also 783). As Karl Rahner elaborates this position in *Sacramentum Mundi*,

> the unique and final culmination of this history of revelation has already occurred and has revealed the absolute and irrevocable unity of God's transcendental self-communication to mankind and its historical mediation in the one God-man Jesus Christ, who is at once God himself as communicated, the human acceptance of this communication and the final historical manifestation of this offer and acceptance.[114]

However, while Teilhard seems to have ignored the difficulty that his insistence upon a continuing process of revelation occasions in relation to this point of Christian doctrine, he in no wise meant to minimize

114. "Revelation" in *SM*, 5:349; *ET*, p. 1462.

the unique and definitive nature of the culmination of revelation in the Incarnation. Instead, he was stressing that the yet-to-be-completed aspect of the revelation of this same Christ will reach its culmination only at the Parousia.[115] Here Rahner's distinction between "transcendental revelation" (i.e., the subjective transcendental encounter with God that could occur to anyone, even without conceptual expression) and "predicamental-historical revelation" (i.e., the historical mediation and conceptual objectification of this former experience[116]) will perhaps serve to throw a helpful light upon the difference between what Teilhard considered the human "mystical current"—with its partial and fragmentary intuitions of God that he saw as nevertheless contributory to revelation—and what he undoubtedly believed was unique and definitive in the biblical revelations culminating in Christ. If Teilhard's position on this matter appears ambiguous, it may be a problem posed more by his terminology than the concepts which, if given a fair study, appear orthodox enough.

Perhaps this same deficiency of distinctions, beyond any debate over the extent and manner of development of doctrine, caused Teilhard's position on a continuing revelatory process likewise to suffer from ambiguity. While he undoubtedly credited this same "mystical current," under the influx of grace, with being a continuing activant of an unfolding revelatory process in respect to humanity today and in the future, he predicted no new revelations in terms of objective content beyond what has already been objectified in Christ. All that is to follow is but the growth, in the ontological as well as gnoseological realm, of that same Christ. Understood thus, Teilhard's "curve" of revelation contains no new "facts" but is the continuing development of what is already coming to be in terms of that doctrine which has already been revealed. Teilhard's switch from a "development of doctrine" to a "curve" of revelation may have been motivated by a concern lest the former be equated too narrowly with an increase in dogmatic definitions rather than representing a continuing actualization of the meaning of the Incarnation within the world still in process.

Similarly, in advocating that Christianity come to a fuller understanding of what at the same time is only the most literal and "physical" sense of Scripture, Teilhard made little or no distinction between revelation and doctrinal development within the Scriptures themselves. Nevertheless, while he occasionally commented in his notes on the differences in the New Testament between the Jesus of the Synoptics and the Christ of John and Paul, his implication is that the latter constitutes a new revelation that transcends the historical Jesus of Matthew, Mark, and Luke, and is not simply an inspired case of doctrinal

---

115. Cf. René Latourelle's paradoxical remarks in this regard in his *Theology of Revelation* (New York: Alba House, 1966), pp. 447-48.
116. Cf. Rahner, *SM*, 5:348; *ET*, p. 1461.

development.[117] But this imprecision, to Teilhard's way of thinking, rather than causing revelation to be specially restricted to the biblical canon, paradoxically caused him to see revelation as continuing through the whole process of the evolution of man's thought.

Despite these conceptual confusions, Teilhard has nevertheless made a unique contribution to the overall theology of revelation and, implicitly, a beginning of a solution to what remains a central problem in the theology of doctrinal development. The problem that according to Rahner underlies both the problem of revelation and the development of doctrine is the one of being and becoming.[118] But this is ultimately the whole metaphysical issue called into question within any evolutionary system of thought. Teilhard's own attempts, despite their imprecisions of expression and incomplete development, to address himself to these problems of the meaning and laws of revelation and doctrinal development from within the context of his whole system could be among the most significant contributions to be found in this area today.[119]

Thus, if this criticism and defense may be pursued a little further

117. Cf. Karl Rahner, "Considerations on the Development of Dogma" in *Theological Investigations* (London: Darton, Longman & Todd, 1966), 4:6.

118. Speaking of the ultimate problem at the root of all discussions of revelation, Rahner writes:

> The fundamental hermeneutical principle required for an answer to this question (i.e. how revelation can be at once of directly divine origin and at the same time constitute the very core of human history) is to be found by considering the most general relationship between God and the world of becoming ("Revelation" in *SM*, 5:348; *ET*, p. 1460.

> This is much the same as what he identifies as the root of any discussion of the development of dogma: ". . . it ultimately reaches down to the obscure depths of a general ontology of being and becoming, of the persistence of identity in change —and also comprises the general metaphysics of knowledge and mind, which forms the same questions in searching for truth with regard to its identity and real historical involvement" ("Considerations on the Development of Dogma," *Theological Investigations*, 4:5).

119. This is not to detract from the significant contributions made by those such as Gabriel Moran in his *Theology of Revelation* (New York: Herder & Herder, 1966). But to suggest that Teilhard's basic "reversal of perspective" (to use Maritain's phrase concerning Teilhard) with its seeming "substitution of becoming in the place of being" (to use another of Maritain's criticisms) certainly takes us closer to the heart of the matter in question, even if Teilhard had never mentioned the problem of revelation, than perhaps any subsequent Catholic author. Moran's speculations, in fact, appear to tie in neatly with Teilhard's despite their dissimilar approach. Speaking of revelation as a *continuing process*, Moran states: "At the resurrection Christ was constituted Son of God for us; at that time he *began* his revelatory-redemptive activity in fullness. . . . There is no question of adding objective truths to the deposit of faith, nor is there a question of going beyond Christ. What is of utmost importance is that the revelational process first accomplished a continuing revelational process" (p. 75). As for the mystery as to how this process continues, Moran suggests that it be understood within the context of the sacramental-moral and liturgical life of the Church. Speaking of the privileged place of Holy Scripture in this ecclesial life, Moran adds: "Holy Scripture, sacred, revealing, salvific as it is, still only mediates the revelation verbally. . . . Holy Scripture of itself is thus oriented towards a bodily expression of revelation not because Scripture is an incomplete part of revelation, but because Scripture must be bodied forth in transforming man" (p. 124).

along the lines suggested by Rahner's speculations, it would seem that Teilhard's uniqueness remains to some extent both in relation to his own time and to what has up to now been elaborated by the theologians. His uniqueness lies in his singular understanding of what is at least one very vital element in the process of recognition and explication of revelation within the process of the development of doctrine. According to Rahner, the ultimate recognition of all development in that reflection known as the *sensus fidelium* remains its least-solved mystery. If this "collective consciousness" (Rahner's words, not Teilhard's) is the final locus of that discernment upon which the magisterium depends in its judgment of the validity of any doctrinal development as being "dogma, *as* revealed by God" (again, Rahner[120]), then Teilhard's contribution leads to the question of where this consensus is to be found. Is it within the confines of the "Mystical Body" as contained within the strict confines of the Catholic Church as it was conceived in most pre-Vatican II theology? Or within an ecumenical "Christendom"? Or within the consensus of all humanity? Without denying the unique historical revelation embodied in Christ and singularly lived within the Christian "phylum" that constitutes the principal locus of the Incarnation today, what Teilhard's speculation contributed is an insistence on an appeal to the consensus of all mankind. This is not because the Church is in anyway incompetent to define its own doctrine under the special guidance of the Spirit, but simply because, in the end, this "Body of Christ" must assume truly pleromic dimensions, embracing all of mankind and the cosmos, which is oriented for mankind's sake toward that Omegic pole which already exists in Christ. If revelation is complete in Christ, it is nevertheless incomplete until his Body assumes the full dimensions of the pleroma, and the *sensus fidelium* as the "mind" of that Body becomes the corporate reflection of all mankind.

If this claim of Teilhard's uniqueness may be pushed one step further, one more thing should be added. If the "curve" of revelation is somehow "convergent," then another reason can be discovered for Teilhard's realignment of this dynamic consciousness of Christianity along the path of a revelation-in-process rather than in terms of doctrinal development. Doctrinal or "dogmatic" development up to now has characterized a pattern of divergent growth in religious consciousness. Whatever has been its benefits toward a unity of faith among adherents to the Catholic communion, the fact remains that each definition has meant the de facto hardening of a further division within the Christian faith, and generally a further separation from the non-Christian world. Such divergence within the general law of complexified growth is inevitable. But there must and will appear another stage, that of the

120. *Theological Investigations*, 4:34, 27.

general convergence that leads to newer and higher awareness. This is also inevitable, although continued resistance and subsequent polarization in respect to it are not. Nevertheless, if Christianity represents the most advanced segment of mankind's religious consciousness—a position that Teilhard was firmly convinced was the case in virtue of its unique relationship to the continuing Incarnation—then the reflective activity of this uniquely privileged consciousness will not only parallel but to some extent anticipate the future development of all human thought. Having run the course of its expansive (and thereby necessarily divergent) phases, Christianity (like all human reflection) will now find itself slowly being brought around by the forces of human planetary compression into a new alignment with those fragmentary and essentially incomplete human mystical currents that have manifested themselves sporadically all through mankind's history. These mystical currents will flare up with a new and insistent intensity in the face of the existentially ultimate questions that increasingly confront man in a world that has already evolved to the point of inescapability of what Teilhard called the "Grand Option"[121]—the decision whether to continue the great effort of evolution or not.

In his growing awareness of the common destiny Teilhard saw an inevitable convergence of human thought, a general reflection of all the thinking surfaces of the cosmos in a combined assault on the ultimate question, that of the real existence of a divine Omega-point, a personal God who can assure us of the irreversibility and ultimate success of the evolutionary process. Christians already see the face of that Omegic personality in the features of Christ, and they have lovingly traced these features in their collective consciousness of faith as it reflects the divine image. Yet that image remains incomplete and shadowy, and to some extent because of the fragmented nature of the surface, the image itself remains fragmented or even distorted by the peculiarities of each facet of this as yet incomplete mirror.

Teilhard consequently saw the future progress of Christian consciousness to be in concert with the progress of human reflection in general. It would not be merely in terms of a development of further doctrine—something that has hitherto been a movement of analysis, of specification and definition. It would instead be a development of revelation, something not so much concerned with propositions as with Person. It would be concerned not only with the modalities of the mediation, but even more with the encounter in itself. Thus the emphasis must be on synthesis more than on further analysis, useful and necessary though the analytical mode of cognition continues to be. In Teilhard's view, at this point of the world's passage from an expansive state to a compressive phase of demographic and psychological de-

121. Cf. "La Grande Option" (1939) in *Oeuvres*, 5:55-82; *FM*, pp. 37-60.

velopment, no new revelations in the definite sense of going beyond Christ are heralded, and probably no new "dogmas" either. Rather what is to be expected is a new synthesis: that of the historical-predicamental revelation of Christ with the transcendental quest of all mankind, past, present, and future—the completion of the pleroma that mirrors God, and through this, the completion of the total reflection-revelation of God himself.

9

Christogenesis:
Confusion or Coherence?

For all its engaging fecundity, one of the most disturbing elements of the current phenomenon of "Teilhardianism" is the apparent inability of many of its more outspoken advocates to grasp its Christological emphasis. More than any accusation of a reversal of Christian perspective (which would imply theological heresy), or of a confusion of levels of knowledge (which would imply epistomological heresy), or replacing being with becoming (which would imply ontological heresy), the actual popularity of a Christ-less Teilhardianism would seem to bear out Jacques Maritain's fear that the espousal of Teilhard's synthesis amounts to a "kneeling before the world." One need only point to the confession of his more humanistic friends (J. Huxley and others) that, impressed as they are with Teilhard's vision, they have been unable to follow him to his conclusions regarding the eventual consummation of the universe in the great "Christ-Omega."

Is it then to be concluded that Teilhard's efforts are capable only of leading in the end to a glorious vision of a hope-filled humanism, one in which the philanthropical energies of modern man might be mobilized to new heights of selflessness, but one incapable of effectively serving as a prolegomenon of Christian faith? This is the question that has motivated this study. Rather, the central theme of Teilhard's whole vision of evolving reality is Christogenesis, which stands at the very heart of that process which he was to summarize as pleromization. Without the "ever-greater Christ," the ultimate Omega remains but a chimera.

Judged in the light of his own requirements—intending to effect a reconciliation between those who believe in the present world and those who believe in the world to come—the outcome of Teilhard's life-project must not only be examined in terms of its inner consistency, but also be analyzed in the light of its power to convince others, for it is only in the light of external criticism that the synthesis that was so luminously clear to Teilhard can be evaluated on the basis of what Teilhard himself claimed for it. Also, it is only in the light of its failure to convince (both believers and unbelievers) and to effect the reconciliation Teilhard so earnestly desired, that the internal flaws in his logic can be evaluated. Leaving aside the power of divine grace to bridge over all gaps in human logic and to overcome all hesitation to commitment, the centrality of Christogenesis (and all claims to the validity of his reinterpretations) stands or falls in relation to its "de facto," necessary relationship to the synthesis; and this not only in the mind of Teilhard, but in the minds of those who find his thought attractive.

A. TEILHARD'S GENERAL METHODOLOGY

Teilhard's principal contribution to modern Catholic thought was to have proposed a new synthesis of scientific and religious thought, a synthesis attempted numerous times before, either through an all-embracing philosophical systematization (as, for example, that by Whitehead) or through what generally turned out to be an ill-fated concordism between evolutionary science and the Bible (perhaps De Nouy's attempt is an example of this). Teilhard's over-all methodology was different; it was, as he so often insisted, "phenomenological," that is, it simply attempted to correlate—in terms of the general drift of evolutionary phenomena (as he interpreted it) and in terms of the religious phenomenon and its expression in revelation—the general convergence of these phenomena in a general pattern of complexity-convergence-consciousness. Thus, while attempting to avoid any metaphysical presuppositions, he saw this correlation between scientific and religious data to be expressible in terms of a general law or "philosophy" of "creative union," which, far from being a general presupposition, was on the contrary the more or less abstract expression of a phenomenologically based "Ultra- " of "Hyper-physics."

Expressed in these terms, Teilhard's synthesis might be visualized as a tripod, whose three legs converge at a single point. Its three distinct "legs" here correspond to the three diciplines of science, philosophy, and theology, each of which possesses its own proper methodology. From the phenomenological viewpoint of evolutionary science, Teilhard saw the culmination of the universe in terms of an "Omega-point," which represents the summit of human consciousness and its collective development. But from this approach, Omega is a mere hypothesis, and an uncertain one at that, given man's instability coupled with his potential for evil as well as good. On the other hand, philosophically speaking, Omega is but "the unknown God," an "existential exigency" whose existence is postulated only in contrast to the despair consequent upon the universe's ultimately being an absurdity. Thus, although these two legs of the tripod—the phenomenological and the philosophical—remain engaging and plausible hypotheses, they cannot stand with any certainty without the third support, which is properly theological. For Teilhard, this third and ultimately stabilizing support is the certain and personal existence of an "Omega-God," who is revealed in Christ. Ultimately then, the justification of Teilhard's synthesis is unabashedly founded in revelation.

Thus, not only is Teilhard's synthesis ultimately theological in its ontological substance, but it is noetically dependent on revelation for its solidity. Consequently, if it has been shown that Teilhard's methodology in dealing with this revealed guarantee of the synthesis is properly theological, (in that it did actually begin with revelation and developed truly in the line of "fidem quaerens intellectum"), then it may be hoped that the centrality of Christ, historic as well as cosmic, will also be seen as absolutely essential to the Teilhardian synthesis. Lacking this, Teilhard's own insistence that his synthesis was not a facile concordism, but simply a case of converging modes of knowledge, would be unfounded.

B. GENERAL REVIEW

This study has attempted to investigate thoroughly the theological foundation of the all-important "convergence" element of Teilhard's synthesis. The investigation has proceeded along the line of an examination of three major points or questions from which one principal unifying conclusion has been drawn.

The first question (the preliminary level of the investigation—Part I) asked to what degree Teilhard actually drew on Sacred Scripture for the theological inspiration and expression of his synthesis. The answer is the one word *extensively*. Although his ways of using the words of Scripture varied enormously, and may often have provided him his initial inspiration (even to the extent of suggesting insights into the evolutionary phenomena as well as serving as a type of "apologetic" conclusion), it may be averred that so extensive was his use of Scripture that his whole synthesis is permeated by it and can even be expressed largely in the terminology of biblical revelation.

The second question (corresponding to Part II) dealt with the extent to which those major scriptural themes in which Teilhard chose to express his synthesis theologically—the Pauline themes of "creation in expectation"; "the Body of Christ"; and the "pleroma," and also some corresponding Johannine themes—were reinterpreted by Teilhard in the light of his own central theme of Christogenesis: the gradual fulfillment of the universe in Christ and Christ in his universe. To determine this, the stages of his thought have been delineated in detail, and in such a way as to have uncovered some serious dialectical difficulties, particularly those which take their origin in the problems of sin and evil, and which caused him both to alter the overeagerness of some of his early interpretations and to attach himself with ever greater tenacity to those interpretations which he was convinced remained unassailable. In contrast to the exegesis of his day and to a considerable portion of that of our own day, Teilhard's understanding and use of these scriptural themes represents a considerable reinterpretation.

In view of Teilhard's conviction of the validity of his reinterpretation, the third question (taken up in Part III) had to be asked. That was, looking back on the development witnessed in Part II, how could Teilhard have suggested that his views, in all their unconventionality (apart from their occasional resemblance to those of certain early Church Fathers), could seriously be considered tenable in the light of modern exegesis? Now that we have seen his concrete approach, what can we say of his methodology, or more exactly, of his hermeneutical presuppositions? In dealing with this question in chapter 7, two other closely related questions arose. First, how did Teilhard typically approach Scripture? As a private reader, an apologist, a biblical theologian, or a systematic theologian? Second, what kind of probative force or "sense" did he assign to Scripture? We have seen that despite occasional variations in his approach, his overall general "attack" resembled the more or less typical methodology of the systematic theologian. And we have seen that Teilhard believed that his interpretations were faithful to the literal sense of Scripture.

This assertion was a startling claim in his day, and it still remains so to many. The claim, as he made it, seems to have been based on a general "hermeneutical" presupposition—that without positing the existence of any hidden *sensus plenior* in the text itself, the literal sense of the Pauline terms in question is ultimately capable of yielding a legitimately revelatory meaning. The revelatory element is discovered in the light of a universally applicable parameter of evolutionary development, which parameter is applied not just to the natural world, but to the process of revelation itself.

In chapter 8 the whole matter comes to rest in the question of "L'Evolutif surnaturel." With this the whole concept of revelation as something "fixed" is contested. What Teilhard understood as the "literal sense" of Scripture obviously undergoes a development in the unfolding of its further meaning for us. It is nevertheless the conclusion of this study, based on his many notes on the subject of revelation, that, while he never denied the uniqueness of the historic manifestation of God in Jesus, Teilhard understood this revelation to be just as incomplete and unfinished in the noetic sense as the Incarnation itself, even in its physical extension. In this sense "revelation" and "Incarnation" are inseparable and coterminous, and the completion of both weighs as a heavy responsibility on redeemed mankind.

C. A HERMENEUTICAL REAPPRAISAL

In the light of the foregoing summary, it now becomes necessary to ask a few probing questions. If the first two legs of the tripod that forms Teilhard's synthesis remain shaky, or incapable of standing alone (despite the enthusiastic endorsement of some admiring humanists), what can be said of Teilhard's claim of the certainty of the third, the theological support? What can be said of this claim when it does in fact remain based, despite its early patristic counterparts, on an interpretation that is a radical reinterpretation of those very texts in which Teilhard claimed to see his synthesis theologically vindicated? For all his personal certainty that he was interpreting St. Paul (and also St. John) in the only way that could possibly make sense to modern man, did not his generally eclectic approach to all Scripture—and even his admittedly discriminating approach to the Pauline epistles and to the Gospel of St. John—leave the door wide open to heresy (in its original sense of "to pick and to choose according to one's tastes")? Without casting doubt on Teilhard's Christian belief or his loyalty to the Catholic Church, what can be said about the interpretive integrity of a man whose understanding of Scripture seems to have been governed by its compatibility with his own vision of the phenomenological world and the existential problems that this vision raised? Does there not lie concealed in this methodology the old problem of circularity of reasoning—of "proving" the faith by the Bible while attesting to the veracity of the Bible from the starting point of faith? Here the facile "solution" of distinguishing between Scripture as history and Scripture as the foundation for statements of belief runs into a more complicated turn. For if Teilhard's certainty about the reality of the "cosmic Christ" (prescinding from his acceptance of the historicity of Jesus of Nazareth and his loyal belief in the Christ of defined Christian doctrine) is based on his own reading of the Pauline "Kyrios-Christos" texts (which has precedents in some patristic interpretations but for the most part remains outside the pale of defined Christian doctrine), then on what grounds can his interpretations lend certainty to a belief in an "Omega" that remains purely hypothetical in the phenomenological and philosophical orders? Indeed, to have based his belief not only on the

"coherence" of the vision that these texts inspired ("coherence" generally to his mind the surest indicator of the truth) but also on its compatibility with the phenomenological order and its power to give a
satisfactory answer to mankind's existential predicament, is to seem to
beg the question. Because of Teilhard's reversion to such admitted
criteria, otherwise admiring friends found it impossible to follow his vision to its conclusion. Also, more vocal critics have since found ready
grounds for deeming his work "theological science-fiction." On these
bases even some theologians and believing philosophers who would
otherwise be inclined to adopt his synthesis (at least with qualifications)
relegate it to the realm of "mysticism."

D. UNFINISHED QUESTIONS

Teilhard's ultimate answer to these problems was to attempt to
evade what he considered to be the unwarranted disjunction between
revelation understood as a "fact" (given and enshrined in the past) and
revelation as a "process" (and as such, highly dependent on the continued growth of the "noosphere"). In effect, Teilhard's solution and ultimate answer to his critics was not an appeal to some other criteria
beyond those he had already adduced (phenomenological consistency,
existential motive-power, and ultimate coherence), but rather a reassertion of these criteria on a more strictly theological level. From this
standpoint, the Incarnation (connected with man's appearance, i.e.,
"biogenesis" on its "hominized" level) and subsequent doctrinal development (a clear instance of "noogenesis" in the theological realm)
combine to suggest a view of revelation that is clearly processive in
nature—a "Christogenesis" of both the ontological and the noetic orders.

That such a practical identification of revelation with the Incarnation
presents difficulties, practical as well as theoretical, cannot be gainsaid.
Just as the concept of a continuing Incarnation presents real difficulties
in regard to the distinction between the unique subject of the hypostatic union and those who become assimilated to it, so an analogous situation exists when a continuing revelation is spoken of in which the "literal sense" of the scriptural texts only yields its fullest meaning in consonance with the reflective evolution of man. Likewise, because of the
parallel relationship it bears to the Incarnation, this same concept of
revelation entails much the same difficulty as the reconciliation of the
more traditional understanding of the pleroma (as being the fullness of
God's self-manifestation, understood in the passive sense) with a more
active understanding of it (as waiting upon evolution for its completion,
which in some way "completes" God).

On the other hand, Teilhard's concept of a revelation continuing in process (under the form of "amorization") beyond the parousial completion of the Incarnation might prove fruitful for an intensified rapport between the "process theologians" and the more traditional Christians who see all things, including revelation, as coming to absolute completion with the Second Coming of Christ. Perhaps some terminological refinements similar to the process theologians' *panentheism* as a replacement for Teilhard's strong (but none too happy) insistence upon Christianity as "the true pantheism" might be in order here as well. But these possibilities suggest a deeper problem, that of which Teilhard's few vague mentions of "Trinitization" as correlative to "pleromization" give some hint: the lack of development of a theological "pneumatology" in Teilhard's synthesis, a lack that some of his disciples might be well advised to remedy. Certainly the transition from a "hyper-physics" that holds all energy to be ultimately "psychic" in nature and the ultimate "Weltstoff" to be "spirit-matter," to a more fully elaborated theology of the Holy Spirit in conjunction with the Incarnation has possibilities. Not the least of these considerations would promise a further understanding of "revelation in process." But this leads to another point.

E. MYSTICISM AND ULTIMATE COHERENCE

In Teilhard's notes and essays the phenomenon of mysticism is so frequently associated with revelation that one gets the impression that he would have considered being judged a mystic more a compliment than a condescending epithet. Indeed, the logic of his own synthesis would lead to this assessment of the situation. For if human awareness is the most obvious measure of progress in evolution, then the highest forms of awareness would have to be considered the highest indication of progress, particularly when this awareness becomes not just an individual activity but is shared by a whole community—and even more as it becomes the common property of the whole developing "noosphere." If research is, as Teilhard maintained, the highest form of human activity, then mysticism is the highest form of research. Such a view —which seems to have been genuinely held by Teilhard, besides giving the lie to such misconceptions of Teilhardian thought as being eminently "activist" in orientation as opposed to a more "contemplative" view of the human vocation—would raise serious doubts about the validity of any theology or philosophy that is not decisively "mystical" in its approach to reality. If anything can be deduced from Teilhard's conclusions about the nature of religion, it is that all religious impulses in mankind are "holistic" in their motivation, ultimately tending to a unitive view of nature and even a "pantheistic" understanding of God.

Aside from the fact that such a view of the human "mystical current" has obvious bearings on the subject of revelation understood from the viewpoint of its relationship to the collective development of human awareness, it at the same time calls into question the ultimate adequacy of all the "pure" sciences to the extent that they content themselves with merely analytic deduction. To the extent that any science, natural or otherwise, ignores the synthetic trends of man's mystical aspirations, there is constant danger that the meaning of the part will be lost in its relationship to the whole, or that the whole will be simply ignored.

This may be the case with those scientists who are unable to follow Teilhard's conclusions to his "Christogenic" vision of Omega, although it must be remembered that faith is a gift that does not automatically result from the quest that many of these same men have begun. It may be that either the inherited dualism of the classical past or the present philosophical hypochondria of existentialism has turned today's theologians and philosophers from seeking a total coherence in their view of reality. But if coherence remains the characteristic of truth in any particular branch of science, the quest for total coherence or consistency in our view of reality cannot be set aside much longer. The search for a new means of "noetic integration"—Julian Huxley's phrase—cannot be delayed except at the risk of promoting even greater human alienation than now exists.

What then of Teilhard's contribution to this quest? Undoubtedly it suffers methodological gaps. But this quest, as this study has shown, demands a readiness to break with the careful limitations of many well-established disciplines, even in the sacred sciences of theology and biblical interpretation, in the interest of greater coherence in the whole and greater consistency among the parts. That such readiness can be achieved only by accepting mystical intuitions of possibilities may seem to some an incalculable risk. But for one who sees the intuition of mysticism confirmed by revelation, the risk is small indeed. For revelation is no mere record of the past that determines the possibilities of the present world, nor is it a set of predictions about another world that will exist far beyond our own. The Incarnation has made such a dichotomous view of revelation untenable. Revelation is, in the final analysis, the completion of "Christogenesis"; and "Christogenesis" is, conversely, the revelation of that Incarnate God who gives all things their coherence and in whom all things shall find their completion—the Christ "in whom all things hold together," the God in whom "all shall become all."

Appendix A

A LIST OF BIBLICAL QUOTATIONS AND ALLUSIONS
AS FOUND IN THE WORKS OF TEILHARD DE CHARDIN[1]
WITH AN INDEX OF REFRENCES TO THIS STUDY[2]

Gen. 1-3	*Dictionnaire apologétique de la foi catholique* 2:502ff.	pp. *234–36*
	10:49-50 (*C&E*, pp. 36-37)	
	10:61-63 (*C&E*, pp. 45-47)	
	10:98-100 (*C&E*, pp. 79-81)	p. *245*;
	10:190-91 (*C&E*, p. 162)	cf. also pp.
	10:222-26 (*C&E*, pp. 190-93)	46–50, 98–99,
		105, 239
Gen. 1:28	**7:72 (*AE*, p. 66)	p. *47*
	**11:195 (*TF*, p. 177)	
Gen. 2:7	3:219 (*VP*, p. 156)	p. *49*
Gen. 11:1-9	5:238 (*FM*, p. 187)	p. 38
Gen 32:23f.	**Ecrits, p. 5 (*WTW*, p. 14)	pp. 38, 40
	Ecrits, p. 51 (*WTW*, p. 62)	
	5:238 (*FM*, p. 187)	
Exod. 20:1-17	**11:85 (*TF*, p. 81)	

---

1. Center column: ** *designates a direct quotation*, * an indirect quotation. All unmarked references are to "allusions" or other citations. (For working definitions of the above terms, see the extensive note at the beginning of Appendix B.) All the published *Ouevres de Teilhard de Chardin* (with the exception of Vol. 12, i.e., *Ecrits*) will be listed simply by their French volume number with the corresponding English reference in parentheses (see bibliography for the title abbreviations). Unpublished essays are designated by their Fondation Teilhard de Chardin archive manuscript number ("*T.A. #*") whenever possible.
2. Right-hand column: the italicized page numbers give reference to quoted examples of Teilhard's use of Scriptures. Those not italicized refer to further discussion of these same scriptural passages in the course of this study.

Matt. 10:39   **Ecrits*, p. 113 (*WTW*, p. 94)   p. *40*
   (Luke 9:23;   **Ecrits*, p. 130 (*WTW*, p. 112)   p. *78*
   17:33)
   (John 12:25)
Matt. 13:52   **11:106 (*TF*, p. 97)
                  **T.A. #92, p. 10   p. *63*

Matt. 14:27-31   **Ecrits*, p. 307 (*WTW*, p. 226)   pp. *38, 40*
   (John 6:10)   **4:171 (*DM*, p. 117)   pp. *38, 43*

Matt. 15:13   *Ecrits*, p. 289 (*WTW*, p. 209)
   (John 15:2)
Matt. 16:15-16   **10:289 (*C&E*, p. 241)   p. *45*

Matt. 16:24   **Ecrits*, p. 130 (*WTW*, p. 111)   p. *78*
   (Mark 8:34)   *Ecrits*, p. 162 (*WTW*, p. 144)
   (Luke 9:23)   10:260 (*C&E*, p. 219)

Matt. 18:7   **10:43 (*C&E*, p. 33)
   (Luke 17:1)   **10:53(*C&E*, p. 40)
                  **4:89 (*DM*, p. 58)   pp. *32, 174*
                  **1:346 (*PM*, p. 312)
                  **10:175 (*C&E*, p. 150)
                  **10:227 (*C&E*, p. 195)   p. 49
                  **11:213 (*TF*, p. 198)   p. 49

Matt. 19:12   **Ecrits*, p. 47 (*WTW*, p. 58)   pp. *36, 111, 156*
                  **Ecrits*, p. 167 (*WTW*, p. 149)   p. *37*

Matt. 22:14   **Ecrits*, p. 349 (*WTW*, 265)   p. *72*

Matt. 24:12   *10:172 (*C&E*, p. 147)   p. 69

Matt. 24:27-28,   **4:196 (*DM*, p. 134)   p. *69*
   24:27-39   9:113 (*S&C*, p. 84)   p. *70*

Mark 9:25   **4:171 (*DM*, p. 117)   pp. *38, 43*

Luke 1:28   **9:43 (*S&C*, p. 18)

Luke 1:34   **4:85 (*DM*, p. 55)

Luke 1:45   **4:168 (*DM*, p. 114)

Luke 2:29   **Ecrits*, p. 129 (*WTW*, p. 111)

Luke 2:34   **Ecrits*, p. 232 (*WTW*, p. 190)

Luke 8:30	*Ecrits*, p. 116 (*WTW*, p. 97)	p. *47*
	Ecrits, p. 223 (*WTW*, p. 181)	p. *47*
Luke 10:27	**Ecrits*, p. 275	
(Deut. 6:5)	**10:215 (*C&E*, p. 184)	pp. *75–76*
	*13:116	p. 76
Luke 11:42	**Ecrits*, p. 401 (*WTW*, pp. 290-91)	
	Ecrits, p. 442 (*HU*, p. 65)	
	4:147 (*DM*, p. 99)	p. *75*
Luke 12:33	**13:27	pp. *32, 67*
Luke 16:26	**10:81 (*C&E*, p. 65)	
Luke 18:41	**4:164 (*DM*, p. 111)	pp. *38, 43*
Luke 19:17	9:60 (*S&C*, p. 34)	
John 1:1	*Ecrits*, p. 124 (*WTW*, p. 106)	
(Col. 1:15)	10:210-11 (*C&E*, pp. 180-81)	
	9:239 (*S&C*, p. 189)	pp. 210, 213,
		241, 284
John 1:9	7:429 (*AE*, p. 406)	
John 1:14[3]	**Ecrits*, p. 40 (*WTW*, p. 50)	pp. 35, *53*,
		109, 214
John 1:29	*10:170 (*C&E*, p. 145)	p. *79*
John 2:1-12	*Ecrits*, p. 349 (*WTW*, p. 264)	p. *60*
John 2:4; 12:	*4:95 (*DM*, p. 62)	
27; 13:1; 17:1		
John 3:10	**10:164 (*C&E*, p. 139)	
John 3:16	**4:11 (*DM*, p. 5)	p. *40*
John 3:21	9:42 (*S&C*, p. 17)	
John 3:30	**Ecrits*, p. 346 (*WTW*, p. 261)	
	**9:101 (*S&C*, p. 72)	
	**4:93 (*DM*, p. 61)	
John 4:14f.	**Ecrits*, p. 41 (*WTW*, p. 52)	p. *110*

3. Because of the large number of references to "The Incarnate Word" in Teilhard's works, no effort has been made to list all these references. For a general treatment of this subject, see chap. 2§D, of this study also chap. 6§B above.

John 4:34	**4:174 (*DM*, p. 119)	p. *215*[4]
John 5:17	**4:165 (*DM*, p. 112)	p. *70*
John 6:20	**4:77 (*DM*, p. 50)	p. *43*
(Matt. 14 :27)	**4:172 (*DM*, p. 117)	p. *43*
(Mark 6:50)		
John 6:44	*Ecrits*, p. 167 (*WTW*, p. 149)	pp. *112*, 215
	**4:164 (*DM*, p. 111)	
John 6:48f.	10:23-4 (*C&E*, pp. 16-18)	pp. 61, *121–22*
John 8:12; 9:5	9:60 (*S&C*, p. 34)	p. *166*
John 8:32	*Ecrits*, p. 49 (*WTW*, p. 59)	p. *46*
	**11:37 (*TF*, p. 31)	
John 11:25	9:60 (*S&C*, p. 34)	p. *166*
John 11:51-52	*Ecrits*, p. 124 (*WTW*, p. 106)	pp. *53–54*, 112
John 12:24	*Ecrits*, p. 131 (*WTW*, p. 113)	p. *78*
John 12:32	**Ecrits*, p. 339 (*WTW*, p. 254)	pp. *44, 116*
John 13:34; 15:12	**6:189 (*HE*, p. 153)	
	6:297 (*VP*, p. 211)	
	**11:37 (*TF*, p. 31)	
	**7:26 (*AE*, p. 20)	
	**7:58 (*AE*, pp. 51-2)	
	**5:124 (*FM*, p. 95)	pp. *75*
John 14:2	**4:142 (*DM*, p. 96)	p. *70*
	**4:180 (*DM*, p. 123)	p. *70*
John 14:6	**10:21 (*C&E*, p. 15)	p. *120*
	10:196 (*C&E*, p. 168)	p. *76*
John 14:9	**10:26 (*C&E*, p. 20)	pp. *56, 125*
John 15:1-6	*Ecrits*, p. 40 (*WTW*, p. 50)	p. *109*
	Ecrits, p. 131 (*WTW*, p. 113)	p. *112*
	Ecrits, p. 289 (*WTW*, p. 209)	p. *72*
	10:21 (*C&E*, p. 15)	pp. 56, *120*
John 15:10	**4:147 (*DM*, p. 99)	p. *75*

4. While they do not appear in his essays, special attention is called to Teilhard's comments on a number of verses from chapters 1 to 7 of St. John's Gospel. See chap. 6§B, 1 above.

John 17:21	**Ecrits*, p. 113 (*WTW*, p. 94)	pp. *40*, 211–12
	**Ecrits*, p. 131 (*WTW*, p. 113)	pp.*74*, *112*, *212*
	6:192 (*HE*, p. 155)	
John 20:29	**Hymne de l'Univers*, p. 34 (*HU*, p. 34)	
John 21:12-3	10:167 (*C&E*, p. 142)	
Acts 17:23	**5:37 (*FM*, p. 24)	p. *45*
Acts 17:27	**Hymne de l'Univers*, p. 24 (*HU*, p. 25)	
	**9:99 (*S&C*, p. 71)	
	**4:164 (*DM*, p. 111)	p. *45*
Acts 17:28	**Ecrits*, p. 37 (*WTW*, p. 47)	pp. *52*, 136
	**Ecrits*, p. 137 (*WTW*, p. 117)	p. 40
	**Ecrits*, p. 293 (*WTW*, p. 214)	p. *52*
	**Ecrits*, p. 342 (*WTW*, p. 257)	p. *116*
	**10:91 (*C&E*, p. 75)	pp. *52*, *168*
	**9:100 (*S&C*, p. 71)	p. *52*
	**4:23 (*DM*, p. 13)	
	**4:134 (*DM*, 89)	p. *52*
	**4:147 (*DM*, p. 99)	
	**4:154 (*DM*, p. 104)	p. *52*
Rom. 5:12	**10:53 (*C&E*, p. 39)	pp. *48–49*
	10:64 (*C&E*, p. 48)	
	**10:100 (*C&E*, p. 81)	pp. *48*, *92*, *225*, *251*
Rom. 5:15-21	10:49 (*C&E*, *p. 36*)	pp. *127–29*
(1 Cor 15:	10:52 (*C&E*, p. 39)	
21-22)	9:109 (*S&C*, p. 80)	
	10:222 (*C&E*, p. 190)	pp. *49*, 144
Rom. 6:9	**10:57 (*C&E*, p. 44)	p. *65*
	10:281-82 (*C&E*, p. 235)	
Rom. 7:24	**Ecrits*, p. 428	p. *87*
Rom. 8:22	**Ecrits*, p. 54 (*WTW*, p. 66)	pp. *46*, *84*
	**Ecrits*, p. 286 (*WTW*, p. 206)	p. *85*
	Ecrits, p. 295 (*WTW*, p. 215)	
	Ecrits, p. 335 (*WTW*, p. 250)	p. *116*n.35
	Ecrits, p. 425	p. *85*
	**10:69 (*C&E*, p. 53)	pp.*70*, *87*
	**10:88 (*C&E*, p. 72)	p. 88

	3:142 (*VP*, p. 102)	p. *89*
	3:192 (*VP*, p. 137)	
	**4:50 (*DM*, p. 31)	pp. *88, 172, 249*n. 64
	T.A. # 92, p. 10	p. *90*
	**9:162 (*S&C*, p. 123)	p. *89*
	1:347 (*PM*, p. 312)	pp. *49, 91*
	7:282 (*AE*, p. 272)	p. *92*
Rom. 8:28	**Ecrits*, p. 57 (*WTW*, p. 69)	p. *32*
	**Ecrits*, p. 191 (*WTW*, p. 170)	p. *32*
	**Ecrits*, p. 320 (*WTW*, p. 238)	p. *33*
	**Ecrits*, p. 343 (*WTW*, p. 258)	pp. *33, 116*
	**10:45 (*C&E*, p. 35)	p. *164*
	**9:101 (*S&C*, p. 73)	
	**4:85 (*DM*, p. 55)	
	**4:90 (*DM*, p. 58)	
	**4:150 (*DM*, p. 101)	pp. *33, 50, 174*
	7:97 (*AE*, p. 90)	
Rom. 8:38	*4:156 (*DM*, p. 106)	
(Eph. 3:18)	10:107 (*C&E*, p. 89)	
Rom. 10:17	**Ecrits*, p. 341 (*WTW*, p. 256)	pp. *44–45*
Rom. 14:7-8	*Ecrits*, p. 275	p. *114*
(Gal. 2:20)	*Ecrits*, p. 344 (*WTW*, p. 259)	pp. *116–17*
(Phil. 1:20)	9:102 (*S&C*, p. 74)	
(1 Thess. 5:10)	*4:133 (*DM*, p. 89)	p. *58*
1 Cor. 3:32- 23	*4:41 (*DM*, p. 25)	pp. *211–12*
1 Cor. 4:7	**4:75 (*DM*, p. 47)	
1 Cor. 7:9(38)	**Ecrits*, p. 258 (*WTW*, p. 197)	
1 Cor.7:25- 29	11:83 (*TF* p. 77)	
1 Cor.10:16-17	*Ecrits*, pp. 375-76	p. *126*
	10:23-24 (*C&E*, p. 17)	p. *119*
1 Cor. 10:23	*11:85 (*TF*, p. 80)	
1 Cor. 10:31	**4:33 (*DM*, p. 18)	
	**4:57 (*DM*, p. 35)	

1 Cor.11:24-25[5]	*Ecrits*, p. 164 (*WTW*, p. 146)	p. *112*
(Matt. 26:27-28)	*Ecrits*, p. 287 (*WTW*, p. 208)	p. *114*
(Mark 14:22-24)	*Ecrits*, p. 289 (*WTW*, p. 210)	
(Luke 22:19-20)	*Ecrits*, p. 375	
	Ecrits, p. 441 (*HU*, p. 23)	
	*10:90 (*C&E*, p. 73)	
	Hymne de l'Univers, pp. 22,31	
	(*HU*, pp. 23,32)	
	*9:94 (*S&C*, p. 65)	p. *56*
	*4:95 (*DM*, p. 66)	p. *73*
	*4:150 (*DM*, p. 102)	
	*4:172 (*DM*, p. 117)	
	*4:181 (*DM*, p. 124)	
1 Cor. 12:15-19	*6:64 (*HE*, p. 50)	pp. *131–32*
1 Cor. 13:12	**4:155 (*DM*, p. 105)	p. *73*
1 Cor. 15:23f.	*9:113 (*S&C*, p. 85)	p. 57
1 Cor. 15:28	*Ecrits*, p. 6 (*WTW*, p. 15)	p. *62*
	**10:91 (*C&E*, p. 75)	
	**9:113-14 (*S&C*, p. 85)	pp. *170, 171*
	**4:139 (*DM*, p. 94)	p. *63*
	**11:59 (*TF*, p. 54)	pp. *63–64,174,175*
	**T.A. # 92, p. 10	p. *63*
	*T.A. # 118, p. 2	p. 176
	**6:87 (*HE*, p. 69)	
	6:103 (*HE*, p. 83)	
	**1:327 (*PM*, p. 294)	p. *181*
	*1:344 (*PM*, p. 310)	
	11:106 (*TF*, p. 97)	p. *182*
	**10:180 (*C&E*, p. 151)	pp. *74, 182, 183*
	**10:200 (*C&E*, p. 171)	p. *64*
	*7:230 (*AE*, pp. 221-22)	
	**7:231-32 (*AE*, p. 223)	pp. *64, 189*
	**7:234 (*AE*, p. 225)	p. *190*
	13:65-66	pp. *190–91*
	**11:228 (*TF*, p. 210)	p. *190*;
		cf. also pp. 80,
		140, 174–84,
		197, 205–6,
		219–20
1 Cor. 15:55	*9:92 (*S&C*, p. 63)	p. 77

5. See n. 8 on page 31 of this study.

2 Cor. 5:2   **11:59 (*TF*, p. 53)

2 Cor. 5:4   **4:122 (*DM*, p. 82)   p. *68*

2 Cor. 11:23   **4:62 (*DM*, p. 39)
                 **9:162 (*S&C*, p. 123)
                 **11:116 (*TF*, p. 104)
                 **9:287 (*S&C*, p. 218)

Gal. 2:20   **Ecrits, p. 344, (*WTW*, p. 259)   pp. *57, 117*

Gal. 3:27   9:153 (*S&C*, p. 116)

Eph. 1:4-5   6:138 (*HE*, p. 111)

Eph. 1:10   9:60 (*S&C*, p. 34)   p. 166
                 *9:140 (*S&C*, p. 107)   p. *134*
                 **9:211 (*S&C*, p. 166)   p. *35*
                 7:272 (*AE*, p. 264)   pp. 104, 133–34
                 10:196 (*C&E*, p. 168)   p. 76
                 **10:290 (*C&E*, p. 242)   cf. also pp. 139,
                                                        148, 153, 203,
                                                        219

Eph. 1:22   *Ecrits, p. 40 (*WTW*, p. 50)   pp. *109*, 148–50

Eph. 1:23   *Ecrits*, pp. 40–41 (*WTW*, pp. 50–51)   pp. *109*, 148–50
(Eph. 4:10)   9:60 (*S&C*, p. 34)   p. *166*
(Col. 2:10)   4:43 (*DM*, p. 26)   p. 136
                 **T.A.* #92, IV, p. 10   p. *175*
                 9:211 (*S&C*, p. 166)   p. *35*; see pp.
                                                        139–40, 200, 202–3,
                                                             205, 210

Eph. 3:18   **9:140 (*S&C*, p. 107)   p. *140*

Eph. 4:9-10   *Ecrits*, p. 273
                 **10:52 (*C&E*, p. 39)   p. *127*
                 **10:56 (*C&E*, p. 43)
                 **9:62 (*S&C*, p. 36)
                 **10:88 (*C&E*, p. 71)   pp. *55*, 88
                 9:82 (*S&C*, p. 54)   pp. 58–60
                 **9:92 (*S&C*, p. 64)   pp. *78, 138, 170*
                 **4:50 (*DM*, p. 30)
                 **4:149 (*DM*, p. 101)   p. *173*
                 **11:79 (*TF*, p. 73)
                 **11:102 (*TF*, p. 97)   p. *263*
                 **11:117 (*TF*, p. 106)   see also pp. 55,
                                                           140, 165, 197

	**4:149 (*DM*, p. 101)	p. *173*
	**11:60 (*TF*, p. 55)	
	**9:153 (*S&C*, p. 117)	
	*10:107 (*C&E*, p. 88)	
	10:121 (*C&E*, p. 100)	
	*5:123 (*FM*, p. 94)	
	**10:168 (*C&E*, p. 143)	p. *264*
	*9:211 (*S&C*, p. 167)	p. *35*
	**10:210 (*C&E*, p. 179)	
	*Sur le Regne de Dieu" (*T.A.*), p. 3	
	**10:223 (*C&E*, pp. 190-91)	pp. *39, 49*
	**10:281 (*C&E*, p. 235)	p. *66*
	**11:236 (*TF*, p. 215)	
	**7:428 (*AE*, p. 407)	
	**13:107	pp. *194–95*, see also pp. *136,137*
Col. 1:18	*Ecrits*, p. 40 (*WTW*, p. 50)	p. *109*
	*Ecrits, p. 339 (*WTW*, p. 254)	p. *116*
	*Ecrits, p. 408 (*WTW*, p. 297)	
	**10:21 (*C&E*, p. 15)	pp. *58, 120, 133*
	*10:107 (*C&E*, p. 88)	
	9:87, (*S&C*, p. 58)	
	*9:43 (*S&C*, p. 26)	pp. *130–31*
	**9:211 (*S&C*, p. 167)	p. *35*
	7:288 (*AE*, p. 277)	
	10:196 (*C&E*, p. 168)	p. *77*; see also pp. *137, 139, 150, 155*
Col. 1:19[6]	*Ecrits*, p. 273-74	p. *156*
(Col. 2:10)	*Ecrits*, pp. 286, 291, 299	pp. *156–57*
(Eph. 4:13)	(*WTW*, pp. 211, 214, 220)	
	Ecrits, pp. 401, 411, 412-3	pp. *158–59*
	(*WTW*, pp. 290-91, 300, 301-2)	
	10:23, 23, 24, (*C&E*, pp. 16-17)	pp. *121,139,160–61*
	9:60 (*S&C*, p. 34)	p. *166*
	10:84, 85, 86, 89 (*C&E*, pp. 67, 69, 70)	pp. *166–67*
	9:88 (*S&C*, p. 59)	p. *169*
	4, esp. pp. 43, 50, 153	
	(*DM*, pp. 25, 85, 130)	pp. *172, 174*
	11:59 (*TF*, p. 54)	p. *175*
	10:102 (*C&E*, p. 83)	pp. *176–77*

6. The "Pleroma"; while it is not feasible, for reasons of space, to list all the references to this single word that Teilhard used so often, the principal examples utilized in the course of this study are listed here under Col. 1:19, except where more definite sources could be located. Accordingly, none of the above references are classed as "quotations," nor are all of them listed separately (their are some eight allusions to or mentions of the Pleroma alone in *Le Milieu divin*).

1 John 5:4	**4:177 (*DM*, p. 121)	p. *44*
Apoc. 1:8(a)[7] (21:1; 22:13)	**Ecrits, p. 116 (*WTW*, p. 98) **9:39 (*S&C*, p. 14) **9:60 (*S&C*, p. 34) **9:163 (*S&C*, p. 124) **6:113 (*HE*, p. 91)	pp. *50–51* p. *166* p. *132;* see also pp. 31, 136, 216–19
Apoc. 1:8(b)	**Ecrits, p. 42 (*WTW*, p. 52) *4:202 (*DM*, p. 138)	pp. *51, 110*
Apoc. 14:4	**11:70 (*TF*, p. 63)	
Apoc. 14:13	**4:41 (*DM*, p. 24)	p. *68*
Apoc. 21:13	**10:84 (*C&E*, p. 67) **9:103 (*S&C*, p. 75)	p. *68* p. *68*
Apoc. 22:20	4:197 (*DM*, p. 135)	pp. *71, 174*

7. In addition to the five short quotations of the phrase *Alpha and Omega* listed above, there are at least eighteen occasions on which the phrase *Christ-Omega* occurs in Teilhard's workds, but they are not listed here.

Appendix B

GENERAL STATISTICS:
Scriptural Quotations, Allusions, and References in
the Works of Teilhard de Chardin

Introductory note:

In the preceding list of quotations and allusions to Sacred Scripture (Appendix A), as well as in the following table of statistics, the following definitions have been adopted for the purposes of this study:

Explicit (direct Quotation—the verbatim (actual or intended) repetition of words, phrases, or sentences, either with direct source references or without. Usually accompanied by quotation marks,˙ although in Teilhard's works, italics (underlining in the original manuscripts) occasionally replace quotation marks for this purpose.

Implicit (indirect) Quotation—not the exact words of a writer or speaker, but a summary of them. Usually written without quotation marks. In Teilhard's works, the use of italics or underlining is generally found in this situation.

Allusion—"a passing or casual reference; an incidental mention of something either directly or by implication" (*Random House Dictionary*). According to *The Oxford Dictionary of the English Language* and *The Oxford Etymological Dictionary of the English Language*, an "allusion" in its proper sense implies a "play on words" of some sort in which the object of reference is not specifically mentioned. However, for the purposes of this study the former (and broader) definition of an allusion as "a passing or casual reference" has been used, in some cases to specify a particular passage from which Teilhard appears to have drawn inspiration, or in other cases to serve as a point of reference for specifically biblical words (such as "Pleroma") that play a major part in this study. Some other such "allusions," such as those to "The Word" or "The Incarnate Word," or the Pauline phrase *in Christo Jesu*, however, were not considered so crucial to this study and were therefore omitted from consideration in these tables.

Reference—a source of identification, whether general (mention of an author or book) or exact (by listing of page or chapter and verse number).

Citation—a passing reference to an author or book by way of invoking authority. (N.B. This term is occasionally used in this study to designate any quotation or reference.)

Book or Author	Total No. of Texts	Explicit Quotes	Implicit Quotes	Allusions or other References	Total No. of Citations
Old Testament	15	12	3	14	29
Matthew	21	28	5	3	36
Mark	1	1			1
Luke	12	11	1	5	17
John	31	25	4	19	48
Gospels total	65	65	10	27	102
Acts	5	14			14
Paul	58	89	47	94	231
Hebrews	1	2		1	3
Cath. Epistles	4	3		1	4
Apocalypse	6	10	1	1	12
Acts. ⎫ Epist. ⎬ *total* Apoc. ⎭	70	105	48	97	249
New Testament (total)	139	189	58	114	351
Grand Total	156	182	61	138	380

Appendix C

A LIST OF EXPLICIT REFERENCES TO ST. PAUL
AND TO ST. JOHN[1] IN THE WORKS OF TEILHARD DE CHAR-
DIN
AS THEY APPEAR IN THIS STUDY[2]

*Ecrits,	p. 39 (WTW, p.50)	p.109
*Ecrits,	p.48 (WTW, p.58)	p.111
*Ecrits,	p.196 (WTW, p.175)	pp.113, 244
*Ecrits,	p.335 (WTW, p.250)	p.116 n.35
10:22	(C&E, p.16)	pp.60, 160
10:52-53	(C&E, pp.39-40)	pp.48, 92, 93
10:88	(C&E, p.72)	p.167
10:91	(C&E, p.75)	p.63
*9:82	(S&C, p.54)	pp.58, 137
9:83	(S&C, p.54)	p.130
9:84	(S&C, p.55)	p.130
9:113	(S&C, p.85)	pp.57, 171
4:32	(DM, p.18)	p.57
4:43	(DM, p.26)	pp.61, 130-31
4:50	(DM, pp.30-31)	p.249 n.64
4:141	(DM, p.95)	p.131
*4:148	(DM, p.100)	p.173
4:150	(DM, p.101)	pp.131, 247
TA#92,	IV, p.10	p.63
11:54	(TF, p.48)	pp.90, 100
11:59	(TF, pp.53-54)	pp.64, 175
11:60	(TF, p.55)	p.175
11:62	(TF, p.57)	p.61
11:63	(TF, p.58)	p.90

1. The asterisks in the first column denote double references, to both St. Paul and St. John. Entries without the asterisk are to St. Paul alone. Entries begin with *Oeuvres de Teilhard de Chardin* volume number unless otherwise indicated.
2. Page numbers referring to this study are in the right-hand column. See also pp. 29 and 208 above and the general index to the *Oeuvres de Teilhard de Chardin*, as compiled by M. Paul L'Archevêque, 13:250, 252.

*TA#*118,	p.2	p.176
6:64	(*HE*, p.50)	p.131
10:100	(*C&E*, p.81)	pp.48, 245
1:327	(*PM*, p.293)	p.180
11:107	(*TF*, p.98)	p.263
11:116	(*TF*, p.104)	p.61
9:210	(*S&C*, p.165)	p.241
9:211	(*S&C*, p.166)	p.246
10:199-200	(*C&E*, p.151)	pp.64, 184
10:223	(*C&E*, p.190)	p.39
*TA#*117		p.62 n.95
11:214	(*TF*, p.198)	p.188
13:65		p.190
7:272	(*AE*, p.264)	p.104
*10:271	(*C&E*, p.227)	p.286
10:290	(*C&E*, p.242)	p.134
13:107		p.194

Appendix D

SELECTED TEXTS OF UNPUBLISHED MATERIAL:
ESSAYS AND CORRESPONDENCE
OF TEILHARD DE CHARDIN

1. Excerpts from unpublished essays and notes arranged chronologically.

a. From "Notes et esquisses," Aug. 15, 1917 (Cahier 3, pp. 20-21):[1]

Historiquement, la conception paradisiaque (paradis terrestre) paraît *extra-historique*, incompatible avec le monde géologique, qui a toujours été un monde de souffrance et de mort. La mort et la concupiscense sont des *stigmates évolutifs* des réalités naturelles (non secondaires ou intrusives).

Il reste que, historiquement, la vue Paulinienne, basée sur une chute historique et palpable, reste "en l'air,"—*vraie*, mais *indémontrable* (et ceci, simplement du fait de la théologie la plus classique, dès lors qu'on admet que la mort et la concupiscense sont naturelles, donc non intrusives, comme St Paul le pensait humainement) (La conception du nudatum et du spoliatum est très adroite, mais franchement, ne devait pas être dans l'esprit de St. Paul. (*Elle concilie un dualisme primitif*) dans une synthèse secondaire.

Ceci, qui doit être *envisagé franchement* et loyalement, amène à regarder l'Evolution du dogme sous une forme très profonde; non pas seulement dans la transformation des formules, mais dans la naissance des dogmes. Il y a une très grande part psychologique. La théorie de

---

1. The above passages contain many abbreviations; however, the full spellings have been given according to the transcriptions provided by the Fondation Teilhard de Chardin, Paris, prior to more recent publication.

la Rédemption est née d'une "fausse" interprétation du problème du Mal . . . (En ce sens que St Paul subjectivé, considérait la mort comme intrusive essentialiter, (non solum historicé).

Et cependant nous aimons le même Christ que St Paul, et ce Christ est dans le plénitude du XX siècle de Vie et d'amour! . . .

b. From "Essai d'integration de l'homme dans l'Univers" Dec. 10, 1930. The fourth of four conferences given at Chadefaud to the "Groupe Marcel Legaut". (T.A. #92, p. 10):

Revenons à St. Paul; rappelons-nous que le surnaturel se nourrit de tout, et acceptons jusqu'au bout ces magnifiques perspectives d'après lesquelles le Christ de St. Paul nous apparaît comme Celui *en qui tout est créé* et Celui en qui le monde entier, avec toute sa *profondeur, sa largeur*, sa grandeur, *sa longueur*, son physique, son spirituel, atteint et prend sa consistance.

Nous entrevoyons alors que dans ce christianisme, grâce à l'influence du Christ, nous trouvons les deux éléments requis par le sens humain; d'abord une unité totale et profonde, unité organique conservant néanmoins les relations individuelles, c'est-à-dire présentant en soi ces perfections dans l'unité que déforme le panthéisme: *"Le Christ est celui en qui tout deveient tout"* (St Paul). De même, dans cette formation plénière, à partir du Christ, de tout, nous trouvons à satisfaire notre besoin d'optimisme, de création. Nous avons tout ce qu'il faut dans nos traditions et nos écritures chrétiennes pour avoir doit, en tant que chrétiens, de croire que le monde, quelle que soit du reste la part d'expiation qu'il demande, est avant tout une oeuvre de création continuée dans le Christ. Pourquoi ne pas revenir à ces grandes sources pronfondes, à la mesure des besoins présents, *"nova et vetera"* comme dit l'évangile?

Si nous accomplissons cette transformation de la notion d'Incarnation, de Christ, de Communion, qui est au fond le grand travail d'une création en union avec Dieu, . . . Nous entrevoyons que dans une Incarnation bien comprise comme création continue de tout l'Univers, s'il y a toujours place pour l'expiation de la faute, il y a place aussi pour l'effort laborieux et la progrès. Ainsi la croix, expression de la souffrance rédemptrice, est, d'abord, le symbole de l'effort créateur, mais laborieux, d'une humanité qui monte vers le Christ qui l'attend.

c. From "Occident et Orient: La Mystique de la Personalité" (1933) from notes taken by Jean Bousquet. (T.A. #118, p. 2):

L'attitude de la mystique occidentale a toutes les vertus du panthéisme oriental sans en avoir les inconvénients; la réunion en Dieu ne se fait pas par évanouissement, mais par épuration et raffinement de ce qu'il y a de plus personnel et de plus clair dans les choses: la vertu du panthéisme est réalisée, Dieu est tout en toutes choses, et elle est d'autant plus grande qu'elles sont unifiées dans leur plus pure essence. Pour St. Paul, par exemple, le figure du monde n'est autre chose qu'une création qui gravite autour du Christ, qui est descendu dans le monde comme dans un grand baptême: il y prend l'essence du monde, les choses les plus pures, les concentre en lui et revient ainsi à son Père.

2. Excepts from Teilhard's correspondence (arranged alphabetically by recipient)

a. To Claude Cuénot (Feb. 15, 1955) (*T.A.* Correspondance "C-F" paragraph 4 and following):

"Personnellement, je répète, j'ai l'impression que le concept de création-efficiente est "enfantine". J'ajouterais qu'il me paraît stérile et dangereux, dans la mesure où il dévalorise le Monde (excès d'extrinsécité et de gratuité du Cosmique par rapport à Dieu) et où il rend inexplicable le Mal (dont toute la responsabilité, finalement retombe sur Dieu,—dans la mesure où celui-ci est regardé comme *absolument libre* de créer ou de ne pas créer).

Par contre, je suis grandement attiré par le concept de *création-informante*, (Dieu n'étant plus conçu par analogie avec une Cause efficiente, mais avec une *cause formelle*). Ici la métaphysique classique s'indigne: soit parce que, dit-elle, un tel mode de création entraînerait l'identité du Créateur et de sa création; soit parce que "l'information" pré-suppose une "puissance" ou "matière" pré-existante. (Ceci est l'objection de Tresmontant; il faut dit-il, distinguer entre "Dieu créant", et "Dieu se donnant").

Mais c'est là justement que je répond à mes "opposants" qu'ils ne comprennent rien au mécanisme expérimental de l'Union.

a) L'union différencie (donc dans le cas d'une création informante pas d'identité entre Créateur et Création).

b) Mais, plus important peut-être encore, l'*UNION CRÉE*. . . . En simple Physique nous savons maintenant que le Mouvement (ou plus exactement l'accélération d'un Mouvement) engendre la Masse (scandale aux veux du philosophe scolastique pour qui le mouvement local est la plus "accidentelle des Qualités . . .) De ce point de vue, il n'est plus nécessaire de distinguer, dans la création, deux temps: l'un pour la constitution d'un "Weltstoff" et l'autre pour l'arrangement de cet "être participé à l'état brut." Mais il faut nous élever à la conception nouvelle d'un processus qui engendre son Objet d'une même acte, du haut en bas tout entier.—Ce qui nous ramène à l'idée (qui vous gêne) d'un Multiple-pur ("Néant-unissable") inévitablement *conjugué* à l'existence de l'Un-pur (ou plus exactement de l'Unum-trinum).—cf. 1948 "Comment je vois" and "Conting. de l'Univers et Goût. . . ."

b. To Jeanne Mortier (Aug. 25, 1950) (*T.A.*, Correspondance à J. Mortier):

Vis-à-vis de l'Encyclique et de l'Assomption, je pense essentiellement comme vous, bien entendu, mais il y a un peu un "scandale" pour les âmes instruites et de bonne volonté. . . . Je crois bien voir ce que Rome a en vue: faire avancer le Marial parallèlement au Christique, et empécher une certaine évaporation du dogme en symboles abstraits. Mais "réalisme" n'est pas nécessairement "littéralisme"; et ce n'est pas faire de l'irénisme et de la conciliation que d'ajuster (d'agrandir et de renforcer) les représentations dogmatiques à un Univers qui a acquis une dimension de plus (le "génétique") (une Cosmogénèse au lieu d'un Cosmos). De ce point de vue, je crains bien que les affirmations d'un "individu Adam" (malgré le caractère symbolique reconnu de la Genèse en ce point!) et d'une incorruption littérale du corps de Marie (impliquant l'évasion hors du cycle cosmique d'un groupe de protéines, se maintenant hors du temps et de l'espace) ne paraissent à la grande majorité des chrétiens ou des gentils réfléchis un défi à ce qu'il y a de plus essentiel et de plus définitif dans la science moderne . . . Rappelez-vous l'article du Card. Ruffini dans l'Osservatore Romano, sur l'Evolution étendue à l'Homme: exactement la position de l'Encyclique . . . (il n'y a que les intégristes pour faire une bête noire ou un épouvantail de irénisme!) Et bien voilà qui me rassure. L'intégrisme, comme le stalinisme, tend à forcer l'Homme au repos: Il ne peut qu'être stérile, et finir par sauter.—Autre chose. . . : définir l'Assomption, c'est affirmer (par les faits) que la "Révélation continue", c'est-à-dire que le dogme croît (qu'il vit): pas de plus magnifique preuve que le Christianisme (comme le Vivant et l'Humain) évolue (au sens correct, "génétique, du mot).

c. To François Richaud (Jan. 18, 1952) (*T.A.*, Correspondance "R" #118)

En ce qui touche Dieu et le Monde, les systèmes intellectuels en présence (Scolastique-Védante, par. ex.) sont toujours pris dans le dilemme: diviniser ou minimiser ("annihiler") le Monde. Et cependant la verité semble bien être dans la notion du "Plérôme" de St Paul: la Création complète ["complétant"] en quelque façon Dieu. Il y a, autrement dit, une sorte de perfection absolue dans la Synthèse de l'Un "a se" et du Multiple. La Plérômisation, "en outre" de la Trinitisation. . . .

d. To P. Auguste Valensin (*T.A.* Correspondance Teilhard-Valensin)

i. on Feb. 2, 1920:

"Comme vous l'avez senti, il (Père Léonce) voudrait affirmer plus que je ne le fais la distinction essentielle (*en même temps* que la nature *physique commune*) des contacts par la grâce et l'Eucharistie. Or ceci

ne peut se faire qu'en traitant la question d'un point de vue plus
général, c'est-à-dire en distinguant *toute une série de zones* successive
dans la "communion" ou union réelle avec le Christ, toutes ces zones
étant *physiques*, mais chacune dans un ordre spécial,—(les divers
ordres n'etant pas fortuits, mais *ebauchés les uns des autres*). Je vois
assez clairement ce qu'il y a à dire sur ce sujet, qui peut réellement, je
crois, donner, en *toute orthodoxie*, une grande unité, et une grande
"physicéité" à la sanctification des âmes et des corps in
Christo. . . . Ce que vous me dites touchant les grands horizons
ouverts par l'idée d'une Eucharistie comprise comme un *rouage* essentiel de la transformation spirituelle (et non comme une simple industrie
d'amour) est exact: et c'est justement ce qui m'effare que si peu de
gens les aperçoivent, alors que la grande majorité des Nôtres, je crois,
sont convaincus (et prêchent) que l'Eucharistie n'est pas un moyen
libre de salut (ex natura entis supernaturalis). (Comment du reste
parler autrement, après St. Jean et St Paul?."

ii. on Dec. 17, 1922:

Notez que je comprends parfaitement les réserves que vous imposait le
Dictionnaire.—Mais tout de même, on a le droit de parler comme St.
Paul!—Ceci soit dit, je le répète, sans préjudice du profond intérêt que
m'a causé votre article. Mais, je vous en prie, ne réfutez pas seulement! assimilez! construisez!

1) "Vous avez tort de mépriser le panthéisme des poètes. Ce
    panthéisme-là est la mystique dont Spinoza et Hegel ont été les
    théologiens. Il représente une force psychologique, et il contient
    une vérité vécue considérable. Il est un panthéisme vivant. Vous
    faites comme un homme qui, dans le Christianisme, dédaignerait
    Ste Thérèse pour ne s'occuper que de St Thomas ou de Cajetan.—"
2) "Vous laissez le lecteur sour l'impression que la position
    spinozienne, par exemple, est simpliciter mala, falsa,—Comment
    n'avez-vous pas laissé entrevoir qu'entre l' "Incarnation"
    spinozienne où Tout est divin hypostatiquement, et l' "Incarnation"
    des Théologiens extrinsécistes et timides où le Plérôme n'est qu'un
    agrégat social, il y a place pour une Incarnation se terminant à
    l'édification d'un Tout organique, où l'union physique au Divin a
    des degr"–?—Vous opposez la morale chrétienne à la morale
    spinozienne en disant que la première nous dit seulement de de-
    venir "semblables à Dieu." Je n'accepte pas l'opposition. Pour le
    Chrétien, être (? ?) c'est participer, sous la similitude de conduite,
    à un être commun;—c'est réellement "devenir le Christ," "devenir
    Dieu."

Bibliography

I. A GENERAL LIST OF WORKS, ESSAYS, AND NOTES OF PIERRE TEILHARD DE CHARDIN UTILIZED IN THIS BOOK

1. The series *Oeuvres de Teilhard de Chardin*, published by Editions du Seuil, Paris, and by William Collins and Sons, Ltd., London (individual volume titles and publication dates given below, along with publisher in the U.S.A.):

   Volume 1, *Le Phénomène humain*. 1955. 349 pp.; *The Phenomenon of Man* (New York: Harper & Row, 1959), 320 pp. (1965, TB 383)

   2, *L'Apparition de l'Homme*. 1956. 375 pp.; *The Appearance of Man* (New York: Harper & Row, 1965), 286 pp.

   3, *La Vision du Passé*. 1956. 391 pp.; *The Vision of the Past* (New York: Harper & Row, 1966), 285 pp.

   4, *Le Milieu divin*, 1957, 203 p.; *The Divine Milieu* (New York: Harper Bros., 1960), 144 pp. (1965 TB 384, 1960 pp.)

   5, *L'Avenir de l'Homme*. 1959. 405 pp.; *The Future of Man* (New York: Harper & Row, 1964), 319 pp.

   6, *L'Energie humaine*. 1962. 223 pp.; *Human Energy* (New York: Harcourt Brace Jovanovich, 1969), 191 pp.

   7, *L'Activation de l'Energie*. 1963. 429 pp.; *Activation of Energy* (New York: Harcourt Brace Jovanovich, 1970), 416 pp.

   8, *La Place de l'Homme dans la Nature* ("Le Groupe zoologique humain") (Paris: Editions Albin Michel, 1956). 173 pp.; *Man's Place in Nature* (New York: Harper & Row, 1966), 124 pp.

9, *Science et Christ*. 1965. 293 pp.; *Science and Christ* (New York: Harper & Row, 1968), 230 pp.

10, *Comment je crois*. 1969. 294 pp.; *Christianity and Evolution* (New York: Harcourt Brace Jovanovich, 1971). 255 pp.

11, *Les Directions de l'Avenir*. 1973. 236 pp.; *Toward the Future* (New York: Harcourt Brace Jovanovich, 1975). 224 pp.

13. "*Le Coeur de la matière.*" 1976. 254 pp.

2. Other published collections of essays and letters:

Accomplir l'Homme (Paris: Grasset, 1968), 281 pp.; *Letters to Two Friends*. edited by Ruth Nanda Anshen (New York: New American Library, Meridian World Pub., 1968), 237 pp.

Blondel et Teilhard. Correspondance commentée par Henri de Lubac sj (Paris: Beauchesne, 1965), 168 pp.; *Pierre Teilhard de Chardin—Maurice Blondel: Correspondence* (New York: Herder & Herder, 1967), 174 pp.

Construire la Terre (Cahiers de Teilhard de Chardin,[1] 1) (Paris: Editions du Seuil, 1958), 46 pp.; *Building the Earth* (Wilkes-Barre, Pa.: Dimension Books, 1965), 125 pp.

La Parole attendue (Cahiers de Teilhard de Chardin, 4) (Paris: Editions du Seuil, 1963), 159 pp. Cf. pp. 22-29.

Ecrits du temps de la guerre (1916-1919) (Paris: Grasset, 1965), 448 pp.; *Writings in Time of War* (London: Collins; New York: Harper, 1968), 315 pp. (Now republished as *Oeuvres*, vol. 12, by Editions du Seuil, Paris.)

Etre Plus, Directives Extraites des Ecrits Publiés ou Inédits du Père, de sa Correspondance et de ses Notes (Paris: Editions du Seuil, 1968), 158 pp.

"L'homme devant les enseignements de l'Eglise et devant la philosophie spritualiste" in *Dictionnaire Apologétique de la Foi Catholique*, 2 (Paris: Beauchesne, 1911): 502-14.

Hymne de l'Univers (Paris: Editions du Seuil, 1961), 176 pp.; *Hymn of The Universe* (London: Collins; New York: Harper & Row, 1965), 158 pp.

Genèse d'un pensée. Lettres 1914-1919 (Paris: Grasset, 1961), 406 pp.; *The Making of a Mind, Letters from a Soldier Priest, 1914-1919* (London: Collins; New York: Harper & Row, 1965), 316 pp.

Je m'explique, Texts choisis et ordonnés par Jean-Pierre Demoulin (Paris: Editions du Seuil, 1966), 253 pp.; *Let Me Explain* (London: Collins, 1970), 189 pp.

1. A series containing some hitherto unpublished essays of Teilhard with accompanying articles; most of these essays have since been published elsewhere. These *Cahiers* are not to be confused with Teilhard's early and still unpublished notebooks or "Cahiers."

Lettres d'Egypte 1905-1908 (Paris: Aubier-Montaigne, 1963), 228 pp.; *Letters from Egypt* (New York: Herder & Herder, 1965), 256 pp.

Lettres d'Hastings et de Paris 1908-1914 (Paris: Aubier-Montaigne, 1965), 463 pp.; *Letters from Hastings, 1908–1912* (New York: Herder & Herder, 1968), 206 pp and *Letters from Paris* (New York: Herder & Herder, 1967), 157 pp.

Lettres à Léontine Zanta (Paris: Desclée, 1965), 142 pp.; *Letters to Leontine Zanta* (New York: Harper, 1969), 127 pp.

Lettres de voyage 1923-1955, Recueilles et présentées par Claude Aragonnés (Paris: Grasset, 1962), 370 pp.; *Letters from a Traveller* (London: Collins; New York: Harper, 1962), 380 pp.

Réflexions sur le Bonheur (Paris: Editions du Seuil, 1966), 91 pp.

3. Unpublished[2] essays, notes, and correspondence of Teilhard researched in the course of this study.

A. Unpublished essays and papers (listed chronologically; Teilhard Archive numbers listed in parenthesis whenever possible).

"La Nature synthetique de l'esprit." 1917 (*T.A.* #106). 1 p.

"A propose de spiritisme: observations sur la synthèse experimentale." 1920 (*T.A.* #27). 3½ pp. typewritten.

"Sur le progrès" (Apr. 24, 1921). (Notes recorded by C. Cuénot). 14 pp. handwritten.

"Engagement demandé au P. Teilhard de Chardin au sujet du péché originel" (Nov. 2, 1924) (*T.A.* #56). 1 p. Typewritten.

"Essai d'intégration de l'Homme dans l'Univers." (Nov.–Dec., 1930) (*T.A.* #92). Typewritten transcripts of four lectures (3d lecture missing). 72 pp. Typewritten.

"Profession of Faith." A statement sent to Lucille Swan, Sept. 28, 1933 (*T.A.* #107). 1 p. Typewritten.

"Orient et Occident: La Mystique de la Personalité", 1933 (*T.A.* #118). 2½ pp. Typewritten.

"Temoignage fraternel." 1936 (*T.A.* #110). 1½ pp. typewritten (Extrait de *Le Trait d'Union*, bulletin de l'Union catholique de Malades 66 [Oct. 1936], pp. 6-9).

"Eclaircissements (à l'usage de ceux qui auront la charité de réviser ce livre)" (Feb. 1941) (*T.A.* #102). 1 p. typewritten (extracts from a letter to R. P. d'Ouince concerning *Le Phénomène humain*).

2. Unpublished, or if published, out of print, or not yet readily available.

"Un troisième infini: loi de la complexité-conscience." 1942 (*T.A.* #96). 4 pp. typewritten.

"Sur le Regne de Dieu (dans le cadre des Exercices de S. Ignace)." 1946 (notes prises au cours d'une conference du R. P. Teilhard de Chardin, Le Chatelard). 3½ pp. typed.

"Equipe 'Science et Conscience" (Debat entre le P. Teilhard de Chardin et Gabriel Marcel) (Jan. 4, 1947) (*T.A.* #67). 6 pp. typewritten.

"Cosmologie et Théologie" (Debat Teilhard—Dubarle) (Jan. 19, 1947). 2 pp. typed ds.

"A quoi sert le monde?" (dialogue between M. Louis Lavelle and Teilhard de Chardin). 1947 (*T.A.* #55). As reported in the *Bulletin de Liaison entre Scientifiques de la Societé de Jésus* 4 (Juin 1947).

"Foi humaine— Foi spirituelle" (Jan. 18, 1948) (*T.A.* #117) (Notes taken by Solange Lemaître and L. Roinet). 6 pp. typed.

"Evolution et Finalité" (Feb. 12, 1948) (*T.A.* #111). 2½ pp. types (a preface by Teilhard for an unpublished book of the same title written by Jean Montassey).

"Comment je vois" (Aug. 26, 1948) (*T.A.* #43). 26 pp. mimeographed.

"Ce que la science nous apprend de l'évolution; conséquences pour notre apostolat"; alias: "Le néohumanisme scientifique moderne et ses réactions sur le christianisme de la masse ouvrière" (conférence donnée à la Session d'études des Aumôniers fédéraux de l'Action catholique ouvrière, Versailles) (Sept. 21, 1948) (*T.A.* #93). 6 pp. typed (from notes taken by l'Abbe Pihan?).

"Note relative à une publication possible du *Le Milieu divin*" (Oct. 1948) (*T.A.* #113). 1 p. typed.

"On the Significance and Trend of Human Socialization" (Feb. 1951) (*T.A.* #72). 1½ pp. typed (in English).

"L'Amour" (dicté à Solange Lemaître) (July 1951) (*T.A.* #105). 1 p. typed.

"On the Biological Meaning of Human Socialization" (May 15, 1952) (*T.A.* #78). 5 pp. typed (in English).
New York: Sheed & Ward, 1968. 309 pp.

"Mal évolutif et Péché originel" (June 19, 1952) (*T.A.* #98). Typed extract from a letter.

"Le phénomène humain" (remarques préparé pour Rueff), June 1953 (*T.A.* #73). 1 p. typed.

"The Antiquity and Planetary Significance of Human Culture" (Oct. 1954) (*T.A.* #52). 11¾ pp. typed (in English).

B. Notes and "Journals" of Teilhard de Chardin[3]

"Notes et esquisses" (nine "Cahiers") 1915-1925 (as transcribed in typewritten form by the Fondation Teilhard de Chardin, Paris. Now being published in two volumes, by Fayard, Paris, Vol. I 1975)

"Journals," 1944-1955 (in possession of the Paris Province of the Society of Jesus) consisting of the following nine volumes:

"Journal 13 (1)," July 18, 1944-Oct. 10, 1945. 161 pp.

"Journal 14 (2)," Oct. 27, 1945-Apr. 6, 1947, 151 pp.

"Journal 15 (3)," Apr. 6, 1947-Dec. 23, 1948, 183 pp.

"Journal 16 (4)," Sept. 30, 1948-Nov. 4, 1948 (section overlapping "Journal 15 (3)") and Jan. 2, 1949-July 30, 1949. 183 pp.

"Journal 17 (5)," Aug. 1, 1949-Oct. 1950, 160 pp.

"Journal 18 (6)," Nov. 1950-June 22, 1952, 161 pp.

"Journal 19 (7)," June 23, 1952-June 18, 1953, 73 pp.

"Journal 20 (8)," June 24, 1953-Oct. 19, 1954, 78 pp. (contains several passages date July, 1952)

"Journal 21 (9)," Oct. 20, 1954-Apr. 7, 1955, 35 pp.

"Carnet de retraits," 1939-1948(?) (Notes in possession of the Paris Province of the Society of Jesus).

C. Correspondence (for the most part unpublished)

The Following system of classification is used by the Fondation Teilhard de Chardin to classify those eleven volumes of correspondence (transcribed in typewritten form) which are available to the general researcher:

"Vol. A-B": "Correspondance Teilhard—l'Abbe Breuil"

Vols. "C-F", "K", "L", "M": "Lettres du P. Teilhard à Jeanne Mortier"

Vols. "N-O-P", "R", "T" (latter does not include letters to members of the Teilhard family):

"Lettres du P. Teilhard au P. August Valensin"

II. COMMENTARIES, BIOGRAPHIES, AND OTHER STUDIES OF TEILHARD

Allegra, Gabriel M., O.F.M. *My Conversations with Teilhard de Chardin on the Primacy of Christ*. Chicago, Ill.: Franciscan Herald Press, 1971. 126 pp.

---

3. The "Cahiers" or "Journals" from 1925 to mid-1944 (nos. 10-12) are missing, having been left behind in Peking in 1946.

Baltassar, Eulalio R. *Teilhard and the Supernatural*. New York: Helicon, 1966. 336 pp.

Barbour, George B. *In the Field with Teilhard de Chardin*. New York: Herder & Herder, 1965.

Barthélemy-Madaule, Madeleine. *Bergson et Teilhard de Chardin*. Paris: Editions du Seuil, 1963. 687 pp.

Bravo, Francisco. *Christ in the Thought of Teilhard de Chardin*. Notre Dame, Inc.: University of Notre Dame Press, 1967. 163 pp.

Chauchard, Paul. *Teilhard de Chardin on Love and Suffering*. Glen Rock, N.J.: Paulist Press, 1966. 93 pp.

Crespy, Georges. *La Pensée théologique de Teilhard de Chardin*. Paris: Editions Universitaires, 1961. 231 pp.

Cuénot, Claude. *Teilhard de Chardin: les grandes étapes de son évolution*. Paris: Plon, 1958. 489 pp.; *Teilhard de Chardin*. New York: Helicon, 1965. 492 pp.

―――. *Science and Faith in Teilhard de Chardin*. London: Garnstone Press, 1967. 109 pp.

Francoeur, Robert, ed. *The World of Teilhard de Chardin*. New York: Helicon, 1961. 208 pp.

Gray, Donald P. *The One and the Many: Teilhard de Chardin's Vision of Unity*. New York: Herder & Herder, 1969. 185 pp.

Hale, Robert, O.S.B. Cam. *Christ and the Universe: Teilhard de Chardin and the Cosmos*. Chicago: Franciscan Herald Press, 1973. 125 pp.

Kopp, Joseph. *Teilhard de Chardin: A New Synthesis of Evolution*. Glen Rock, N.J.: Paulist Press, 1964. 72 pp.

Lubac, Henri de, S.J. *La Pensée religieuse du Père Teilhard de Chardin*. Paris: Aubier, 1962. 374 (1) pp.; *The Religion of Teilhard de Chardin*. New York: Desclee; London: Collins, 1967. 380 pp.

―――: *La Prière du Père Teilhard de Chardin*. Paris: Fayard, 1964. 223 pp.; *Teilhard de Chardin: The Man and his Meaning*. New York: Hawthorn, 1965. 203 (10) pp.

―――. *Teilhard de Chardin, Missionaire et apologiste*. Toulouse, Editions de Prière et vie, 1966. 110 (1) pp.; *Teilhard Explained*. New York: Paulist Press, 1968. 115 pp.

Maloney, George A., S.J. *The Cosmic Christ: from Paul to Teilhard*.

Mooney, Christopher F., S.J. *Teilhard de Chardin and the Mystery of Christ*. New York: Harper & Row, 1964. 288 pp.

North, Robert, S.J., S.S.D. *Teilhard and the Creation of the Soul*. Milwaukee: Bruce, 1967. 317 pp.

O'Manique, John. *Energy in Evolution, Teilhard's Physics of the*

Future. London: Garnstone Press, 1969. 113 pp.

Philippe de la Trinité. *Teilhard de Chardin: foi au Christ universel*. Paris: La Table Ronde, 1968. 249 pp.

———. *Teilhard de Chardin: Vision cosmique et Christique*. Paris: La Table Ronde, 1968. 332 pp.

Rabut, Oliver, o.p. *Dialogue avec Teilhard de Chardin*. Paris: Editions du Cerf, 1958. 210 pp.; *Teilhard de Chardin: A Critical Study*. New York: Sheed & Ward, 1961. 247 pp.

Rideau, Emile. *La Pensée du Père Teilhard de Chardin*. Paris: Editions de Seuil, 1965. 590 pp.; *Teilhard de Chardin: A Guide to his Thought*. London: Collins, 1967. 672 pp.

Smulders, Piet, sj. *La Vision de Teilhard de Chardin*. Bruges: Desclée de Brouwer, 1964. 278 pp.; *The Design of Teilhard de Chardin*. Westminster, Md.: Newman, 1967. 310 pp.

Solages, Mgr. Bruno de. *Teilhard de Chardin: Temoignage et étude sur le dévéloppement de sa pensée*. Paris: Privat, 1967. 397 pp.

Speaight, Robert. *Teilhard de Chardin: A Biography*. London: Collins, 1967. 360 pp.

Towers, Bernard. *Teilhard de Chardin* (Makers of Contemporary Theology Series). Richmond, Va.: Knox, 1966. 45 pp.

Szekeres, Atilla, ed. *Le Christ Cosmique de Teilhard de Chardin*. Paris: Editions du Seuil, 1969. 439 pp.

Wildiers, N. M. *An Introduction to Teilhard de Chardin*. New York: Harper, 1968. 191 pp.

III. BIBLICAL STUDIES (BOOKS AND ARTICLES) OF PARTICULAR USEFULNESS TO THIS BOOK

Andriessen, Paul. "La nouvelle Eve, corps du nouvel Adam," in *Recherches Biblique* 7 (Paris, Bruges, 1964): 87-109.

Barrett, C. K. *From First Adam to Last: A Study in Pauline Theology*. London: Adam & Charles Black, 1962. 124 pp.

Barth, Karl. *Christ and Adam: Man and Humanity in Romans 5*. Edinburgh: Oliver & Boyd, 1963. 45 pp.

Benoît, Pierre, op. *Exégèse et théologie*. Paris: Editions du Cerf, vol.

1, 1961. 416 pp.; vol. 2, 1961, 447 pp.; vol. 3, 1968, 441 pp.

Bover, J. M. *Téologia de San Pablo*. Madrid: Biblioteca de Autores Christianos, 1946. 952 pp.

Brown, Raymond, S.S. "Hermeneutics" in *The Jerome Biblical Commentary*. Englewood Cliffs, N.J.: Prentice-Hall, 1968. pp. 605-23.

———. *The "Sensus Plenior" of Sacred Scripture*. Baltimore, Md.: St. Mary's Seminary, 1955. 161 pp.

———. "The 'Sensus Plenior' Ten Years After" in *The Catholic Biblical Quarterly* 25 (1963): 263-85.

Bultmann, Rudolf. *The Old and New Man in the Letters of St. Paul*. Richmond, Va.: Knox Press, 1967. 79 pp.

———. *Theology of the New Testament*. London: SCM, 1952. 2 vols.

Cerfaux, Lucien, et Cambier, Jules. *L'Apocalypse de saint Jean*. Paris: Editions du Cerf, 1955. 238 pp.

———. *Le Christ dans la Théologie de S. Paul*. Paris: Editions du Cerf, 1951. 435 pp.; *Christ in the Theology of St. Paul*. New York: Herder & Herder, 1959. 559 pp.

———. *La Théologie de l'Eglise suivant saint Paul*. Paris: Editions du Cerf, 1942, 1948. 334 pp., 430 pp.; *The Church in the Theology of St. Paul*. New York: Herder & Herder, 1959. 568 pp.

———. *Une Lecture de l'Epître aux Romains*. Tournai: Casterman, 1947. 139 pp.

Cornelius a Lapide. *Commentarius in Scripturas Sacras*. Paris: L. Vivès, 1868. Vols. 16, 18, & 19.

Cornely, Rudolpho, sj. *Commentarius in S. Pauli Epistolarum (Cursus Scripturae Sacrae* 7). Paris: Lethielleux, 1927.

Craddock, F. B. " 'All Things in Him': A Critical Note on Col. 1:15-20" in *New Testament Studies* 12 (1965-66): 331.

Culliton, Joseph T., C.S.B. "Lucien Cerfaux's Contribution Concerning 'The Body of Christ' " in *The Catholic Biblical Quarterly* 29 (1967): 41-59.

Dahl, M. E. *The Resurrection of the Body (Studies in Biblical Theology* 36). London: SCM, 1962. 120 pp.

Dubarle, A-M., o.p. "Le gémissement des créatures dans l'ordre divin du cosmos: (Rom. 8:19-22)" in *Revue des Sciences philosophique et théologiques* 38 (1954): 445-65.

Durand, Alfred, sj. *Evangile selon Saint Jean*. 6th ed. Paris: Beauchesne, 1930. 591 pp.

Durwell, F. X. *La Résurrection de Jésus: mystère de salut*. Paris: Editions Xavier Mappus, 1958. 397 pp.; *The Resurrection: A Bibli-*

cal Study. New York: Sheed & Ward, 1960. 371 pp.

Ernst, Josef. "The Significance of Christ's Eucharistic Body for the Unity of Church and Cosmos" in *Concilium: Scripture: No. 4* (1968). Pp. 55-60.

Feuillet, André. *L'Apocalypse*. Paris, Bruges: Desclée de Brouwer, 1963. 122 pp.

――――. *Le Christ sagesse de Dieu*. Paris: Gabalda, 1966. 460 pp.

――――. "La création de l'univers dans le Christ d'après l'Epître aux Col. 1:16a" in *New Testament Studies* 12, no. 1 (Oct. 1965): 1-9.

Fitzmeyer, Joseph A., S.J. "Pauline Theology" in *The Jerome Biblical Commentary*. Englewood Cliffs, N.J.: Prentice-Hall, 1968. Pp. 800-827.

Gager, John G. Jr. "Paul's End-Time Language" in *The Journal of Biblical Literature* 89, no. 3 (Sept. 1970): pp. 325-37.

Henry, Paul, sj. *Compléments de Christologie*. Paris: Publ. Institut Catholique de Paris, no. 7. 171 pp.

Käsemann, E. *Essays on New Testament Themes* (*Studies in Biblical Theology 41*). London: SCM, 1964. 200 pp.

――――. *Perspectives on Paul*. Philadelphia, Pa.: Fortress Press, 1971. 173 pp.

Knabenbauer, Jos. sj. *Evangelium secundem Joannem* (*Cursus Scripturae Sacrae*, 7). Paris: Lethielleux, 1898.

――――. *Epistolas ad Ephesios, Philippenses, Colossenses* (*Cursus Scripturae Sacrae*, 9). Paris: Lethielleux, 1912.

Lagrange, M-J., o.p. *Evangile selon saint Jean*. Paris: Lecoffre, 1925. 555 pp.

――――. *St. Paul: Epître aux Romains*. Paris: Gabalda, 1931. 395 pp.

LaPointe, Roger, D.E.S. *Les trois dimensions de l'herméneutique*. Paris: Gabalda, 1967. 151 pp.

Latourelle, René. *Theology of Revelation*. New York: Alba House, 1966. 509 pp.

Lehmann, Karl. "Hermeneutics" in *Sacramentum Mundi*, 3. New York: Herder & Herder, 1968. Pp. 23-27.

Lightfoot, J. B. *Notes on the Epistles of St. Paul*. London: Macmillan, 1895. 336 pp.

Lohse, Eduard. "Pauline Theology in the Letter to the Colossians" in *New Testament Studies* 15, no. 2 (1969): 201-20.

Lyonnet, Stanislas, s.j. "La Rédemption de l'univers" in *Lumière et Vie* 48 (1960): 43-62.

Manson, T. W. *On Paul and John* (*Studies in Biblical Theology*, 38).

London: SCM, 1963. 168 pp.

Moran, Gabriel, F.Y.C. *Theology of Revelation*. New York: Herder & Herder, 1966. 223 pp.

Moulton-Milligan. *The Vocabulary of the Greek New Testament*. Grand Rapids, Mich.: Eerdmans, 1963. 750 pp.

Prat, Ferdinand, s.j. *Théologie de St Paul*. 4 vols. Paris: Beauchesne, 1909. 604 pp., 612 pp.; 1912, 608 pp., 612 pp.; *The Theology of St. Paul*. 2 vols. Westminster, Md.: Newman Press, 1952. 523 pp., 516 pp.

Rahner, Karl. S.J. "Revelation, B. Theological Interpretation" in *Sacramentum Mundi*, 5, New York: Herder & Herder, 1969. Pp. 348-54; also in *Encyclopedia of Theology*. New York: Seabury, 1975, pp. 1460-73.

————. *Theological Investigations*. Baltimore, Md.: Helicon; London: Darton, Longman & Todd. Vols. 1 & 4, 1961, 1966.

————. "On the Theology of the Incarnation," in *Word and Mystery*, ed. Leo O'Donovan, S.J., New York: Paulist-Newman Press, 1968.

Rissi, Mathias. *Alpha und Omega*. Basel: F. Reinhardt Verlag, 1966. 221 pp.

Robinson, H. Wheeler. *Corporate Personality in Ancient Israel*. Philadelphia, Pa.: Fortress Press, 1965.

Robinson, J. A. T. *The Body: A Study in Pauline Theology (Studies in Biblical Theology*, 5). London: SCM, 1952. 95 pp.

Robinson, James M. "A Formal Analysis of Col. 1:15-20" in *The Journal of Biblical Literature* 76 (1957): 270-87.

Scheffczyk, Leo. "Die 'Christogenesis' Teilhard de Chardins und der Kosmische Christus bei Paulus" in *Theologische Quartalschrift* 143 (1963): 137-74.

Schiffers, Norbert. "Revelation: Concept of: Basic Notion" in *Sacramentum Mundi*, 5. New York: Herder & Herder, 1969. Pp. 342-48.

Schnackenburg, Rudolf, *The Gospel According to St. John (Das Johannesevangelium*, 1965). Freiburg: Herder, 1968. 638 pp.

Schweitzer, A. *Die Mystik des Apostels Paulus*. Tübingen: J.C.B. Mohr, 1930. 405 pp.; *The Mysticism of Paul the Apostle*. New York: Seabury Press, 1968. 411 pp.

Vawter, Bruce, CM. "The Colossians Hymn and the Principle of Redaction" in *The Catholic Biblical Quarterly* 33 (1971): 62-81.

————. "Johannine Theology" in *The Jerome Biblical Commentary*. Englewood Cliffs, N.J.: Prentice-Hall, 1968. Pp. 828-39.

Viard, A. o.p. " 'Expectatio Creaturae' (Rom., VII, 19-22)" in *Revue biblique* 59 (1952): 337-54.

Vögtle, G. A. *Das Neue Testament und die Zukunft des Kosmos* (*Kommentare und Beiträge* zum AT und NT). Düsseldorf, 1970. 259 pp.

IV. OTHER WORKS UTILIZED OR REFERRED TO

Aquinas, Thomas. *Compendium of Theology*. London, St. Louis, Mo.: B. Herder Book Co., 1947. 336 pp.

Benz, Ernst. *Evolution and Christian Hope: Man's Concept of the Future from the Early Fathers to Teilhard de Chardin*. New York: Doubleday & Co. (Anchor Books, Garden City, N.Y.) 1966. 270 pp.

Bergson, Henri. *L'Evolution créatrice*. Paris: Alcan, 30th. ed, 1930. 403 pp.; *Creative Evolution*. New York: Modern Library, 1944. 453 pp.

Blondel, Maurice. *L'Action* (1893). Paris: Presses universitaires de France, 1950. 495 pp.

Fransen, Piet, S.J. *Intelligent Theology*. 3 vols. Chicago: Franciscan Herald Press, 1969. 148 pp., 157 pp., 183 pp.

Hardon, John A., S.J. *Christianity in the Twentieth Century*. Garden City, N.Y.: Doubleday, 1971. 527 pp.

Huxley, Aldous. *The Perennial Philosophy*. London: Chatto & Windus, 1946.

Huxley, Julian. *Essays of a Humanist*. New York: Harper & Row, 1964. 287 pp.

———. *Knowledge, Morality, & Destiny*. New York: Mentor Books, 1957. 287 pp.

———. *Religion without Revelation*. New York: Mentor Books, 1959.

Maritain, Jacques. *The Peasant of the Garonne*. New York: Holt, Rinehart, Winston, 1968. 227 pp.

Moltmann, Jürgen. *Theologie der Hoffnung*. Munich: Chr. Kaiser Verlag, 1965. 340 pp.; *Theology of Hope*. New York: Harper & Row, 1967. 342 pp.

Newman, John Henry. *Essay on the Development of Christian Doctrine*. New York: Doubleday Image, 1960. 434 pp.

Pieper, Josef. *Hoffnung und Geschichte*. New York: Herder, 1967; *Hope and History*. New York: Herder & Herder, 1969. 106 pp.

Richards, I. A. *The Philosophy of Rhetoric*. New York: Galaxy (Oxford University Press), 1965.

Scheeben, M.-J. *La Dogmatique*. Translated by L'abbé P. Bélet. 4 vols. Paris: V. Palmé, 1881.

————. *Die Mysterien des Christentums*. Freiburg: Herder, 1865. 777 pp.; *Les mystères du Christianisme*. Paris: Desclée de Brouwer, 1947. 841 pp.

Whitehead, Alfred North. *Process and Reality, An Essay in Cosmology*. New York: Harper Torchbooks, 1960. 544 pp.

Index